HISTORY OF IMPERIAL CHINA

Timothy Brook, General Editor

THE EARLY CHINESE EMPIRES

QIN AND HAN

Mark Edward Lewis

THE BELKNAP PRESS OF
HARVARD UNIVERSITY PRESS
Cambridge, Massachusetts
London, England
2007

Cataloging-in-Publication Data available from the
Library of Congress
Library of Congress catalog card number: 2006043039
ISBN-13: 978-0-674-02477-9 (alk. paper)
ISBN-10: 0-674-02477-x (alk. paper)

CONTENTS

MAPS

THE EARLY CHINESE EMPIRES

QIN AND HAN

INTRODUCTION

IN THE Western imagination, China's history has been inextricably linked to the notion of "empire." But in fact, more than a millennium of Chinese history passed before anything resembling an empire ever existed. For centuries, six separate states battled for military supremacy, until in 221 B.C. the Qin dynasty defeated the last of its rivals and unified the country. Military conquest is only part of the imperial story, however. China owes its ability to endure across time, and to re-form itself again and again after periods of disunity, to a fundamental reshaping of Chinese culture by the earliest dynasties, the Qin and the Han. Politics and military institutions were reconfigured, of course. But so were literary and religious practices, kinship structure, village life, and even cityscapes.

Taken together, the Qin and Han empires constitute the "classical" era of Chinese civilization, as did the Greeks and Romans in the West. Like the Greco-Roman Mediterranean, Chinese culture during this period is distinct from the societies that evolved out of it. Yet what was to come cannot be understood without a grasp of China's first period of unification and how it was achieved. Five major features of the classical period will be explored in depth in the chapters that follow. They are: (1) the distinct regional cultures whose divisions were transcended, but not eradicated, by the imperial order; (2) the consolidation of a political structure centered on the person of the emperor; (3) the cultivation of literacy based on a non-alphabetic script and of a state-sponsored literary canon that sanctioned the state's existence; (4) demilitarization of the interior, with military activity assigned to marginal peoples at the frontier; (5) the flourishing of wealthy families in the countryside who maintained order and linked the villages to the center of power.

The defining characteristics of the Chinese empire—and, indeed, of all empires—were its large scale and the diversity of its peoples. While all of China's inhabitants have retroactively become "Chinese" today, this term is anachronistic for the pre-imperial period. The peoples of that time would have been known as the Qin, Qi, Chu, or by the name of one of the other Warring States, or as the inhabitants of a particular region (for example, the people "within the mountain passes"). The Qin's conquests united these groups politically in the third century B.C., but distinct regional cultures and "temperaments" survived. Such regional variations were not an inconvenient fact of life but, rather, became essential to an empire that justified itself by making just this kind of hierarchical distinction—between the universal, superior culture of the imperial center and the limited, particular cultures of regions and localities. This fundamental distinction manifested itself in political service, religion, literature, and many other aspects of Chinese life.

The second basic innovation in classical China was the invention of the figure of the emperor. He was not merely the supreme ruler, chief judge, and high priest but the very embodiment of the political realm. The state radiated out from his person: everyone in state service was his servant and held office entirely at his behest. The state was the emperor, along with his retinue of servants, and without him there could be no state. This centrality was manifested in the sumptuary regulations that exalted his person, for example, the creation of fabric patterns that only he could wear or roads that only he could use. But it was also expressed in a new urban form, the imperial capital, in new cults of which he was privileged priest and sacrificer, and even in new models of the universe where he served as the unique link between Heaven and Earth. In this centralized political system, whoever stood in closest physical proximity to the emperor wielded enormous power, for good or ill.

A third critical change brought about by the Qin conquest was the universal use of a single non-alphabetic script. By standardizing written communication among groups that did not speak mutually intelligible tongues, this innovation bound together all the regions of the empire and allowed the establishment of a state-sanctioned literary canon.[1] In later periods even areas that did not become part of modern China—Korea, Japan, and Vietnam—shared significant elements of culture through their use of a common written script. The state canon, in turn, provided both a sanction for the emperor as the chief exponent and defender of the values articulated within the state, models for exemplary individuals who enacted those values, and the basis of a shared education and intellectual life. Eventually, a common literary culture linked all those engaged in, or aspiring to, state service. In later centuries literacy would permeate lower levels of society, through Chinese theater, popular fiction, and simplified manuals of instruction.

In the centuries following the Qin conquest, the gradual demilitarization of both peasant and urban populations and the delegation of military service to marginal elements of society reversed an earlier trend among the competing states which had extended military service throughout the peasantry. In 31 A.D. universal military service was formally abolished, not to reappear until after the end of the last empire in 1911. In place of a mobilized peasantry, military service was provided by non-Chinese tribesmen, who were particularly skilled in the forms of warfare used at the frontier, and by convicts or other violent elements of the population, who were transported from the interior to the major zones of military action at the outskirts of the empire. This demilitarization of the interior blocked the establishment of local powers that could challenge the empire, but also led to a recurrent pattern in which alien peoples conquered and ruled China.

Finally, "empire" as it developed in early China depended on the emergence of a new social elite—great families throughout the realm who combined landlordism and trade with political office-holding. These families dominated local society through their wealth, which they invested primarily in land, and their ability to mobilize large numbers of kin and dependents. In the classical period, law and custom divided inherited property among sons, and therefore landed wealth was subject to constant dispersal. Even large estates (although no estates in this period were large by Western standards) devolved into a multitude of small plots within a few generations. In order to reproduce their wealth over time, families were obliged to find sources of income outside agriculture. Trade and moneylending were vital occupations among the gentry, but the greatest source of wealth was imperial office-holding.

Over time, powerful local families became economically dependent on state service to maintain their position, and the formal education required to obtain such service steeped their sons and grandsons in the imperial literary culture. Combining local power with a commitment to the state, these great families forged the primary link between the countryside and the imperial court. They imposed the emperor's will throughout the land in a manner that an understaffed bureaucracy could never have achieved. In later periods, as the population of the empire grew and the ratio of officials to population declined, these powerful families, dispersed throughout the empire, became even more important to the state—and could make even greater demands upon its largesse.

Over the centuries, as China's empire waxed and waned, the five features of state and society introduced during the classical period themselves underwent constant change. The attributes and functions of an emperor, as well as his religious nature, evolved under the pressures of politics. The contents of the canon, its relation to other elements of literary culture, and the way it was disseminated and used to recruit people for imperial offices also varied with the shifting political scene. Whenever alien peoples conquered China and formed new dynasties, they reorganized the state's military institutions and reconceived the relation of armies to the court. Meanwhile, over time and from region to region, the great families modified the ways they reproduced wealth and exerted local influence, as well as the means by which they were drawn into state service. But in one form or another, these features endured across the two millennia of imperial Chinese history, in service to an idea of state and society that continues to inform Chinese culture and influence the contemporary world.

I

THE GEOGRAPHY OF EMPIRE

GEOGRAPHY is a human science, not just the stu.ly of land forms, riverways, and soil types. It investigates the manner in which human beings shape, and are shaped by, their physical environment, and the way they interact with one another in space. Since the Neolithic period, people throughout the world have extracted their subsistence from the soil. But Chinese civilization in particular is noted for its ties to a landscape that has formed many of its basic characteristics and which has itself been transformed since the paleolithic through the toil of hundreds of generations of peasants. Mastering nature in this way entails asserting power over others, through control of natural resources and the methods for extracting a livelihood from them. The control of land and water was fundamental to the structure of the Qin and Han empires and to the course of their history.[1]

The Regions of Early Imperial China

Like all of Chinese history, the geography of the early empires is a tale of the country's many distinct regions. The state created by the Qin dynasty was not the modern China familiar from our maps. The western third of contemporary China (modern Xinjiang and Tibet) was an alien world unknown to the Qin and the early Han (Map 1). Modern Inner Mongolia and Manchuria also lay outside their frontiers, as did the southwestern regions of modern Yunnan and Guizhou. While the modern southeast quadrant (Fujian, Guangdong, and Guangxi) was militarily occupied, it also remained outside the Chinese cultural sphere. The China of the early

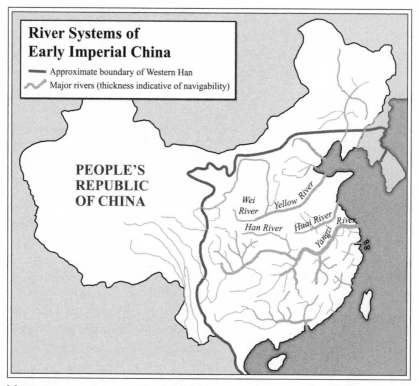

**River Systems of
Early Imperial China**

━━━ Approximate boundary of Western Han
〜 Major rivers (thickness indicative of navigability)

PEOPLE'S
REPUBLIC
OF CHINA

Wei
River

Yellow River

Han River   Huai River   River

Yangzi

MAP 1

imperial period, and of much of its later history, consisted of the drainage basins of the Yellow River and the Yangzi. This area comprised all of the land that was flat enough and wet enough to be suitable for agriculture, and thus defined the historical limits of the Chinese heartland.

This area has several distinctive geographic features. First, it is very hilly. Consequently, until the introduction of American food crops, much of the land was not amenable to cultivation. This scarcity resulted in highly concentrated populations, isolated from one another for the most part before the advent of the railroad and airplane. The limited arable land was further compartmentalized into a series of core areas—alluvial plains, coastlands, and interior basins—separated by high mountain chains or elevated plateaus that divided the Chinese heartland into distinct regions.[2]

In the Roman Empire, it was cheaper to ship grain or wine all the way from one end of the Mediterranean Sea to the other than to transport it just a hundred miles overland by wagon. Regions without water links were not integrated into the Mediterranean economy. The same was true of China. Prior to the construction of railroads in the nineteenth century, carrying grain more than a hundred miles by pack animal cost more than producing the grain itself. Except for luxury goods such as spices, silks, or gems, where small amounts produced large profits, hauling goods overland was prohibitively expensive. And a lack of good natural harbors in north China made trade up and down the coast uneconomical. Consequently, almost all bulk trade relied on inland waterways. But even this mode of transportation had its limitations. Both of the major rivers—the Yellow River and the Yangzi—flowed from west to east, with no navigable water links between them. No natural intersecting lines of transport moved north and south.

Rivers erode rock and soil in the western highlands and carry it down into the plains, where it is deposited as silt. Moving swiftly in narrow channels through the mountains, the Yellow River carries off a great deal of soil. In most rivers in the world, a silt content of 5 percent is considered high, but the Yellow River has been known to carry as much as 46 percent, and one of its tributaries carries 63 percent. This huge concentration of silt makes the water murky and explains the origin of the river's name. For the last 500 miles of its course, there are no major tributaries, so the river slows down and deposits its silt as sediment.

Over time, as the bottom of the channel gradually rose, the river overflowed its banks. Dikes were built ever higher to prevent flooding, and in some places the river started to flow above the surrounding countryside. Today, in a stretch of about 1,100 miles, the Yellow River moves along 11 yards above the plain. But dikes do not control silting, and floods continued to occur on an ever larger scale. On more than 1,500 occasions during the history of imperial China the Yellow River burst its dikes, destroying farmland, killing villagers, and earning its description as "China's sorrow."

Under the Qin and Han empires, the Yellow River was the core of Chinese civilization, home to around 90 percent of the population (Map 2). It was separated by mountains and hills into a northwestern region (modern Gansu and northern Shaanxi), the central loess highlands (modern Shaanxi, Shanxi, and Western Henan), and the alluvial floodplain (modern Henan, southern Hebei, Shandong, northern Anhui, and northern Jiangsu). The Yangzi drainage basin, still a frontier region in this period, was also naturally divided into three regions: the mountain-ringed Min River basin (modern Sichuan), the middle Yangzi (Hubei, Hunan, and Jiangxi), and the lower Yangzi (Zhejiang, southern Anhui, and Jiangsu).

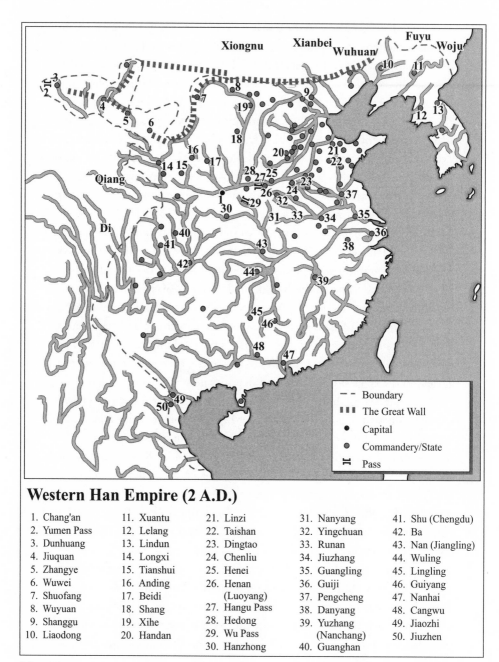

Western Han Empire (2 A.D.)

1. Chang'an	11. Xuantu	21. Linzi	31. Nanyang	41. Shu (Chengdu)
2. Yumen Pass	12. Lelang	22. Taishan	32. Yingchuan	42. Ba
3. Dunhuang	13. Lindun	23. Dingtao	33. Runan	43. Nan (Jiangling)
4. Jiuquan	14. Longxi	24. Chenliu	34. Jiuzhang	44. Wuling
5. Zhangye	15. Tianshui	25. Henei	35. Guangling	45. Lingling
6. Wuwei	16. Anding	26. Henan	36. Guiji	46. Guiyang
7. Shuofang	17. Beidi	(Luoyang)	37. Pengcheng	47. Nanhai
8. Wuyuan	18. Shang	27. Hangu Pass	38. Danyang	48. Cangwu
9. Shanggu	19. Xihe	28. Hedong	39. Yuzhang	49. Jiaozhi
10. Liaodong	20. Handan	29. Wu Pass	(Nanchang)	50. Jiuzhen
		30. Hanzhong	40. Guanghan	

MAP 2

In the Yellow River valley, the wind-deposited (aeolian) loess of the central highlands offered little resistance to wooden digging sticks. Capillary action in this uniform, friable (easily crumbled), and porous soil provided sufficient moisture to grow the standard crops of millet and wheat in a region where annual rainfall now averages only 10 to 20 inches (though it may have been slightly wetter at the time of the Qin conquest). Because of the dry climate, the soil was not leached by rainfall and remained highly fertile and alkaline. The piling up of the loess into mounds across the landscape had the further advantage of providing relative security from flooding.

In the great plain to the east, by contrast, the soil was deposited by the river. Though more fertile than the loess, this sedimentary soil was also more vulnerable to flooding and salinization. Rainfall followed a modified monsoon pattern, with about 70 percent falling in August, and very little in spring and early summer. Just at the peak of the growing season, when water was needed most, and despite the runoff from melted snow in the western mountains, the Yellow River fell to a quite low level, and irrigation with river water was impossible. Farmers depended on wells that were owned by wealthy families and dug by small groups of peasants. The enormous system of dikes, on the other hand, was maintained by the imperial state. This combination of a large-scale government-financed flood control system with a small-scale, family-owned irrigation system shaped the political economy of north China, as we will see.

In contrast to the rolling loess mounds and flat alluvial plain of the Yellow River basin, high mountains and rugged hills dominate the landscape from the Yangzi southward. Agriculture is possible only in the low river valleys, deltas, and marshlands. The chief environmental threat in the south was not drought or flood but excessive wetness, which made the lowlands too swampy for cultivation but provided a fertile breeding ground for disease. In literature ranging over a millennium, from the Han through the Tang periods, the south is described as a region of swamps and jungles, diseases and poisonous plants, savage animals and even more savage tattooed tribesmen. Even the southern regions that had been absorbed into the Chinese world by the Zhou state were still treated as culturally distinct and less than entirely civilized during the Warring States period and the Qin empire. The south was a place of exile, from which many a disgraced official never returned.

These major regional divisions provided the geographic underpinning of the Warring States in the fifth century B.C. The area of the loess highlands west of the Hangu Pass (essentially the Wei River valley) formed

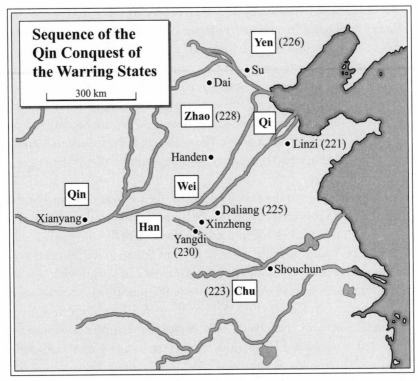

Sequence of the Qin Conquest of the Warring States

├─ 300 km ─┤

Yen (226)

• Su

• Dai

Zhao (228)

Qi

Handen •

• Linzi (221)

Qin

Wei

Xianyang •

Han

• Daliang (225)

• Xinzheng

Yangdi (230)

• Shouchun

(223) Chu

MAP 3

the core of the Qin state, which expanded to include the Min River basin of Sichuan. At the other end of the Yellow River valley, the alluvial flood plain was dominated by Qi state. Located between these two powers, the central loess highlands and western parts of the alluvial plain were divided among the successor states of Jin: Han, Wei, and Zhao. To the south, the Middle Yangzi was the core of the Chu state, while the lower Yangzi defined the states of Wu and Yue, which after briefly rising to dominance had been absorbed by Chu (Map 3).[3] Thus, the division of China into regions and the distinctive character of those regions, although based on the physical structure of the land, were translated into the cultural realm in the form of states and the perceived characteristics of their peoples.

According to the first great Han historian, Sima Qian (ca. 145–86 B.C.), the united empire of the Qin-Han period inherited these regions, each centered on a major city.[4] Most important was the area surrounding the Qin capital city of Xianyang (and later the nearby Han city of Chang'an). This region, focused on the Wei River, was connected to the Gansu corridor and Central Asia in the northwest, to Sichuan in the south, and to the central plain of the Yellow River valley to the east. The second great region, centered on the old Qi capital of Linzi, was the flood plain of the Yellow River (modern Shandong province). The Sichuan region was centered on Chengdu and defined by the mountain-ringed Min River valley. In his account Sima Qian divided the middle and lower Yangzi into three regions centered on Jiangling, Wu, and Shouchun, but they were relatively undeveloped and in economic terms are probably best understood as a single region. One might also speak of a Lingnan region roughly equivalent to modern Guangdong and North Vietnam. But apart from the great ports of Panyu (Canton) and Lianlou (Hanoi), this remained wild jungle territory only loosely connected to the imperial structure.

Region and Custom

The Zhou state, which lasted from ca. 1140 to 236 B.C.—longer than any other in Chinese history—was dominated by an aristocracy that shared a largely common culture. Regional variations were, for these aristocrats, hallmarks of the lower classes. Similarly, the conquering Qin state viewed regions and their distinctive cultures as antithetical to the project of unification. However, beneath this largely negative rhetoric from the Zhou and Qin, one can make out traces of the distinctive regional cultures that underlay the divisions of the Warring States period.

Throughout this turbulent time, the aspiration toward unification and the reality of regional division were in tension. Nowhere is this more evident than in the *Tribute of Yu* (*Yu gong*), probably composed in the middle of the Warring States period (fourth century B.C.). This sketch of the entire known world divides China into nine regions, each marked by the distinctive character of its people and products, which are described in some detail. The overarching theme of the text is how these nine regions were united into a single state by the travels of the sage Yu and by the sending of each region's unique products as tribute to the capital. Thus, the regional separation produced by mountains and rivers and expressed in local products and customs was transcended in the person of the ruler, who moved throughout the realm and drew its varied and bountiful production to himself.[5]

In the late Warring States period, the discourse on regional differences took several forms. Military texts discussed regional cultures in order to assess the strengths and weaknesses of each state. Other texts followed the model of the *Tribute of Yu* in using distinctive regional products as the material equivalents of regional character. Meanwhile, the traditions of statecraft distinguished the various regions and their customs by their administrative practices, in order to contrast them with the sweeping legal reforms advocated by the imperial power. In the Han period this tradition would develop into a standard trope that criticized even Qin law as merely the product of local custom, like fruits and handicrafts.

The key text in the military discourse on regional customs is "Evaluating the Enemy" in the *Master Wu (Wuzi)*, a Warring States military treatise. In response to a question from Marquis Wu of Wei state about how to cope with the six hostile powers that surrounded him, Wu Qi discusses each state under a fixed set of rubrics: their people's nature or character, their land or territory, their government policies, the conduct of their armies, and the way to defeat them. He expounds upon the links between the terrain, character, and government of each region.

> Qin's nature is strong. Its terrain is difficult. Its government is severe. Its rewards and punishments are reliable. Its people do not yield; they are all belligerent. Therefore they scatter and fight as individuals. As the way to attack them, one must first entice them with profit and lead them away. Their officers are greedy for gain and will separate from their generals. Take advantage of their separation to attack them when scattered, set traps and seize the key moment, then their generals can be captured.
>
> Chu's nature is weak. Its terrain is broad. Its government is disorderly. Its people are weary. Therefore when placed in formations they cannot maintain them long. As the way to attack them, strike and cause disorder in their camp. First ruin their morale by nimbly advancing and then rapidly withdrawing. Cause them fatigue and toil. Do not join in actual combat, and their army can be destroyed.[6]

In this interpretation, the difficulty of Qin's terrain fosters the unyielding character of its people, which in turn induces severe government, manifested in extreme rewards and punishments. Chu's terrain, by contrast, is broad, open, and watery. This manifests itself in weak character and disorderly government, which lead to lassitude among the people. An army of such men cannot hold together for long. Wu Qi subjects each of the other states to a similar analysis.

These ideas also figure in a chapter on the military in the *Master Xun (Xunzi)*, a third-century B.C. Confucian philosophical text. It speaks only

This reference to the fiery and impetuous nature of southerners figures in other texts, and a belief in the "poisonous words" of certain people also appears in Qin legal documents.[8]

That so many regional particularities could be transcended only through tribute paid to a unitary state was a theme of both the *Tribute of Yu* and the *Master Xun*. After describing the products that distinguish each region, the *Master Xun* asserts that all local products must converge in the central state or in the person of the ruler:

> The north sea has running horses and barking dogs, but the central states obtain, raise, and command them. The south sea has feathers, plumes, elephant tusks, rhinoceros hides, copper, and cinnabar; but the central states obtain them and turn them into wealth. The eastern sea has purple-dye plants, white silks, fish, and salt; but the central states obtain them and wear or eat them. The western sea has skins, hides, and patterned yak tails; but the central states obtain and employ them.[9]

This geographic schema was carried forward into the Han. Its clearest expression is in Sima Qian's *Shi ji* (*Records of the Historian/Astrologer*), the first great history of China, completed around 90 B.C. In a section focused on prominent merchants and manufacturers, Sima Qian states that the Han united the world, opened up trade and communication between regions, and moved the former ruling houses and regionally powerful families to the capital. He then divides China into a set of regions identified with the former Warring States and describes each one in terms of its location, distinctive products, and the characteristic temperament or behavior of its people:

> Zou and Lu border on the Zhu and Si rivers. They still have the lingering influence of the Duke of Zhou, so by custom they are fond of the classicists and do everything by ritual. Consequently their people are fussy and punctilious. They have a considerable industry in sericulture [growing silkworms] and hemp, but no wealth from forests or wetlands. The territory is small and people numerous, so the people are very frugal. They have an aversion to crimes and avoid heterodoxy. In their decline, however, they have grown fond of trade and pursue profit, in this regard being worse than the men of Zhou.[10]

of the leading military powers Qi, Wei, and Qin. Like the Λ
text emphasizes how the difficulty of Qin's terrain prod\
sturdy people who were controllable only through rigorous
punishments. However, it gives a more elaborate account o.
narrowness and isolation of Qin's topography, features that w
prominently in Han criticisms of that state: "As for the peop
[the land] from which they are provisioned is narrow and cut c
control of the people is stern and harsh. They are coerced by ge\
conditions and isolated. They are made accustomed [to service
wards and manipulated by punishments."[7]

The *Master Xun* further argues that these Warring States armies
not match those of the sage founders of the earlier Shang and Zho\
nasties, even though the earlier armies were small and equipped \
primitive weapons. This was because regional armies fighting under
sway of local customs supposedly were no match for an idealized a
conquering authority based on ritual and moral perfection. This autho,
ity transcends custom because it derives from the textual and ritual pro
gram of the classicist tradition. The *Master Xun* follows the *Master Wu*
in most respects, except that the moral power of the sage, rather than the
strategic skills of the commander, is the force that conquers soldiers acting within the limitations of their local customs.

The derivation of character from physical environment also appears in
texts that explain the differences between the Chinese and their neighbors to the north and south. In these texts, the north is the realm of extreme yin (shady, dark, and cold), while the south is yang (bright, sunny,
and hot). The distinctive physiques and cultures of the peoples in these
regions derive from this difference. A related argument in a first-century
A.D. text describes the south as a zone of disease and death and then ex-
pands this poisonous atmosphere to include human nature and conduct:

The fiery air of the sun regularly produces poison. This air is hot.
The people living in the land of the sun are impetuous. The mouths
and tongues of these impetuous people become venomous. Thus, the
inhabitants of Chu and Yue [middle and lower Yangzi] are impetuous and passionate. When they talk with others, and a drop of their
saliva strikes their interlocutors, the arteries of the latter begin to
swell and ulcerate. The southern commanderies are a very hot region. When the people there curse a tree, it withers, and when they
spit on a bird it drops down dead.

Sima Qian's text carries forward the theme that a unified polity encompasses and rules regions marked by distinctive products and customs. But he introduces several significant innovations.

First, local customs and temperament are central to Sima Qian's presentation. Goods and their exchange are mentioned, but the focus of his attention is the characteristic emotions and behavior of the people. Second, he identifies the regions with the old Warring States. Here, the Han dynasty, with its unified empire, plays the role attributed in the *Master Xun* to the sage ruler, and the regions are the formerly independent states that were absorbed into the empire. Local custom is thus identified with a period of great political and cultural strife—an identification so strong that the early Western Han scholar Jia Yi (201–169 B.C.) referred to the states allied against Qin as "the diverse customs," and when Sima Qian divided Chu into three distinct regions he referred to them as "the three customs."[11]

Advocates of unification considered local "customs" to be marks of intellectual limitation and lack of refinement. In philosophical terms, customs embodied the errors of conventional wisdom, against which the intellectual traditions of the Qin and the Han defined themselves. In political terms, a creature of custom was an inferior and a subject. Regional customs were partial and limited, as opposed to the text-based, universal wisdom of the sage.

> The sons of craftsmen and carpenters all carry on their fathers' work, and the people of cities and countries are all comfortable in and used to their own customs. Dwelling in Chu one becomes a person of Chu; dwelling in Yue one becomes a person of Yue; dwelling in Xia [the central Chinese states] one becomes a person of Xia. This is not inborn nature, but caused by accumulation and polishing. Thus, if a man is able to carefully focus on his actions, to be cautious against growing habituated to customs, and to greatly accumulate and polish, then he will become a gentleman.[12]

In this geography of class, ordinary people are bound by the power of custom, knowing only the inherited occupations of their natal land. Commoners are inferior to scholars, and rural villagers are inferior to courtiers, while only the sage ruler is truly liberated by his universal wisdom.

Trapped in their immediate physical environment, commoners and villagers become obsessed by material objects. In contrast to the superior man who "makes things serve him," the petty man is "reduced to the service of things." As summarized in the *Springs and Autumns of Master Lü* (*Lüshichun qiu*), an encyclopedic text sponsored by the chief minister of Qin just before unification, "One who is prince over the people and desires to cause the lands beyond the seas to submit must restrain to the highest degree his use of things and place no value on petty profit. Having his senses escape from the sway of custom, he can bring order to the age." This exalted claim justified the Qin conquest of the other Warring States, which, according to stone inscriptions composed for the first emperor, led to the "inspection" and then the "cleansing of customs."[13]

Qin and Han writers thus adapted the criticism of custom developed by their philosophers to formulate a spatial theory of empire in which the governments of the Warring States were dismissed as products of limited regional cultures. What had been good government in the age of competing states now became partiality, ignorance, and greed. In its place the imperial authors proposed a standard based on the textual wisdom of sages that negated topography and transcended locality.

Although the Qin and Han states thus claimed to have risen above geography and custom, the history of this period was defined by a shifting balance of power between regions and by variations in the imperial government's relation to the land it claimed to rule. The remaining sections of this chapter will sketch these shifts and variations, which will be explored in more detail in the chapters that follow.[14]

Qin and the Geographic Limits of Unification (897–202 B.C.)

The core of Chinese civilization—the Yellow River valley—was divided into the area to the east of the Hangu pass (Guandong) and the area "within the passes" (Guanzhong) west of the Hangu pass and south of Tong pass. Qin state controlled Guanzhong and in the middle of the Warring States period had occupied the Sichuan basin as well. Thus, Qin's conquest of the other Warring States, completed in 221 B.C., marked the triumph of the Guanzhong region over Guandong and the Yangzi drainage basin. The first century and a half of imperial Chinese history was shaped by this fact. Long a frontier region consisting of loess highlands, mountains, and two river valleys, Guanzhong, under the Qin, had developed strong military traditions during warfare with hostile peoples to its north and west and later to the east. These traditions were still recognized in the Han popular saying that "Guanzhong produces generals, while Guandong produces ministers."

Indeed, the Guandong region was distinguished by its cultivation of the arts of administration and literature. All the major philosophical traditions had originated in the east, which remained the center of text-based learning. The region was also the demographic center of the empire. By the end of the Western Han it possessed half a dozen commanderies with populations of more than 1,500,000, while the three commanderies immediately around the capital had only 1,000,000 apiece. Of the dozen largest cities, all but the old capital and Chengdu were in the east. The area was the most agriculturally fertile in the empire, and also the center of craft production, as indicated by the fact that eight out ten government craft offices were there.

While less important than Guanzhong or Guandong, the region of the Yangzi drainage basin possessed a colorful history and culture defined by the legacy of the earlier Chu state. During the late Zhou and Warring States periods, Chu had been part of the Chinese cultural sphere but was marked by its own traditions in art, literature, and religion. The perception of Chu as a realm apart is indicated by a remark from a frustrated adviser to Xiang Yu, the Chu commander who would eventually overthrow the Qin: the adviser had "heard that Chu people were just monkeys in clothes." Other stories, linked to the doctrine of hot climates producing hot-tempered people, refer to the tendency of Chu people to resort to violence at the least provocation. Whatever the basis of these stereotypes, the Han imperial house originated in Chu, and much of the tastes of the Western Han court in dress, music, and poetry derived from this southern culture.[15]

Originally established in 897 B.C. as a small dependency to raise horses for the Zhou royal house, the Qin state expanded for the next two centuries until it reached the edge of the Yellow River. Since it was in the far west, Qin had no organized foes to the west or the south, and it also enjoyed good natural defenses. Jia Yi in the early Western Han period noted this fortunate geographic situation: "The territory of Qin was made secure through being ringed by mountains and bounded by the Yellow River, thus protected on every side."[16]

Qin's first incursion into the central regions occurred in 672 B.C. But only after it had secured its own position in the west through the conquest of neighboring tribesmen in the fourth century B.C. did Qin begin to figure prominently in the political rivalries among the Warring States.

Over the course of the next century and a half Qin defeated all its opponents. Its new empire was organized into thirty-six commanderies, which in turn were subdivided into more than a thousand districts. In this way, throughout the Chinese world, Qin imposed direct rule on all its newly conquered regions.[17]

Qin's ultimate military and political success was grounded in agrarian reforms instituted by Shang Yang, the chief minister in the middle of the fourth century B.C. From 350 B.C. onward, the Qin government legally recognized ownership of land by individual peasant households, along with the right to buy and sell it. At the same time, families from overpopulated states to the east were encouraged to resettle in sparsely populated Qin. In exchange for recognition of their land ownership, peasants were obliged to pay taxes and provide service, especially military service, to the state. Qin's heartland in the Wei River valley was gridded by pathways and irrigation ditches into uniform plots that could be given away as rewards or inducements for loyalty to the government. This transformation of the structure of Qin agricultural lands and the relation of its people to that structure underlay the state's rise to power.

The reform of landholding was accompanied by the division of the state into territories administered by officials appointed by the ruler. The court's authority in the countryside increased as a result, and the influence of holders of hereditary fiefs declined. Administrative districts under court appointees had been introduced in the successor states of Jin, from which Shang Yang imported the institution, but the Qin state carried it through more systematically than its rivals.

Despite these successes, some hereditary fiefs were still being awarded in Qin in the late third century. When officials complained to the first emperor of Qin that he was not awarding enough fiefs, nor giving them to his own sons or meritorious ministers in the manner of the Zhou kings, the chancellor Li Si rejected the criticism. He pointed out that the enfeoffed descendants of the previous Zhou dynasty had eventually turned against both their king and one another, thereby fragmenting the state. The new empire would include no kingdoms but would entirely be directly ruled by appointees of the emperor.

At the same time that it reshaped its own lands, Qin opened new regions to cultivation. It conquered the Shu and Ba peoples in what is now Sichuan and began the irrigation networks that made the Chengdu plain a fertile region—networks still in use today. A canal built by Zheng Guo drew water from the Wei River beginning in 246 B.C. to irrigate the alka-

line land of central Shanxi. Although the canal was not a major feat of
engineering by later standards, being only about twenty miles long, it
made a major contribution to Qin wealth: "Thereupon the land within
the passes became a fertile plain, and there were no more bad years. Qin
thus became rich and powerful, and ended by conquering the feudal
lords." This passage exaggerates in its focus on a single cause, but its insistence on the fundamental importance of improved water control to the
rise of Qin is indisputable.[18]

The administrative uniformity imposed by Qin masked the fact that it
remained one state ruling others, with a clear division between Qin and
its recently conquered rivals. Qin's rapid fall to the rebellious Chu in 206
B.C., only fifteen years after it conquered the last Warring State, precipi-
tated a debate about whether a unified empire transcending regional
states was indeed possible. The Qin collapse led to a resurgence of calls
for distribution of political power among the regions. This idea had already been adopted by the last Qin ruler, who in 207 B.C. declared himself to be one king among others, rather than an emperor, in an attempt
to preserve what was left of his crumbling authority. His kingship, however, was short-lived, and he was put to death a year later by one of the
chief rebels, Xiang Yu.

Yet Xiang Yu pursued a similar vision of restoring a confederacy of
states in the image of the Eastern Zhou. Making himself king of Chu, he
sought to divide the rest of the empire into eighteen states held loosely
under his authority. These kingdoms were distributed to his generals and
to rivals whom he hoped to appease. One of the latter was Liu Bang, who
became king over a state in the valley of the Han River, one of three
carved out of the old Qin state. Now known as the king of Han, Liu Bang
went on to defeat Xiang Yu and found the Han dynasty.

In contrast to Xiang Yu, Liu Bang (later the emperor Han Gaozu,
r. 202–195 B.C.) established an imperial state that largely adopted Qin institutions, while making concessions to the power of regional loyalties
and the need to reward his allies. After briefly establishing his capital at
Luoyang, he recognized the geographic advantages of the Qin state and
shifted his capital to the new city of Chang'an, just across the Wei River
to the south of the old Qin capital. While preserving simplified versions
of Qin institutions in the western half of the empire, he divided the more
populous east and the Yangzi valley into ten kingdoms that were distributed as rewards to his leading followers. Laws were instituted to separate
the imperial realm from the states to the east. However, within six years

Gaozu had contrived to replace all but one of the kings with his own brothers or sons, thus affirming the principle that "all under Heaven was the realm of the Liu clan."

Nevertheless, the administrative division between Guanzhong and the rest of the empire remained in place. This was marked by a whole set of regulations, including a ban on the exportation of horses from Guanzhong (to reduce the military threat of the kingdoms to the east), the stipulation that anyone who served in the courts of the kings could not serve in the central imperial court, and the requirement of travel documents issued by the state for anyone going through the passes.[19] In short, the structure of the early Han state retained, in modified form, the domination of the Guanzhong region over the rest of the empire.

The Suppression of Regional Powers (202–87 B.C.)

Granting kingdoms to imperial relatives still posed the dangers that Li Si had warned against, and in time several of the states began to detach themselves from the imperial center. Some even threatened to form alliances with nomads to the north of the Han frontier. To counter these threats, the third and fourth Han emperors, Wen (r. 179–157 B.C.) and Jing (r. 156–141 B.C.), weakened the regional kingdoms in four ways.

First, when the ruler of a large kingdom died, his lands were divided among his children or among other Liu relatives. Thus, the state of Qi was divided into six states within forty years of its foundation. Second, if a king left no heirs, then his kingdom reverted to direct imperial control. Third, part of the territory of several rulers was confiscated as a penalty for supposed crimes. Finally, the imperial court carved up the kingdoms of rebels, supposed or real. For example, when the king of Huainan was convicted of plotting rebellion (on the basis of an accusation made under torture by a former subordinate), he was sent into exile, where he committed suicide, and his state was divided. This systematic assault on the power of the feudatory kingdoms led to a rebellion in 154 B.C., when the king of Wu led an alliance of seven states against the Han court. The suppression of this rebellion brought on a wave of confiscations and divisions that ended the political threat of the feudatory states.

By the reign of Emperor Wu (r. 140–87 B.C.), the interior of China was firmly under imperial control, so the emperor turned his attention outward. From 134 to 119 B.C. the main effort was a war against the Xiongnu, the great nomadic empire that ruled the lands to the north and the northwest of the Han. Seeking allies, the dispatched Zhang Qian in 138 B.C. to find the Yuezhi, a nomadic people who had been enemies of the Xiongnu. Although taken prisoner by the Xiongnu and held for over a decade, Zhang Qian became familiar with the city-states of Eastern Central Asia (modern Xinjiang), which were inhabited by Indo-European peoples who lived off trade and irrigation-based agriculture. In subsequent decades these states became linked to the Han by many economic, political, and cultural ties.

In the same period, as Han forces advanced into the south, the southwest, Korea, and Eastern Central Asia, the empire attained its greatest size, with eighty-four commanderies and eighteen kingdoms. North China was largely free of raids, and the empire's expansion into Eastern Central Asia led to the acquisition of new crops such as clover, pomegranates, and grapes, as well as new styles of music and cosmetics. To celebrate his triumphs, Emperor Wu introduced a multitude of cultic reforms, culminating in the greatest religious rituals known in Han China, the *feng* and *shan* sacrifices at Mount Tai. In these rites the emperor asserted his sovereignty over the world, proclaimed his success to the highest gods, and like the first emperor sought to cap his worldly triumphs with the ultimate prize of immortality. Indeed, the acquisition of land and the pursuit of immortality were closely linked, for immortals lived at the edges of the earth or on the peaks of mountains, which only a world-ruling monarch could bring within his realm.

Landlordism and Resurgence of Regionalism
(87 B.C.–88 A.D.)

While the Han state was devoting its wealth and manpower to military expansion, the real threat to the sovereign's territorial control was the gradual emergence of landlordism. In Emperor Wu's reign, officials sought to transform the temporary wealth of a government post into the permanent security of land. Writers began to call attention to the widening gap between wealthy landowners and poor peasants. Dong Zhongshu (ca. 179–104 B.C.), a failed courtier but a leading figure in Confucian scholasticism, blamed this development on Qin's introduction of private ownership of land, allowing those with money to buy up the holdings of anyone who fell on hard times. As a result, "The rich are able to join up block after block of land, while the poor lacked even enough land on which to stand an awl."[20] To counter this concentration of landholding, he advocated reviving the mythic "well-field" grid system of equal blocks of land described in the fourth-century B.C. philosophical text *Mencius*.

But contrary to Dong Zhongshu's assertions, the roots of landlordism lay not in Qin but in Han agricultural policies. The wars of Emperor Wu required taxes that drained the meager resources of the peasants. The burden was exacerbated by the practice of collecting capitation taxes in cash. When the harvest was good and the value of grain dropped, a peasant had to sell a larger share of his harvest to raise the necessary cash. When the harvest was bad and grain became expensive, he had little grain to sell. Forced to borrow money to meet their obligations, peasants sank deeper into debt and eventually had to sell their sole asset, their land.

A second destructive aspect of Han policy was also linked to the financing of wars. Emperor Wu instituted a property tax based on the total value of a household's holdings. Failure to fully report wealth was punishable by confiscation of all property, and any informer received a share of what the state took. Mercantile wealth was taxed at twice the rate of land, so merchants seeking to protect their wealth bought up real estate. Officials trying to convert the temporary windfall of a high salary into permanent wealth also bought fields and farms. Thus, large numbers of peasants ruined by the government had to sell their land to merchants and officials pushed by the same government into buying them out. The result was social inequities on a vast scale.

Technological developments also played a role in the concentration of landholding. A farmer with enough money to buy iron tools and ox-drawn plows could cultivate more land than those who relied on wooden implements and their own back-breaking labor. Later innovations that combined ox-drawn plows with seeders that could be operated by a single worker exacerbated the difference in productivity between rich and poor. Even the brick-lined wells needed for irrigation in the Yellow River valley required considerable wealth to build. Those with the capital to adopt the most advanced technology worked larger areas and obtained higher yields than those who could not, thereby further concentrating wealth and land in the hands of the few rather than the many.

This shift in land control eventually ended the practice of moving locally powerful families to the capital region, primarily to towns associated with imperial tombs. Both the first emperor and Han Gaozu had done this in order to mitigate regional powers, and the practice was repeated six more times in the Western Han. In 20 B.C. a courtier persuaded the emperor to attempt a seventh forcible resettlement: "For more than thirty years nobody in the empire has moved to live in towns associated with imperial tombs. There is an increasing mass of wealthy people east of the passes, most of whom have fixed their claim to the best fields and are causing the poor to serve them. They ought to be moved to the new tomb, in order to strengthen the imperial capital and weaken the regional nobility. This would also facilitate equalizing the rich and the poor."[21]

Although the emperor approved the proposal, it could not be carried out, for by this time the power of the great families matched that of the court. This defeat, in which the ruler acknowledged that he could not command his subjects to leave the graves of their own ancestors in order to tend those of the emperors, was a striking symbol of the shifting balance of power between the court and the regions. At roughly the same time, the shrines of the imperial lineage established in every commandery of the empire were suppressed in the name of frugality and filial piety: forcing officials and local worthies to make offerings to men who were not their ancestors violated a major principle of Confucian thought.

Another sign of a weakening dynastic center was the increasing control over the court exercised by families of the emperors' consorts. If an emperor died young, the empress dowager (his mother, who was linked to the imperial family by marriage only) chose not just his successor but also the regent and sometimes the imperial tutor. These last two were often members of the dowager's family. Wang Zhengjun, the mother of Emperor Cheng (r. 32–7 B.C.), installed her brothers and nephews in positions of power in just this way when her son and his two successors, Emperors Ai (r. 6–1 B.C.) and Ping (r. 1 B.C.–5 A.D.), died without heirs. She channeled more and more power to her nephew Wang Mang, who was twice appointed regent and who finally installed himself as acting emperor. In 9 A.D. he declared the Han line finished and accepted the abdication of the last Western Han ruler.

However, Wang Mang's Xin dynasty lasted only seventeen years. Having lived his entire life at court, nourished on the statist fantasies of the *Rituals of Zhou* and other Confucian texts, he sought to carry out the radical restoration of imagined Zhou institutions, as advocated by so many earlier scholars. All land was to be confiscated and redistributed in equal plots, while slavery and tenancy were to be abolished. The reform met such resistance that it was abandoned after three years. Nevertheless, due to the hostility that had been generated among the great families, when a peasant rebellion challenged Wang Mang's authority, the leading families of the east China plain joined the rebellion, overthrew his Xin dynasty, and helped to establish a distant relative of the Liu lineage as first emperor of a "restored" Han in a new eastern capital.

Isolation of the Eastern Han (25–168 A.D.)

In many ways the revived Eastern Han dynasty bore little resemblance to its western predecessor. Although this fact was disguised in the early reigns, the Han revival marked the triumph of locally powerful families over the central court and the consequent shift of authority from the capital toward the regions. Basic institutions, such as universal military service, were abandoned, as were all attempts to restrict the concentration of land ownership. Emperor Guangwu (r. 25–57 A.D.), a ninth-generation Liu whose nearest imperial relative was the third-generation Emperor Jing, demoted all the kings and replaced them with closer relations. Fewer than ten major clans of the Western Han maintained their eminence in the Eastern Han.

When Emperor Gaozu founded the Western Han, his eighteen chief followers had received the highest offices, but once they died their families rapidly declined. Emperor Guangwu, by contrast, was from a landlord family, and other landlords had assisted his rise. When these men died, their families continued to hold power in their communities and often to secure offices at court, because they held long-established local bases and considerable wealth. Much of Eastern Han history is consequently a history of lineages and factions with regional power bases, such as the Yin clan of Nanyang in modern Henan, or the Ma clan of the Wei River valley.

Perhaps of even greater significance was the shift of the capital from the region within the passes to the flood plain of the Yellow River east of the Hangu pass. The opposition between these two regions, which had defined much of Warring States and Qin history, had continued to be crucial in the early Han period and in Han law. The transfer of the capital from Chang'an to Luoyang represented a shift from an area that had dominated through strategic position and military force to one that claimed supremacy in the spheres of literary and economic production. This meant not only the seizure of political pre-eminence by landlords and merchants who had accumulated estates and wealth during the Western Han period but also the rejection of the military traditions of the Qin region and the assertion of the primacy of literary and artistic cultivation.

The shift of the capital was the geographic foundation for the "triumph of Confucianism"—a phrase often used to describe intellectual developments in Han China. Major works of Eastern Han history and literature expatiated on the superiority of the new capital, with its associated ritual reforms, to the former capital, which had been little more than a continuation of the Qin empire. Similarly, the late first-century A.D. writings of Ban Gu linked the Western Han with the Qin in an age of violence and barbarism, while celebrating the triumph of culture and ritual in the Eastern Han.

Yet the Western Han order was not completely abandoned, for the new dynasty traced its legitimacy back through the Liu lineage. This was shown in a dispute over who were considered ancestors of the founding Emperor Guangwu. Early in his reign he erected shrines in Luoyang to his own ancestors, men who had never been emperors nor even enfeoffed as kings. When this led to vociferous protests about corrupting the imperial line, Guangwu moved the shrines from the capital to his old home at Nanyang, just to the south of Luoyang. In their place he worshiped the seventh- and eighth-generation emperors Xuan (r. 74–49 B.C.) and Yuan (r. 49–33 B.C.) as his own father and grandfather. A fictive family was thus created that grafted the revived dynasty onto the last ruler of the Western Han who had produced an heir.

Other changes took place in the geography of China during the first three reigns of the Eastern Han. As Emperor Guangwu abandoned the earlier offensive strategy on the northern frontier, the Xiongnu engaged in substantial raids. A large-scale flight to the south ensued, eventually leaving vast regions depopulated and hundreds of districts abolished. Eastern Han rulers began to resettle nomads in these abandoned regions within the frontiers and to use them to provide cavalry against the Xiongnu. While militarily effective, this policy intensified pressures for southward migration. Between 2 and 140 A.D. the registered population in the northwest dropped by 70 percent, while the population in the south rose substantially—in some districts by as much as 100 percent. Despite this population shift, the Yangzi valley and regions to the south remained a frontier region, with most of the registered population there concentrated in a few urban centers.

By the time the Eastern Han dynasty was coming to an end, scholars were already looking back on its first three reigns as a golden age. Beginning with Emperor He (r. 89–106) the court became increasingly isolated, cut off from both its frontier and the interior. At the frontiers, the Xiongnu federation was destroyed forever at the end of the 80s, only to be replaced by their former subjects, the Xianbei, as threats. These tribesmen had received massive payments for killing Xiongnu, but their very success caused the subsidies to dry up. The Xianbei consequently began to extract wealth from the Chinese population by force. On the western border, Qiang nomads had been resettled inside the Han frontiers to provide labor and replace the population that had fled the region. Brutal treatment at the hands of Han landlords and officials led to a major rebellion in 110. The Eastern Han court, no longer greatly concerned with affairs in the distant "barbarian" west, decided to cut its losses by abandoning four provinces. Those Chinese who were unwilling to move saw their homes and crops burned by the local government. Not surprisingly, a large group of disgruntled frontiersmen joined the Qiang against the Han.

Bursts of interest on the part of the court led to a partial reconquest and the temporary reestablishment of military colonies, but they did not last long. By 168 the Ordos region and areas adjoining the former capital had been lost. Rebellions also rose in the south in 137, but rather than sending armies it no longer commanded, the court dispatched senior officials to bribe local chiefs with promises of marquisates. This solution worked for a few years, but in the 140s rebels arose from the south, killing governors in interior commanderies and desecrating imperial tombs.

Thus the court lost control not only of frontier populations but of frontier armies as well. During the Western Han and the first century of Eastern Han rule, generals had been appointed for the duration of a campaign. In the second century A.D. frontier commanders remained at their posts for decades. Their armies—made up of convicts, nomad tribesmen, and professional soldiers who had replaced the peasant levies—had no ties to the Han state. Instead, they developed strong personal bonds with their immediate commanders, who paid their wages and represented their sole link to the court. By the last decades of the Eastern Han, the court was no more able to command the imperial armies than it was able to control the nomads resettled inside the frontiers.

The empire did not fare any better in the interior. There, the court lost control over commanderies through impoverishment and ineptitude. From the beginning of the second century A.D., as the government's coffers ran low, the court ordered local officials to deal with floods or other

disasters, but without providing the means to do so. In 143 official salaries were reduced, and the court began to borrow money from kings and
nobles. Regional inspectors began to act as semi-independent governors
of entire provinces, recruiting soldiers on their own initiative and pursuing policies of their own choosing.

The central government, for its part, was increasingly cut off from
local society by the growing power of the "Inner Court" secretariat composed of eunuchs. The official bureaucracy, staffed by members of powerful lineages with regional bases who had formed the primary link between the court and local society, lost all its authority. The split became
critical after large numbers of courtiers were banned from holding office
in the Great Proscription of 169, which followed an unsuccessful attempt
to destroy eunuch power by force. The landlord author Cui Shi (d. 170)
quoted a popular saying that summarized the court's loss of authority in
local society: "Orders from the provincial and commandery governments
arrive like thunderbolts; imperial edicts are merely hung upon the wall
[as decoration]."[22]

The local reaction to disorder and the inability of the imperial government to cope with it was to band together for self-defense. In areas dominated by powerful lineages, landlords formed private armies made up
of their tenants and neighboring free peasants. In areas without landlords (usually poorer and more backward regions), whole villages under
the leadership of their elders moved up into the hills and built walled settlements. Such migrations inspired Tao Yuanming's fourth-century A.D.
story of the hidden, egalitarian utopia of the "Peach Blossom Spring."

Warlordism and the Breakdown into Regions (A.D. 169–220)

Finally, in certain areas peasants and local scholars began to form religious associations, organizing themselves into military units and often es-
pousing millenarian doctrines. One of the largest of these associations
was organized by Zhang Jue, who taught that disease resulted from sin
and could be healed by confession. He came to believe that the Han lineage was exhausted and that his fate was to establish a new dynasty under the rising Yellow Heaven. He organized his followers into military
units and gave them titles.

The court discovered followers of Zhang Jue among the palace guards,
but it was still taken by surprise in 184 when news arrived that a rebellion had broken out in sixteen commanderies, sweeping aside the local

troops, seizing several cities, and kidnapping kings. These rebels, called Yellow Turbans because of the headdress that showed their allegiance to the new Heaven, were defeated within a year, but only with the assistance of the private armies of powerful lineages. Moreover, other rebellions inspired by the Yellow Turbans soon broke out. The most significant was the Five Pecks of Grain movement in Sichuan, which established an independent Daoist theocracy for several decades. By 188 most of the Han empire was divided between independent provincial governors and local strongmen—categories that had become virtually indistinguishable.

In 189 Dong Zhuo, a frontier general from the northwest, brought his army to within 70 miles of Luoyang. Invited into the city by officials who had massacred the eunuchs, Dong Zhuo seized the capital and kidnapped the boy emperor. Unsure of his position so far from his base, Dong Zhuo burned the eastern capital to the ground and took the emperor back to Chang'an. The rebel was killed in the northwest in 192, and the young emperor was passed from warlord to warlord, as the empire broke up into eight regions. The leader of one region, Yuan Shu, declared himself emperor in 197, but his own people deserted him, and he died in misery two years later. He failed because the Han emperor, powerless though he was, still embodied the vanished unity to which all the warlords aspired but which none was able to attain. Until such time as one of the aspirants was in a position of unchallenged supremacy, the last emperor remained a vital pawn on the political chessboard.

One of the warlords, Cao Cao, described the hopeless situation as follows:

> My armor has been worn so long that lice breed in it,
> Myriad lineages have perished.
> White bones exposed in the fields,
> For a thousand *li* not even a cock is heard.
> Only one out of a hundred survives,
> Thinking of it rends my entrails.[23]

Cao Cao finally took charge of the emperor and held him as a virtual prisoner for more than twenty years. Although he did not dare to take the title of emperor for himself, Cao Cao encroached on the privilege of the imperial line by declaring himself king of Wei in 216, a title previously reserved for the Liu lineage. However, Cao Cao could not repeat the success of the first emperor or Han Gaozu in directly administering the land

and the peasant population. With most territory controlled by landlords, he had to be content with establishing military colonies in those areas that had been depopulated by war and flood. These colonies were allotted to refugees who served in his armies or provided taxes, men who became effectively tenants of the imperial house. The government thus came to rely on state-owned lands worked by a hereditary soldiery, asserting its authority only as the greatest of the landlords with the largest private army.

Cao Cao conquered the Yellow River valley, thereby reuniting the north. However, his abortive attempt to impose his authority in the Yangzi valley ended in disaster at the battle of Red Cliff, where he was defeated by the youthful warlord Sun Quan. When the last Han emperor finally abdicated to Cao Cao's son, Cao Pi, in 220, only three warlords remained: Cao Pi in the north, Sun Quan in the lower Yangzi, and Liu Bei in Sichuan. Each declared himself emperor—of Wei, Wu, and Shu, respectively—thus initiating the period of the Three Kingdoms. This was followed by three centuries in which the Chinese state that had been governed as a unity in the early imperial period was divided into northern and southern regions defined by the valleys of the Yellow River and the Yangzi.

2

A STATE ORGANIZED FOR WAR

THE QIN state's conquests of its neighbors and the unified empire that emerged were built on a foundation of reforms that Shang Yang, a minister from the state of Wey, carried out in the years following 359 B.C. His radical, thoroughgoing transformations of Qin military and civil life grew out of practices that were first pioneered in Qi and in Jin and its successors. Internecine wars among the Zhou nobility following the monarchy's loss of power and the eastward shift of the capital in 770 B.C. had put pressure on Qi and Jin to increase the size of their armies. Gradually these states extended military service from the nobility and its followers to the entire population of the capital, and then on to certain segments of the rural population. Under Shang Yang's adaptation of these practices, Qin peasants who served in the army were rewarded with land that their individual households could hold and work and on which they paid taxes. But there were severe punishments as well as rewards.

The discovery of over a thousand Qin dynasty bamboo strips at Shuihudi in 1975 produced an abundance of new materials for the study of late Warring States Qin. These sources, however, have not changed the basic outlines of our understanding of Shang Yang's reforms as described around the turn of the first century B.C. in Sima Qian's *Shi ji* (*Records of the Historian/ Astrologer*):

> He commanded that the people be divided into tens and fives and that they supervise each other and be mutually liable. Anyone who failed to report criminal activity would be chopped in two at the waist, while those who reported it would receive the same reward as

that for obtaining the head of an enemy. Anyone who actively hid a criminal would be treated the same as one who surrendered to an enemy [he would be executed and all property confiscated]. Any family with more than two adult males who did not divide the household would pay a double military tax. Those who had achievements in the army would in proportion receive an increase in rank [in the twenty-rank hierarchy in which the entire populace was rated]. Those who engaged in private quarrels would be punished with a severity that accorded with the gravity of their quarrel. Those who devoted themselves to the fundamental enterprises and through their farming and weaving contributed much grain and cloth would be remitted [from tax and corvée], while those who worked for peripheral profits [in trade and crafts] and those who were idle or poor would be confiscated as slaves. Those in the royal family who had no military merit would not be listed in the registers of [royal] relatives . . . For the fields he opened up the *qian* and *mo* [horizontal and vertical pathways] and set up boundaries. He equalized the military levies and land tax and standardized the measures of capacity, weight, and length.[1]

These reforms, and others, radically altered the nature of both the army and the state in several ways.

First, they made possible a substantial increase in the size of armies, which from the middle of the sixth century were increasingly composed primarily of infantry. In the sixth and fifth centuries B.C., Wu and Yue, located in the lower Yangzi valley, had introduced reliance on infantry to the Yellow River valley through their northward expansion. In the two centuries between the introduction of infantry and the reforms of Shang Yang, mass infantry armies composed of peasant levies, supplemented by cavalry in the fourth century B.C., supplanted the chariot armies of the aristocracy.

Soldiers on foot required fewer specialized military skills and far less expensive equipment than the chariot-based nobility. And with new sources of manpower made available by the extension of levies into the countryside, states and noble lineages could rapidly create armies of infantry that dwarfed the old chariot armies. Finally, technological innovations—the invention of the crossbow, the development of lamellar armor (composed of rows of leather plates, sometimes lacquered, sewn together), the improvement and general propagation of swords (again, introduced by Wu and Yue), and the increasing use of iron weapons—made the infantry army a truly formidable force. In the internecine wars of the period, those states that developed mass infantry armies, equipped with the new weaponry, soon swallowed up rivals who failed to do so.

A seventh-century army would not have exceeded 10,000 men, and even greatly expanded forces in the late sixth century consisted of no more than 50,000 soldiers. Warring States armies, on the other hand, may have numbered in the hundreds of thousands, with the largest force mentioned numbering 600,000. Even if most armies in the field had only about 100,000 soldiers, the expansion in size was still considerable. Consequently, any state that hoped to survive was required to recruit soldiers from an ever-larger base. This was possible only if the state could expand military service to lower and lower levels of the population, and to wider ranges of the hinterland.

A second transformation growing out of Shang Yang's reforms was that city-states—the dominant political unit prior to the Warring States— became obsolete in the face of these enormous armies. Defeated city-states were absorbed by their conquerors, who redistributed the land to their own population in exchange for military service and taxes. Land gained through conquest was supplemented with territory cleared from forests or made farmable through irrigation. As city-states disappeared, the old city-based nobility lost its central place in the state order, just as it lost its prominence in the army. In place of the nobility, the state was increasingly dominated by a single autocratic ruler, whose agents registered the peasants and mobilized them into state service and collected taxes to support the ruler's military ambitions.[2]

Third, Shang Yang's policies established a uniform administration for the entire population, based on military service. His five-man squads were responsible for enforcement of laws within their own units and for the performance of their units in battle. Identification of the social order with the army was strengthened through a system of ranks imposed throughout the population. Other states had tried this, but nowhere as systematically as the Qin. Anyone who gained merit in battle by slaying enemies or commanding victorious units was rewarded with promotion in a twenty-rank hierarchy. Depending on their rank, people would receive stipulated amounts of land, numbers of dwellings, and quotas of slaves. These ranks could be used to remit penalties for violations of the law or to redeem relatives from penal bondage.

Ranks were not hereditary, but if a man died heroically in battle his descendants received the number of ranks he would have gained. The hierarchy of military merit fixed by these ranks was intended to be the only measure of honor and distinction in Qin society. All social status was a direct reflection of military performance. Even members of the royal family depended upon merit earned through military service to maintain their elite status.

Under Shang Yang the Qin state transformed military districts called *xian* into the basis of local civil government. The word *xian* had first referred to the land outside a walled city which was inhabited by farm laborers and servants of the nobility. However, in the late Spring-and-Autumn period (770-481 B.C.) these *xian* became the primary source of peasant recruits for the military, and lineages or states began to recognize their strategic importance. Eventually, the entire Qin state was divided into *xian* and *jun* (originally a subunit of the *xian*), thus making universal military service the foundation of the state's entire administrative apparatus.

Shang Yang's final major reform was the construction of a network of paths that formed a rectangular grid over agricultural fields and divided the countryside into equal-sized blocks of land (Fig. 1). According to one historic source, this grid covered the entire state of Qin. Supporting evidence comes from a modern study using large-scale topographical maps to examine the layout of fields in China. It has shown that throughout much of the north, particularly the areas of Qin and Jin, roads and footpaths form a striking rectilinear pattern, everywhere oriented north-south and east-west. Regularity on this scale would have been impossible without state intervention.

Reshaping the countryside into blocks was integral to the Qin's system of military service and civil control. Shang Yang argued that agriculture was the root of all wealth, and his ideal state was a land of small-scale peasant farmers guided by a detailed code of laws. Each family received land of a size that a single adult male could work. By distributing land in this way, the state kept the maximum acreage in cultivation and made the highest possible number of adult males eligible for military service and taxes. Since those who earned high rank on the twenty-point scale received additional land and servants, the systematic partition of the land provided a fixed unit for standardized rewards. In Shang Yang's view, non-peasants such as merchants and craftsmen were dangerous parasites. They were recorded on separate registers and were sometimes subjected to servitude in state workshops or to military service in frontier garrisons.

In these ways, Shang Yang's reforms broke down the social and institu-

Fig. 1   Harvest scene set on a grid of irrigation channels. Mulberry trees have
been planted at the field's edge.

tional barriers between city and hinterland that had defined the Zhou
state. He divided the entire countryside into a rectangular grid, the entire
population into military units, and the administration into military districts; and then he mapped the individual households of the population
onto the grid in accordance with merits earned in battle or through agriculture. This identity of military and civil order and the dedication of the
entire society to military conquest were hallmarks of the Warring States
period and the foundation on which the first empire was built. Shang
Yang's reforms ultimately brought an end to the Zhou nobility and to the
armed lineages in semi-independent city-states that had used their military and cultic power to extract sustenance from the rural villages under
their control.

Along with the noble lineages, the peasant village as a unit of fiscal organization also vanished. All military power and claims to service and
tribute were now concentrated in the hands of the rulers of the territorial
states, while the only significant unit for the definition of kin ties or the
offering of service and taxation was the individual household. Whereas

political organization and kin structures had previously been merged, now they were separated into a state order under a single, absolute prince and a kin realm composed of individual households, each ruled by its own paterfamilias.[3]

Reshaped by Shang Yang's new institutions, the Qin state—hitherto a peripheral power that had figured only in historical narratives focused on more central states—made a dramatic entry onto the political stage. Shang Yang himself commanded the armies that defeated the state of Wei in the center of the Yellow River valley in 340 B.C. Winning battle after battle, Qin extended its control beyond the Hangu pass and ultimately forced Wei to accept a position as a subordinate "ally."

In 316 B.C. Qin completed its conquest, begun 130 years earlier, of the southwestern states of Shu and Ba in what is now the Sichuan basin and imposed its own law, landholding patterns, and military service on these non-Chinese neighbors. In 314 B.C. it defeated the last hostile Rong tribe and thus ended all threats to the west. In 312 B.C. Qin forces conquered the central Yangzi state of Chu at Danyang and secured the Hanzhong region. This linked the Qin heartland to Ba and Shu as a single territorial block. Combined with expansion at the expense of Wei into the central plain, these victories made Qin virtually impervious to attack. One integral state, ringed by mountains, now controlled the entire Guanzhong region.

Qin's expansion to the south opened up a new source of economic wealth that gradually made the state predominant among its rivals. In 310 B.C. Qin began construction of a new capital for Shu in Chengdu, a city modeled on the Qin capital of Xianyang. From this base Qin developed the Sichuan basin as a major agricultural center, most notably through the famous irrigation project at what is now Dujiangyan. This entailed dividing the flow of the Min River and routing the reduced flow in the new channel into a series of irrigation canals (Map 4). This irrigation system, which is still functioning today, turned the Min River basin into the major source of grain for Qin armies.[4]

The Rise of the Autocrat

While Shang Yang's policies transformed the old noble-based city-states into peasant-based warring macrostates, they did not secure the dominance of the individual ruler. Shang Yang himself was executed in 338 B.C. by a new leader who was angered when his own tutor fell victim to

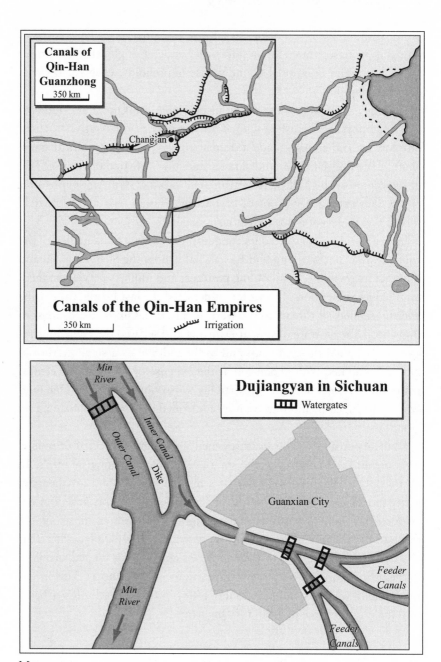

Canals of Qin-Han Guanzhong

|__ 350 km __|

Chang'an

Canals of the Qin-Han Empires

|__ 350 km __| ⌇⌇⌇ Irrigation

Dujiangyan in Sichuan

▥▥▥ Watergates

Min River

Inner Canal

Outer Canal

Dike

Guanxian City

Min River

Feeder Canals

Feeder Canals

MAP 4

Shang Yang's principle that the law applied even to members of the ruling house. A succession struggle in 307 B.C. left Qin's court at the mercy of a coalition of enfeoffed courtiers, who were all beneficiaries of a new version of fiefs that granted not political authority over towns or cities but the tax income extracted from a specified geographic area.[5]

Weakened by these setbacks, Qin was defeated by the combined armies of the other Warring States in 295. After a brief recovery, Qin suffered a disastrous defeat at the hands of the Zhao state, which used cavalry in combat. While part of the Qin forces were fighting a losing battle against Zhao, its other armies were dispatched to Qi in the Shandong peninsula, where Qin's chief minister Wei Ran expanded the enclave around his prize fief of Dingtao.

Here the history of Qin took a significant turn through the introduction of new policies to strengthen the position of the ruler. The rhetorician Fan Sui traveled to the Qin court, where he attacked the failings of Wei Ran and propounded the doctrine of "allying oneself with those who are distant [that is, the Qi state, which Wei Ran was invading] to attack those nearby [originally Han, ultimately Zhao]." The king of Qin accepted these arguments and appointed Fan Sui as a minister. Fan Sui then persuaded the king of the virtues of direct royal rule, targeting the queen dowager and Wei Ran, who had controlled the court since 307. In 266 the king dismissed the queen dowager (his mother) and banished Wei Ran and his allies. Fan Sui was then appointed chief minister.

This was a significant event, for Fan Sui was the first politician to articulate a policy of irrevocable expansionism for Qin. Abandoning the old practice of making and unmaking alliances to suit the needs of the moment and seizing territories scattered far and wide (for example, Dingtao in the east), he asserted that the way to expand was to wage war against one's neighbors through alliances with distant powers. This was, in his view, the only way to expand the state as an integrated territorial unit. To reinforce this policy of a unitary state, he insisted that "each inch or foot gained was the king's foot or inch."

This was a criticism not only of Wei Ran, enfeoffed as marquis of Rang, but also of the widespread practice of enfeoffing royal relatives and high officials. Such holders of fiefs often dominated the governments of their states, accumulated large personal fortunes, and assembled armies of personal followers, thereby challenging the monarch's authority. Fan Sui halted these practices in order to concentrate power in the person of the ruler and strengthen Qin state against its enemies.

The ruler's power was further enhanced by the introduction of elite military commands composed of full-time professionals. These men were granted a variety of legal privileges and were kept at the disposal of the ruler. The earliest recorded cases of such elite units come from the reign of King Helü of Wu (r. 510-496 B.C.), who had a personal retinue of 500 men and a corps of 3,000 runners celebrated for their endurance.

The philosophical text *Master Xun* describes the elite troops of the king of Wei, who were trained to wear heavy armor, carry a large crossbow with fifty arrows, strap halberds to their backs, buckle helmets to their heads and swords at their sides, pack a three-day supply of food, and then quick-march 100 *li* (just over twenty-five miles) in a single day. Those who met these standards earned an exemption from corvée labor and taxes for their entire household.[6] Similar troops were adopted by Shang Yang in Qin, and they provided the early model for the soldiers depicted in the famous terracotta army of the first emperor. Because the emperor's personal guard defended his position as unchallenged autocrat in life, replicas of these soldiers were placed in his tomb to continue to defend him in the afterlife.

A final maxim of Fan Sui was to not only seize territory but also attack people. The aim was not merely territorial expansion but also the destruction of armies on such a scale that rival states could not recover and fight back. As a result of this new policy, several campaigns and battles in the third century B.C. produced slaughter on a scale previously unknown in Chinese history. The greatest bloodshed, according to sources of the period, occurred when Qin defeated Zhao in the campaign at Changping in 260 B.C., a battle that supposedly ended with the death of 400,000 Zhao soldiers. Although Qin's own massive losses in this campaign and a subsequent defeat at the hands of an allied army postponed for several decades the final conquests that created the first empire, the crushing defeat of Zhao left Qin with no serious rival. All that remained was the destruction between 230 and 221 of the remaining six Warring States.[7]

In summary, the rise of Qin to dominance and its ultimate success in creating a unified empire depended on two major developments. First, under Shang Yang it achieved the most systematic version of the reforms that characterized the Warring States. These reforms entailed the registration and mobilization of all adult males for military service and the payment of taxes. While all Warring States were organized for war, Qin was unique in the extension of this pattern to every level of society, and in the manner in which every aspect of administration was devoted to mobilizing and provisioning its forces for conquest. Second, through the policies introduced by Fan Sui, Qin alone successfully concentrated power in the person of the ruler. While other states were still dispersing authority and prestige among enfeoffed administrators and royal kin, Qin was largely able to make the ruler the single locus of undivided authority.

Qin Nationality and "All under Heaven"

One major consequence of the reconstruction of the Qin state was the emergence of a distinctive national character. Qin increasingly defined itself, and was defined by others, as a land and a people apart. In the earlier Zhou state, Qin had been one state among others, linked to the rest by a shared elite culture of ritual vessels, music, and verse. Qin's elimination of the nobility and its incorporation of the lower strata of society into military and civil service meant that local or regional traditions became definitive of Qin nationality.[8]

The clearest evidence of a distinctive Qin national culture is the fairly rapid emergence of a new discourse that associated Qin with non-Chinese barbarians and linked barbarian culture to Qin's political reforms. Prior to the middle of the Warring States period, texts such as the *Transmission of Master Zuo* (*Zuo zhuan*), the *Words of the States* (*Guo yu*), the *Analects* (*Lun yu*), the *Master Mo* (*Mozi*), and the *Mencius* (*Mengzi*) seldom mention Qin, and when they do they never indicate Qin's supposed cultural otherness. The archaeological record also shows that the Qin nobility shared a common culture with states of the central plain. In their graphs and bronze bells, the Qin conservatively clung to the older Zhou forms even when more popular revised forms of graphs and bells were introduced in other states.[9] The Qin clearly did not consider themselves to be cultural outsiders associated with barbarians, as they would be described after 300 B.C., and especially under the Han.

In the late Warring States period several texts began to speak of Qin people as alien or backward in relation to the states of the central plain— a character derived from their intermingling with barbarians whose customs they presumably had absorbed. The *Gongyang Commentary to the Spring-and-Autumn Annals* (*Chun qiu Gongyang zhuan*), a Confucian text compiled sometime between 320 and 233 B.C., was one of the first to emphasize the opposition between "Chinese" and "barbarian," and it clearly identified Qin with the barbarians: "When the ruler of Qin died, the *Annals* did not record his name. Why is this? Because Qin are barbarians."[10]

Texts from the very end of the Warring States period often refer to Qin's having barbarian customs, either as an original condition or through absorption. The *Stratagems of the Warring States* (*Zhanguo ce*), a collection of model speeches attributed to historical figures from the Warring States period, asserts: "Qin has the same customs as the [barbarians] Rong and Di. It has the heart of a tiger or wolf; greedy, loving profit, and untrustworthy, knowing nothing of ritual, duty or virtuous conduct." A speaker in the same text describes Qin as "a state of tigers and wolves" that greedily desires "to swallow the whole world," but he goes even further in stating that "Qin is the mortal enemy of 'All under Heaven,'" thus treating it not merely as barbaric but as the antithesis of civilization or humanity.[11]

In the Han empire, these remarks on Qin's savage nature were conflated with its topography into a general model that accounted for the origins of the coercive laws of Shang Yang, the cruelty of the first emperor, and the fall of Qin. The early Han philosophical compendium, the *Master of Huainan* (*Huainanzi*), said:

> The customs of Qin consisted of wolf-like greed and violence. The people lacked a sense of duty and pursued profit. They could be intimidated through punishments, but could not be transformed through goodness. They could be encouraged with rewards, but could not be urged on with reputation. Enveloped in difficult terrain and belted by the Yellow River, they were cut off on all sides and thus secure. The land was profitable and the topography beneficial, so they accumulated great wealth. Lord Xiao wanted to use his tiger-like or wolf-like power to swallow up the feudal lords. The laws of Lord Shang were produced from this situation.[12]

The Han historian Sima Qian made a similar observation in the preface to his table on the comparative chronology of the Warring States: "Now Qin state mixed in the customs of the Rong and Di barbarians, so it placed violence and cruelty first and treated humanity and duty as secondary. Its position was that of frontier vassal, but it offered suburban sacrifices [like the Son of Heaven]. This terrified the true gentleman." Here, the cruelty of Qin laws and the martial tendencies of its people are explicitly attributed to Qin's being a frontier state located in a region inhabited by non-Chinese people.[13]

Sima Qian also echoes the *Master of Huainan* when he places the following remarks in Shang Yang's mouth: "Lord Shang said, 'Qin had the teachings of the Rong and Di. There was no distinction between fathers and sons, who dwelt together in the same room. Now I have reformed their teachings, and established for them the division between men and women. I have built the great Jique Palace, and set up a capital like that of Lu or Wei.'"[14] The theme of Qin barbarism is the same, but here Shang Yang's policies are intended to correct them. The remarks about building a palace and capital like those of the eastern states Lu or Wei indicate Qin's status as a backward state that sought to imitate its cultural betters.

The Han criticism of Qin as a creature of savage custom and of Qin law as an expression of barbaric local practices reached its apogee with the first great Han critic of Qin, Jia Yi, who wrote under Emperor Wen. His most celebrated discussion of Qin, "The Discursive Judgment Censuring Qin," connected Qin's terrain, its customs, and its rulers to one another and to its ultimate downfall. Its account of Qin history begins: "Qin's territory was enveloped by mountains and belted by the Yellow River, so that it was secure. It was a state cut off on all sides." Qin's excellent strategic position was the source of its security and also of its isolation.

This image of isolation reappears in Jia Yi's description of Qin's imperial rulers. "The king of Qin [the first emperor] thought he was sufficient to himself and never asked others, so he committed errors without being corrected. The second emperor inherited this, following his father without changing. Through violence and cruelty he doubled the calamity. Ziying [the third Qin ruler] was completely alone without intimates, imperiled and young he had no assistance."[15] Jia Yi follows this account of the rulers' isolation with the explanation that the "customs of Qin" placed a taboo on all criticism, so that when the rulers committed errors, no officials remonstrated with them. In contrast with the Zhou dynasty, which had established feudal lords who allowed it to survive even after it lost real power, the Qin relied entirely on "numerous laws and stern punishments" and thus had no supporters at the end. The geographically induced isolation of Qin shaped its customs, which in turn led to the isolation of the rulers and their exclusive reliance on punishments. These alien customs were specifically contrasted with the Zhou practices that had defined the civilization of the Chinese heartland.

Other writings by Jia Yi made the link between custom, law, and the fate of Qin even more explicit. The chapter "The Changing of the Times" in his *Xin shu* explains the decline of Qin customs in the following manner:

> Lord Shang turned against ritual and duty, abandoned proper human relations, and put his whole heart and mind into expansion. After practicing this for two years, Qin's customs grew worse by the day. Whenever Qin people had sons who grew to adulthood, if the family was rich they sent them out as separate households, and if they were poor they sent them out as indentured laborers. If someone lent his father a rake, hoe, staff, or broom, then he put on airs of great generosity. If a mother took a gourd dipper, bowl, dustpan, or broom, then her offspring would immediately upbraid her. Women suckled their infants in the presence of their fathers-in-law, and if the wife and mother-in-law were not on good terms then they snarled and glared at one another. Loving their young children and material gain while holding their parents in contempt and having no proper relations, they were scarcely different from animals.[16]

Here Shang Yang's reforms cause families to break up into individual nuclear households, which leads to devaluation of kin ties. The greed and the animal-like nature of the Qin people, which figured in earlier texts as inborn character, appear here as a consequence of culture, specifically Shang Yang's reforms. Jia Yi laments that his own Han dynasty carried on these corrupted Qin customs.[17]

A version of many of these ideas occurs in the *Guliang Commentary to the Spring-and-Autumn Annals* (*Chun qiu Guliang zhuan*), a work probably written in the Han period and closely related to the *Gongyang*. This text treats Qin's barbarism as something that developed in the span of recorded history, but it does not link barbarism to the reforms of Shang Yang. Instead, it traces it to an unprincipled campaign waged by Lord Mu in 627 B.C. However, it also incorporates Jia Yi's idea that the failure of Qin government manifested itself in the breakdown of proper family relations, particularly the instruction of children and the separation of men and women.[18]

These remarks on the barbaric, backward, and alien culture of Qin could be interpreted as simply the emergence of anti-Qin polemics after it became the dominant power in the region. However, scattered evidence from traditional texts, along with newly discovered materials, suggests that, in the same period, the Qin state itself adopted this persona of a state distinct from and hostile to the culture of the central plain. Thus, the accusation of the *Stratagems* that Qin was the enemy of "All under Heaven" figures also in the opening chapter of the late Warring States philosophical text *Master Han Fei* (*Han Feizi*), but since this is presented as a speech from Han Fei to the king of Qin (later the first emperor), it is clear that the authors felt that Qin accepted and perhaps even prided itself on this adversarial relation.[19]

A better-known example of Qin's sense of its own otherness is Li Si's account of the music of Qin. Himself an alien statesman who became chief minister in Qin, Li Si, in arguing against a proposal to expel foreigners, offered as precedent a supposed Qin adoption of foreign music: "The true sounds of Qin are to delight the ear by singing *woo-woo* while striking a water jar and banging a pot, strumming the zither and slapping the thigh. The music of Zheng and Wei, the *Sangjian*, *Zhao*, *Yu*, *Wu*, and *Xiang* are the music of alien states. But now you have abandoned striking water jars and banging pots to adopt the music of Zheng and Wei; set aside strumming zithers and slapping thighs to take up the *Zhao* and *Yu*." Since the comment quoted here was part of a persuasion addressed to the Qin court, this reference to "the music of alien states" was clearly not intended as an insult, as it is depicted in an anecdote from an earlier century. That Li Si and the Qin courtiers both accept the false argument that the music of the central states is a recent importation suggests that Qin had come to pride itself on its presumed cultural distinctiveness. The vulgar nature of the "true" Qin music might also suggest some pride in popular, regional practice, as opposed to the refined music of the court.[20]

The perceived separation between Qin culture and that of the other states is demonstrated in several Qin documents, both official and private, discovered in tombs. A text found at Shuihudi in the tomb of a local official serving in an area of Chu that had only recently been conquered states:

In ancient times the people each had their local custom, so what they regarded as profitable, liked, or hated were different. This was not beneficial to the people, and it was harmful to the state. Therefore the sage kings made laws and measures in order to correct and rectify the people, to eliminate their deviant boorishness, and to purge their wicked customs . . . Now the legal codes and decrees are complete, but the people do not use them. Dissipated people controlled by local custom do not cease, which means abandoning the ruler's enlightened laws.[21]

This contrast between the enlightened laws of the ruler and the benighted rule of custom indicates the difficulties faced by Qin's central government in imposing its will both on powerful local families and conquered territories.[22] The argument presupposes a cultural gulf between the people of Qin and those of Chu (which was, admittedly, not one of the central states).

Further evidence comes from letters written by Qin conscripts found in another tomb from the same time and place. The author of one of the letters complains that the natives in this recently conquered territory do not obey the occupying forces. He warns the recipient of the letter not to travel to these "new territories" which are inhabited by "bandits." This reciprocal hostility is also indicated in the received literary sources, as in the prophetic saying that "even if only three households remain in Chu, it will be Chu that destroys Qin." Such feelings would be found in any case of military occupation, but they doubtless did much to increase the sense that the two sides represented foreign and hostile cultures.[23]

This split between Qin and the central states was written into Qin law, as shown in legal documents found at Yunmeng.[24] Thus, by the end of the Warring States period, the idea that Qin was culturally distinct from the other parts of the old Zhou realm, as well as from the southern state of Chu, was not merely conventionally accepted both outside and inside Qin but was even a formal principle in Qin government practice.

Such a development fits well with our current models of pre-imperial Chinese history. Under the Zhou a vast area—including most of the Yellow River valley, the central and lower Yangzi, and to a degree the area of present-day Sichuan—had been linked by a shared elite culture. During the Warring States period the gradual disappearance of the hereditary nobility eliminated the exponents and embodiments of this culture. At the same time, the incorporation of commoners into the state, primarily through universal military service, meant that local or regional traits became definitive of those who were active in state service. Since Qin introduced the most comprehensive forms of the new institutions, it may well have achieved the highest degree of regional integration and self-consciousness.

One important element in this model was an increase in social mobility in the period. With the disappearance of hereditary offices, people from the lower aristocracy and even commoners were able to rise through the ranks in the army and government, carrying with them their indigenous ideas about music, food, literature, religion, and other aspects of life. This new social mobility is reflected in texts found in tombs, notably the Almanacs (Ri shu, literally Books of Days). Examples from Shuihudi and Fangmatan indicate that the life possibilities for a typical newborn child in Qin covered a wide range, from servant or concubine, to local bravo, to official, to a high minister or noble. Additional evidence from tombs is a fourth-century change in Qin mortuary practices which introduced, or re-introduced, catacomb burials (these had been a local feature many centuries before) and the flexing of the corpse rather than extending it in the Zhou manner. This suggests the incorporation of regional practices into elite culture.[25]

Shared military service and exposure to non-Qin people as enemies or hostile subjects would have facilitated the development of an "us-them" mentality in Qin. This took tangible form in the widespread practice in the period of building walls along the frontiers between states. Likewise a departure from Qin, according to the Almanacs, required a ritual of exorcism, similar to the ritual performed before departing from one's native town.[26]

This increasingly clear divide between states seems to have reached a crescendo in the decades immediately prior to unification. The chapter "Bringing People In [lai min]" of the late Warring States political text Book of Lord Shang (Shang Jun shu), probably written around 250 B.C., insists that only natives of Qin should be recruited into the army, while new immigrants should engage in agriculture. Somewhat later, Qin ministers proposed the expulsion of foreign officials and advisers, arguing that they were all spies in the service of their states of origin. The minister Li Si disputed and defeated this anti-foreigner policy, but when the philosopher Han Fei was brought to the Qin court at the behest of the first emperor, Li Si argued the opposite side: "Han Fei is a member of the Han royal lineage," he said. "Now Your Majesty desires to unite all the states, but Fei to the end will work for Han, and not for Qin. This is basic human nature . . . It would be best to use some violation of the laws as a pretext to execute him." Li Si's argument, based on the assumption that loyalty to one's own state was a natural human sentiment, led to Han Fei's execution.[27]

This evidence, though admittedly sparse, challenges the claims of modern scholars in China that unification was a natural and inevitable result of increasing trade and cultural exchange among the Warring States. To the contrary, nationalist or regionalist sentiments seem to have been on an up-swing throughout the Warring States period and to have grown even stronger at the very end. These tendencies were mitigated in part by the mobility of intellectuals, who moved from state to state in search of education, patronage, or office and thereby developed a commitment to a broader realm of "All under Heaven."[28] Indeed, the anti-foreign sentiment at the Qin court might have been in part a reaction to the increasing prominence of foreign "guest-ministers" who supplanted other parties at court.

The clear self-definition of Qin as a realm apart was also blurred by the constant shifting of its boundaries during the period. Even the solid inter-state walls had to be rebuilt along new lines as the borders shifted.[29] However, on balance I would argue that the predominant tendency of the late Warring States was toward sharper divisions between nations, and that countervailing tendencies were limited to a small segment of the in-tellectual elite.

The *Book of Lord Shang* and the Dilemma of Qin

We have thus far encountered Shang Yang as the creator of reforms that led to Qin dominance and as a semi-mythic figure who figured in later thought as the source or emblem of a distinctive Qin culture that blurred into barbarism. He also served as the eponym for a manual of political thought and methods known as the *Book of Lord Shang* (*Shang Jun shu*). This text was largely compiled after his death, some of it perhaps as late as the Han. However, the title is not arbitrary, for its key chapters present a theoretical systematization of the principles underlying the institutions of Shang Yang and hence of late Warring States Qin. Some of the chap-ters claim to present actual policies or laws of Qin state, but the most sig-nificant are those that elaborate the basic principles by which an ideal warring state should operate.[30]

The overarching principle is the identity of the army with the peasant populace, which enables the entire state to be mobilized for war: "The means by which a ruler encourages his people are offices and rank; the means by which a state arises are agriculture and war."[31] This vision fig-ures throughout the book, which constantly discusses how to encourage people to devote themselves to agriculture and warfare—the rewards that will result from doing so and the disasters that would flow from failure to do so.

People's desires being myriad and profit coming from a single [source], if the people are not united there is no way to attain their desires. Therefore you unite them, and then their energy will be concentrated. Their energy being concentrated, you will be strong. If they are strong and you use their energy, you will be doubly strong. Therefore the state that can both create energy and destroy it is called "a state that attacks the enemy," and it is inevitably strong. Block up all private means by which they can gratify their ambitions, open up a single gate for them to attain their desires, make it so that the people must first do what they hate and only then attain their desires, and then their energy will be great.[32]

When agriculture is the sole source of energy (the "single gate"), and warfare its only outlet, the people will risk mutilation and death ("what they hate") to serve the state. By concentrating all the people's efforts on these two activities, the state produces the energy and manpower it needs to fight. The effective ruler gets the people to "forget their lives for the sake of their superiors" and makes them "delight in war" so that they "act like hungry wolves on seeing meat."[33] All other human values or activities become threats to the state order.

These threats are variously described as "lice" or "evils": the "six lice" (longevity, good food, beauty, love, ambition, and virtuous conduct); the "ten evils" (rites, music, odes, history, virtue, moral culture, filial piety, brotherly love, integrity, and sophistry); or the "twelve lice" (rites, music, odes, history, moral culture, filial piety, brotherly love, sincerity, benevolence, duty, criticism of the army, and being ashamed of fighting).[34] Most of these vices were virtues in philosophical texts, especially those studied by Confucian scholars. A repeated target in the *Book of Lord Shang* is the practice of granting office or patronage to scholars, which seduces people away from agriculture and war.

Although the *Book of Lord Shang* is sometimes described as a program for a totalitarian bureaucracy, officialdom itself is an object of suspicion and critique—yet another mode of escaping from agriculture and war. The second chapter of the book lists "deviant officials" being "idle in office," as well as generosity in their salaries, as a threat to the state, worse than granting office for literary attainments, or allowing merchants to profit through sale of grain, or making luxuries available to those with money. A substantial bureaucracy threatens the ruler because it separates him from the facts about his realm: "In the institutions of a well-governed state, the people cannot escape punishment just as the eyes cannot hide what they see from the mind. But chaotic states of the present day are not like this. They rely on a multitude of officials and a host of clerks. Even though these clerks are numerous they have the same tasks and form a single body. Consequently they cannot supervise one another."[35]

The Qin laws found at Shuihudi show this same suspicion of officials, as does the late Warring States political treatise the *Master Han Fei*. Rather than relying on officials, who try to enhance their positions by deceiving the ruler and avoiding agriculture and war, the *Book of Lord Shang* advocates employing the five-man units of mutual surveillance established by Shang Yang. If the people can be made to supervise and report on one another, then the bureaucracy can be set aside and the state reduced to the ruler and his people:

> In regulating the state, if legal judgments are made in the households then it attains the kingship; if they are made among the officials then it will be merely strong; if they are made by the ruler it will be weak . . . If a criminal is invariably denounced, then the people pass judgments in their minds. If when the prince gives a command the people respond, so that the method of enforcing the law takes shape in the households and is simply carried out by officials, then the judgments over affairs are made in the households. Therefore, with a true king rewards and punishments are decided in the people's minds, and the means of enforcing the law are decided in the households.[36]

In the well-governed state the people are the ruler's eyes and ears, and the instrument of his judgments. Merchants, scholars, and officials are at best a necessary evil, to be reduced to a bare minimum and kept rigorously in check.

However, if judgments are to be made in the households, then the ruler himself plays no active role in the administration of the state. Apart from the insistence that the ruler must make sure that the state is devoted to agriculture and war and must ward off assorted parasites, there is in fact no discussion of the techniques or character of the ruler. This is in striking contrast to the *Master Han Fei* and works of political philosophy in most cultures. The only active role assigned to the ruler is as the source of law.

This is the theme of the first chapter of the text, in which Shang Yang persuades the lord of Qin that the changing state of the world requires new laws and institutions: "Ordinary people are at ease in their habits, and scholars are immersed in what they have learned. These two types are the sort to fill offices and preserve the law, but you cannot discuss with them that which lies beyond the law. The Three Dynasties became kings through different rites, and the Five Hegemons dominated the world with different laws. So the wise man creates laws, while the stupid man is controlled by them. The worthy change the rites, while the unworthy are constrained by them."[37] The ruler acts only as the creator of laws, which are then distributed among the people who are to enforce them through mutual surveillance.

But this leads to a paradox. On the one hand, a complete set of laws is to be stored in a special sealed chamber in the ruler's palace, and anyone who without permission enters this chamber or tampers with one graph of the written law is to be put to death with no possibility of pardon. On the other hand, the ruler's charge is to promulgate the law to special officials who must answer any questions about the meaning of the laws put to them by other officials or by the common people. Failure to provide this information results in punishment. "Therefore all the clerks and commoners in the world without exception will know the laws. The clerks clearly knowing that the people know the laws, they will not dare to treat the people contrary to the law, nor will the people dare to violate the law . . . Therefore all the clerks and commoners of the world, no matter how worthy or clever in speech will be unable to speak a single word that would distort the law." This emphasis on officials and the people asking questions about the law is reflected in Qin legal documents, a substantial section of which consists of such questions and answers.[38]

The law in the *Book of Lord Shang* was thus both hidden away in the palace with the ruler and distributed in its entirety to every person in the world. In both cases it was immune to the altering or twisting of a single graph or word. This reinforced the identification of the ruler with the law, for both were simultaneously to be hidden in the palace and distributed throughout the empire in the bodies of the self-policing subjects.

Perhaps the most striking and significant idea in the *Book of Lord Shang* emerged directly from the notion that any surplus within the state would turn functioning elements into self-indulgent parasites. The "six lice" derive directly from the "three constant functions": farming, trade, and government office. If farmers have a surplus, they become concerned about living a long life and eating well; if merchants have a surplus, they become concerned about obtaining female beauty and affection; if officials have time to spare, they become concerned about personal ambitions and a reputation for virtue. Not only are functions outside agriculture and war to be discouraged, but any surplus available to the people becomes a threat or danger. War serves not only to conquer enemies and seize their resources but also to consume any internal surplus that would otherwise destroy the state. A truly strong state must know not only how to create energy but how to destroy it.

This argument recurs throughout the text, usually describing any accumulation of energy and resources as a form of "poison": "One who uses a strong people to attack the strong will perish; one who uses a weak people to attack the strong will become king. If a state is strong and does not engage in war, then the poison is shipped into the interior. Rituals, music, and parasitic officials arise, and the state will inevitably be whittled away. But if the country is strong and carries out war, then the poison is shipped to the enemy. The state will have no rituals, music, or parasitic officials, and it will inevitably be strong." Other versions of this doctrine state that one must destroy the people's energy by attacking the enemy, and that failure to do so will lead to villainy and the growth of parasites. For the state to be orderly, the people must be weak, and they can be kept weak only by the constant dispersal of their wealth and energies in war.[39]

Thus, the state organized for war, as analyzed in the *Book of Lord Shang*, requires not only that all the energies of the people be devoted to agriculture and war but that there must always be another war to fight, another enemy to defeat. Ultimately, war was fought not for gain but for loss, to expend energies and wealth that would otherwise accumulate in the hands of those who, by virtue of their growing prosperity, would come to serve their own interests rather than those of the state.

Such a state sucks in more and more resources to be consumed in wars that no longer serve any purpose save to keep the machine running. Sooner or later the energy and resources expended in the wars become too great for the state to bear, at which point it implodes. It is a "suicide state," "destined to self-destruct."[40] As we shall see, this fate, which is implicit in the *Book of Lord Shang*, would work itself out explicitly in the fall of the Qin empire.

3

THE PARADOXES OF EMPIRE

WHEN THE fall of his last rival left the king of Qin master of the civilized world, he and his court were fully aware of the unprecedented nature of their achievement. As one courtier remarked, they had surpassed the greatest feats of the legendary sages of antiquity. And now they would set about enacting visionary programs designed to institutionalize a new era in human history, the era of total unity.[1]

Yet as Jia Yi would later observe, the Qin dynasty collapsed within two decades because it did not change enough. Despite its proclamations of making a new start in a world utterly transformed, the Qin carried forward the fundamental institutions of the Warring State era, seeking to rule a unified realm with the techniques they had used to conquer it. The Qin's grandiose visions of transformation failed to confront the extensive changes that the end of permanent warfare had brought about. It fell to the Han, who took over the realm after the Qin dynasty's defeat, to carry out the major institutional programs and cultural innovations that gave form to the vision of world empire.

The scale of the problems that confronted the Qin in creating an imperial order can be seen in the changes they attempted to make during their brief rule.

Centralization under the First Emperor

The first change carried out by the Qin was to create a new title and model for the ruler. Unification required institutions and values that could transcend regional ties, and the ultimate authority for these institutions and values would be a semi-divinized monarch who ruled as the agent of celestial powers. Imposed from on high, the dynasty of such a ruler must be detached from the regions that made up his realm. To become servants of this celestial monarch, agents of the state would be required to forswear loyalties to family and home. The emperor's officials, though raised above local society, would be servants of the monarch, drawing their authority from him.

The king of Qin claimed for himself the title of *huangdi*, which we inadequately translate as "emperor." *Di* had been the high god of the Shang, the first historical state in China that ruled the central Yellow River valley in the second half of the first millennium B.C. However, by the Warring States period its meaning had changed. The mythic culture-hero sages who had supposedly created human civilization were called *di*, indicating their superhuman power. And the four high gods of Qin religion were known as *di*, corresponding to the points of the compass and thus embodying the cosmos.

In claiming the title *di* for himself, the king of Qin asserted his godlike power, strengthened by the addition of *huang*, which meant "shining" or "splendid" and was most frequently used as an epithet of Heaven. Declaring himself the first *huangdi*, the First Emperor claimed to be the initiator of a new era and, the progenitor of a second, third, and fourth *huangdi*, a dynasty that would reach to the end of time, just as his realm reached to the limits of space. To transcend his human state and become an immortal, the First Emperor initiated the *feng* and *shan* sacrifices in which he ascended Mount Tai to communicate with the highest god.

To ground the cosmic claims of his title, the First Emperor toured his new realm and inscribed his achievements in verse on the peaks of mountains. The texts of six of these inscriptions have been preserved, and in them the emperor spoke of how his blessings had been bestowed upon all within the four seas, "wherever sun and moon shine," "wherever human tracks reach," descending even to the beasts and the plants. The range of his power and beneficence was universal.[2]

This new vision of the ruler was also articulated in a philosophical work sponsored by the king of Qin's first chief minister, Lü Buwei. This text, the *Springs and Autumns of Master Lü* (*Lü shi chun qiu*), was structured according to the calendar, and it argued that the ruler followed the pattern of Heaven. In a closely associated move, the First Emperor claimed that a cosmic cycle, the so-called Five Phases cycle, brought about his rise to power and made it an inevitable part of the divine plan.

A major building program was undertaken to transform the capital city into a microcosm of the universe. The emperor's new palace was patterned on the North Star and the Big Dipper, the fixed center of the sky. Great statues cast from the confiscated weapons of defeated states represented constellations, and replicas of all the palaces of the conquered states served as a microcosm of the Earth.

These ceremonial and architectural assertions of the emperor's godhead were accompanied by institutional programs that aimed to centralize and unify all aspects of Chinese life. The most important of these lay in the intellectual sphere. Whereas each of the Warring States had its own writing system, the Qin government created a new, simplified nonalphabetic script to be used throughout the empire. It reduced the complex and variable Large Seal script with its curving lines—the kind of writing used on Zhou ritual vessels—into simpler, more rectilinear forms. The Qin writing system may have suppressed as much as twenty-five percent of the pre-Qin graphs.

The new standardized script allowed swifter writing with brush and ink—essential for imperial record keeping. It was propagated across the empire through public displays of graphs on stone inscriptions, on objects manufactured in government workshops, and in official documents. The result was a graphic koine—a language shared by diverse peoples without being the first language of any of them. This artificial written language existed only in texts and was distinct from the mutually unintelligible languages spoken in different parts of the empire. It allowed written communication between people who would not have been able to communicate orally because they would have pronounced the graphs differently. Still in use through most of the Western Han period, this script was eventually replaced by an even simpler variant known as "secretarial" script, which could be written even more quickly.

The development of a pan-imperial writing system led to the founding of an imperial academy intended to control the dissemination of texts and the interpretation of their meanings. In Han and later accounts this event was described as the "burning of the books," but it was actually a policy of unification rather than destruction. When a scholar argued that the First Emperor should imitate the Zhou founders by enfeoffing his relatives, the chief minister, Li Si, retorted that what the state should do was put an end to such criticism of current institutions through reference to an idealized antiquity.

Acting on this principle, he removed all copies of the *Canon of Odes*

(*Shi jing*), *Canon of Documents* (*Shang shu*), and the texts of the philosophical traditions from private hands, stored them in the imperial library, and made them available for study only under government-appointed scholars. Books on utilitarian matters such as medicine, divination, agriculture, and forestry were not confiscated. Persuaded that a unitary empire required a unitary doctrine, the Qin government tried to control political thought by limiting access to written texts, but there was no systematic destruction of them. That damage was done in 206 B.C. when Xiang Yu sacked the Qin capital and burned the imperial library to the ground.

Essential to state control of political discourse was the appointment of scholars who would study the relevant texts and transmit their knowledge to students. While Han accounts depict the Qin as hostile to scholarship, particularly classical studies based in the Confucian tradition, this was clearly not the case. The First Emperor consulted classicist scholars regarding his performance of the *feng* and *shan* sacrifices, and his stone inscriptions are replete with classical citations, composed entirely in verse using the same rhyme groups as the *Canon of Odes*. The aforementioned *Springs and Autumns of Master Lü* comprised all of the intellectual traditions, including the classicists. Contrary to the Han's claims, their own intellectual policies in the early Han period followed the Qin precedent, and early Han scholastics were either former Qin scholars or their intellectual heirs. The Han's establishment of the classical Confucian canon as the state orthodoxy represented not a radical reversal of the Qin practice but simply a narrowing of scope.

Standardization was extended into administration and business by establishing a single scale of weights and measures throughout the realm. Even the widths of axles were supposed to be equalized, so that carts and chariots could all run in the same ruts in the roads. Cast bronze models for units of length, weight, and volume were distributed to local government offices and imposed on all merchants, thus facilitating trade. Examples of these official bronze measures have been found in excavations as distant as Manchuria. Government workshops were ordered to annually check and correct their weights, measures, and balances, and all vessels of a given type were to have identical lengths and widths. The mark of the office or shop and the responsible official were engraved or affixed to the bottom of all objects as a guarantee that they met regulations. Failure to meet these standards was punishable by law.[3]

To create uniform measures of value, the Qin minted bronze coins that bore the characters "half of a *liang*" (equal to about eight grams), which was the actual weight of the coin. Warring States coins had inscribed values that were not related to their weight. The *Book of Han* reports that with the advent of bronze coins, "such things as pearls, jade, tortoise shells, cowry shells, silver and tin became objects only used for decoration or as precious treasures, and were no longer used as money."[4]

The standardization of script, the textual canon, measures, coinage, and law (as we will see in Chapter 10) seems conventional today, and it requires a leap of imagination to realize what innovations they were in the third century B.C. Many of these advances did not appear in Europe until the French Revolution, over two millennia later. A unified empire was an entirely new political form in China, and standardization was crucial to its efficient administration across vast distances, and to the daily lives of the realm's inhabitants. Many of these innovations also gave a tangible form to the new office of emperor, and conveyed a sense that the ruler and his government must be obeyed.

To physically bind his domain together, and exclude those who lay outside it, the First Emperor initiated a network of roads that radiated out like a fan from the capital in Xianyang. It would be used to dispatch troops, officials, and messengers, as well as to facilitate commerce. One road, called the "Straight Road," ran 600 miles from the capital to Inner Mongolia.[5] Remnants of this road, over which materials for building the first Great Wall were transported, still survive today (Map 5). Qin's imperial highways extended about 4,250 miles, and the Han enlarged the network even farther. These roads were not simply dirt paths. China's varied terrain required stone bridges, trestles, reinforcements over or through mountains, and roadways suspended from wooden posts to run along cliffs. Illustrations of these appear on the walls of Han tombs (Fig. 2). Similarly, Han funerary inscriptions for local officials or worthies cite their efforts in creating road networks. The transportation system included rest houses where travelers could eat and sleep, as well as relay buildings and post stations where messengers exchanged exhausted horses for fresh ones.

From the Shuihudi legal documents we know that the Qin set up checkpoints along the roads where travelers had to pay a tax and show passports in order to continue. This institution lasted into the Han dynasty. Records show that passports were sometimes forged, and in times of famine passport restrictions for those transporting grain were waived.[6] Several texts speak of passports for going into or out of the capital re-

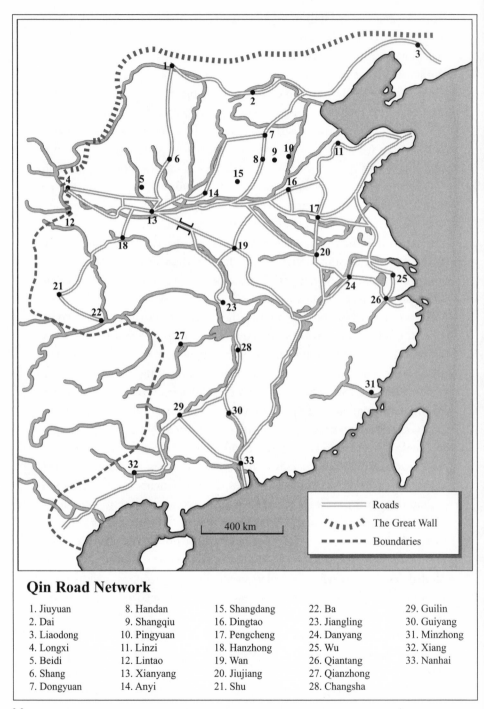

Qin Road Network

1. Jiuyuan	8. Handan	15. Shangdang	22. Ba	29. Guilin
2. Dai	9. Shangqiu	16. Dingtao	23. Jiangling	30. Guiyang
3. Liaodong	10. Pingyuan	17. Pengcheng	24. Danyang	31. Minzhong
4. Longxi	11. Linzi	18. Hanzhong	25. Wu	32. Xiang
5. Beidi	12. Lintao	19. Wan	26. Qiantang	33. Nanhai
6. Shang	13. Xianyang	20. Jiujiang	27. Qianzhong	
7. Dongyuan	14. Anyi	21. Shu	28. Changsha	

Map 5

Fig. 2   Official chariot crossing a bridge. The canopy and outrider are markers of status.

gion, prohibitions against traveling in winter, bans on households moving away from the frontiers, and the detention of strangers traveling on the roads. Stations for inspecting passports also served as jails when necessary. Roads allowed movement throughout China, but it was a highly controlled movement to serve the purposes of the state.

The network of roads facilitated a major ritual of unification known as the imperial progress, during which the emperor personally inspected the programs under way throughout his domain. The First Emperor made no fewer than five tours of his new eastern provinces in ten years (Map 6). Many Han emperors, particularly during the Western Han period, did likewise. At a lower level, an official's status was measured by the size of the retinue that accompanied him when he traveled on government business throughout the empire. Han tomb murals depict scenes of such carriage processions.

In addition to roadways, the Qin used rivers for transport in the north, and built several canals in the Guanzhong region. Travel by water was even more common in the south, where topography made road construction difficult and travel by boat more suitable.

Qin Frontiers and Qin Shihuang's Imperial Progresses

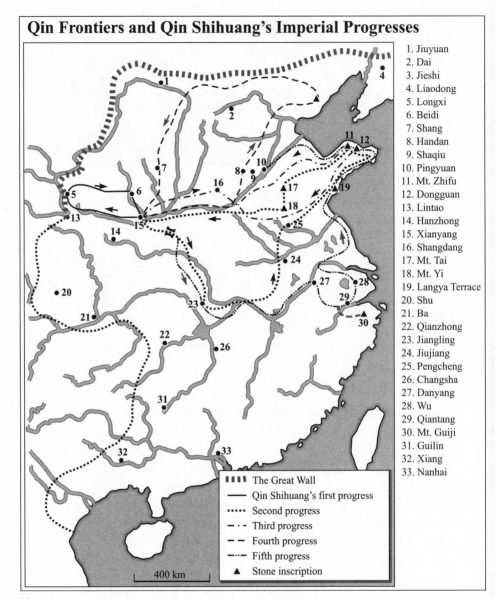

1. Jiuyuan
2. Dai
3. Jieshi
4. Liaodong
5. Longxi
6. Beidi
7. Shang
8. Handan
9. Shaqiu
10. Pingyuan
11. Mt. Zhifu
12. Dongguan
13. Lintao
14. Hanzhong
15. Xianyang
16. Shangdang
17. Mt. Tai
18. Mt. Yi
19. Langya Terrace
20. Shu
21. Ba
22. Qianzhong
23. Jiangling
24. Jiujiang
25. Pengcheng
26. Changsha
27. Danyang
28. Wu
29. Qiantang
30. Mt. Guiji
31. Guilin
32. Xiang
33. Nanhai

▎▎▎▎ The Great Wall
—— Qin Shihuang's first progress
•••• Second progress
— • — Third progress
— — Fourth progress
—•••— Fifth progress
▲ Stone inscription

400 km

MAP 6

While the Qin engaged in major building projects to link together the regions of their new realm, they also worked to restrict movement between their own territory and the lands that lay beyond. In the first half of the first millennium B.C. many peoples to the north of what became China gradually developed a new mode of living based on transhumant nomadism—the transfer of livestock from one grazing ground to another depending on the season. During the Warring States period, northern Chinese states had expanded into the grasslands being used by these northern peoples, and had built walls to secure their expansion. As they became increasingly aware of these people to the north and their distinctive mode of life, the Chinese people began to define their own state as "central," in contrast with an "outer" world defined not merely in terms of geography but also of culture. Just as the Greeks defined themselves through a set of contrasts with their Persian enemies (free vs. slave, stern and hardy vs. effete and sensual), so an emerging sense of contrasts with the "barbarians" played a crucial role in the invention of the Chinese empire.

This sense of contrast was marked by wall building. It culminated in the Qin's attempt to secure their realm by connecting the earlier walls at the northern frontier into a single defense system. After having driven the northern tribesmen completely out of the great bend in the Yellow River, the Qin put the road builder Meng Tian in charge of building a system of rammed-earth walls and watchtowers to protect this newly conquered territory, as well as the rest of the northern frontier. The wall's purpose was to hold back the northern tribesmen, particularly the Xiongnu, so that they "no longer dared to come south to pasture their horses and their men dared not take up their bows to avenge their grudges."[7] Sima Qian's *Shi ji* states that Meng Tian commanded 300,000 workers on this project, which was carried out in harsh terrain that was difficult to reach. For every man working at the actual sites of construction, dozens must have been needed to build service roads and transport supplies. Although this structure is often described as the Qin-Han Great Wall, there is no evidence that it ran continuously from Central Asia to the sea, in the manner of the later Ming wall.

The final aspect of centralization was to systematize the extraction of labor and service from the peasants. Taxes took two main forms: a harvest tax and a poll tax. The harvest tax in the early Han amounted to one-fifteenth of the harvest, later lowered to one-thirtieth. While this tax was officially levied on crops, the state lacked the capacity to measure individual harvests, so it was actually levied on the basis of the amount of land owned, multiplied by the expected yield per plot. Even though the tax represented a small percentage of an average harvest, in bad years when the yield was seriously reduced it could have proved a considerable burden.

The capitation (head) tax was usually paid in cash every year. Children were taxed at half the figure for adults. The Qin used this tax on individuals to modify behavior. For example, since fathers and adult sons living together were liable to a double tax, they had an incentive to set up separate households, thereby cultivating the maximum possible amount of land. Doubling the number of households, in turn, increased the number of men available for military service.

In addition to paying taxes, the peasants' second obligation to the state was to provide annual labor service on public projects. Although the ages at which men were liable for such service varied over time, the basic principle was that all adult males had to work without pay for a stipulated period of time (one month per year under the Han) on construction projects and miscellaneous duties in the commanderies and counties. They transported goods such as grain or hemp cloth, built palaces and official quarters, mined or carried the salt and iron that was produced in state-sponsored monopolies, and repaired roads, bridges, and waterways. By the Eastern Han period, this obligation was routinely commuted into a cash payment which was used to hire full-time laborers, who could develop a higher level of skill than peasants serving on rota.

The Han as Qin's Heir and Negation

When the Qin dynasty collapsed after only two decades, it was succeeded, after several years of civil war, by the Han dynasty. Since the Qin had been the first state to impose its rule on the whole Chinese world, it remained the unique model of how an empire should be administered. The Han dynasty thus inherited many Qin practices. However, the long-term survival of the Han depended on the alteration, usually groping and gradual, of these Qin practices, and the adoption, often unwilling, of new modes of control.

One generation of imperial Qin was not sufficient to eradicate local loyalties and secure universal acceptance of an absolute autocrat. The First Emperor's Qin was in reality one regional state ruling others; and Qin's insistence on its unique status blocked the creation of a unitary empire. The ruling houses and leading families of the old Warring States figured both as actors and as foci in the rebellion that toppled the dynasty, and the Han's subsequent policy of enfeoffment acknowledged the enduring reality of the old Warring States. The emergence of a true emperorship would require considerable changes.

The humble background of the Han founder, Liu Bang, which at first appeared as a weakness, ultimately proved to be an asset. The Liu family originated in Chu, but Liu Bang (later known as Emperor Han Gaozu) set up his first capital in Luoyang and then moved, for strategic considerations, to Guanzhong. Thus, from the very beginning the Han dynasty was defined by the absence of ties to any locality. Its claims to rule were based entirely on the merit and potency of the founder and the transmission of these traits down through the generations of the Liu clan.

The beginnings of the re-invention of the ruler appear in a discussion in the *Shi ji* of how he triumphed over his chief rival, Xiang Yu:

> Gaozu held a banquet in the Southern Palace of Luoyang. He said, "My lords and commanders, speak frankly to me and dare to hide nothing. Why did I gain the empire? Why did Xiang Yu lose it?" Gao Qi and Wang Ling replied, "Your majesty is careless and insults others, while Xiang Yu was kind and loving. But when you sent someone to attack a city or occupy territory, you gave them what they conquered, sharing your gains with the whole world. Xiang Yu was jealous of worth and ability. He harmed those who achieved merit and was suspicious of the worthy. When victorious in battle he gave others no credit, and when he obtained land he gave others no benefit. This is why he lost the empire."
>
> . . . Gaozu said, "You have recognized one point, but failed to recognize a second. As for calculating strategies within the commander's tent and thereby assuring victory a thousand miles away, I am not as good as Zhang Liang. As for ordering a state, making the people content, providing rations for troops and assuring that supply lines are not cut, I am not as good as Xiao He. As for assembling a million-man army, winning every battle fought, and taking every city attacked, I am not as good as Han Xin. These three are great men, and I was able to employ them. That is why I gained the empire. Xiang Yu had only Fan Zeng and he could not use him. That is why he was slain by me."[8]

The hallmarks of the dynastic founder, and by extension the ruler, were his defeat of the Qin and his willingness to share success with his followers. The ruler brought peace to the world, and gathered the most talented men of the realm. These ideas had been elaborated by Warring States political theorists, and some had already figured in Qin stone inscriptions. They justified rule through the monarch's claims to the highest excellence, as demonstrated by his achievement of universal order and by his generosity in sharing its fruits.

As with the First Emperor, appeals to worldly success were supplemented with claims to divine sanction, although in the Han dynasty these took the form of supernatural assistance more than cosmic process. Writing a century after the Han founding, Sima Qian related that Emperor Gaozu's mother had been impregnated by a dragon, the Red God (*di*). Consequently Gaozu had a remarkable physiognomy that presaged his rise to world rulership, and multi-colored clouds or dragons hovered above him. On his deathbed Gaozu attributed his miraculous rise to the support of Heaven.[9] Finally, the Han court followed Qin's adoption of the Five Phases theory, claiming that their rise to power signaled the ascent of a new cosmic phase. This theory was prefigured in the story that when Gaozu, son of the Red God, first rebelled against Qin he slew a great serpent that turned out to be the son of the White God. The succession of the god of one color by another marked the conquest of one phase by its inheritor.

Over the course of the dynasty the justifications of imperial authority grew more grandiose. Emperor Wu introduced many new cults to exalt imperial authority, most notably sacrifices to the Grand Unity and the Empress Earth, and he followed the First Emperor in performing the *feng* and *shan* sacrifices to the high god. The rise to intellectual dominance of Confucian classicism was marked in the religious sphere by the establishment of the cult of Heaven. The Eastern Han also witnessed the revival of the old Zhou doctrine that the emperor ruled as the "Son of Heaven" on the basis of a "mandate" received from this highest celestial power. This became the classic form for the claim that imperial authority was bestowed by celestial powers, and that the emperor ruled as the agent of Heaven on Earth.

This unique status of the emperor was enacted in many practices and institutions. The emperor was the embodiment of the government, even being called "*guo jia* (state)" in some Eastern Han writings. All offices and salaries were his gift, although he delegated the authority to make lower-level appointments, and all officials were his "servants" (*chen*). Moreover, the ranks of merit awarded to peasants were also gifts from the emperor, as were special staffs awarded to people over seventy. He was the supreme judge, the last court of appeal, and could order executions at will. He also had the power to grant amnesty to those sentenced to death, a power that he exercised with great frequency. The dynasty's

legal code was based on the decrees of the founder, with imperial proclamations automatically having the force of law. All lands not under cultivation were considered his personal property, a claim that justified the
creation of the great imperial hunting parks celebrated in Han poetry, as
well as the state monopolies of iron and salt.[10]

In addition to these administrative, legal, and economic powers, a
range of ritual practices and sumptuary regulations also distinguished the
emperor. The palaces of the imperial family and buildings pertaining to
the court occupied half the capital. These buildings were the scenes of
elaborate rituals in which all members of the court prostrated themselves
before the emperor. In addition, the imperial tombs gradually formed a
line of artificial mountains that visibly towered over Chang'an, and they
were the scenes of repeated sacrifices, accompanied by song and dance.
These tombs were maintained by the populations of satellite cities created solely for their upkeep. During the Western Han, temples for the
first two emperors were established in every commandery. The emperor
had a unique term for self-reference (*zhen*) and a unique word to refer to
his death (*beng*). Certain colors and patterns of ornament were reserved
for him, as were types of banners and chariots. Each gate in the capital's
wall flanked a three-lane road, with the central lane reserved for the emperor's use. Any entry into a palace compound required his permission.
Any threat to the emperor or destruction of objects associated with the
imperial line was punishable by death.

In all these ways the emperor was defined as the center of the realm
and the source of political authority. Some Western scholars, attacking
the cliché of "oriental despotism," have argued that the bureaucracy developed methods to check the emperor's power by appeals to Heaven as
marked by omens, thus achieving a semblance of "division of powers."
Others have gone so far as to argue that true power resided in the bureaucracy, while the emperor, like the present-day monarch of Great Britain,
"reigned but did not rule." However laudable the intent behind these arguments, they are wrong.

The clearest demonstration of this is a pattern in which policy-making
power shifted from the formal bureaucracy to whatever group of people—largely eunuchs or imperial affines (relatives by marriage)—surrounded the emperor's person. This shift of power from "outer" court to
"inner" court was institutionalized by the reign of Emperor Wu, and was
repeated throughout early imperial and medieval China, when emperors
were less autocratic than in late imperial China. The formal bureaucracy

had no effective base of independent power. Far from developing the power to check the emperor or significantly affect policy, the bureaucrats of early imperial China sank into impotence, serving only to execute policies formulated by others.

As chief administrator, high judge, and chief priest, the emperor knew no limits to his authority except the not-inconsiderable ones imposed by biology. Since he was the descendant of earlier emperors, his proposals for major changes in law or cult could be criticized as unfilial. Yet, throughout the Han dynasty, whenever an emperor chose to alter the practices of his ancestors, he was able to do so. Nevertheless, emperors relied on other people to provide them with information, and they were thus constrained by their ignorance of the world outside the court. They also depended upon officials to carry out their commands in distant provinces. Similarly, many emperors, like other people, preferred leisure to work, and were happy to leave the governing to others.

And perhaps most importantly, as long as an emperor was young, power devolved to whoever could speak in his name. Since it was in the interest of the court to have a weak emperor in power, Han history is marked by an increasing tendency toward young emperors. Several early deaths of emperors or heirs even suggest the possibility of murder as a means of securing a pliable ruler. This reached a climax in the last century of the dynasty, when no adult ever acceded to the throne. But, even when the emperor was incapable of ruling in his own right, he remained the sole source of authority at court, so it was the eunuchs or affines controlling his person who dominated government policy. The emperor continued to be the sole locus of authority even at the very end of the Han, when competing warlords struggled to gain possession of the last boy emperor.

In addition to strengthening the institution of the emperor, the Han government carried forward virtually all the policies by which the Qin had sought to impose unity on its newly conquered realm. The unified Qin script was used for writing, though simplification continued. The Qin imperial academy, designed to make the capital the center of intellectual life, also endured, although its intellectual range and its links to office holding were modified. Similarly, the empire-wide legal code remained a central tool of imperial unification. Although the Han initially attempted to simplify Qin laws and make them less brutal, it soon reverted to largely following the Qin pattern.

The Han also pursued the Qin policies of standard measures and coinage. Models used to fix the state-sanctioned units of measure employed in the market have been found in several Han tombs. The Qin *ban liang* gave way to the smaller *wu zhu* coin in the Han. This coin weighed five *zhu* (hence its name), about three grams, and it continued in use until the Tang dynasty (618–906 A.D.). The government monopolized coin production, and the quality of the coins was so good that forgeries eventually became unprofitable. Coins were also edged with a hard lip to prevent forgers from clipping bits off of coins, which could then be used to cast new ones.

In the last century of the Western Han, according to one report, twenty-eight billion coins were made. Such large-scale minting is surprising, although the mandatory payment in coins of capitation and other taxes may help explain it. Still, this vast amount of currency suggests a considerable monetization of the economy, which was only possible through the government's ability to impose a uniform, abstracted measure of value in the form of denominated pieces of metal. In the Eastern Han, gifts from the emperor and personal wealth were routinely measured in cash, and disaster relief—such as burying flood victims—was awarded in terms of so many coins per head. Coinage also facilitated the commutation of the one-month period of labor service and military duty into a cash payment that the government used to hire full-time professionals.

As in so many other things, the Han carried forward the Qin calendar. However, in 104 B.C. Emperor Wu declared a "Grand Beginning" for a new phase in the Five Phase cycle, and he had the calendar modified accordingly. He also initiated the use of reign periods named for a great event or achievement that the emperor wanted to immortalize. In addition to the "Grand Beginning" (*tai chu*) for his calendar reform, he declared an "Original *Feng*" (*yuan feng*) for his first performance of the *feng* and *shan* sacrifices, and so on. This inscribing of the emperor and his achievements into the structure of time was a significant element in the creation of a common imperial culture. Two further refinements to the calendar were made in the Xin and Eastern Han dynasties, as the measurement of time and the observation of natural cycles in the heavens became more and more precise.

We take accurate calendars for granted today, but they required millennia of careful astronomical observation and correction. Precise calendars were needed in the Han to control payment of salaries, timing of transfers or promotions, and granting of leaves from office. They were also necessary at the frontiers to track military duty and to co-ordinate actions across the northern border. Chinese calendars were based on the lunar month, but since the lunar month varies between twenty-nine and thirty days, a formal calendar ensured that everyone in the empire knew which months were twenty-nine days and which ones were thirty. And since the solar year of approximately three hundred and sixty-five days, which controls the seasons, is not precisely twelve lunar months, every few years an extra "intercalary" month was added to synchronize the two. Failure to synchronize with what we today call a "leap year" would have meant, for example, that the first month of the year, which marked the beginning of spring, would arrive a few days earlier every year until eventually it would fall in mid-winter.

The Han inherited the Qin practice of levying a cash capitation tax, and of setting tax rates to influence people's behavior. To encourage marriage, the early Western Han imposed a poll tax on unmarried women between the ages of fifteen and thirty that was five times the normal tax. In the Eastern Han, women who had given birth received a three-year tax exemption and their husbands a one-year exemption—measures aimed at increasing the population. Double taxes on merchants sought to discourage that career, and tax exemptions for the elderly expressed filial piety. However, such taxes could modify behavior in unforeseen ways. When some parents started killing their babies in order to avoid paying taxes, the government eventually exempted children under six years of age from the capitation tax.[11]

The government probably collected taxes in cash because it was easier to transport than large amounts of grain. However, coming up with enough cash for taxes required that peasants either perform extra work for wages or sell their grain. Wage labor was sometimes available, but selling produce was the most common way to earn tax money. In good years, prices for grain went down, and peasants had to sell a larger proportion of their harvest to pay the tax. In bad years they risked starvation when they sold their meager harvest to meet their obligations. The cash tax eventually ruined the peasantry and was a major factor in the rise of landlordism. One unresolved question is how or where peasants sold their crop. Those living near a city or large town could have taken their produce to market, but those farther away probably sold their grain to wealthy local families or to mobile merchants, who exploited the poor farmers' need for cash to impose a low price.

Living in the shadow of Qin's fall and dependent on his own allies, the Han founder had enfeoffed his major followers as kings, reserving for himself only the key strategic area of Guanzhong. Although he devised pretexts to destroy his former allies and replace them with his own kin, for the first half-century of the Han dynasty semi-independent kings ruled more than half the empire. Only after the defeat of the feudatories in 154 B.C. did the Han recreate a truly unitary empire. Over the two and a half centuries that followed, the consequences of political unification forced them gradually to shift away from the Qin model in several basic ways.

The first shift was the abandonment of universal military service and the associated direct rule of the peasant population. The mass mobilization of peasants for military service—the organizing principle of the Warring States polity and the Qin state—remained useful until the defeat of the feudatories in 154 B.C. Subsequently, general war inside China ceased to be a real possibility. For the war that the Han did have to fight—against the nomadic Xiongnu at the northern frontiers—an army of infantry was useless and impossible to provision. Moreover, short terms of duty could not maintain standing garrisons, and horsemanship and expertise with the crossbow—necessary military skills by this time—could not be gained under the old system of one or two years of active service followed by brief, annual training sessions. To man garrisons and mount long expeditions into the grasslands required a new form of army (Fig. 3).

Gradually the Han ceased mobilizing and training peasants, instead levying a tax to hire long-term professionals and to recruit non-Chinese cavalry. When rebellions against Wang Mang demonstrated that armed peasant levies within the interior of China could threaten the imperial court, the routine mobilization and training of peasants was abolished altogether, along with the offices associated with this practice. From then until the end of imperial China, no government restored the practice of imposing military service on the peasantry.[12]

A second major shift after 154 B.C. was in state-sponsored patronage of the arts and literature. The Warring States polity had been an engine of war, and the maxim that guided policies and justified authority was "enrich the state and make the army strong." With the disappearance of the feudatory states in 154 B.C., the old justification through military power faded. Instead, the state increasingly claimed to rule as the patron of a Chinese civilization embodied in the canon, the imperial academy, and the classical virtues. Thus the devotion of the state and its agents to the defense and extension of the cultural patrimony became central to the imperial project. In the reign of Emperor Wu, the office of academician was restricted to students of the Zhou classics—in practice, largely

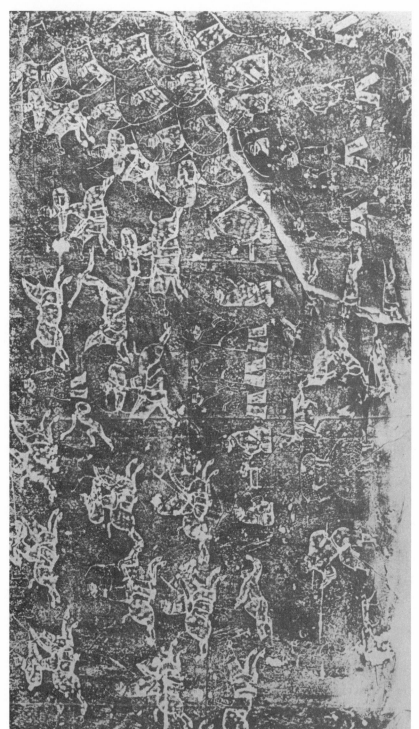

Fig. 3   Cavalry battle between Chinese and nomads.

Confucians. By the end of the Western Han more than 30,000 students attended the imperial academy, and it had become one of the primary routes to court office. The canon was even more highly honored under Wang Mang, who claimed to rule as a Confucian sage and established the cult of Heaven. Under the Eastern Han, the texts inherited from Zhou became the crown of the imperial edifice.[13]

The final major shift in the Han order was the rise of a new form of elite that combined a commitment to imperial service with local power based on land and social networks. Unlike the end of the peasant levy and the development of the imperial academy, this change had no basis in imperial policies and indeed was actively opposed by the Western Han court. However, in the long run it proved to be the most crucial change, the one that allowed the imperial system to survive the downfall of individual dynasties.

Qin had attempted to break the power of the Warring States elites by moving them to the capital region. Powerful local families had revived during the civil war and the early Han, but Emperor Wu appointed special legal agents charged with their destruction. However, at the same time that he was eliminating the vestiges of earlier elites, his policies were creating a new form of local power. His anti-merchant policies persuaded people to use wealth from trade to buy land. Likewise, any individual who was earning large sums of money from a high office at court or the command of a local prefecture or commandery had an incentive to turn this fleeting plenitude into lasting wealth through investment in real estate. Increased taxes pushed marginal peasants into the arms of moneylenders and ultimately into bankruptcy. Forced to sell their land cheaply to those with cash, they now had to work for these landlords as tenants.

In the last century B.C. the government made a series of laws to limit the concentration of landholding and prevent small-scale freeholders from becoming tenants. This was less out of compassion for the peasantry—whom the state squeezed mercilessly—than out of a desire to maintain its source of taxes and service. Wang Mang tried to nationalize all land and abolish slavery in an attempt to halt the development of landed estates and the rise of locally powerful families. His failure ended the government's resistance to the rise of landlordism.

Several developments help to explain why landlordism triumphed. Perhaps most important is the fact that the Eastern Han had been established by a coalition of large landowners that included the founding emperor. The eastern-dominated court rejected the military traditions of

Guanzhong, which were closely linked to the state's reliance on free smallholders. With the abolition of universal military service, control of the individual peasant household ceased to be the basis of state power, and the court's concern for the free peasantry largely vanished.

Whereas earlier local elites had been detached from and often hostile to the imperial state, many of the new landlords had risen to wealth and eminence through state service. Their newfound family traditions of study and conspicuous morality gave them every hope of maintaining access to office. Entry to the imperial academy or other avenues to office came through periodic recommendations solicited from eminent local families known to the central court or local officials, so powerful landlord families assured themselves of continued access to office through their control of these recommendations. The income from imperial offices allowed them to restore their estates after the partition that followed the death of the head of the family. Since the disappearance of the nobility, only the ruling house practiced primogeniture, while commoner families used partible inheritance, that is, the division of the father's property among the sons.

Merchants who had shifted their wealth into land followed the same course of action. Consequently, often the same family would run an estate, market the products of that estate or engage in money lending, and educate its sons in the classical texts, with the expectation of securing government offices. No longer based on the extraction of service from the peasantry, the state now secured its foundations through the loyalty of the powerful families who looked to it as their armed protector and a source of profitable appointments. This remained the pattern for imperial control throughout later dynasties.

The Failure of Qin and Its Later Mythology

Qin's twin role as both *the* model of empire and a target of criticism was reflected in the historical mythology that grew up around it. Its rapid rise and fall left a mark on all later Chinese thought about Qin and the nature of empire.

Within four years of the First Emperor's death in 210 B.C., the newly established empire collapsed in general rebellion. Its once invincible armies suffered defeat after defeat, its newly built capital was burned to the ground, and the last Qin ruler was slain. The reasons for this catastrophe were a constant topic of discussion in the early decades of the Han. While these musings often focused on supposed moral or intellectual deficiencies, such as overly cruel laws and the rejection of the wisdom of the ancients, the archaeological and textual evidence exposes these criticisms as self-serving Han propaganda with little relation to Qin policy or its failures. In fact, the Han incorporated Qin practice virtually intact at first, and the few modifications such as simplification of the laws and establishment of fiefs were soon abandoned.

So why did the Qin dynasty fail? The most insightful discussion of this catastrophe is also the earliest. Writing only a couple of decades after the Qin collapse, the early Han scholar Jia Yi argued: "One who conquers the lands of others places priority on deceit and force, but one who brings peace and stability honors obedience to authority. This means that seizing, and guarding what you have seized, do not use the same techniques. Qin separated from the Warring States period and became ruler of the whole world, but it did not change its ways or alter its government. Thus, there was no difference in the means by which they conquered and the means by which they tried to hold it."[14]

For all the ambition of the Qin reforms, with their vision of a new world where measures, laws, and truths flowed from a single source, the implementers of these reforms carried the basic institutions and practices of the Warring States unchanged into the empire. The direct administration of peasant households who were mobilized for military service continued as the organizing principle of the state, with a large servile labor pool formed from those who violated any of the numerous laws. No longer necessary for inter-state warfare, this giant machine for extracting service had become a tool in search of a use.

To occupy these conscripts, the Qin state engaged in an orgy of expansion and building that had little logic except employing Warring States institutions that had been rendered obsolete by their own success. Armies were launched on massive, pointless expeditions to the south, north, and northeast. Colossal projects to construct roads, a new capital, and the First Emperor's tomb were initiated. Laborers were dispatched to the northern frontier to link old defenses into the first Great Wall. A state created for warfare and expansion, Qin wasted its strength—and alienated its newly conquered people—by fighting and expanding when there were no useful worlds left to conquer. Mutinies by labor gangs led to a general rebellion of Qin officers and people against their rulers, and the first Chinese empire went down in flames only fifteen years after it was created.

The Han, though the heirs of the Qin, needed to dissociate themselves from the disaster of the first imperial dynasty's collapse. However, adopting Qin's practices even while condemning them produced a fundamental contradiction. The Han finally resolved it by dropping their critique of Qin's institutions and instead demonizing the First Emperor. The failures of Qin were explained by the brutality and megalomania of its founder and the barbarism of the Qin dynasty's political tradition. The result was a myth about cruel Qin laws that savagely attacked China's intellectual and political heritage. The Han portrayed themselves as patrons of the classical intellectual traditions and moral government that the First Emperor had tried to destroy.

This myth, however, simply masked the contradictions in the Han position. In painting the First Emperor as a monster, Han writers, along with those of later dynasties, developed literary tropes in which policies that provided the model for imperial practice and ideology figured as evidence of megalomania and villainy. As a result, throughout the history of imperial China the actual characteristics of the political system defined by the First Emperor were condemned as criminal. In their place was erected a moralizing façade, which some have described as the "hypocritization" of Chinese political culture. The remaining history of imperial China thus fell under the sway of a false consciousness of denunciation, focused on making a monster of the man who had provided the very model of imperial rule.

To take one example, the earliest accounts describe the Qin conquest as an attempt to impose the First Emperor's will upon Heaven and Earth, in a war against nature. Jia Yi describes how the First Emperor "cracked his long whip to drive the universe before him," "flogged the entire world," and "shook the four seas": "He toppled famous walls, killed local leaders, gathered the weapons of the world into Xianyang where he melted them down into bells and to cast twelve statues of giant men, in order to weaken the common people. Then he trod upon Mount Hua as his city wall and used the Yellow River as his moat. Based on this towering wall he gazed down into the fathomless depths and thought that he was secure."[15]

Sima Qian extended this pattern by describing how the First Emperor denuded Mount Xiang of trees because a storm caused by the goddess of a local shrine blocked his river passage. He cut through mountains and filled up valleys in order to run a road straight from Jiuyuan in the northwest to Yunyang, near the old Qin capital. When seeking the isles of the immortals, he dreamt that he was wrestling with a sea god, who blocked him. He armed himself and the boats he dispatched with repeating crossbows to kill the whales that threatened his search, and at one point shot and killed one. His practice of ascending numerous peaks and placing stone inscriptions there to recount his merits is yet another form of attempting to impose, or literally inscribe, his will upon the natural world.[16]

Several of these inscriptions contain lines on the theme of commanding nature. One inscription states that the First Emperor's laws and standards "extend wherever sun and moon shine," as though these astral bodies were his agents, and that "his blessings reach the oxen and horses." Another inscription describes how the emperor's power "shakes the four extremities of the Earth" and "regulates the universe." A third inscription narrates how the emperor destroyed walls, cut through embankments to open up the courses of rivers, and leveled steep and dangerous defiles to eliminate obstructions. This whole process is described as "fixing the shape of the land."[17]

The idea that the First Emperor in his hubris sought to control the universe became a standard theme in later Chinese literature. When Nanjing became a capital in the fourth century A.D., accounts told how in his travels the First Emperor had passed through the Nanjing region and learned that it had the topography of a future capital. In order to thwart this prophecy, which entailed the fall of his dynasty, the emperor commanded that the top of a mountain be lopped off. Other accounts describe his attempts to construct a bridge across the eastern sea in order to reach the isles of the immortals. Jiang Yan's sixth-century A.D. "Rhapsody on Resentment" repeats much of Jia Yi and Sima Qian's criticism, and then tells how the First Emperor constructed a bridge from sea turtles. A century later the poet Li Bo (Li Bai) employed a version in which a sorcerer brought stones to life, and the First Emperor whipped them in order to make them march into the sea to form his bridge. In this account he also tried to shoot a whale that blocked his passage to the isles.[18]

The early stories treat the First Emperor as a megalomaniac. The later poems employ him as an Ozymandias figure, ending with reflections on his death and the collapse of his works. Nevertheless, they highlight unacknowledged aspects of emperorship. First, the idea that the emperor's rule included the entire natural world, including trees and rocks, was generally accepted in imperial China. Second, the vision of the emperor commanding powerful spirits and making war on deities was not limited to the First Emperor. For example, the greatest poet of the Western Han,

Sima Xiangru, wrote a "Great Man Rhapsody" in which he depicted Emperor Wu commanding a retinue of gods to storm the gates of Heaven and carry off a jade maiden. Emperor Wu's own poem on sealing up the breach in the Yellow River's dike portrays him commanding the god of the river.[19] Finally, the building of a canonical imperial capital—with its rectangular walls, grids, and towers—entails the imposition of imperial will upon the landscape. The practices of the First Emperor in imperial city design, such as the building of palaces on celestial patterns and the incorporation of replica palaces or their stylistic elements from around the empire, were carried forward in the Han and later dynasties.

While the First Emperor's actions were a topic for censure, they also provided an unacknowledged pattern for later imperial power, a pure case or ideal type at the origin which later rulers emulated in muted, disguised versions. This role of the First Emperor as unacknowledged model embodies in a single mythic figure the hidden role of Qin as prototype for a permanent Chinese empire.

4

IMPERIAL CITIES

THE CITY is one of the largest structures on earth and the realm of artifice par excellence, the place where people can model their visions of the ideal society and the cosmos. With its walls designed to separate people from their surroundings, the city represents a uniquely human space, filled with the products and practices that make up a civilization. Major loci of political power, urban centers provide both the gathering place for rulers and administrators and the stage on which they display their authority. And in the realm of trade, cities are focal points of circulation and exchange, drawing in people and precious objects and in turn producing new goods that will flow outward to other cities or to lesser clusters of human habitation.

Prior to the Warring States period, Chinese cities were cultic and political entities inhabited by the nobility and their followers. They were, for the most part, lineage centers, with a population of at most a few tens of thousands and a single city wall. With the collapse of Zhou royal power, most of these cultic centers became independent city-states ruled by a ducal house and its noble followers who controlled the subject populations of their immediate hinterlands. Only gradually were these city-states incorporated into the large territories of the fifth-century B.C. Warring States.

Warring States and Early Imperial Cities

Recent archaeological excavations show that the number and complexity of cities increased during the Warring States period, as urban population, craft production, and trade grew. Defensive city walls became longer, and secondary walls inside the city were built to separate political and ceremonial districts from commercial and residential ones.[1] This physical separation of political activity from daily life captures a crucial moment in Chinese urban history, when the Warring States incorporated cities into their larger administrative network and replaced the local nobility with their own agents. From this point forward, cities in China were both physically and politically divided against themselves, with one part of the city devoted to crafts and commerce while the other was tied to political authority. These two urban realms coexisted in a degree of mutual suspicion.

This suspicion was articulated in laws that placed merchants on special registers and banned them and their descendants from holding office, wearing silk, riding horses, or owning land.[2] In practice only smaller traders were registered, while wealthy merchants who engaged in long-distance trade in luxuries escaped the bans. Nevertheless, the growing division between merchants and officials, both of whom were necessarily urban inhabitants, replaced the ancient division between city dwellers and rural populace as the central legal divide of the imperial period.

This legal and physical division corresponded to the new social model propounded by the philosophers of the period, in which the ruler's agents were an occupational category distinguished from all other forms of work through their cultivation of mind and their freedom from slavery to the objects built and exchanged by the rest.[3] Thus, even as the boundaries between town and country dissolved in the administrative models of the territorial state, new and sharper lines were imposed within the city itself.

Evidence for the division of the city and the pre-eminence of its political district comes from the Eastern Han tomb of the Colonel Protecting the Wuhuan (a nomadic people living to the northeast of the Han). Wall paintings tracing the career of the occupant depict five cities in which he served as an official. They are all portrayed as dual cities with two walled compounds, one for the general populace and the other for government buildings. While little information about the residential areas, other than the walls and gate towers, is provided, the layout, buildings, inhabitants, and activities of the government district are painted in great detail (Fig. 4). Many buildings are labeled to explain their identity or function. In one city, the market where the Colonel Protector supervised trade to buy horses from the Wuhuan—a trade that made this region one of the richest in the empire in the late second century A.D.—is also painted. This for-

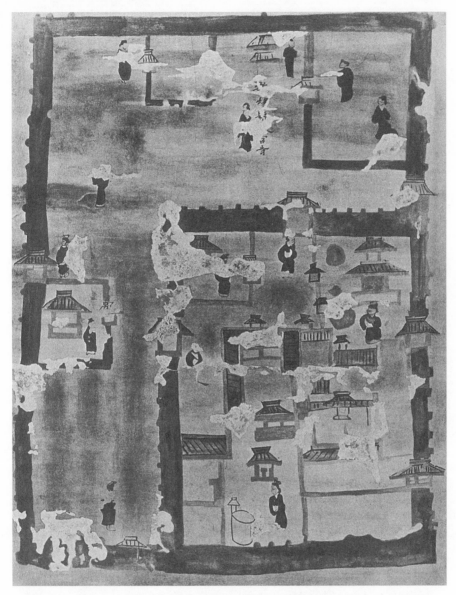

Fig. 4   City walls and government buildings of Fanyang district capital, Hebei.

mulaic portrayal of cities confirms what is suggested in texts, that imperial cities were divided in two, and the essential element was the palace
compound, with its state functions and political elite.

In the Warring States cities, new architectural elements appeared that
emphasized the ruler's power through height and verticality. Towers, pil-

lar gates, terraces, and raised buildings demonstrated both the visibility and the vision that marked the emperor's power, and suggested his ties to celestial spirits and divine forces rather than to ancestral ghosts. The importance of height and range of vision is demonstrated in a parable by the Eastern Han scholar Wang Chong (27–ca. 100 A.D.): "To mount a high tower and glimpse as far as the four neighboring states is what people desire. To sit hidden in a closed room, turning inward into the darkness, boring into a grave and sleeping in a cave, reaching to the edge of the Yellow Springs [realm of the dead] is what people hate. Someone with a closed mind and sealed-off thoughts who does not gaze from the heights is a companion of the dead."[4]

Anecdotes about towers exaggerated their great height, in one case boasting that the tower was 160 meters high and reached the clouds. Such height allowed a ruler to survey his own domain and possibly spy into neighboring states. In one passage, the loftiness of the tower is said to demonstrate the profundity of its builder's stratagems, and it elicits a collective toast and vow of loyalty from a group of visiting lords.[5]

In the Warring States period, pillar gates or gate towers (*que*) in the city wall were elaborated into lofty displays of the ruler's authority. In the middle of the fourth century B.C., when Shang Yang began constructing the new Qin capital at Xianyang, the first items built were the Ji gate towers. Similarly, at the end of the third century B.C. in the new Han capital of Chang'an, the gate towers received primary attention. Han ritual texts and poetry asserted that only the Son of Heaven was entitled to a gate flanked by two towers, that the height of the towers must correspond to the rank of the palace's occupant, and that towers flanking a gate were necessary because they "distinguished the superior from the inferior." Thus, beginning in the Warring States and well into the Han empire, the gateway with its towers became a more prominent symbol of authority than the surrounding wall. In the tomb art of the Eastern Han, gate towers to the city or to a great family's defensive compound are the most commonly depicted architectural structures (Fig. 5).[6]

Terraces with platforms were also built to intimidate foreign visitors by demonstrating the wealth of the owner and the extent of his gaze. Archaeological excavations have revealed the massive, packed-earth foundation mounds for these terraces, dating back to the Warring States. Pictorial bronzes from that period depict mounds flanked by steps and topped with large wooden platforms where ceremonies are being performed. Sometimes a series of ascending terraces was employed. Archi-

Fig. 5   Towers of a city gate, flanking an official.

tectural remains around these terraces indicate that they were the most visible elements of large palace complexes during the Warring States period.

Terraces could also form the core of an architectural structure composed of a series of rooms and corridors built around the earthen mound so as to give the impression of multiple stories. In an age that still lacked the ability to construct true multistoried buildings, this design allowed for structures that seemed to rise above the city. The most important example, and the one whose reconstructed image has been most frequently reproduced, was the Palace of the Ji Gate Towers in the Qin capital.[7]

Such palace buildings towering above the flat, horizontal plane of the residential and business district displayed the ruler's powers of observation—he was able to fix all within his gaze and at the same time to show people that they were observed. But equally important, these lofty new structures served as tools of invisibility. They made the ruler's presence known while concealing his person. They demonstrated his ability to study the activities of his people and his foes without himself being observed. The image of the ruler as an all-seeing, invisible eye (anticipating by two millennia Foucault's meditations on Bentham's panopticon) gave tangible form to the idea, expressed in such philosophical texts as the *Canon of the Way and Its Power* (*Dao de jing*) and the *Master Han Fei*, that the sage or ruler must remain hidden and unknowable.[8]

One of the masters of esoteric arts who advised the First Emperor argued that the ruler should move in secret to avoid evil spirits and should never let others know where he was. Moreover, since aerial or celestial spirits could be approached through physical ascent, the ruler should live in towers and move on elevated walkways to meet them and achieve immortality. In response to this advice, the First Emperor built elevated walks and walled roads to connect all 270 of his palaces and towers. Anyone who revealed where, in this vast complex, the emperor was visiting would be put to death. The emperor communicated orders only from his main palace in Xianyang, and at all other times remained in hiding. Fittingly, when the emperor died while journeying along the eastern sea, his body was transported in a sealed carriage to the capital, and the carriage was filled with fish to cover the smell of decay and conceal its contents.[9]

Raised walkways to mask the emperor's movements continued into the Han, and eventually withdrawal of the emperor from the gaze of the populace and even of the court became a principle of imperial political power. Throughout the imperial era, the Chinese ruler was sequestered behind a series of walls (a mythicizing version of which appears in the Kafka parable) in the "forbidden city."[10] To be allowed to see him was a privilege even for his officials, and to actually come into his presence was the highest of honors. Unlike ancient Rome, medieval Europe, or India, where the ruler showed himself to his people, received petitions, and publicly dispensed justice as a ritual of royalty, the ruler in China derived status from being hidden or invisible.

We know less about the other part of dual cities, the area for residence, commerce, and manufacture. The further one moves from the government sphere, the sparser the written records and archaeological finds become. The residential areas of the Han capitals were divided by a grid of major thoroughfares and then subdivided into walled wards under a low-level government administrator and a group of influential residents. It is unclear whether this system existed in other cities of early imperial China, but since this grid was a method for controlling the population, it is likely that major cities of the period were structured in this manner.

The chief thoroughfares were lined with houses of the noble and wealthy, while the alleys were inhabited by poorer people such as the philosopher Zhuang Zhou, who "lived in a poverty-stricken alley of a poor neighborhood, impecunious and weaving sandals." Alleys were too narrow to accommodate the large carriages that moved up and down the major boulevards, and the houses there were crumbling or miserable. Their inhabitants were often described as penniless writers, low-class wastrels who indulged in song and cheap liquor, or criminals. By contrast, the major boulevards were filled with high officials wearing their court hats and robes.[11]

One center of the residential district was the market. Tomb art indicates that the main features of the imperial capital's market also appeared in major provincial cities, with local variations. The markets and their surrounding neighborhoods were the chief site for the activities of merchants and craftsmen, but they were also the locus of government power within the outer city. They replicated on a reduced scale the division between the government and the populace that defined the dual city. The market's multistory tower served as a vertical symbol and site of authority, like the palaces, while its grid echoed the government order imposed on the outer city. Yet in spite of these physical manifestations of authority, the market remained a place of popular assemblies and a setting for many activities that challenged the prescribed order.

The most visible expression of government control was a multistory tower that housed the officials in charge of the market. In the Eastern Han capital of Luoyang, the market chief and his deputy had a staff of thirty-six men. They were responsible for guaranteeing that goods sold in the market were of sufficient quality and that all prices were in accord with the standards imposed after a monthly review of authorized agreements between buyers and sellers. According to Qin law, objects for sale in the market had to have price tags hung on them stating the exact cost. Records of all transactions and the moneys involved were to be placed in special boxes that officials could inspect at the end of the day to collect the government's tax share.[12]

Officials also sold government surplus commodities or the products of government workshops and may have charged a fee to notarize contracts recording purchases. The tower had a flag on top and a drum in the upper chamber to signal the opening and closing of the market. The towers in the Chang'an markets are described in an Eastern Han poem as being five stories high, while a Han tomb tile depicting the market in Chengdu shows one that is only two stories.[13] In either case, the tower would have been the highest structure in the market, visible to everyone.

The second manifestation of government power in the markets was the imposition of a grid, like that of the residential districts. The tomb tile depicting Chengdu's market shows a perfect square with a gate on each side

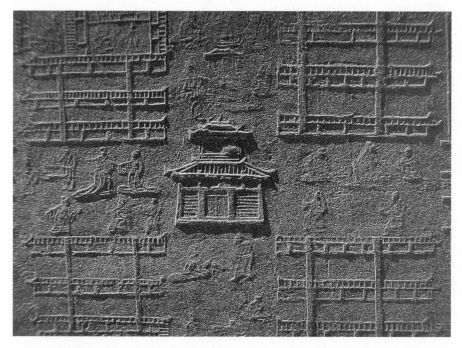

Fig. 6   Grid of the Chengdu market, with the tower in the center.

and two major roads running between the gates in a simple cross pattern. The two-story tower is exactly at the center. The image shows the market as a reduced version of the canonical ideal of a capital city, as described in the *Records for the Scrutiny of Crafts* (*Kao gong ji*), a late Warring States text about construction that was appended to the *Rituals of Zhou* (*Zhou li*) (Fig. 6).

Each of the market's four quarters is in turn divided by rows of one-story buildings. These presumably housed shops, which were grouped by product. Human figures move about on the four main streets. The most important shops may have lined the major thoroughfares, while lesser shops and stalls lined the alleyways. Such a pattern existed in the Tang capital markets, and it probably existed in the Han. This grid of shops in the market figures in the poetry and other texts of the period, which emphasize the regularity of the lines of shops as evidence of imperial greatness and social order. Several tomb images also depict the arrayed stalls in lines or as a grid, and Qin legal documents insist on the regularity of stalls.

Archaeological excavations and newly discovered texts have provided additional evidence regarding the Han capital markets. Chang'an had two markets, an eastern market of 500,000 square meters (25 percent larger than the largest shopping mall in the United States) and a western one of 250,000 square meters. Both were surrounded by walls 5 to 6 meters thick, against which merchants built warehouse facilities. The eastern market was largely devoted to merchandise stalls, but the western market was also a major manufacturing center, with a kiln that produced terracotta human figures for imperial burials, a mint, a state iron-casting site, and a privately run workshop making funerary figurines of people, horses, and birds.

Whereas the Chengdu tile market was divided into four sectors, the capital markets were divided into nine. These were in turn divided by the regular lines of stalls, as stipulated by Qin law (Fig. 7). All merchants selling a particular category of goods were placed together, and each line of stalls was under the supervision of a senior merchant who had to vouch for the integrity of all merchants on his row. Like the population at large, these merchants were divided into five-man groups of mutual legal liability who had to observe one another and denounce any misbehavior.[14]

The market was also used for public punishments, both beatings and executions. The heads or whole corpses of major criminals were fre-

Fig. 7   Scenes of market stalls, with the market tower and signal drum on the right.

quently on display. Passages in the *Records of Ritual* (*Li ji*), a Han compendium of essays on rites, and the *Methods of the Commandant* (*Sima fa*), a Warring States military treatise, pair the market with the court as respective sites of punishment and reward, the "two handles" of the ruler's power in legalist political theory.[15]

The market hosted less violent displays of authority as well as political performances seeking a wider audience. When Lü Buwei, chief minister of Qin during the youth of the First Emperor, desired to mark the completion of the *Springs and Autumns of Master Lü*, the philosophical compendium of which he was the patron, and to assert that it contained all significant knowledge, he placed the text at the entrance to the market of Xianyang, suspended one thousand pieces of gold above the text, and offered the gold to whoever could remove or add a single character. A similar anecdote tells how Shang Yang demonstrated to the people of Qin that his rewards were trustworthy by announcing in the market that he would give cash to whoever performed a specified simple task, and in fact gave such a reward.[16]

As the one place where the people could legally gather in large numbers, the market was the privileged site for the communication of messages from the rulers to the people, whether those messages took the form of words, texts, money, or dismembered bodies. As a site of crowds, merchant wealth, and public spectacles, however, the market was not completely under the government's control. Unsanctioned activities took several forms, associated with merchants, "wandering swordsmen" with gangs of youthful idlers, and masters of esoteric arts related to shamanic cults, particularly diviners and doctors. Each of these groups challenged the state in its own way.

While merchants posed no direct political challenge to the state, their wealth allowed a life of luxury surpassing that of their political superiors. The merchants' ostentatious wealth tempted officials to corruption and poor peasants away from a life of toil, taxes, and service to the state. This tension between a merchant order, defined by wealth, and an official order, defined by rank, was built into the structure of the dual cities and exacerbated by laws banning registered merchants and their descendants from holding office. The merchants' violation of the state's sumptuary order and their ability to purchase land and services from free peasants pervade the writings of the period.

In addition to flouting the sumptuary order, mercantile wealth also challenged the efficacy of the laws. While in theory no one was exempt from punishments, it was a common saying that the sons of rich families would never die in the market place, that is, be publicly executed. Officials responsible for coinage sometimes collaborated with merchants in schemes to forge cash and manipulate currency. Thus, the market was feared by supporters of the state as a site where men gained power and status not awarded by the government, where this power and wealth were routinely displayed in violation of sumptuary regulations, and where wealth itself was manipulated to the detriment of criminal law and government administration.[17]

Crowds regularly gathered in the marketplace to entertain themselves with spectacles and amusements or to listen to men of political ambition. The most common spectacle was the departure or arrival of eminent people in their fine carriages and elaborate costumes. Less frequent were the performances of political pretenders seeking to gain attention or support. The costumes of the urban elite, as in so many societies, became the standard for others to emulate.

> In the city, if they love to have their hair dressed up high,
> Then everywhere else they dress their hair an inch higher.
> In the city, if they love to enlarge their eyebrows,
> Then everywhere else they will make their eyebrows cover half
>   their foreheads.
> In the city, if they love large sleeves,
> Then everywhere else they will use up whole bolts of silk.

Urban dwellers' authority in fashion challenged the state, for in the political texts of the period it was the tastes in attire of the ruler that were supposed to set the model for others to follow.[18]

The market's violence and criminality were generally associated with butchers and "wicked youths" but most importantly with "wandering swordsmen" or gangsters (you xia)—men who devoted themselves to an ethic of vengeance, faithfulness to oaths, and devotion to the death. The poems on Han capitals place these men and their gangs of sworn followers in the markets. The histories situate them in the "alleys" and "wards" of the major cities. Like other denizens of the market, they are described as acting for profit, in this case as bandits, kidnappers, grave robbers, and hired assassins rather than merchants. Gangsters formed associations of professional killers who intimidated or bribed officials. Memorials written in the Eastern Han described them as the creators of a "private law" based on vengeance that threatened to supplant the state's legal codes.[19]

Butchers, who were accustomed to hacking flesh and shedding blood, made up another category of violent men in the marketplace. They were located in one area, distinguished from other trades not just by their products but by the prestige and wealth of clients who came in search of men willing to cut more than fresh meat.

"Wicked youths" were a broader social category closely tied to the other two through their violent tendencies. Most of the leading criminals described in Sima Qian's Records of the Historian/Astrologer were admired by gangs of youths, who emulated them or assisted in their illegal activities. The "youths of the wards and alleys" often became gangsters or swordsmen in order to earn money, and one band of youths acted as accomplices for a wayward imperial prince who engaged in robbery and murder for sport. The "cruel clerks" employed by the state to destroy powerful local families were sometimes recruited from among these gangs or worked with them. Many "wicked youths" were sent on expeditions to Central Asia to get them out of the city.

In peacetime, "wicked youths" were portrayed as wastrels with no proper occupations, who passed their time in the market gambling, cock fighting, and coursing hounds. These activities were so common that they were depicted on tomb tiles. In times of disorder, however, these urban gangs formed a reservoir of recruits for those engaged in large-scale vendettas or rebellion. The biographies of many leaders in the uprising against Qin show that their first followers were recruited from among the youths.

The Han founder himself is depicted as a classic wastrel who refused to work on his family's property, spent his time in bars drinking and eating with his friends, and was regarded by his father as "worthless and unreliable." His earliest followers (Xiao He, Cao Can, and Fan Kuai) are described as "youths and bold clerks"—wild young men or aspirant swordsmen who had low-level government posts. Reliance on idle youths to initiate a rebellion also figures in the fall of Wang Mang. The early histories suggest that the gangsters and youths who gathered in the markets were simple criminals in times of order but played an important role in the toppling of dynasties in times of chaos.[20]

The final social element that gathered in the market and challenged the authority of the state comprised the masters of esoteric techniques, particularly diviners and "shaman doctors." This group was accused of claiming supernatural powers in order to swindle peasants. And because divination, medicine, and related religious practices were a source of wealth, the group was denounced for luring idle young people away from proper occupations and into their own disreputable pursuits.

A standard example of such a polemic appears in the first-century B.C. *Discourse on Salt and Iron (Yan tie lun)*, supposedly a record of a debate about the state monopolies: "Following the customs of the age, hypocrites practice deceit and become shamans and invocators for the common people in order to extract payments from them. With brazen effrontery and powerful tongues, some of them establish enterprises and attain wealth. Therefore those who dread work abandon agriculture to study with them." The *Discourses of a Hidden Man (Qian fu lun)*, the collected essays of the late Eastern Han writer Wang Fu (ca. 90–165 A.D.), makes similar accusations, except that it focuses on the role of women as both followers of the shamans and their victims, and it argues that curing disease through appeals to spirits is the method by which shamans swindle people and attract followers.

The market was often the scene of the kind of pushing and shoving that risked turning a crowd into a mob or a riot. Prostitutes plied their trade in the market and its nearby drinking establishments, an added attraction for a certain clientele. And of course there were beggars—at best a pitiful nuisance, at worst celebrated avengers like Wu Zixu and Yu Rang, who kept themselves and their violent schemes alive by begging for food.[21]

In summary, the physical partitioning of cities in the Warring States led to a permanent legal and social division that left the imperial Chinese city forever divided against itself. In the early imperial period the state was formed from a hierarchical network of palace cities, with their surrounding agricultural lands. The outer cities made up of residences, workshops, and markets were necessary to the production and exchange of goods, but in both ideology and fiscal practice they were marginal and potentially threatening to the state. Despite attempts to impose order through grids in streets and markets, the populations of the outer cities remained alien to the government's ideal patterns of service and hierarchy. Even their licit population, the merchants and craftsmen, threatened the state by creating alternative hierarchies based on wealth that lured miserable rural people to abandon their work and seek wealth in the city.

In addition, markets attracted marginal people into the cities to seek their fortunes in illicit occupations. Condemned as "lazy" or "wicked" by most writers, these people survived through non-registered businesses, criminality, the mantic arts, and prostitution. Sharing a common space in the market and a common status as unsanctioned or unregistered enterprises, they helped to create a distinctive urban culture that lay outside the force-field of the state. They also interacted across the empire in webs of trade and criminality that paralleled the network of official cities, but remained permanently apart from it.

Invention of the Imperial Capital

Shang Yang, the minister who laid the foundations for Qin's rise to power, initiated construction of the Qin capital Xianyang in the middle of the fourth century B.C. This city followed the pattern of Warring States capitals but was expanded beyond its walls under subsequent rulers. This expansion reached a peak under the First Emperor, who launched a major rebuilding program to create a new type of capital that would mark the creation of the first state to rule all of China. In 220 B.C. he built the Xin Palace south of the Wei River (the capital proper was to the north of the river) and then renamed the palace the Apex Temple, as the earthly image of the Heavenly Apex Star. This star was the center of Heaven and the palace of the High God, or in some texts his celestial essence. Sima Qian would begin his account of the organization of the sky with this star.[22] The First Emperor patterned elements of his capital on the sky to mark his role as the earthly agent of celestial power, thereby creating a new style of capital to mark his unprecedented achievements.

In 212 B.C. he constructed a great palace in the Shanglin park south of the Wei River. The two peaks of the Southern Mountains served as the gates of this palace, which was to boast an upper hall that could hold 10,000 people. From this hall the emperor planned to build a covered walk to South Mountain, on the summit of which he had placed a plaque declaring the mountain to be the gate tower of the palace. Another elevated walk for secret movement was built to connect this new palace to the old one north of the river "in imitation of the way in which in the Heavens a corridor leads from the Heavenly Apex Star across the Milky Way to the Royal Chamber Star." In a flurry of construction, the First Emperor built "300 palaces within the passes," according to the *Shi ji*, with elevated walks and walled roads linking them and ensuring that he could move from palaces to villas to towers like a spirit, without being observed.[23]

It was not enough for the capital to represent the Heavens; it must also become a microcosm of the Chinese empire on Earth. Each time Qin conquered a Warring State, a replica of that state's palace was built on the northern bank of the Wei River, facing the new palace to the south. These replica palaces were also connected by covered walkways with walled-in towers, and they were filled with musical instruments and singing girls from the vanquished states. Because palaces were seen as the embodiment of states, the Qin could symbolically annex a state by destroying its original palace and rebuilding a "captive" replica in its own capital.[24]

Continuing in this vein, the First Emperor resettled 120,000 of the most powerful families of the conquered states in Xianyang. Later he also resettled families to tend his future tomb, his summer palace at Sweet Springs, and even one of the stone inscriptions that he placed on the mountains in the east.[25] This policy of drawing the empire's people into the center reduced the possibility of resistance in what were now provinces, placed dangerous elements within the immediate purview of the emperor and his court, and through the capital's new inhabitants and buildings demonstrated that Xianyang was the center and epitome of empire. It gave literal form to the early Chinese idea that the power of a ruler was revealed in his ability to cause people from far away to come to his court.

The First Emperor also collected captured weapons from across the empire, melted them down, and cast them into twelve statues of giants. These probably depicted immortals whose appearance signaled approval of the First Emperor's achievements and his future attainment of immortality.[26]

The replication of the newly conquered world figured in another building project of the First Emperor, his tomb mound at Mount Li. The *Springs and Autumns of Master Lü* notes that late Warring States rulers had built great tomb complexes that imitated their palace cities. This is confirmed by a model of the fourth century B.C. tomb complex of the king of Zhongshan that was found in his tomb. The culmination of this practice was the artificial mountain erected by the First Emperor, the tomb now best known for its terracotta army. This carried on the Qin tradition of erecting an earthen grave mound (tumulus) and then building wood-framed architectural complexes beside it. It also adopted the eastern tradition of ringing this complex with a double wall, lending it the status of a palace city.

But the First Emperor adapted this Warring States idea of replication to his new claim as ruler not of a state but of the entire world. His central tomb was filled with models of palaces and towers, sculptures of officials, and numerous rare objects. All those concubines who had not given birth to children were also to be slain and buried in this replica of the court. This was then surrounded by a model of the earth, with seas and rivers made from liquid mercury and representations of the Heavens on the ceiling.[27] From recent excavations, which have reached only the outskirts of the tomb, we know that the area between the inner and outer walls contained sculptures of even more officials, entertainers, and the terra-cotta army of more than 6,000 soldiers and horses. These in turn were ringed by the actual tombs of high officials, members of the royal family, and an underground replica of a stable. Thus the tomb complex copied both the Qin state and the world.

Despite all this building, several features of the capital reveal the limits of Qin's transition from a state organized for war into a universal empire. First, Xianyang was ritually empty. All the major altars of state were elsewhere in Qin. The most important were the Fu Altar and the Four Altars of Mount Wu, which were in the hills around the old capital of Yong. These included the altars for the four directional deities (the highest Qin gods), for the Treasures of Chen, and for most celestial and meteorological phenomena. The earlier capital in Longxi had several dozen shrines, and numerous shrines to minor gods and spirits were scattered across Qin.[28]

As the First Emperor went through his newly conquered lands, ascending mountains and leaving inscriptions to celebrate his achievements, he also conducted sacrifices or made offerings to major regional gods, notably the Eight Spirits in Qi. He performed the *feng* and *shan* sacrifices on Mount Tai and Mount Liangfu, once again attributing the highest spiritual potency to sacrifices far away from Qin's capital. Finally, he standardized the cults of major mountains and rivers, deciding which major natural features would receive sacrifices—natural features that were necessarily dispersed throughout the realm.

Mount Hua was the sole piece of sacred landscape that was anywhere close to the capital. The emperor's only attempt to attribute ritual importance to the city was to assign to seven lesser rivers near Xianyang—the Ba, Chan, Changshui, Feng, Lao, Jing, and Wei—the same ritual status that he accorded to the major rivers. But in practice they did not receive all the offerings granted to the truly great rivers.[29]

Thus, in both Qin and the conquered territories, the religious policy consisted of recognizing and rationalizing existing regional cults. These reflected not the centralization of power in the new empire but the features of natural geography and the dispersed cultic practices that had evolved in past centuries. Whether this indicates a general lack of interest in religious ritual on the part of the First Emperor or a devotion to received practice, it is quite different from the understanding that emerged in the Han empire of the capital as the center for the highest religious rituals.

The second limit to the imperial transformation of Xianyang lies in the very features by which the First Emperor made it a new style of capital: the replica palaces, the statues cast from confiscated weapons, and the resettled population. The primary purpose of these projects was to fashion a monument to Qin's victory over the other Warring States. The replica palaces and the giant statues eternalized this victory and in so doing guaranteed that the war would never truly end in the minds of the vanquished or the victors. In the same way, the First Emperor's inscriptions proclaimed his creation of a new world, but they also froze in stone the celebration of Qin's triumph over its rivals. Thus the First Emperor's capital dramatically embodied the failure of Qin to rule its conquered peoples with different methods than it had used to defeat them.

The Qin empire's ambitious building program had not been completed in 206 B.C. when most of the capital was destroyed by Xiang Yu's army. When the Han founder, Liu Bang, decided that for security he should also make his capital in the Qin heartland, he had to build a new city largely from scratch. One of the Qin emperor's surviving summer retreats, the Xingle Palace, located south of the river, was renamed Changle and adopted as the Han founder's primary palace. As a result, the Han capital, Chang'an, was established on the south side of the Wei River. Here, Shusun Tong, a classicist scholar who had served the Qin, staged the first great imperial ritual for the Han, one in which all the courtiers prostrated themselves to the Han founder and saluted his triumph.[30] Thus began the creation of a Han imperial capital centered around ritual performance.

The Han founder was a man of Chu state in the south, and the decision to place his capital in the Wei River valley uprooted his dynasty from its place of origin. This deliberate breaking of geographical and cultural ties was a first step in the creation of an artificial imperial culture marked by the absence of local attachments.[31] The *Records of the Historian/Astrologer* portrays the founder, Emperor Gaozu (as Liu Bang became known), as a man who lacked loyalty to family and home, and it attributes his triumph to this very characteristic. This facet of Gaozu's character was shown in many ways.

First, he adopted the myth that his true father was a dragon. This divine paternity was not only a standard element in the mythology of sages and dynastic founders, but it also justified a lack of loyalty to his earthly father and to his ancestral home. As a youth, Gaozu refused to work in his family's business and instead spent his time drinking and carousing with similarly inclined friends. During his rise to power, Gaozu even tried to throw his own children out of a carriage to aid his escape. When his father was taken prisoner by Xiang Yu and threatened with being boiled and eaten, Gaozu asked to share the soup. After becoming emperor, he richly rewarded a follower who persuaded Gaozu's father to serve as a subject in Gaozu's empire, since there could be only one sun in the sky.[32]

Gaozu's lack of connection to his family and place of origin stands in stark contrast with that of his chief rival, Xiang Yu, in a story told by Sima Qian. Advised that, having occupied and sacked the Qin capital, he should make his own capital there, Xiang Yu instead chose to return to Chu, rule in his home, and enfeoff his allies across the north of China: "To become rich and famous and then not go back to your old home is like putting on an embroidered coat and going out walking in the night. Who would know about it?"[33] He could not leave his old home for the sake of an empire. Gaozu could, and so he triumphed. This parable, within the larger pattern of Gaozu's conduct, shows the importance that Sima Qian attributed to the renunciation of local ties as the key to founding an empire.

Although Gaozu spent most of his time away from Chang'an, much work was done to establish the new city as a capital. The Han government constructed an armory, a granary, and an official market, but there is no record of an ancestral temple, probably since as a commoner Gaozu could trace his genealogy back no further than his grandfather. The chief minister, Xiao He, supervised the construction of a larger palace, the Weiyang, just to the southwest of the Changle Palace, on the Dragon Head Hills—appropriately named, since the dragon was the emperor's symbol. A series of ascending terraces were built into the hillside, and a lofty palace towered over the city.

After Gaozu criticized Xiao He for wasting money on the capital when the empire itself was not yet secure, Xiao He explained his logic this way: "It is precisely because the fate of the empire is still uncertain that we must build such palaces and halls. A true Son of Heaven takes all within the four seas to be his family. If he does not dwell in magnificence and beauty, he will have no way to manifest his authority, nor will he leave anything for his heirs to build upon." The construction of a palace rising above his capital demonstrated Gaozu's authority and the dynasty's immortality. The palace was the "foundation" of the empire, with the emperor as the center of the new state. Whereas the fourth-century B.C. *Transmissions of Master Zuo* (*Zuo zhuan*) had defined a capital as a "city with an ancestral temple," the Han dictionary *Explaining Words* (*Shi ming*) said that the "capital is the seat of the emperor."[34]

The second Han ruler, Emperor Hui, a child who was guided by his tutor Shusun Tong, began to shape the city according to the precepts for the ideal capital described in the *Record for the Scrutiny of Crafts* (*Kao gong ji*): "When the chief carpenter constructs the capital, it is a square of nine li per side. Each side has three gates. In the capital there are nine north-south boulevards and nine east-west. The north-south ones are nine carriage tracks wide. On the left is the ancestral temple, on the right the altar of the soil, in front the court, and in the rear the market."[35] Emperor Hui followed parts of this program.

First, he built an ancestral temple for Gaozu, to the east of the Weiyang Palace. Then he built a new market, the West Market, to the north of his palace. He erected an icehouse in the Weiyang Palace, and finally he built an outer wall to contain the palaces, temples, and markets. Under Gaozu, the imperial palaces were ringed with walls, but no outer walls had defined the entire city. Because the outer wall built by Emperor Hui incorporated the walls of existing structures, it was highly irregular rather than square, as stipulated by the *Record for the Scrutiny of Crafts*. However, the outer wall followed the text in having twelve gates, although four of them were blocked by the Weiyang and Changle Palaces and thus existed only to conform to orthodoxy.

Emperor Hui's orthodoxy was not obsessive. Due to the scale and locations of the palace complexes, major streets did not form a grid. However, they had a special lane reserved for the emperor's use, a feature without textual foundation. When it was noted that the procession carrying Gaozu's crown and robes from his mausoleum to his temple had to pass under an elevated walkway used by Emperor Hui—which was judged to be unfilial—the ancestral temple was moved from the capital city to the mausoleum north of the river. This major ritual reform would affect the later practice of the Han ancestral cult.[36]

The last great builder in Chang'an was the fifth ruler, Emperor Wu. His

two immediate predecessors had been abstemious rulers who accumulated wealth in the imperial treasury, suppressed the major feudatories,
and concentrated power at the imperial court. Emperor Wu renovated
the two existing palaces and filled out the space within the city walls by
building three new palaces. He also constructed a massive sacrificial center to the northwest of the capital, where a Qin summer palace had been
located. However, his most ambitious work was the restoration of the
Shanglin hunting park to the southwest of Chang'an (Map 7).

Once the site of Qin palaces and pavilions, the Shanglin park had
largely fallen into disuse. Emperor Wu filled it with dozens of new structures, carved out a large artificial lake, and erected statues of the Weaving
Maid and Cowherd stars in order to create a replica of the Milky Way.
He placed a statue of a whale in the middle of the lake to make it a microcosm of the ocean, which was the earthly equivalent of the Milky Way.
All three statues have been found in recent excavations. In the park he
built the massive Jianzhang Palace complex, whose main gate was named
Changhe after the gate of Heaven and whose primary building was the
Jade Hall, the name of the Heavenly Emperor's palace. This building was
surrounded by a labyrinth of corridors and topped with a gilded phoenix
weather vane. It rose above even the Weiyang Palace, to which it was to
be a celestial equivalent. The hunting park in many ways supplanted the
capital itself as both primary imperial residence and the major center for
rituals.

Throughout the park, Emperor Wu installed rare plants, animals, and
rocks that he had received as tribute from distant peoples, as booty from
expeditions to Central Asia, or as confiscations from private collectors.
The emperor's exotica included a black rhinoceros, a white elephant,
talking birds, and tropical forests. It not only proved the ruler's charismatic power to attract tribute from distant places but also transformed
the park into an equivalent of the Isles of the Immortals, which were depicted in Han art as covered with strange animals and birds.

In building up this great park next to the capital, Emperor Wu displayed his own vision of cosmic lordship and his dream of personal immortality. The dream was in vain, of course; and like his predecessors,
Emperor Wu was buried beneath an artificial mountain north of the Wei
River. These imperial grave mounds, beginning with that of Gaozu at
Changling and continuing for each of the Western Han emperors who
followed, gradually formed a line of artificial "mountains" rising to the
north of the capital (Map 8).

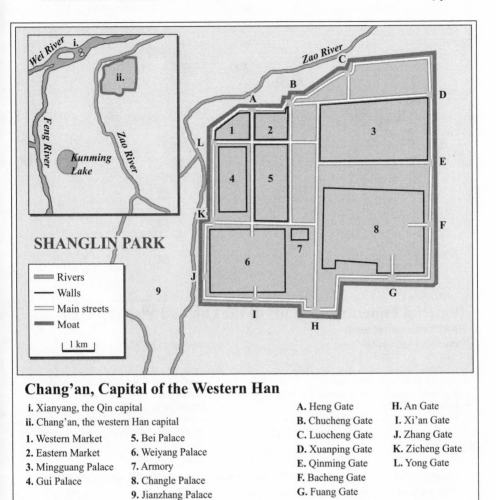

Chang'an, Capital of the Western Han

i. Xianyang, the Qin capital
ii. Chang'an, the western Han capital

1. Western Market   5. Bei Palace
2. Eastern Market   6. Weiyang Palace
3. Mingguang Palace   7. Armory
4. Gui Palace   8. Changle Palace
                      9. Jianzhang Palace

A. Heng Gate   H. An Gate
B. Chucheng Gate   I. Xi'an Gate
C. Luocheng Gate   J. Zhang Gate
D. Xuanping Gate   K. Zicheng Gate
E. Qinming Gate   L. Yong Gate
F. Bacheng Gate
G. Fuang Gate

After Wang Zhongshu, *Han Civilization,* tr. K. C. Chang (New Haven: Yale University, 1982)

MAP 7

Each tumulus had wooden buildings for the performance of rituals, and these were maintained by the populations of towns created for the upkeep of the imperial tombs. Gaozu had initiated this policy by populating a town attached to his father's tomb with leading families of the empire, who were resettled in the capital region in imitation of Qin practice. His successors continued the practice. The populations of these towns may have reached 300,000 people each. According to a census of 2 A.D., more people lived in the tomb towns of the Emperors Wu and Xuan than within the walls of Chang'an. Many leading officials and scholars of the Han dynasty came from these towns or lived there while serving at the

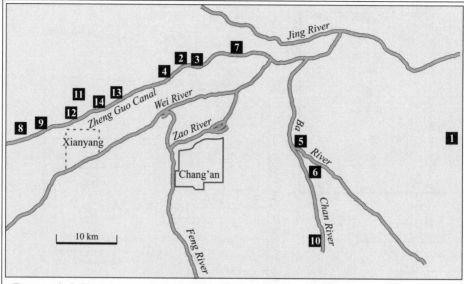

Imperial Funerary Mounds of the Qin and Western Han
Ruler and name of tomb

1. Qin Shihuang (r. 221–210 B.C.)
2. Emperor Gao (r. 202–195) Changling
3. Dowager Empress Lü (regent 188–180)
4. Emperor Hui (r. 195–188) Anling
5. Emperor Wen (r. 180–157) Baling
6. Empress Bo, Nanling
7. Emperor Jing (r. 157–141) Yangling

8. Emperor Wu (r. 141–87) Maoling
9. Emperor Zhao (r. 87–74) Pingling
10. Emperor Xuan (r.74–49) Duling
11. Emperor Yuan (r. 49–33) Weiling
12. Emperor Cheng (r. 33–7) Yanling
13. Emperor Ai (r. 7–1) Yiling
14. Emperor Ping (1 B.C.–A.D. 6) Kangling

MAP 8

court. The growth and maintenance of the ancestral cult thus served to draw population and wealth into the capital area.

Two centuries of resettlement greatly expanded the population of Guanzhong, making it increasingly reliant on imported grain. These new-comers formed the single greatest pool for the recruitment of imperial officials; and like the imperial family itself, they originally found the re-gional customs of Guanzhong alien. However, as the policy of resettle-ment weakened the ability of regions to challenge the center, it also cre-ated a distinctive capital culture based on imperial service performed by these people with few local attachments. Chang'an established the pat-tern in which the capital became the unique physical embodiment of the empire, and its population the true exponents of an imperial culture.

Nevertheless, certain features of Chang'an limited its success as an imperial capital. For the first century of the Han, power was partially dispersed among feudatory states. The courts of Huainan, Hejian, and

Liang all were major centers for the patronage of intellectual and religious activities, and many leading scholars and writers chose the feudatory courts over the imperial one. Only the eclipse of the feudatories in
the second century of Han rule eliminated these rivals to the imperial
capital.

A more important limitation, signaled by the importance of the mausoleum towns, was that the first Han capital, like its predecessor, represented largely a ritual void. The ancestral temple within the walls played
a lesser role than the tomb-side temples at the mausoleums. More important, temples to Gaozu and later emperors were established in every prefecture in the empire, reducing the centrality of the capital in ancestral
cults and associated rituals.

The major cults to cosmic and natural deities followed the Qin pattern
and were scattered across the realm. Sacrifices to mountains and rivers
were carried on in their traditional sites. Those to the directional *di*,
which were among the chief deities in the Han, were located in the temples around Yong. The addition of a fifth *di* by Gaozu simply increased
the importance of the old Yong site. He set up sacrifices to Hou Ji in every
prefecture, feudal kingdom, and district, rather than centralizing this ritual. In Chang'an itself, Gaozu imported shamans from throughout the
empire to perform cults in the palace, and he established a short-lived altar to the war god Chi You.[37]

Emperor Wen, the third Han ruler, had established the cult of the five
di north of the capital, but the *jiao* (suburban) sacrifice continued to be
performed at Yong, and the cult to the *di* remained there as well. Emperor Wu introduced numerous cults, some near Chang'an and some
more distant. The cult of the Grand Unity was first installed to the southeast of the capital. The altar to the Empress Earth was set up at Fenyin, a
considerable distance away. Emperor Wu also turned the old Qin summer palace at Sweet Springs into a major ritual center, where he moved
the chief altar to the Grand Unity. The greatest sacrifices of the Western
Han, the *feng* and *shan*, were performed at Mount Tai in Shandong, and
the Hall of Light, which many scholars suggested should be built in the
capital, was erected instead near Mount Tai.

When the classicists began to gain influence at the court in the last decades of the Western Han, they complained that the massive expense of
maintaining ancestral temples dispersed throughout the empire was un-
warranted, and that these sacrifices required unfilial offerings from non-
kin. The fact that the emperor had to travel to Yong, Sweet Springs,

Fenyin, and Mount Tai for all the major state sacrifices displeased them as well. Even the concentration of temples and palaces in Shanglin Park undercut the ritual status of the capital proper, they claimed.[38]

After the death of Emperor Wu, little construction was carried out in Chang'an. The Jianzhang Palace and many buildings in Shanglin Park were torn down by Wang Mang at the end of the Western Han to provide material for his Hall of Light and related ritual structures prescribed in the classics. These in turn were largely destroyed in the civil war that toppled Wang Mang and led to the transfer of the capital to the Eastern Han city of Luoyang.

This capital was smaller in area than Chang'an but more densely populated. Its wall was nearly a perfect rectangle with proper directional orientation, and it had the requisite twelve gates, although not at regular intervals. It had two palace compounds, like Chang'an, properly aligned on a north-south axis. The palaces and government buildings occupied a much smaller proportion of the city's surface area, which allowed the creation of a more regular grid of major boulevards. Luoyang's architecture was also much more austere than Chang'an's. Luoyang was intended to demonstrate in its austerity and regular spatial arrangements the establishment of the classical canon as the state orthodoxy (Map 9).[39]

This point is made most clearly in the "Rhapsody on the Two Capitals" by Ban Gu (32–92 A.D.), a leading historian and poet. Presented to the Han court in 65 A.D., it follows the model set by the leading Western Han poet Sima Xiangru of a series of rhetorical set pieces in which fictive speakers celebrate their respective courts. By the end, the earlier speakers are reduced to submission, stammering apologies for their ignorance and folly. Sima Xiangru had used the form to celebrate the imperial hunting park and thereby glorify the triumph of imperial power over the feudatories. His focus on the hunting park rather than the city proper confirms, however, that the Western Han capital was not the true center of the empire.

Ban Gu adapted the genre of the rhapsody to glorify the Eastern Han court through a poetic triumph over the Western Han, as well as a personal triumph over Sima Xiangru. He sought to demonstrate the superiority of morally serious literature to the baroque fancies of Sima Xiangru, and the superiority of the ritually proper Luoyang to the corrupt ornamentations of Chang'an. The poem concluded with songs in praise of the textually sanctioned capital ritual complex, consisting of the Hall of Light, the Circular Moat, and the Numinous Tower.

Luoyang, Capital of the Eastern Han

1. Altar of the Earth
2. Imperial Garden
3. Northern Palace
4. Grand Granary
5. Armory
6. Yong'an Palace
7. Altars of the Gods of Grain and Soil
8. Stone Bridge
9. Gold Market
10. Southern Palace
11. Horse Market
12. Chief government offices
13. Southern Market
14. Numinous Terrace
15. Bright Hall
16. Biyong
17. Grand Academy
18. Pontoon Bridge
19. Altar of Heaven

A. Xia Gate
B. Gu Gate
C. Shangdong Gate
D. Zhongdong Gate
E. Mao Gate
F. Kaiyang Gate
G. Pingcheng Gate
H. Yiaoyuan Gate
I. Jin Gate
J. Guangyang Gate
K. Yong Gate
L. Shangxi Gate

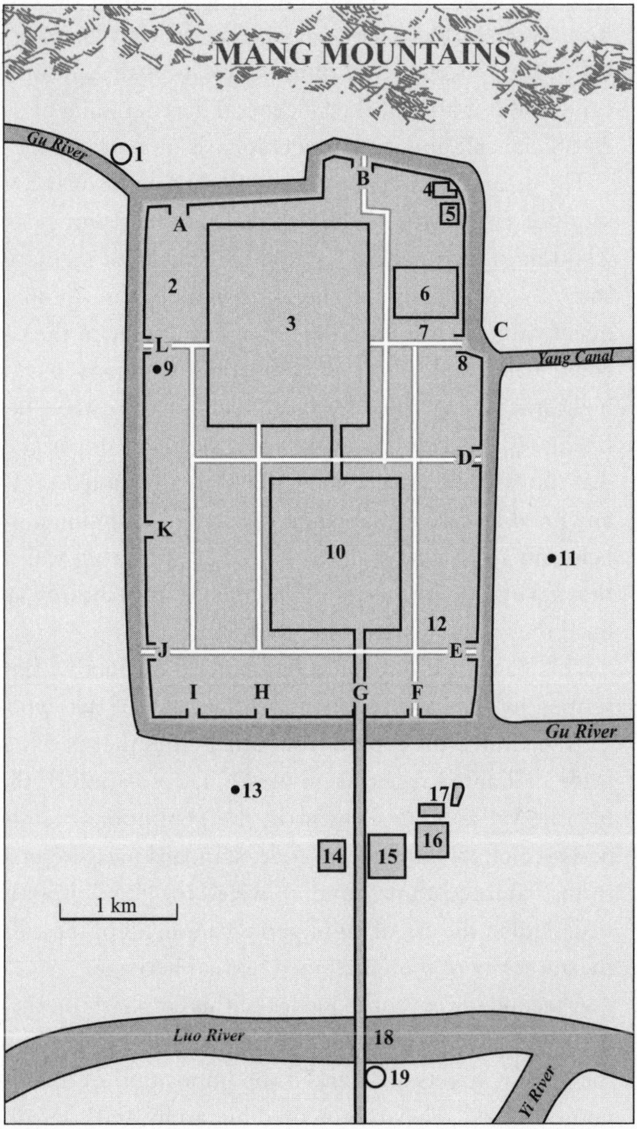

1 km

After Wang Zhongshu, *Han Civilization,* tr. K. C. Chang (New Haven: Yale University, 1982) and Hans Bielenstein, "Lo-yang in the Later Han Times," *BMFEA* 48 (1976), pp. 3–142.

MAP 9

This poetry dramatizes the transformation of the capital into a great ritual center in the last decades of the Western Han, as classicism's influence began to rise. The elimination of ancestral temples in the prefectures around 30 B.C., at the same time that the cult of Heaven first received Han imperial sponsorship, was dictated not simply by questions of economy, as is often claimed, but by the rising influence of the classicist belief that only descendants could make sacrifices to ancestors and that therefore these sacrifices by local officials to Han ancestors were illicit. This led to the concentration of imperial ancestral cult in the environs of the capital. But it also marked a general downgrading of ancestor worship as an official cult and increased emphasis on more public or cosmic cults.

The greatest cosmic cult that emerged under Wang Mang was the altar sacrifice to Heaven. While this is often presented as harking back to Zhou, it in fact marked a ritual realization of the nature of the imperial state. By being placed in the southern suburbs of Luoyang (or any subsequent capital), it asserted the ritual centrality of the capital. As the altar could be shifted wherever the capital was moved, it also detached the highest state cult from any fixed locality and established the unbreakable linkage of this cult to the Han and all future imperial dynasties. The cult was movable because it was offered to an omnipresent sky rather than to any fixed feature of the landscape such as a mountain or river. Far from being an archaic revival, the Han cult of Heaven was a ritual innovation that gave cultic form to the detachment from locality and custom that defined the imperial state and its capital.

This new style of capital had several distinctive features. First, as described in Han poetry, it was the creation of the dynasty or its founder. This separated the capital from other cities that developed naturally from trade or limited regional powers.[40] The creation of the capital city thus became yet another element in the institutional establishment of a dynasty—along with the legal code, standard measures and weights, graphic forms, court costumes, and above all the ritual program to which it was tied. And in the era of an imperial canon, all of these aspects were tied to the authority of the sanctioned textual heritage.

A second, direct consequence of this emphasis on the capital as a political creation is an insistence on its artificiality. The walls, the gates, and the grid of streets all marked the imposition of human design upon the natural world. They represented hierarchy and control over a potentially unruly populace. This artifice was also expressed in the realms of fashion and taste, for which the ruler and his court were to be the ultimate sources and exemplars.

A final characteristic of the new capital is the buried theme of transience. While no one could speak of the death of an emperor or the fall of a dynasty, everyone knew that such events were inevitable. The capital, as a creation of the dynasty, collapsed with the ruling house that created it.

Artificial and evanescent, created by decree out of nothing, it returned to nothing when those decrees lost their hold. Reliance on wood construction underscored this temporality. Whereas the stone ruins of ancient Rome and Greece survived as sources for study and meditation in the West, the ancient capitals of China were burned to the ground whenever a new dynasty took control. Thus Xianyang was destroyed by Xiang Yu; Chang'an was devastated by civil war at the end of the Western Han; and Luoyang was destroyed by Dong Zhuo at the end of the Eastern Han.[41]

The Eastern Han capital of Luoyang survived only in literature, as exemplified by Cao Zhi's celebrated poem of the third century. Cao Zhi had never visited the city, but he assumed the poetic voice of a former inhabitant to lament its demise:

> Climbing to the ridge of Beimang Mountain
> From afar I look down on Luoyang.
> Luoyang, how lonesome and still!
> Palaces and houses all burnt to ashes.
> Walls and fences all broken and gaping,
> Thorns and brambles rising to the sky.
> I do not see the old men;
> I only see the new youths.
> I turn aside, no straight road to walk.
> Waste fields, no longer ploughed.
> I have been away so long
> That I do not recognize the paths.
> Amidst the fields, how sad and desolate.
> A thousand miles without chimney smoke.
> Thinking of the house I lived in all those years.
> My emotions twisted, I cannot speak.[42]

5

RURAL SOCIETY

ALTHOUGH more than nine-tenths of the population worked on the land during the Qin and Han empires, little was written about peasants. Elites preferred the color and excitement of cities and the allure of power at court. Bound to the soil, rural life smacked of the brutish and vulgar. However, Shen Nong, the so-called Divine Farmer, figured in the Han pantheon. Credited with the invention of agriculture, he was the patron sage of a Warring States tradition that insisted all men should grow their own food. An early Han philosophical compendium *Master of Huainan* (*Huainanzi*) quotes him as a law-giver: "Therefore the law of Shen Nong says, 'If in the prime of life a man does not plow, someone in the world will go hungry. If in the prime of life a woman does not weave, someone in the world will be cold.' Therefore he himself plowed with his own hands, and his wife herself wove, to set an example to the world."[1]

Some writers adapted this doctrine to support the Qin regime, which was dependent on rural households' productivity and suspicious of merchants' wealth, and it was carried forward into the Han. Farming was even incorporated into a rarely performed ritual in which Han emperors initiated the agricultural season with three pushes of a plow in a special field. Major officials then took a turn, in order to show through simulated labor the court's interest in agriculture. The empress did her part by engaging in ceremonial weaving for the feast of the First Sericulturist.[2] Although neither ritual was performed regularly, the state did pursue a number of policies intended to maintain a rural system of small, free-holding peasants.

Iron, Irrigation, and Economies of Scale

Several major technological advances were introduced in the centuries preceding the Qin empire, including irrigation systems, fertilizers, and iron implements such as animal-drawn plows. Organic fertilizers in particular played an important role, increasing yield and "turning bad land into good," according to the third-century B.C. compendium *Springs and Autumns of Master Lü*. But the introduction of a technology does not lead automatically to its widespread use. Iron plowshares could plow deeper, especially when pulled by two oxen, and pottery bricks assisted the construction of wells for irrigation, but the Han period saw great regional variations in the adoption of new technology. The historical records tell of areas where the most advanced techniques were not yet in use and where officials attempted to develop and encourage new practices.[3]

For example, at the beginning of the Western Han, farmers broke up the soil with a rake and then used a spade to dig narrow furrows or trenches (about 8 inches wide) in the field, with wide ridges (about 65 inches) between them. They then sowed crops of millet, wheat, or barley on this ridge and later weeded the crop or thinned it out while standing in the furrow. Water was also run through the furrows to reach the roots of the crops. Except for the initial breaking up of the soil, oxen and plows were of little use in this system, and most farmers did not own them.

In Emperor Wu's reign, Zhao Guo advocated a new "alternating fields method" of agriculture. Wider furrows were plowed and seeds were planted in the furrows, not on the ridges. In the course of weeding, the earth fell from the ridges into the furrows, resulting in deeper root systems that were better protected from summer droughts. By midsummer the field would be level. The following year the positions of the furrows and ridges were reversed (hence the name "alternating"), thus supposedly preserving soil nutrients and reducing the need for fertilizer or fallowing (leaving fields uncultivated for a period of time). Wind no longer blew the seeds away from the tops of the ridges, and water was more easily conserved. The use of oxen allowed a larger area to be cultivated with the same amount of human labor.

This productive innovation—introduced on state-owned lands worked by convicts before being disseminated by officials in districts around the capital—entailed a larger capital investment, however. Only a farmer

Fig. 8   Metal-tipped plow drawn by four oxen guided by a single man. He is flanked by another man carrying water and a third using a hoe.

who could afford two oxen and a metal plow could use it (Fig. 8). While in theory a group of poor peasants might have collectively purchased oxen and a plow, questions of actual ownership and responsibility for feeding and maintenance would have made it largely unworkable in practice. Wealthy peasants or landlords thus enjoyed a major advantage in productivity over their poorer neighbors, and each year poor peasants using wooden tools and working by hand fell further behind and were much less likely to survive the inevitable bad years.

The introduction of brick linings meant that wells could be sunk much deeper and yield more water. Irrigation in the North China Plain, particularly the flood plain of the Yellow River, relied on water from such wells. This improvement in irrigation had the same effect on productivity as plowing. Wealthier farmers sank deeper wells and obtained more water, which allowed them to enjoy higher yields and endure lower rainfall. Small farmers, burdened with increasing taxes to pay for foreign wars and lacking capital to build wells, soon fell into debt. High interest rates guaranteed that once money had been borrowed it could seldom be repaid. Consequently, many peasants were forced to sell their land or forfeit it to a local magnate, who kept them on as sharecropping tenants. But because the new techniques allowed land to be worked with less human labor, demand for agricultural workers gradually declined and many peasants were eventually forced off the land altogether.

While the plow used in Zhao Guo's system required a pair of oxen and three men, Eastern Han farmers developed a nose ring that allowed a single man to control both the oxen and the plow. When farmers developed a combined plow and seeder, an individual could both plow and plant in one operation.[4] But once again, these advances were available only to wealthy families and their tenants. As the comparative advantage of the former grew, more farmers were forced off the land.

Only a few steps in the agricultural process were mechanized. Soil preparation, weeding, application of fertilizer, irrigation, and harvesting were still done by hand in the old-fashioned labor-intensive way. The economies of scale obtained through large capital investments were possible only for plowing and seeding.

In the Yangzi valley, agriculture and its associated social history were quite different. The wetter south was far less susceptible to droughts. The primary problem there was excess water, for much land was too marshy to be used until new drainage techniques were developed after the fall of the Eastern Han. Most farmers burned off weeds and vegetation, leaving a fertilizing ash, planted rice in the soil, and then flooded the field. After the plants had grown a bit, weeds were removed and more water was added. There was no transplantation of rice seedlings grown in special beds, as practiced in later China and Japan. Relying on burned material for fertilization required that the field be left fallow every other year so that vegetation could grow back. The result was considerably lower yields than in the north.

Nevertheless, the total acreage devoted to rice cultivation in the south gradually increased, as peasants fleeing flood or invasion in the north resettled in the central and lower Yangzi. Because most of these refugees were poor farmers and the technology of rice production did not allow for major capital investments, landlordism was less prevalent than in the north. Some powerful families pioneered a new irrigation method of damming one end of a small valley to create a lake from which water for the fields could be drawn by a sluice. However, since the chief problem was not irrigation but drainage, this innovation did not transform agriculture in the south. Great families established themselves there in significant numbers only after the massive immigration in the early fourth century A.D. The introduction of new drainage techniques shortly thereafter opened up vast amounts of land and encouraged widespread landlordism.

Almost everyone in Qin and Han China whose writings survive agreed that the government's economic priorities were to stimulate agriculture and protect the peasants. Like the physiocrats of early modern Europe, they believed that agriculture was the only true source of wealth. Manufacture and commerce, if not carefully controlled, threatened to lure peasants away from their farms or reduce them to tenants who no longer provided tax and service to the state. Although some thinkers noted the benefits of a division of labor, these benefits were invoked mainly to justify the activities of scholars and officials rather than those of merchants.[5]

In the Warring States and early empires, the taxes and service of peasants provided the material and labor required by the imperial house and their officials. Taxing merchants was much more difficult (as it is in all societies), because their wealth was easier to hide. A peasant's land was visible, easy to measure, impossible to move, and its expected annual yield could be readily calculated. A merchant could store his wealth in goods or cash and move it from one place to another. A tax on declared property temporarily allowed the state to extract taxes from merchants, but only at the cost of pushing them to invest in land and become land-lords. Landlordism, in turn, reduced the number of registered peasants and weakened the state's permanent base. Enforcing the tax on declared property also risked igniting a virtual war between the government and the most powerful families. After the reign of Emperor Wu, enforcement of this tax was abandoned.

Thus, an accurate perception of the fiscal foundations of the imperial state combined with a mistaken idea of the bases of productivity (the perception of agriculture as the sole source of wealth) encouraged policies aimed at discouraging trade, inhibiting landlordism, and protecting the small-scale peasants, but the policies aimed at the first goal worked against the second two.

Under the Qin and the first Han emperor, taxes and services took several forms. Every adult male was registered by the state between the ages of fifteen and seventeen. Anyone shorter than a specified height would be registered as "small" and given only light duties, or registered as handicapped and excused from service altogether.[6] After 186 B.C. men were registered between the ages of twenty and twenty-four, depending on the rank of their father in the twenty-rank hierarchy, and they were exempted from service at some point between the ages of fifty-eight and sixty-five, again depending on their rank. Women were not legally required to provide corvée labor, but in exceptional circumstances they were recruited for state work projects.

Registered males had to give two full years of military service, one in the capital or at the frontier and one as regular soldiers in their own commanderies. Selected individuals were trained as "skilled soldiers" (expert in using the crossbow), "cavalrymen," or sailors on a "towered warship." All of these received higher ranks and salaries than ordinary infantrymen. After leaving active service, each man performed one month's labor service every year. Only one adult per household was actually conscripted for service, and those above rank nine (that is, officials and aristocrats), those who paid a certain sum of money, and those who were granted exemptions by the emperor were all relieved of service. This corvée was not considered distinct from the two years of service in the army; both were part of a single system of obligation to the state.

While all free adult males provided military service, campaign armies were drawn from the three elite groups: skilled soldiers, cavalrymen, and sailors. Other soldiers served as porters, guards, and spear carriers, but the burden of combat was born by the specially trained elite troops. This division of armed forces into crack units responsible for significant combat and conscripts providing support and the weight of massed bodies was inherited from Warring States practice and continued under the Qin empire.

In addition to providing military forces at the frontier, the army was responsible for defense on the home front. Each year, in the eighth month, every commandery held an inspection in which troops, under the direction of the commandant (the local military official), demonstrated their skills to the grand administrator (head of the local government). This annual training session and inspection guaranteed a substantial pool of peasants who were sufficiently familiar with weapons to function as a local constabulary against large-scale banditry or low-level incursions.[7]

The only state officials with whom a peasant normally came into contact were those at the district level. A district generally included one walled town, and district populations varied from as much as 200,000 to less than 10,000. Even with a low population, it was impossible for officials to meet face-to-face with a significant percentage of the people in their charge, so they relied on locally eminent families to assist them.[8] Nevertheless, to mitigate peasant suffering and slow down, if only temporarily, the drift into debt and sharecropping, in times of scarcity some local officials issued grain, and in times of disaster they distributed cash provided by the central court.

Such activities figure prominently in several stone inscriptions dedicated to virtuous local officials, such as the one for the Eastern Han official Cao Quan: "He took pity on the people's needs, comforted the aged, and cared for widows and widowers. He used his own money to buy grain to give to the infirm and the blind . . . His generous rule spread faster than [messages on] the courier network. The common people, carrying their children on their backs, converged like clouds. He had the walls and houses put in order and laid out stalls in the market. The weather was seasonable and there was an abundant harvest. The farming men, weaving women, and artisans were respectful and grateful."[9]

Although such inscriptions were sponsored by relatives or subordinates of the deceased and hence were not reliable indicators of popular feeling, it is possible that some local officials had more success than their superiors at court in protecting the well-being and livelihood of the peasants in their charge.

Villages and Farms

The district was subdivided into townships (*xiang*), the townships into communes (*ting*, whose chief acted as the local police official), and the communes into villages or hamlets (*li*, which also meant "ward" in a city). All these units had their own, locally appointed, quasi-official leaders, the lowest being the village headman (*likui*).

Government documents, especially those recovered from Shuihudi, provide our most detailed glimpse of village life from the Qin period. Typical is this extract from the "Statute on Stables and Parks":

> In the fourth, seventh, tenth, and first months the oxen used in agriculture are measured. When the year ends, in the first month they are subject to a great evaluation. For good results the Overseer of Agriculture is granted a bottle of wine and a bundle of dried meat; the corral keepers are relieved one turn of duty and the chief of the cattlemen is granted thirty days [exemption from service]. For bad results the Overseer of Agriculture is berated, the corral keepers are fined two months [extra service]. If the oxen used in agricultural work have decreased in girth, the person in charge is bastinadoed with ten strokes for each inch. The oxen are also evaluated per village. For good results the Village Headman is granted ten days. For bad results he is bastinadoed thirty strokes.[10]

The degree of surveillance and control imposed on local governments and peasants is evident from the following: "How many rat holes in a granary warrant sentencing or berating? It is the practice of the court that for three or more rat holes the fine is [the purchase of] one shield and for two or fewer [the responsible official] is berated. Three mouse holes are equal to one rat hole."[11] Although the Han carried on many Qin practices, we cannot be certain how accurate these statutes are as a picture of Han village life.

We do know that Han peasants encountered officials when they registered for the census, when they paid taxes in coin or in kind (which had to be brought to designated collection points), when they fulfilled their service obligations, and when they borrowed seed grain for the season. Peasants could also encounter officials through their mutual responsibility units of five or ten people and through the misfortune of running afoul of the law. The single known example of a Han will indicates that officials witnessed the signing of wills involving the distribution of land.

A typical village consisted of about a hundred families, all of whom owned small amounts of land. Neighbors were usually not kin, unless a powerful lineage had developed in the town. Individual status was graded in a system of titles that established a state-imposed order among the villagers. The Han had twenty ranks; the eight lowest were bestowed on male commoners apart from slaves, while the higher ranks were reserved for officials. These titles had originated in the Qin, where they rewarded military service or the contribution of grain to the army. In the Han empire, they were awarded to *all* adult males on particular occasions, such as the establishment of an imperial heir-apparent, so that rank often correlated with age. Records of about two hundred such bestowals during the Han period have survived. In addition, certain localities, groups, or individuals earned ranks for meritorious service. Rewards for individual merit were generally reserved for officials or army officers. When the state needed cash, titles were also sold outright.

Rank entailed several privileges. First, those holding higher ranks were exempt from some statutory service. Ranks also could be surrendered to the state for stipulated benefits—for example, reduced punishments for certain crimes, or redemption of a parent from bond service. Finally, ranks determined status in the village, reflected in the seating and distribution of meat and wine at banquets sponsored by the state to mark happy occasions. A question in a Han mathematical text reads: "There are five men each holding different ranks from the first to the fifth. They caught five deer. How should they share the meat in proportion to their ranks?"[12] Through the fixing of rank and its associated privileges, the state sought to eliminate any "natural" local hierarchy and impose its own authority and standards.

Farms in Han China varied widely depending on time, place, and social class. Most common was the small free-holding farm worked by a family of four or five members. An account by the imperial counselor Chao Cuo (d. 154 B.C.) portrayed farmers living constantly on the brink of ruin:

> Now in a farming family of five members, at least two are required to render labor service. Their arable land is no more than one hundred *mu* [11.3 acres], the yield from which does not exceed one hundred *dan* [about 2,000 quarts]. Farmers plow in spring, weed in

summer, reap in autumn, and store in winter. They cut undergrowth and wood for fuel and render labor services to the government. They cannot avoid wind and dust in spring, sultry heat in summer, dampness and rain in autumn, and cold and ice in winter. Thus all year round they cannot afford to take even a day's rest . . .

Furthermore they have to welcome guests on their arrival and see them off on their departure. They have to mourn the dead and inquire after the sick. In addition they have to bring up infants. Although they work as hard as this they still have to bear calamities of flood and drought. Sometimes [extra] taxes are collected quite unexpectedly. If the orders are issued in the morning they must be prepared to pay by the evening. To meet this demand farmers have to sell their possessions at half price, and those who are destitute have to borrow money at two-hundred percent interest. Eventually they have to sell fields and dwellings, or sometimes even sell children and grandchildren into slavery in order to pay back the loan.[13]

Eastern Han statistics indicate that the average farm was even smaller than Chao Cuo estimated for his day, usually about seven to eight acres. By contrast, the life of a landlord in the late Eastern Han was quite comfortable: "May I live in a place with good fields and an ample house, with hills to the back and facing a stream, surrounded by waterways, encircled by bamboo and trees. Let a threshing ground and vegetable gardens be in front and an orchard behind. May there be sufficient carriages and boats to relieve the tedium of walking and wading and enough servants to ease my four limbs from hard work. For nourishing my relatives, there should be fine foods. My wife and children should not have to suffer any hard labor."[14] Of course neither of these images—one brutally analytic and the other lyrical—depicts an actual farm; the first describes a schematic type, the second an ambitious ideal.

If a newly landless peasant was lucky enough to remain a tenant sharecropper, he would have the use of land, tools, oxen, and a house in exchange for one-half to two-thirds of his crop. If, as often happened, he was removed from the local registers by his master and thereby escaped tax and corvée, his life probably improved. With his rent set as a fixed percentage of his harvest, he could escape misery in all but the worst years, while avoiding the need to convert crops into cash to pay poll tax to the state (Fig. 9). He also had access to oxen and tools that he could never have afforded on his own (Fig. 10).

Fig. 9 Share-cropping tenant farmer transferring grain rent from his cart to a receptacle. He is witnessed by a landlord with counting sticks seated in front of his raised granary.

Fig. 10 Peasants husking grain with a treadle-worked grain pounder in front of a raised granary.

Millet, barley, wheat, and soybeans were not the only products of Han farms, since women manufactured textiles there. This pairing of agriculture with cloth production, each activity linked to a gender, was articulated in the "law of Shen Nong" and had become a cliché long before the Han. Most fabrics were woven from hemp or nettle, and cloth was used as a medium of exchange. Qin statutes stipulate the shape and condition of a bolt of cloth that could circulate as currency, and the exchange rate for cash was also determined. When Emperor Wu established an "equal-supply system" intended to stabilize prices by buying up products when they were abundant and cheap and then releasing them onto the market in times of scarcity, he collected several million bolts of cloth, showing that great quantities of privately manufactured textiles were in circulation.[15]

Of all textiles, silk was the most precious. As early as the *Canon of Odes* (*Shi jing*, 1000–600 B.C.), poems describe the process of cloth production, from gathering mulberry leaves for the silkworms to weaving and dyeing. While large-scale production of cloth in workshops owned by the state or great families used some male labor, many workers in such enterprises were women. Han records refer to great families that employed as many as seven hundred women to weave silk cloth both for use by the mistress of the house and for sale. Wives in wealthy households, as depicted in Han poetry and tomb art, also produced cloth (Fig. 11). That weaving was women's work was even built into the pattern of the sky, where the Weaver Girl asterism (a small constellation) played a prominent role.[16]

Cultivated silk is made by reeling the cocoon's long filaments—which reach several hundred meters—in continuous lengths. This can be achieved only by keeping a rigorous watch over the life cycle of the worms and then reeling the silk before it is spoiled or broken by natural processes. At key moments the women of the household had to live among the silkworms. These worms supported a major sector of the Han economy and society. As the philosophical text *Master Xun* described it in a chapter of rhyming riddles:

> How naked its external form,
> Yet it continually transforms like a spirit.
> Its achievement covers the world,
> For it has created ornament for a myriad generations.

Fig. 11 Women spinning and weaving, with rolls of cloth hung above them on a rack.

Ritual ceremonies and musical performances are completed
   through it;
Noble and humble are distinguished with it.
Young and old rely on it;
For with it alone can one survive.[17]

Silk supplemented metal currency as a medium of exchange, and the government sometimes used silk to pay its armies. It was the primary item in Chinese payments to nomadic confederacies, whether tribute to the Xiongnu (30,000 bales in one year) or bounties to allied tribes. Silk was also the major product traded by the Chinese in frontier markets such as Ningcheng. This cloth was resold in Central Asia and then in India, gradually finding its way to Rome. Pliny the Elder complained that all Rome's gold and silver was flowing to the East to pay for the diaphanous fabrics in which Roman women displayed their charms. Roman gold, wool, amber, ivory, and glass were traded for silk in the Near East, and through the same chain of intermediaries along this ancient "Silk Road" these goods gradually worked their way back to Han China. Such trade in luxuries had little impact on the life of peasants.

The Great Families

As they purchased peasant land, the great families of landlords and merchants, two groups that merged over the course of the Han, did not build up huge estates to be worked by hired labor. The largest family estates described in Han records are less than a tenth the size of a major Roman estate or that of a major medieval monastery. Instead of expanding unitary estates, the great families divided and subdivided their land among their sons in the practice of partible inheritance. These smaller farms were worked either by kin or tenant sharecroppers. The ambition of the great families was not simply to amass land and wealth, but rather to use this land and wealth to build up extensive networks of kin, clients, and neighbors whose loyalties they could command.

The typical household in Han China, as noted by Chao Cuo, consisted of a nuclear family of four to six people. During the last years of aged parents' lives this could turn into a household of up to eight. Some scholars have argued that wealthy families, with their greater resources, kept more generations together in a single compound, as happened in later imperial China. However, the limited surviving evidence shows that families of three generations or more were extremely rare, and nothing indicates that wealthy families were committed to larger households where brothers lived together and cared for parents. Quite the contrary: it was poorer families that could not survive on their small plots if they divided the family farm between brothers. Division of property among kinsmen was characteristic of wealthier families who could afford such distribution. To the extent that the households of great families were larger, it was through the inclusion of retainers or servants.[18]

Most locally powerful lineages divided themselves into many—in some cases hundreds—of nuclear households. They then dominated their districts, commanderies, or regions through alliances of these households and marriage ties with other great surnames. A family that was not included in these networks or cliques was described as a "lone family," "lone gate," "orphan gate," "lone and cold," "lone and obscure," "orphaned and obscure," or "orphaned and provincial." These terms of isolation were applied even to wealthy families that lacked high status or influence.

The Discourse on Salt and Iron (Yan tie lun) argues that to be cut off from human relations is the highest form of punishment: "In the *Spring-and-Autumn Annals* criminals have no names, and when it refers to them it just says, 'Bandits.' By this means it humbles criminals and cuts them off from human relations. Therefore a ruler will not take them as minister, a scholar will not take them as a friend, and they will not be allowed in the wards and villages."[19] Defining lower status and even criminality through isolation suggests that status in imperial China was marked by the extent of a family's network.

This emphasis on social ties underlies the literary sources' obsession with forming links and establishing contacts. This is marked by the recurrence of such terms as "to connect (*jie*)," "to contact (*jiao*)," or "to communicate (*tong*)," which often appear as compounds and have a large range of meanings. They can indicate a formal relation of friendship entered into by people through an explicit compact. Thus, in the biography of a certain Wang Dan, two individuals ask to enter into a relation with him (*jie jiao*), but both are rejected because he disapproves of them. Almost any deliberate association to work toward a common purpose, such as forming an army in times of civil war or conspiring to rebel, was also identified by these terms, as were the relations between patron and retainer, the associations of gangsters (*xia*), and bands of violent youths.[20]

So fundamental were personal links and social networks that an Eastern Han scholar named Zhu Mu wrote an essay "Cutting Connections" in which he argued that in antiquity men had not formed private networks but assembled only in the court or at public gatherings dictated by regulations. In contrast, men now devoted themselves to forming connections for private benefit. He also wrote a letter to Liu Bosheng with a poem on this theme. In a corrupt age, Zhu Mu argued, one should withdraw from the world of social networks and cultivate oneself in isolation. In reply, the famous writer Cai Yong wrote an essay "Correcting Connections," arguing that the profusion of corrupt cliques was due to the decline of government, and that associations based on moral worth, rather than on wealth or power, were acceptable. While he agreed with Zhu Mu's rejection of cliques based on private interest and the pursuit of power, he maintained that it was proper for like-minded scholars to join in study and the cultivation of virtue, on the model of Confucius and his disciples.[21]

The Hidden Tally of Duke Tai, a philosophical text of which only a small fragment survives, went beyond this discourse on proper and improper connections. It listed ten faults that would destroy a state, including such items as strong patrilines that bullied the peasants and private wealth that surpassed the state's. One item is "reputations reaching one hundred *li*, or social connections reaching one thousand *li*." This emphasizes the danger of networks that cover great distances and thus bring whole regions under the control of private alliances. It views networks not as a moral problem but a political one, where the key distinction is the geographic range of influence. The danger of networks is an extension of the dangers of powerful lineages and excessive private wealth.

Lineages extended their contacts and geographic range in a number of ways. Marriage as a means of elevating a family's status is found in virtually all civilizations, and it had a classic precedent in the Han. The emperor Gaozu's father-in-law gave him his daughter in marriage only because his physiognomy revealed a glorious future that would exalt his relatives. In Han sources, intermarriage between leading lineages is a conventional procedure through which they enhance their power. In the rebellions against Wang Mang, rebel forces were sometimes assembled by combining one man's lineage with his relatives by marriage.

Han lineages attempted to marry a daughter to someone whose family background or talent and reputation made him a valuable resource as a kinsman. One such marriage is explicitly described as a means of "linking support and establishing a party/clique." When a proposed son-in-law rejected the tactical marriage being arranged by his family, he demonstrated his lofty character, it was said. But even in such parables, the regular practice of arranging marriages with outstanding individuals or lineages in order to strengthen the patriline was taken for granted.[22]

Scholars of late imperial and contemporary China have noted that the practice of dividing households generally accompanies a focus on marriage ties. Dividing households when sons marry emphasizes the conjugal tie, strengthens links with the wife's relatives, and elevates the status of the wife, who is protected by distance from her mother-in-law. Such quarrels between mothers-in-law and daughters-in-law were certainly an issue in Han China, as shown in poetry and by the fact that a book of medical and magical "recipes" discovered at Mawangdui contains a spell to prevent the problem.

That Han patrilines were comparatively weak is indicated by the absence of such later features as an annual festival for grave offerings, collective cemeteries for the lineage, and collective property. Together with the practices that emphasized marriage ties, this would have furthered Han families' reliance on extensive social networks.[23]

A classic example of a great family and the methods by which it secured power in rural society is the Fan clan of Nantang. They were described as an eminent family in their home villages who "for generations were skilled at farming and at accumulating wealth." With labor provided by dependent households, they built up an estate of about 1,200 hectares, with fishponds and some animal husbandry—a relatively small estate by European standards. The total number of people in the household was probably no more than a couple dozen. In terms of number of people and amount of land it could command, this clan was more powerful than its neighbors but of little consequence above the local level. However, with its wealth the Fan clan "relieved and financially supported lineage and kin, and bestowed charity on the villages where they lived."

When the rebellion against Wang Mang broke out, Fan Hong's wife was seized as a hostage. But the state did not dare to execute her because the Fan clan's conspicuous charity had won devoted local support. After her release, the Fan clan led families of their patriline and kin to build a fort in which more than one thousand families took shelter and were preserved from the Red Eyebrows (the peasant rebels whose uprising triggered the wars that overthrew Wang Mang).[24]

What made the Fan clan important actors in their region and able to act at the imperial level was not their own relatively small estate or their immediate family members and servants. It was their ties of obligation and loyalty with large numbers of households. This network had begun with those who shared their surname but eventually was extended to their neighbors in general. This practice of establishing networks with households sharing first common ancestry and then local residence allowed leading families to call upon the services of thousands of people and thus to dominate their more modest neighbors.

It is useful to situate this practice within a broader historical context. The Warring States and early empires had been created through establishing artificial ties between individuals. Appearing first in the recruitment of free-floating agents created by the destruction of states and clans, such personal ties—consecrated by oaths or appointments and based on exchanging devotion for recognition—underlay the states' bureaucracies, the leagues of gangsters, and the intellectual traditions.[25] Just as the new forms of polity, organized criminality, and intellectual association had all achieved power through establishing and maintaining networks of personal relations, so certain families or lineages became important political actors by using their material or intellectual capital to place others in their debt and then command their services.

However, unlike the ties of government, gangsters, and scholars, the networks of the great families were not created entirely from bonds between individuals. They emerged from a graded series of links that began with the household proper, were extended to other households that shared a common ancestor, then to retainers (ke), then to neighbors from the same or nearby villages, and finally to people from across the region or distant families linked by study or political service.

Owing to this progressive extension of networks, the range of collective legal responsibility for crimes in the Eastern Han went beyond the conventional three generations that defined the largest households. Thus, in the Great Proscription in the 160s A.D. the ban on office-holding was extended to kin who shared a common ancestor five generations earlier, and even to those linked only by patron-client ties. Other sensitive crimes also entailed collective punishments well beyond the range of the household, extending into the broader kin and social networks that defined political power. The scale of such collective action and ensuing punishments was so large that in politically important cases more than 10,000 people might be held responsible and executed.[26]

Such widening social networks also figured in other circumstances. In the list provided by the Eastern Han landlord Cui Shi (d. ca. 170 A.D.) in his *Monthly Ordinances for the Four Classes of People* (*Si min yue ling*), he names those to whom people pay greetings at the New Year in the form of a widening circle. The Fan clan made a list of its charity recipients, which moved from distant kin of the same surname to neighbors. When the Yin lineage allied with Liu Bosheng to rebel against Wang Mang, they led a force of two thousand men composed of "sons and younger brothers, other lineages of the patriline, and retainers." When Li Tong allied with Liu Bosheng and Liu Xiu to rebel, Wang Mang executed all his relations in the capital and Nanyang. The latter totaled sixty-four people, divided into "brothers and households of the patriline" whose corpses were burned in the marketplace. The presence of kin in Chang'an and Nanyang shows that the politically relevant group for a major magnate or lineage went far beyond their own household and estate.[27]

This extension of leading households' authority through networks based on gifts or services meant that a major lineage's power could cover districts, commanderies, and whole regions. Thus, the target of the Han state's suspicion of regions was actually the powerful lineages who resided there, or more precisely the leagues of households and villages formed around them. The earliest were the old ruling houses that had formed the Warring States elite. Such families had served as figureheads for many of the rebellions against Qin and had been forcibly resettled in the capital. They were eliminated during the reign of Emperor Wu in the second century B.C. For Han social history, the important lineages were those such as Fan and Yin who gained wealth through office-holding, trade, and the accumulation of land and used this wealth to establish their prestige and influence.[28]

By the first century of Han rule, several single surname groups had divided themselves into three hundred or more residential households who traced their heritage back to a common ancestor. This had almost certainly come about through generation after generation of property division between brothers, who remained in the same area, living close together and acting as a political unit in opposing the central government. When Emperor Wu moved these powerful families to the capital region, he forbade their living near one another precisely to avoid this kind of dangerous alliance. By the end of the Han, a patriline could consist of more than a thousand families, as demonstrated by Han Rong, who gathered this many members of his patriline and more distant kin in a fortified compound.[29]

Both major Han histories, the *Shi ji* and the *Book of the Han* (*Han *shu*), refer to wealthy people by their branch surnames rather than their households. Thus, in the section following its account of local customs, the *Shi ji* cites the Zhuo, the Shi, the Kong, the Bing, the Ren, the Tian, the Li, and the Du. The Tian consisted of multiple families, and the Du existed in several geographically distinct branches. The great lineages that were moved to the capital region were also often identified by their branch surnames rather than their households. The same term is applied to the locally powerful lineages attacked by the "cruel clerks" of Emperors Jing and Wu, the leading lineages involved in the underworld, those who dominated commanderies, and imperial affines (relatives by marriage).[30]

Ban Gu, the author of the *Book of the Han*, concludes his geographical monograph with a section echoing Sima Qian's account of the regions and their customs or character, but he links these more closely to patrilines. In Henei, for example, "the customs encourage an inflexible strength, so there are many powerful families who encroach and seize land. They treat kindness and ritual as unimportant, and are fond of dividing property while the father is still living." The people of Yingchuan by custom are extravagant and violent. Because they hide their wealth from the government they are difficult to administer. Moreover, due to their greed they constantly engage in lawsuits and divide property while the father is still living. Powerful families in Taiyuan and Shangdang battle one another through cunning and force. They frequently resort to vengeance and vendetta against the family members and more distant kin of their enemies. The people of Qi are extravagant and form political cliques. In many regions, according to Ban Gu, rich families are prone to excess and waste in their wedding ceremonies and funerals.[31]

The shift in the two centuries between the *Shi ji* and the *Book of the Han* in their accounts of the dangers of regionalism is highly significant. In the former, the problems posed by the regions are linked to the character of the people and treated as an extension of their history and terrain. In the latter, however, accounts of the failings of local people and the difficulty of governing them often cite the problems created by powerful families and wealthy merchants. By the middle of the Eastern Han, in other words, the problem of regionalism had become inseparable from the existence of major lineages that used either wealth or force of arms to establish extensive leagues at the village, district, commandery, or even regional level that challenged government authority.[32]

Villages typically consisted of a hundred or more households, and in those dominated by a powerful lineage a significant percentage of those households might share a surname. Any family not belonging to that patriline would almost certainly become an ally or client. Thus the entire village was in effect an extension of the great family's household. This was recognized by the state, which appointed locally powerful people as "fathers and elders" to serve as intermediaries between the state and the village. Similarly, the elder women of the village were referred to as the "village mothers" or the "various mothers."[33]

That the patriline and village could overlap had other political implications, often dire. The Eastern Han scholar Wang Chong explained the First Emperor's supposed execution of the entire village of his attempted assassin, Jing Ke, by pointing out this overlap: "In the twentieth year of the King of Qin, the state of Yan had sent Jing Ke to assassinate the king. The King of Qin discovered it, and the body of Jing Ke was dismembered in order to teach the people a lesson. [Texts] say nothing about executing his village. Perhaps they executed Ke's patriline. An entire patriline would be extremely numerous and would live in the same village. If one killed the entire patriline, then virtually the entire village would be eliminated."[34]

When the retiring official Shu Guang received a parting gift of gold from the emperor, the list of those invited to share in the feasts and banquets paid for by the gift included his "patriline, old acquaintances, and retainers." Shu Guang's immediate family worried that he was spending all the household's money, so they asked "brothers and village elders" whom he trusted to persuade him to use the money to purchase land to secure the family's future. Shu Guang replied:

How could I be so old and muddleheaded as to not think of my descendants? I have my old fields and shacks, and if my descendants will work diligently in them they are sufficient to provide food and clothing as good as those of ordinary people. Now if I should further increase them in order to have a surplus, I would just cause my descendants to be lazy. For the worthy man, having much wealth diminishes his ambition. For the stupid man, having much wealth augments his faults. Moreover, wealth is what is hated and resented by the masses. Since I am unable to morally transform my descendants, I do not desire to augment their faults and produce resentment against them. Moreover, the money that I am spending is that which was granted by the sage ruler to nourish his old servant.

Therefore I am happy to enjoy what he has given me together with my fellow villagers and members of my patriline, and thus live out my remaining days.[35]

Those who participated in the feasts were villagers and members of the patriline, and Shu Guang felt justified in dispersing his wealth for the benefit of these people rather than reserving it for his immediate family. For powerful and ambitious lineages, the patriline and the village were not opposed concepts; rather, the extended kin group at its broadest level determined the structure of village society.

Like the account of the Fan lineage, this passage also shows the importance of conspicuous generosity in the conduct of eminent families. This was already noted by Sima Qian, who asserted that charity was the key to enduring local power. Shu Guang further justified the regular dispersal of wealth throughout the village by arguing that a "moral economy" existed in the peasant village. Village society was constituted in reciprocal obligations created by the regular exchange of gifts or services. Richer members were under moral pressure to distribute their wealth among their poorer neighbors, in exchange for which they received status and certain customary forms of service.[36] This pattern of reducing inequalities, as well as establishing moral and emotional links, was still visible in late imperial and republican China, where wealthier families sponsored feasts, operas, and religious festivals that secured their own status and gained the support of their neighbors.

As Shu Guang argued, wealth was of value only when circulated. If hoarded, it poisoned both the household and village, but when dispersed it turned potential enemies into allies and dependents. In the process of sharing this gift from the emperor, Shu Guang was both imitating the ruler as a giver of gifts and extending the emperor's work to the village level. The emperor himself made a point of granting charity to the poor, the orphaned, and the widowed, in addition to distributing gifts to his officials. The emphasis on charity radiating outward figures in the late Eastern Han landlord Cui Shi's *Monthly Ordinances* and in Han tomb art of landlords, suggesting its importance to their idealized self-image (Fig. 12). Accounts of charity at the local level also appear in stone inscriptions. A certain Wu Zhongshan is described as giving loans to those in need, never demanding repayment, and secretly giving leftovers from his banquets to orphans. Similar charitable actions are credited to a general who distributed among his men all the gifts he received from the emperor.

Fig. 12   Seated landlord with servant who pours grain into the receptacle of a kneeling, aged peasant holding a dove staff.

The chapter in the *Book of the Later Han* (*Hou Han shu*) on "unique conduct," which tells of men who refused office and cultivated virtue in retirement, contains several stories of exemplary generosity. Some of these deal with wealthy families who routinely aided neighbors or rescued hundreds from death in times of famine or civil war. Others focus on kindnesses to individuals. Still other passages in the dynastic histories note how individuals or lineages expended all their wealth rescuing those in need. As a result, the generous families were left with no surplus, while "the orphaned and widowed, both within the patriline and from the outside, took refuge with them."[37]

The importance of charity and gift-giving became legendary in tales of how the wealth and power of certain clans derived from the earlier generosity of their members. This generosity took the form of either "secret kindness" to strangers who turned out to be spirits, or devotion to sacrifices. When a certain He Bigan sheltered more than eighty white-haired old men from a heavy rain, they gave him nine hundred and ninety counting rods, announcing that He's descendants who attained office would be as numerous as the rods. In another story a member of the Zhang clan sheltered a bird at his breast. It turned into a belt buckle, and as long as the lineage kept this buckle its wealth flourished. The Yin clan made annual sacrifices to Guan Zhong of Qi state. One New Year's morning the Stove God appeared to them, paid his greetings, and received the sacrifice of a yellow sheep. From that time on they grew fabulously wealthy, and the sacrifice of a yellow sheep to the Stove God at the New Year became a family tradition. Several of these stories became the topic of popular sayings in the capital region. These tales in which charity magically led to great wealth present in the form of parables or folk tales the social reality of lineages that employed public generosity to secure prestige and power.

The generosity of great families also found more questionable channels to power and influence. In addition to transferring wealth to poorer neighbors, lineages secured office by giving bribes or gifts to those in power. These were considered a form of generosity (directed upward) that established networks in order to strengthen the lineage. A prominent local scholar defended the practice of villagers making gifts to a worthy local official, as long as he did not demand them. High officials conspicuously showered gifts on guests and potential clients in order to curry favor with supporters and strengthen their lineage. A merchant family used gifts to leading nobles to establish links to people with political power, and then wielded the fear inspired by these connections to guarantee repayment of loans.

Ma Rong, a famous scholar, was reputed to be greedy and of low moral character, and in some stories both he and his son awarded offices for cash payments. A low official in the late Han used all his wealth to offer gifts to the servants of an official who dominated the court and thereby "established links of intimacy and generosity with them." On the basis of the debt established by his generosity, he passed by crowds of petitioners and went directly into the presence of the official, from whom he received a post.[38] This story reveals the thin line between charity and bribes. It suggests that as long as the gifts were given over a period of time, with reciprocation delayed for a decent interval, they were not bribes. And the fact that the recipients were themselves of humble status, being merely servants of the official, helps make the case for this kind of "charity."

Aid to kin and villagers moved within the face-to-face world of the local community, and at most would expand to cover a district or commandery. Ties to officials and retainers, on the other hand, often crossed great distances. The clearest evidence of this geographic range comes from stone inscriptions, where the obligations of clients to patrons often included contributing to the erection of a memorial stele. The stele for

Liu Kuan lists the names of over three hundred clients from across north-central China, while that for Kong Zhou was erected by forty-three clients from ten different commanderies.[39]

Many of the clients listed on the inscriptions of leading political figures are described as students. Although this does not always indicate educational links, literary sources describe people who shun political office, devote themselves to teaching, and in so doing establish networks of hundreds or thousands of reverential students. In the case of Fan Zhen, "disciples came from great distances," and some of these students joined together to erect a laudatory stone inscription even before his death.

Other passages elaborate on the vast range of territory covered by scholars in search of the best teachers, and the social ties created in the process. Because his own region in Shandong had no important scholars, the famous scholar Zheng Xuan went to Guanzhong to study with Ma Rong, who already had more than four hundred disciples. Zheng Xuan spent more than a decade studying in different parts of the empire before returning home and likewise gathering hundreds of disciples. So important were the ties between teacher and acolyte that a teacher might give his daughter in marriage to a prize disciple in order to cement the link.[40] Education as well as politics thus provided a means by which lineages extended their influence beyond their home region.

A final form of association used by the great families was local cults. The right to sacrifice to specified deities had been a hallmark of power and status in China at least since the Shang dynasty in the second millennium B.C. and continued to be so through the Han and later imperial China. The "Royal Institutions" chapter of the *Records of Ritual* (*Li ji*) specified: "The Son of Heaven sacrifices to Heaven and Earth. The feudal lords sacrifice to the altars of soil and grain. The hereditary officials make the household sacrifices. The Son of Heaven sacrifices to the world's famous peaks and great rivers. For the five sacred peaks he does it like the Three Lords, and for the four great rivers like the feudal lords. The feudal lords sacrifice to the famous mountains and great rivers within their own territories."[41] The great families used this logic to establish control of cults to mountains, immortals, or other local eminences whose worship was not sanctioned by the state, or only sanctioned after the fact.

The division of property among siblings, arranging of ties through marriage, dispersal of money in banquets and charity, travels of scholars, and leadership in local cults all multiplied the number of households attached to a great family and maximized the number of people whose services the family could command. To maximize wealth and power, these lineages—like the state—aimed to accumulate people rather than land or cash. Since agricultural practices of the period relied on intensive manual labor in an almost horticultural style of farming, with only plowing and seeding producing economies of scale, there was little advantage to converting small holdings into unitary large estates. Great families left tenants to work their own plots, and used the income collected from sharecroppers to extend their networks.

Even when the power of the central state collapsed with the fall of the Eastern Han, locally powerful families did not shift toward a pattern of primogeniture in an effort to preserve their estates intact. Instead, they continued to divide their property among sons and to seek marriage alliances in order to increase the number of their followers and the geographic range of their influence.

6

THE OUTER WORLD

THE GEOGRAPHIC limits of the Qin empire roughly defined the enduring borders of the Chinese people and their culture. Although the empire was sometimes extended into the northern steppes, Central Asia, southern Manchuria, Korea, and continental southeast Asia, these expansions were generally brief. The peoples of these regions remained beyond Chinese control until the final, non-Chinese Qing dynasty.

The people surrounding China can be divided into two groups. To the north and west lay nomadic societies that lived on grasslands and formed states radically different from the Chinese model. Except for the oasis city-states of Central Asia, these regions would remain outside the Chinese cultural sphere. By contrast, the watery regions of the south and southeast, as well as the highland plateaus of the southwest, were progressively settled by Chinese emigrants. There, and in the northeast, sedentary agrarian states would gradually adopt Chinese forms of writing and state organization, but these developments had scarcely begun during the early imperial dynasties.[1]

The Qin-Han epoch was marked by interlinked but opposing developments: the emergence of the notion of a permanent frontier zone separating the sedentary agrarian Chinese from their nomadic northern neighbors, and the ideal of an all-encompassing world empire in which foreign peoples would come to the imperial court to offer tribute and submission. Chinese emperors in part measured their power by their ability to draw these alien peoples into China. Thus, surrounding peoples helped to shape the policies of the Chinese state as well as many features of Chinese civilization. The very definition of a common "Chinese" culture was derived through a set of systematic oppositions with these alien groups, particularly the northern nomads.

Nomadism and the Xiongnu

The history of the rise of nomadism as a mode of life relies entirely on archaeological evidence, and many points of interpretation remain open to dispute. Nevertheless, it is clear that full-blown transhumant nomadism—reliance on flocks that were moved according to a seasonal cycle to obtain sufficient grass and water—developed as the socioeconomic basis of the northern peoples during the first millennium B.C. (roughly corresponding to the Eastern Zhou dynasty, 770–221 B.C.). In the previous millennium, Central Asians had combined agriculture with pastoralism, growing crops around oases or rivers and raising herds in adjacent grasslands. Perhaps because of overpopulation or increasing aridity, some groups gave up agriculture and devoted themselves to nomadic pastoralism, along with hunting and trade. Other groups migrated to river valleys and adopted plow-based agriculture.[2]

Many non-Chinese bronzes, particularly knives and other weapons, discovered in Shang tombs suggest that in an amorphous area known as the "northern zone," between the grasslands and the Yellow River valley, exchanges flourished between the Shang and a bronze-age culture to the north. The chariot was introduced into China from Central Asia through this so-called "northern zone" in the late Shang period, around 1200 B.C.[3] Evidence of the rise of full-blown nomadism in the north, in the ninth through the seventh centuries, includes the greater number of horse fittings and weapons among burial goods, along with other indications of an economy increasingly dominated by animal husbandry.

In the middle of the fifth century B.C. northward expansion by Chinese states brought them into increasing contact with the now nomadic peoples, whom they named the Hu. The state of Zhao adopted cavalry forces, wearing clothing the nomads had adapted for riding. As cavalry became a major component of Chinese armies, trade in horses dominated economic activity in the frontier markets.[4] Finds from the sixth through the fourth centuries B.C. show the earliest appearance in northern tombs of the "Scythian triad" assemblage, named for the nomads described in Herodotus: weapons, horse gear, and objects decorated in the animal style. This era is also marked by the increasing prominence of iron metallurgy rather than bronze.

China's relations with the outside world in the late Warring States were defined by wall building along the frontiers. Eager to secure grasslands to rear horses for their armies, the northern Chinese states seized territory previously used by the nomads, and the walls served to secure this territory. Walls in this period were built from tamped earth and stone, generally following the lines of ridges and hills. They in no way resembled the brick-built Ming wall so familiar to us, and they did not mark an ecological divide between the steppe and the sown, as some have claimed.

The use of walls against nomads was only one version of a wider cultural practice. The Warring States built walls and watchtowers not only in the north but along many of their borders with other Chinese states.[5] Wall building in the north reached its climax with Qin's construction of a single system of walls and watchtowers to mark its expansion into the steppe. In the immediate wake of this development, and to some degree in response to it, the nomadic peoples were united into a single great empire under the Xiongnu tribe. Two models have been suggested for this rise of a nomadic empire only two decades after the unification of China.

One model argues that the nomadic state's rise depended on China. Living off the products of their flocks and handicrafts, the nomadic tribes either needed additional goods from the sedentary peoples to their south in order to survive, or desired them to improve their lives. Skilled in archery and horsemanship, nomads formed a natural army in which every adult male could perform military duties. Political power derived primarily from success in battle against other tribes and in raids on the sedentary Chinese, with the successful war chief securing the loyalty of his followers by distributing booty. Because their elite derived power from distributing goods taken from the Chinese, nomadic polities evolved in close association with the Chinese state. The increasing power of Chinese states required that the nomads field larger armies themselves, and the prosperity of a united China offered wealth that large nomadic empires could extract in the form of payments from the Chinese ruler. This redistribution of wealth northward generated the political power of the nomadic rulers.[6]

Other scholars argue that no clear division between nomads and sedentary peoples at the frontier existed, that nomadic peoples such as the Xiongnu had agriculturists living in their midst, and that the oasis city-states of Central Asia provided whatever goods the nomads and their agriculturist dependents lacked. Thus the nomadic states did not rely on the great sedentary kingdoms of Persia in the west or China to the east for their existence. Goods were extracted from China through trading, raiding, and tribute, to be sure, but these products were not essential for the people's survival or the rulers' privileged position.[7]

According to this model, the small economic surplus of nomadic societies—small of necessity, because they carried it with them—made virtually impossible the rise of a ruling class significantly removed from their people. Violence in such societies consisted not of full-blown warfare but of small-scale raids or vendettas to avenge a wrong, enlarge a herd, or steal a wife. A major crisis, on the other hand, produced by bad weather, internal rebellions against previously dominant tribes, or expansion by sedentary peoples, could shatter the society's already marginal balance. Forced to migrate into new areas or menaced by armed attackers, tribes survived only by organizing large-scale military organizations. These were formed by charismatic warrior chiefs who gathered warriors as a personal bodyguard and then recruited more warriors with the prestige and booty gained through early successes. This process of gradual militarization culminated in the establishment of a centralized state under a supra-tribal leader who ruled as "khan" through the "protection of Heaven" that his victories demonstrated. This new supreme chief transformed tribal aristocracies into a state aristocracy by distributing booty to secure the loyalty of his followers.

The emergence of the Xiongnu state follows this pattern. When the Qin occupied all the territory south of the great bend of the Yellow River, driving away the Xiongnu and other inhabitants, this created an economic crisis. According to the *Shi ji*, Modun, the founder of the Xiongnu empire, gathered and trained a bodyguard that obeyed him to the death, a force with which he killed his own father and seized the title of *chanyu*, "supreme leader."[8] This was followed by a series of victories from Manchuria to Central Asia, with tribe after tribe submitting to the rising Xiongnu power. The campaign culminated in the emergence of a pyramidal structure of lesser hereditary kings or aristocrats under the supreme leader.

This pyramidal structure is described in the *Shi ji*: "There are Left and Right Wise Kings, Left and Right *Luli* Kings, Left and Right Generals, Left and Right Commandants, Left and Right Household Administrators, and Left and Right *Gudu* Marquises. The Xiongnu word for 'wise' is '*tuqi*,' so they often refer to the Heir Apparent as the *Tuqi* King of the Left. From the Left and Right Wise Kings, down to the Household Administrators, the most important men command ten thousand horsemen, the least important a few thousand. As a group they consist of twenty-four great officers, and each of them is called 'Ten Thousand Horsemen.'"[9] The Xiongnu "kings" were chiefs who held part of the empire as appanages—land from the *chanyu* over which they exercised semi-independent rule. Lesser chiefs were members of the high council. The basic features of this system—appanages, pairing of high posts as left and right (east and west), decimal military structure, and a few top-ranking men in the council—recur in later Central Asian states.

These two models of the Xiongnu state—economic dependence on the Chinese empire, military response to the Chinese empire—are not mutually exclusive. The second describes how a centralized state emerged around the *chanyu*, while the first emphasizes the financial bases of his power. Even advocates of the second model agree that the Xiongnu state used revenues extracted from the states around them to pay for its courts and armies. However, exponents of the first model emphasize China as the exclusive or predominant source of the nomads' income, while exponents of the second note that the Xiongnu extracted tribute from vanquished nomadic states as well as from city-states in the Tarim Basin.[10] Given China's great wealth, there is little doubt that it became the greatest source of wealth for Xiongnu rulers, and the *chanyu*'s ability to extract income from the Chinese empire set him apart from his rival chieftains. Nevertheless, the argument that the Xiongnu state depended on income from China for survival is certainly an overstatement.

Modun's new empire reversed the balance of power between the Chinese and their nomadic neighbors. In preceding centuries, Chinese states had expanded northward at the expense of nomadic peoples. But in 200 B.C., the Han founder suffered a disastrous defeat at the hands of the Xiongnu. Consequently, the Han adopted a policy of "peace and kinship" (*he qin*) in which gold, silk, and grain were annually sent to the *chanyu*, along with the periodic gift of Han princesses for his harem. In exchange, the Xiongnu agreed not to attack China. While this was essentially a form of peacemaking through tribute, some Chinese suggested that in the long-run this policy would weaken the Xiongnu. Tribesmen would be corrupted by their taste for Chinese luxuries, and thus dependent upon China. And when sons of Han princesses became rulers in the Xiongnu state, their chiefs would become junior kin of the Han court. A key assumption of this argument was that the Xiongnu differed from the Chinese only in culture, not in kind, and that the adoption of Chinese traditions would ultimately lead to their assimilation into the empire.[11]

In addition to the payment of tribute and gift of women, the *he qin* system entailed the recognition of diplomatic equality between China and the Xiongnu. The Xiongnu chief was given the right to refer to his family name in addressing the Chinese emperor, unlike the Chinese themselves, who, being slaves of the emperor, used only their personal names. In addition, the title *chanyu* was recognized as equal to the Chinese *huangdi*, and the two rulers were described as "brothers." In 162 B.C. the Chinese Emperor Wen wrote: "I and the *chanyu* are the parents of the people. Problems that emerged in the past from the misdeeds of our subordinates should not ruin our brotherly happiness. I have heard that Heaven does not cover just one side, and Earth is not partial to anyone. I and the *chanyu* should cast aside the trivial problems of the past and together follow the great Way."[12] Not only were the two rulers equals in fictive kinship, but the reference to Heaven and Earth suggests that each state comprised one part of an all-encompassing whole.

A similar vision of the world was articulated in a diplomatic communication from the *chanyu* to Emperor Wen: "With the aid of Heaven, the talent of our officers and soldiers, and the strength of our horses, the Wise King of the Right has destroyed the Yuezhi [the nomads who had dominated the north prior to the Xiongnu] and mercilessly slain them to make them submit. Loulan, the Wusun, the Hujie, and the other twenty-six neighboring states are now part of the Xiongnu state. All people who draw the bow have become one family and the northern region has been pacified." A treaty signed a few years later in 162 B.C. adopted this principle: the *chanyu* should rule over all the archers who lived to the north of the great wall, while the settled people to its south, who "wore hats and sashes," were to be governed by the Chinese emperor.[13] This divided the world into two great cultural zones—the realm of the nomads and that of the Chinese—each forming its own empire. It also entailed the rulers' recognition of each other's domination of the lesser states within their respective spheres (Map 10).

This vision of a bipolar world divided between two cultural spheres manifested itself in Chinese thought. Under Emperor Jing, Chao Cuo systematically compared the Xiongnu and the Chinese, portraying the former as an inversion or negation of the latter. The nomads ate meat and drank milk; the Chinese ate grain. The Xiongnu wore skins and furs; the Chinese wore hemp and silk. The Chinese had walled towns, fields, and houses; the Xiongnu, according to Chao Cuo, had none (not in fact true, but it demonstrates how he imagined the two sides as complete inver-

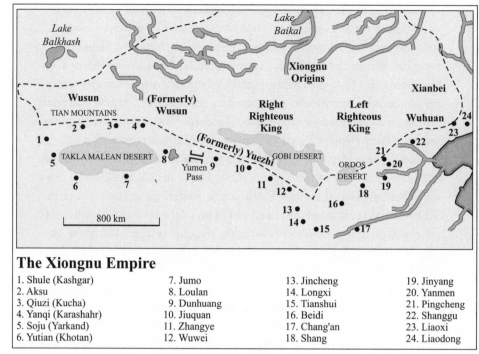

The Xiongnu Empire

1. Shule (Kashgar)	7. Jumo	13. Jincheng	19. Jinyang
2. Aksu	8. Loulan	14. Longxi	20. Yanmen
3. Qiuzi (Kucha)	9. Dunhuang	15. Tianshui	21. Pingcheng
4. Yanqi (Karashahr)	10. Jiuquan	16. Beidi	22. Shanggu
5. Soju (Yarkand)	11. Zhangye	17. Chang'an	23. Liaoxi
6. Yutian (Khotan)	12. Wuwei	18. Shang	24. Liaodong

MAP 10

sions). Finally, the nomads were like flying birds or running beasts that moved constantly until they found good grass and fresh water; the Chinese were rooted in fields and towns. Chao Cuo extended these cultural oppositions to explain the strategic and tactical balance of forces between the two.[14]

Some decades later the *Shi ji*, in a more accurate proto-ethnographic account of Xiongnu customs, described the animals they reared, their techniques of divination, their major state sacrifices and burial customs, their use of verbal agreements instead of writing, and a number of Xiongnu words. But this work is still embedded in a definition of the Xiongnu as the polar opposite of the Chinese. It begins with the conventional reference to their mobility and dependence on their herds. Discussion of the Xiongnu's diet of meat and wardrobe of furs is followed immediately by a conventional attack on the nomads for honoring only youth and strength while treating the aged with contempt. The *Shi ji*'s author, Sima Qian, also offers a standard piece of Chinese moralizing by stating that the Xiongnu sons marry their widowed stepmothers and that brothers marry the widows of deceased siblings. Echoing earlier accounts of nomadic combat, he remarks that the Xiongnu did not find it shameful to retreat when a battle went badly. Sima Qian turns this empirical observation into a moral contrast between the Chinese, who are bound by their sense of duty, and the nomads, who recognize only self-interest.[15]

Defining the two peoples by mutual oppositions is not invariably at the expense of the Xiongnu, however. Sima Qian cites arguments attributed to Zhonghang Yue, a Chinese who went over to the Xiongnu and assisted them against the Han. He showed the necessity of the Xiongnu's honoring youth over age and marrying the widows of kin, and also noted the relaxed relations between the Xiongnu ruler and his subjects, in contrast with the rigid hierarchies of the Chinese court. In this way, accounts of nomadic customs became a method of criticizing some Chinese practices.

Sima Qian adopted a similar stance in discussing Xiongnu law: "Those who in ordinary times draw a sword a foot from the scabbard are condemned to death; those convicted of theft have their property confiscated; those guilty of minor offences are flogged; and those guilty of major ones are executed. No one is kept in jail awaiting sentence longer than ten days, and the number of imprisoned men in the whole country does not exceed a handful."[16] Here the simple principles and equitable punishments of Xiongnu law echo the simplified code imposed by the Han founder, and stand in sharp contrast with the complexities and brutalities of the legal practice of Sima Qian's own day.

According to Chao Cuo, the territory of the Xiongnu was "a place of accumulated *yin* [shade and cold]. The tree bark is three inches thick, and the thickness of ice reaches as many as six feet. The people eat meat and drink kumiss [a yogurt-like drink]. They have a thick skin, and the animals have much fur, so the nature of people and animals is adapted to the cold."[17] This analysis—part of an implied triad with the south as extreme *yang* and China as the balanced middle—traces differences among peoples to cosmic laws.

By the Warring States period some constellations were associated with certain states. Sima Qian's treatise extends this practice to the nomads, who became the earthly equivalents of specified constellations. The bipolar division of the world on the basis of culture and politics reappeared in the structure of the Heavens, with the dividing line of the Heavenly Route matching the frontier between Chinese and nomads. Based on this principle, Sima Qian read many astronomical events in the stipulated regions as signs of the fate in battle of the two competing powers.[18]

In contrast with the Warring States period, when regional cultures constituted the primary divisions in the Chinese sphere, the imagining of a world divided between nomads and Chinese marked a major step. It posited the fundamental unity of a single Chinese civilization defined by what was not nomadic, and it reduced regional divisions to secondary status. China first emerged as a unity through the invention of a Chinese/nomad dichotomy, and this bipolar concept remained central to Chinese civilization in later periods.

It is ironic, then, that the political partition of the world into two spheres lasted only a few decades. In spite of increasing payments, Xiongnu incursions did not cease. Each agreement lasted a few years, only to be broken by a new invasion, which was followed in turn by demands for a resumption of peaceful relations based on an increase in payments. The Chinese attributed this to barbarian perfidy, but it reflected the nature of the Xiongnu state. While the Chinese emperor was unchallenged as chief lawgiver, judge, and administrator, power within the Xiongnu state was constrained and divided by kin bonds, customary practice, and horizontal segmentation between clans or tribes. The *chanyu* maintained control over his subordinate chiefs only by constant negotiations in which he was first among equals rather than an absolute authority. Consensus on his power hinged on his success in battle and distribution of booty.

In such a system, the *chanyu* could not refrain from military action indefinitely. Nor could he stop his subordinates from attacking on their own, for the power and prestige of chiefs likewise depended on their success in battle and distribution of booty. Sometimes they invaded because of tensions with local Chinese officials, sometimes because of resentment of the *chanyu*. The *he qin* policy failed because it relied on a structure of authority that did not exist among the Xiongnu.[19]

As treaty after treaty was violated, debates at the Chinese court were increasingly dominated by calls for war. Decades of peace had given the Chinese time to develop a new style of army based on cavalry and crossbows that could successfully engage the Xiongnu in the field. In 134 B.C. Emperor Wu finally undertook to destroy the Xiongnu through military action. Although his attempted ambush of the *chanyu* failed, in the decades that followed, Chinese armies pushed deep into Central Asia and inflicted substantial losses of both men and flocks on the Xiongnu.

However, Han losses were also considerable, and repeated campaigns drained the treasury without achieving any decisive result. Difficulties in transporting supplies and harsh weather meant that no army could spend even as much as one hundred days in the field, so victories could not be translated into an enduring occupation. Emperor Wu's successors consequently abandoned his policy of launching expeditions and instead retired behind a defensive line, while refusing to pay tribute. This policy was successful, for it deprived the *chanyu* of Han tribute and also reduced his role as defender against Han invasions. The position of the *chanyu* deteriorated, and in 120 B.C. a dissident Xiongnu king surrendered to the Han with 40,000 men. In subsequent decades other chiefs refused to attend the *chanyu's* court.[20] Between 115 and 60 B.C. the Han also secured control of the former Xiongnu sphere of influence in eastern Central Asia (modern Xinjiang).

A battle over succession split the Xiongnu empire in 57 B.C., with no fewer than five kings claiming the title of *chanyu*. After several years one king acknowledged Han suzerainty, visited the Han court, and resettled inside China. This proved to be highly advantageous, for in exchange for obeisance he received generous gifts from the Han. He repeated his visit to the court in 49 and 33 B.C. and sent a son there as a hostage, whose well-being depended on his father's good conduct and who learned Han culture. The wealth that the vassal chieftain gained allowed him to build up his following and defeat his rivals. Eventually, he grew powerful enough to return to the north and resume the old pattern of demanding tribute, until a second succession struggle renewed the civil war in 48 A.D. This led to a permanent split between the southern Xiongnu, who dwelt in China and submitted to the emperor, and the northern Xiongnu, who resided beyond the boundaries of the Han empire.

The southern Xiongnu became dependent on Han assistance, as indicated in 88 A.D. in a memorial from the southern *chanyu*: "Your servant humbly thinks back on how since his ancestor submitted to the Han we have been blessed with your support, keeping a sharp watch on the passes and providing strong armies for more than forty years. Your subjects have been born and reared in Han territory and have depended entirely on the Han for food. Each year we received gifts counted in the hundreds of millions [of cash]."[21] This policy of resettling nomads still grouped in their tribes inside the Chinese empire would have disastrous long-term consequences, as we will see, leading to a breakdown in civil order in the northwest and the southward flight of large numbers of Han Chinese.

Although the northern Xiongnu continued to defy the Han, they were defeated on several occasions by allied armies of the Han and the southern Xiongnu. Moreover, other tribal peoples such as the Wuhuan and

Xianbei broke away from the Xiongnu and received large bounties from the Han for killing Xiongnu. In 87 A.D. a Xianbei army defeated the Xiongnu, killed the northern *chanyu*, and flayed his body. More than 200,000 Xiongnu tribesmen surrendered after this defeat, and a great Han victory in 89 A.D. completed the destruction of the Xiongnu state.

Frontier Armies

One of the key transformations of Chinese society during the Han was the abolition of universal military service, an institution that had underpinned the Warring States and the Qin.[22] With the Han's defeat of the feudatory kingdoms in 154 B.C., the possibility of large-scale warfare in the interior of China vanished, leaving only the threat of the Xiongnu on the northern border. The inability of peasants serving one-year terms to master horsemanship and the crossbow left them ill-equipped for expeditionary forces. Their relatively short terms also made them unsuitable for long-term garrison duty. Emperor Wu allowed some peasants to pay a tax in lieu of military service and used this money to recruit professionals. Nomadic enemies of the Xiongnu and dissident elements of the Xiongnu themselves were also recruited to provide skilled cavalry. In some cases convicts were sent to the frontiers to man garrisons. Thus, during the last century B.C. the Chinese army began to shift away from peasant levies to an army based on professionals, nomads, and criminals.

The rebellion against Wang Mang turned this gradual and informal process into official policy. The rebellion had demonstrated that peasant conscripts could be turned against the state, especially during the autumn training session, when adult males of a commandery gathered for inspection. It also showed that peasants would follow locally powerful families to whom they were bound rather than officials. Training peasants to fight thus simply provided potential rebels with a superior quality of soldier. Furthermore, in the course of the rebellions, much of the population had been displaced, and loss of registered population meant a drastic decrease in tax income for the court. Motivated by the need to decrease expenditures and reduce internal threats, and by the uselessness of conscripts on the frontier, the newly established Eastern Han regime abolished both the annual training sessions and the local military officials. This did away with a formal peasant army, and left only a small, professional army stationed around the capital.

Following the split of the Xiongnu into southern and northern confederacies in 48 A.D., nomads were internally resettled on a large scale. To supervise these new inhabitants, the Eastern Han government set up standing army commands in camps at the frontier, one command for each major nomadic group resettled in China. These standing armies were manned by professional Han soldiers. The total number of troops in the camps is not recorded, but scattered citations indicate that they were in the tens of thousands. These camps remained a permanent feature of the Han army, and their troops took part in most of the major campaigns of the second century A.D.

Expeditionary armies were distinct from the standing armies, and drew their forces primarily from resettled barbarians. Most of the cavalry in the campaigns of the first century A.D. that destroyed the Xiongnu confederacy consisted of nomad soldiers. The Han founder had already employed tribal soldiers during the civil war. After the reign of Emperor Wu, these tribes were usually classified as "dependent states" and allowed to keep their own leaders and customs, under the supervision of a commandant. But the Eastern Han went beyond the policy of "using barbarians to control barbarians." Non-Han soldiers also quelled internal rebellions, much as foreign mercenaries did for monarchs in early modern Europe. The histories record more than fifty cases of the participation of non-Han soldiers in Chinese armies. Twenty-seven of these list no Han troops in the forces involved, and six were under the command of tribal chieftains.

From this evidence it is clear that after the middle of the first century A.D. the primary source of mounted warriors was non-Han soldiers. State-controlled grasslands and stables for rearing military horses, which the Western Han had maintained since the reign of Emperor Jing in the second century B.C., were largely abandoned. The warlords of the Three Kingdoms period (220–280 A.D.) continued to rely on non-Han peoples to provide their cavalry.

In addition to using non-Han troops in their army, the Han also paid bounties for the heads of slain enemies. Xianbei chieftains, before submitting to the Han, received payments for the heads of Xiongnu. In 58 A.D. they again received payments for crushing a force of invading Wuhuan, and at that time they formally submitted. They received annual payments of 270,000,000 cash, and in return they controlled the Wuhuan and killed Xiongnu. Thus the most common military man in the Eastern Han was the nomad warrior serving the empire under the command of his tribal chieftain.

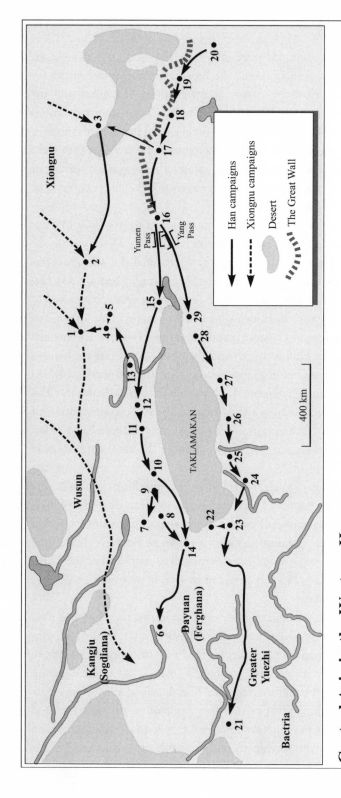

Central Asia in the Western Han

1. Wutugu
2. Pulei
3. Chigu
4. Jiaohe
5. Gaochang

6. Guishan
7. Chigu
8. Juyan
9. Aksu
10. Gumo

11. Qiuzi (Kucha)
12. Luntai (Western Regions Governor General)
13. Yanqi (Karashahr)
14. Shule (Kashgar)
15. Loulan

16. Dunhuang
17. Jiuquan
18. Zhangye
19. Wuwei
20. Jincheng

21. Lanshi
22. Soju (Yarkand)
23. Pishan
24. Yutian (Khotan)
25. Yumi

26. Jingjue
27. Jumo
28. Yixun
29. Yumi

MAP 11

The Western Regions

Like the north, the Western Regions (now Xinjiang and the eastern regions of what was Soviet Central Asia) were inhabited by nomadic peoples such as the Wusun, as well as city-states that had developed near water. With the rise of Modun's northern empire, the Western Regions became part of the Xiongnu sphere of influence. It was a particularly important region for the Xiongnu, described in the texts of the period as their "right arm," because the sedentary inhabitants of the city-states that ringed the Tarim Basin provided the nomads with agricultural goods and the products of urban craftsmen.

When the Han first contemplated attacking the Xiongnu, they sent an emissary named Zhang Qian with one hundred men to seek out the Yuezhi people in the Western Regions as potential allies. The Yuezhi had previously dominated the northern steppes, before being driven west by the Xiongnu, so the Han hoped to receive support from them against their old adversaries. The Han party was captured by the Xiongnu, however, who sent this irate message back to the court: "The Yuezhi lie to the north of us. How can the Han send envoys there? If we wished to send envoys to Yue [to the southeast of China], would the Han allow us to do so?"[23] Zhang Qian remained a prisoner for ten years before finally being allowed to return to China in 126 B.C. with the first detailed information on the Western Regions (Map 11).

Expansion into Central Asia began with the surrender of a subordinate Xiongnu king in 120 B.C. The region he controlled lay between the Han and the Western Regions, so his surrender opened a gateway to the west. As Zhang Qian noted: "If we use this opportunity to send rich gifts to the Wusun, persuade them to move east and occupy their former territory, and send them a princess as a wife, then the Han could conclude an alliance of brotherhood with them. Under the circumstances they would surely obey us. If we make them obey us, this would cut off the right arm of the Xiongnu. Once we have established an alliance with the Wusun, then Daxia [Bactria] and the other countries to the west could all be persuaded to come to our court and acknowledge themselves our foreign vassals."[24] The court approved this proposal, which defined the course of Han policy in Central Asia.

Some scholars have argued that the Chinese moved into Central Asia for economic reasons, either to open a market for silk and other goods or to supplant the Xiongnu in controlling trade routes through Xinjiang.

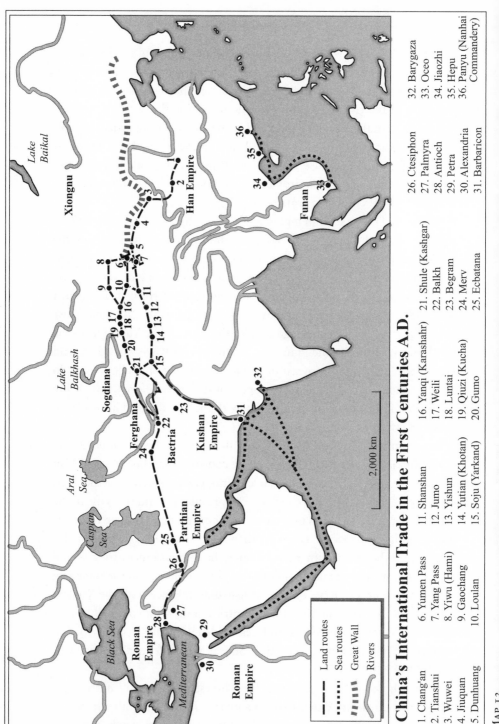

China's International Trade in the First Centuries A.D.

1. Chang'an	6. Yumen Pass	11. Shanshan	16. Yanqi (Karashahr)	21. Shule (Kashgar)	26. Ctesiphon	32. Barygaza
2. Tianshui	7. Yang Pass	12. Jumo	17. Weili	22. Balkh	27. Palmyra	33. Oceo
3. Wuwei	8. Yiwu (Hami)	13. Yishun	18. Luntai	23. Begram	28. Antioch	34. Jiaozhi
4. Juquan	9. Gaochang	14. Yutian (Khotan)	19. Qiuzi (Kucha)	24. Merv	29. Petra	35. Hepu
5. Dunhuang	10. Loulan	15. Soju (Yarkand)	20. Gumo	25. Ecbatana	30. Alexandria	36. Panyu (Nanhai
					31. Barbaricon	Commandery)

MAP 12

But there is no evidence of substantial trade between China and the Western Regions prior to the first century B.C., and the transcontinental trade route conventionally called the "Silk Road" did not exist when the Han first sent missions to Central Asia. The initial motive was political—part of the conflict with the Xiongnu—and trade increased only as a consequence of those first missions.

As for the idea of a "Silk Road," the term was coined by a German geographer in the late nineteenth century. Neither the Chinese nor the Romans, who constituted its two termini, were aware of the existence of such a route or even of the existence of one another. The Romans knew only that somewhere the "Seres," the "silk people," produced the fabric that appeared in Roman markets. The Chinese heard vague rumors of a "Great Qin" empire in the far west, a mythic realm of fantastic plants and animals. Not only were the supposed parties of trade on the "Silk Road" ignorant of one another, but no merchant ever traveled the length of such a route. China's frontier trade and political gift-giving moved large amounts of silk into Central Asian markets, where it was sold to points further west. From Xinjiang it proceeded to the area of modern Afghanistan and India, then to Persia, and finally to the eastern provinces of the Roman empire. The transcontinental trade route was a series of regional trade routes that, in steps, transported quantities of silk from China to Rome. Each participant was conscious of only one or two steps along the way (Map 12).[25]

The Han's first attempt to secure an alliance with the Wusun had mixed results. While the Wusun king agreed to marry a Han princess, he also accepted a bride from the Xiongnu and granted ritual priority to the latter.[26] This became common in the Western Regions, where small states tried to maintain independence by simultaneously offering concessions and pledges to both great powers. In 108 B.C. and again in 92, the state of Loulan sent one prince as a hostage to the Han court and one to the Xiongnu. When the king of Loulan died, the Xiongnu rushed their hostage home and put him on the throne before the news reached China. This initiated a period of anti-Han policies that lasted until 77 B.C., when a Han agent arranged the assassination of the pro-Xiongnu ruler.

The Han's first major military campaign into the region took place in 108 B.C., and it led to agreements with the Wusun and Loulan. In a second and more important campaign, Ferghana was conquered in 101 B.C. The great distance of Ferghana from the capital demonstrated the range of Han power, and securing the region's breed of exotic horses was such a

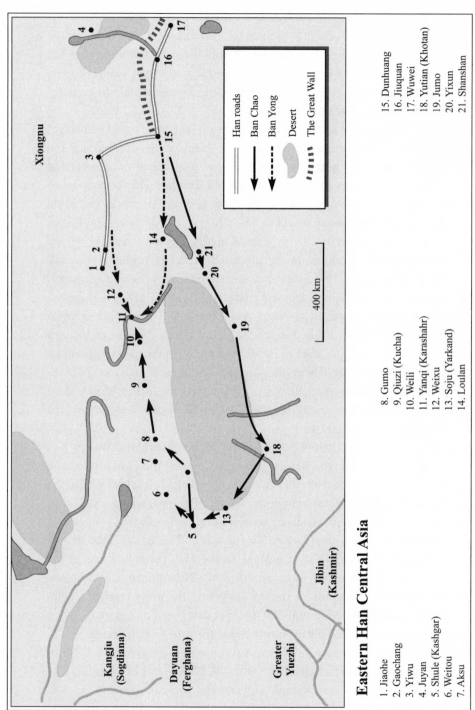

Eastern Han Central Asia

1. Jiaohe
2. Gaochang
3. Yiwu
4. Juyan
5. Shule (Kashgar)
6. Weitou
7. Aksu

8. Gumo
9. Qiuzi (Kucha)
10. Weili
11. Yanqi (Karashahr)
12. Weixu
13. Soju (Yarkand)
14. Loulan

15. Dunhuang
16. Jiuquan
17. Wuwei
18. Yutian (Khotan)
19. Jumo
20. Yixun
21. Shanshan

MAP 13

victory for the Han court that it was celebrated in hymns composed for performance in the ancestral temple.[27] The successful campaign, the longest and most expensive ever mounted by the Han, led most of the Central Asian states to send tribute and hostages to the Han court.

The successful campaign against Turfan in 90 B.C. was significant because this state was the closest to the Xiongnu and hence a key to their access to the west. The armies for this expedition were drawn from six states of the Western Regions, indicating the degree of influence the Han had attained by that time. After a brief Xiongnu resurgence in the area, another major Han victory in 71 B.C. led to the eclipse of Xiongnu power in Turfan.

These military successes culminated in the establishment of the office of the protector-general of the Western Regions in 60 B.C. Located near the earlier base of the Xiongnu chief in the Western Regions, this office was the Han military and political headquarters. The Han also set up agricultural colonies and extended the frontier network of walls and watchtowers into Central Asia. Two garrisons at Dunhuang and Juyan produced numerous wooden strips with Han administrative records, which have been discovered in the twentieth century and which provide details of Han life there.

Central Asia's ties to the Han rose and fell. At the end of the Western Han the Chinese pulled out of the Western Regions, and the northern Xiongnu re-established their dominance. After 91 A.D. Chinese authority recovered, through the success of the protector-general Ban Chao (brother of the historian and poet Ban Gu) and his son Ban Yong (Map 13).

Discussions of China's relations to the outer world have traditionally focused on the so-called tribute system, in which foreign states sent distinctive native products as gifts to the emperor in token of their submission. Whatever its role in later dynasties, tribute certainly did not constitute a formal system under the early empires, as recent scholarship has shown. Tribute was presented by alien states under some circumstances, but the practice remained improvised and inchoate. The notion of tribute (*gong*) was not limited to foreign relations: even candidates for office sent to the court were considered "tribute," as were some taxes.[28]

Nevertheless, the submission of the southern Xiongnu entailed presenting gifts to the emperor, and the giving of gifts became a fundamental element in the relation of the Western Regions to the Han court, as described in the *History of the Later Han (Hou Han shu)*: "Overawed by our military strength and attracted by our wealth, all the rulers presented exotic local products as tribute and their beloved sons as hostages. They bared their heads and kneeled down toward the east to pay homage to the Son of Heaven. Then the office of the Wuji Colonel was established to take care of their affairs and the command of the protector-general established to exercise authority. Those who submitted from the beginning received money and official seals as imperial gifts, but those who surrendered later were taken to the capital to receive punishment."[29]

Just as in earlier accounts each region of China had sent its typical products to the ruler as a symbol of the region as a whole, so the crucial feature of foreign tribute was that it should be distinctive of the area from which it came. In exchange for such exotic items, the Chinese ruler sent gifts of precious metals or silk to the foreign rulers, in addition to bestowing Chinese titles upon them. In these exchanges the value of what the Chinese gave was greater than what they received, an imbalance intended to demonstrate the superiority of the Chinese in the relationship. For many Central Asian states, however, tribute-bearing missions were simply pretexts for trade. In the late first century B.C. the state of Kashmir, in a particularly blatant example, did not even formally submit to China but nevertheless sent envoys bearing tribute. An official pointed out that these envoys were not officials from Kashmir but ordinary merchants coming to trade.[30]

Surrendered Xiongnu kings and the rulers of Central Asian states were routinely granted titles by the Han emperor, along with an official seal of office and other credentials. This honor underscored their status as subordinates of the Chinese ruler. Generally the ruler of a tributary state was designated a marquis, and his major followers received titles as chancellors, generals, or colonels. Recognition from the Chinese empire acquired great prestige among the peoples of Central Asia. When a man named Lü Guang conquered Kucha in 383 A.D., many states from the region came to submit to him. To indicate their loyalty to China, they showed him seals that they had received from the Han court and preserved for two centuries after the fall of the dynasty.[31]

These titles were not empty honorifics or signs of submission. They entailed the performance of administrative functions that were technically under the supervision of the protector-general. In one case several Wusun officials received Han titles sometime between 48–46 B.C. A few decades later when the Wusun king was assassinated, these officials were judged to have been negligent in their duties and were stripped of their seals and credentials. Similarly in 153 A.D. a Chinese officer transferred to another local ruler the seals and credentials of a vassal king in the Turfan area who had failed to preserve order.

The Qiang and the Wuhuan

One western people deserving special note is the Qiang, because their uprisings in the first half of the second century A.D. were a major cause of the Han's decline. People with this name figured in the Shang oracle inscriptions, and they were spread across much of the west from modern Gansu south to Yunnan. The graph for their name indicates a sheep, and they are described as herdsmen of oxen, horses, sheep, donkeys, and camels. From at least the early Warring States period they had also adopted agriculture, so that records refer to their farmlands and the quantities of wheat they produced.[32]

While the Qiang were in contact with the Xiongnu and in the early period allied with them against the Han, they never formed a larger state or federation. The Chinese defined the Qiang by this tendency to break up into numerous mutually hostile tribes: "They did not establish the ruler-subject relationship, nor use the authority of elders to stay unified. When someone grew strong then he would split his group and be their chief, but when he declined he would become the follower of another." As described by the Chinese general Zhao Chongguo in 63 B.C.: "The reason why it is easy to control the Qiang is that as soon as there are influential men they attack each other, so naturally they cannot unite."[33] Ironically, this tendency toward repeated division made it impossible to defeat them using the methods that had worked against the Xiongnu. If a Qiang chieftain was beaten, the effects of defeat spread no further than his own tribe, but if he achieved success, then his forces swelled into a major insurrection. Peace agreements were also limited in range.

The Qiang resettled inside Han China as early as the second century B.C., sometimes with Han permission, sometimes without. During the civil war against Wang Mang and the early decades of the Eastern Han, many Qiang moved into the Han northwest. When Guangwu, the founder of the Eastern Han, reoccupied Gansu, he found the Qiang controlling large areas. The Han government sought to deal with this problem by dispersing the Qiang into the interior, even resettling them near the old capital Chang'an in 35 and 50 A.D. This only intensified the Qiang rebellions and led to proposals to abandon the counties around the former capital. So large was the resettlement and so rapid Qiang population growth that by the fourth century A.D. approximately half the population of the Guanzhong region was non-Chinese.[34]

This intermingling of the Qiang and the Han in western China provided numerous occasions for conflict. In 33 B.C. a memorial pointed out that "recently the Western Qiang have guarded our frontier, and thus come into regular contact with Han people. Minor officials and greedy commoners have robbed the Qiang of cattle, women, and children. This has provoked the Qiang's hatred, so they have risen in rebellion for generation after generation." Sixty years later nothing had changed: "Now in every part of Liangzhou [Gansu] there are surrendered Qiang who still wear their hair unbound and button their lapels on the left [non-Chinese customs] but live mixed with the Chinese. Since their customs are different and languages unintelligible, they are frequently robbed by minor officials and scheming people. Thoroughly enraged and yet helpless, they rebel. All barbarian disturbances are due to this."[35] Most officials at court believed that the root of the problem with the Qiang lay in the misconduct of local officials in league with powerful commoners.

To quell these uprisings, the Han government instituted the office of "Inspecting Commandant who Protects the Qiang" in 111 B.C. He was to assist the Qiang living within Han borders, to investigate their complaints, and to maintain a staff of translators to handle communication with Qiang beyond the frontiers. He was responsible for organizing agricultural colonies to provision garrisons that could thus handle local rebellions without assistance from the central armies. These local garrisons proved largely ineffective when the rebellions actually occurred, and assistance from the imperial armies often did not come.[36]

The Han practice of incorporating non-Chinese peoples as dependent states, as a preliminary to recruiting their warriors as allied forces for the army, dates back to the beginning of the dynasty.[37] The earliest Qiang dependent state was established in 60 B.C., and by the time of the Eastern Han there were Qiang dependent states in the Ordos, Gansu, and Sichuan, along with dependent states of the Xiongnu and several other Central Asian states. In theory, members of a dependent state continued to live according to their own customs and under their traditional rulers. Han administrators were not supposed to control them but to secure obedience to special dictates imposed by the Han court.

To become "inner" subjects of Han China, surrendered barbarians had to render service to the Han government as laborers or soldiers. The

Qiang figure prominently in Eastern Han campaigns against nomads on the frontier, providing the "ears and eyes" of the government on the border. They may also have paid some taxes. Surrendered Qiang chieftains, if they were powerful enough, brought tribute to the Han court and paid homage to the ruler. Minor chieftains of small tribes were left in peace. Those who did attend the court could receive titles and seals in the same manner as the rulers of the Western Regions.[38]

This policy of loose control and minimal service was often ignored. Inspecting commandants routinely exacted money and service from the Qiang to enrich themselves. When Zhang Huan was appointed to the post in A.D. 55, he discovered that his eight predecessors had all exploited the Qiang for personal gain.[39] His refusal to accept horses and gold offered by Qiang chieftains is cited as a demonstration of integrity, but this shows that high officials sent out by the court were usually as savage in their extortion as the dishonest local officials criticized in the memorials.

The nature of the commandant's office changed as increasing resettlement forced the creation of more dependent states. In A.D. 94 more than half a million Qiang submitted as "inner" subjects, and in 107 and 108 several tens of thousands submitted. As these people could not be incorporated under Han administration, they formed dependent states under the supervision of newly established commandants. Whenever local order broke down, the powers of the office of inspecting commandant were extended. Established as a military office charged with mobilizing allies for military service, it was gradually given administrative powers equivalent to those of the head of a commandery. In the areas under their control the inspecting commandants governed not only surrendered barbarians but also frontier Chinese. Thus, internal resettlement of non-Chinese eventually led to the militarization of local society and administration on the frontier.[40]

In addition to the Qiang and the Xiongnu, the peoples most commonly placed under military supervision as dependent states were the Wuhuan, who along with the Xianbei were called "eastern barbarians." These nomadic peoples, dwelling largely in what is now Inner Mongolia, had been defeated by Modun and incorporated into the Xiongnu state. As subordinate states, they provided regular payments of furs, horses, and livestock, along with troops for Xiongnu wars against the Han.

This situation was transformed in 119 B.C. when a Han victory pushed the *chanyu*'s court out of Inner Mongolia, allowing the Wuhuan a degree of independence. The Han resettled them in commanderies beyond the great wall in the northeast, where they were placed under the supervision of an "Inspecting Commandant who Protects the Wuhuan," with head-quarters near modern Beijing. However, throughout the Western Han the Xiongnu continued to compel payments from many Wuhuan, who still raided the Han.

The relations between the Han and the Wuhuan changed again in 49 A.D. when the Han emperor persuaded the leading Wuhuan chieftains to submit. Almost a thousand chiefs came to the Han court to pay homage and offer tribute in slaves, horses, oxen, bows, and furs. The emperor reciprocated with a great banquet and precious gifts. Later in the year the chieftains requested to become "inner" subjects, and eighty-one of them received titles as marquises. Kin of the leading chiefs were kept as hostages.[41]

The Wuhuan resettled inside the Han frontier, which they guarded in exchange for regular payments of food and clothing. They also received bounties for the heads of slain enemies. Although the exact number is uncertain, as many as three million Wuhuan may have lived inside the Han frontiers by the late second century. Following this resettlement, the office of the inspecting commandant was re-established, this time with its headquarters at Ningcheng. Wall paintings in the tomb of one Inspecting Commandant depict the city's walls, administrative offices, military installations, and markets. These paintings contain valuable information about the lives of the Wuhuan, showing their clothing and shaved heads, as well as the goods they bought and sold in the market. Another wall painting depicts a nomad's tent, an exotic structure soon to become fashionable among the Han elite.[42]

Dependent states of the Wuhuan not only fought the Xiongnu and then the Xianbei, who had united the northern nomads against the Han after the Xiongnu's defeat, but also suppressed rebellions inside China proper and in the far south.[43] Moreover, trade in the market at Ningcheng made the region where the Wuhuan resided one of the wealthiest in China at the end of the second century. The cooperation between the Wuhuan and Han officials became so close that in 187 A.D. two Han officials led the nomads in a rebellion against the court.

In 184 A.D., when the Yellow Turbans rebelled against the Han in Shangdong and the northeast, more than one million Chinese fled to the region around Ningcheng. Again in A.D. 205, when the warlord Cao Cao's armies, which included large numbers of Wuhuan cavalry, invaded the northern commanderies, more than 100,000 Chinese households sought protection with the Wuhuan.[44] Such widespread trust in the Wuhuan, and a preference for their protection to that of a Chinese warlord, indicates the degree to which nomadic dependent states had become a constitutive element of China by the end of the Han.

Sedentary Neighbors and the Cult of Exotics

To its northeast, southeast, and southwest, China was ringed by sedentary peoples rather than nomads. These regions were of little political or economic importance to the Han, since they posed no military threat and their territories were difficult to reach. Also, the damp southern climate encouraged diseases fatal to northerners. Later the peoples in these areas would adopt many aspects of Chinese life, including bureaucratic administration and script, so that by the seventh century A.D. China was surrounded by lesser replicas of itself. But with the exception of Korea, this acculturation had scarcely begun during the Han.

In what is now North Korea, a combination of trade and settlement introduced a local Chinese administration in the late second century B.C. But by the first century A.D. Korean peoples had begun to form their own states, particularly Koguryŏ, and in A.D. 106 the Han administration was temporarily expelled. Although the Chinese continued to rule parts of Korea until the end of the Han and beyond, this region had no lasting future as part of China (Map 14).

In the far south (modern Guangdong, Guangxi, and northern Vietnam) and southeast (modern Fujian), the Qin and then the Han set up commanderies that were little more than military garrisons. They also granted titles and seals to favored local chieftains, who made nominal submission to the Han court and sent tribute in the form of exotic goods. Chinese settlements in these areas ranged from sparse to nonexistent, and the Han records contain little more than narratives of the loyalty or rebellion of some local chiefs.

Han incursions into the southwest (modern Yunnan and Guizhou) were similar, combining brief military interventions with attempts to win over local chiefs through the gift of titles. Some people at the Han court became interested in the region because of reports of possible trade through the southwest to more distant lands. In 135 B.C. a courtier proposed an exploratory mission to seek out trade routes between the southwestern state of Yelang and the far southern region of Nan Yue. At about the same time, the celebrated poet Sima Xiangru, a westerner from

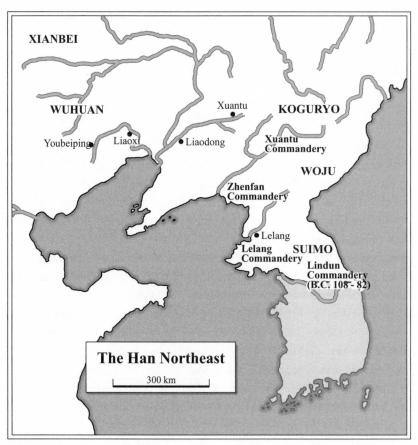

MAP 14

Sichuan, tried to establish contacts between southwestern Sichuan and what are now Myanmar and India. A couple of decades later Zhang Qian, the captured emissary who had first explored Central Asia for the Han court, reported observing Chinese goods in Bactria that had passed from Sichuan through the southwest. However, all such trade routes proved too difficult to be of regular use. Although a few commanderies were established and the kings of Yelang and Dian were granted titles, Chinese contacts with the region remained episodic and superficial.[45]

While these states were of little military or political interest, the Han were fascinated with rare goods from these regions as well as from the northern and Western Regions. The Han obsession with rare objects from distant places originated in the idea that the ruler's power was measured by his ability to attract people and their products to his court. The greater the distance from which people came, and the more exotic the product, the more potent was the ruler.

The most elaborate depictions of this theme are in the writings of Sima Xiangru, particularly his poem "Rhapsody on the Imperial Hunting Park," which mingles animals presented by northern nomads and peoples of Central Asia with creatures of fantasy and myth:

> The sun rises from its eastern ponds
> And sets among the slopes of the west;
> In the southern part of the park,
> Where grasses grow in the dead of winter
> And the waters leap, unbound by ice,
> Live zebras, yaks, tapirs, and black oxen,
> Water buffalo, elk, antelope,
> "Red-crowns" and "round-heads,"
> Aurochs, elephants, and rhinoceroses.
> In the north, where in the midst of summer
> The ground is cracked and blotched with ice
> And one may walk the frozen streams or wade the rivulets,
> Roam unicorns and boars,
> Wild asses and camels,
> Onagers and mares,
> Swift stallions, donkeys, and mules.[46]

In the late first century A.D. Wang Chong wrote two essays denouncing the tendency to celebrate the ancient Zhou as the greatest dynasty, while criticizing the Han. He pointed out that the Han dynasty had received exotic tribute from distant lands of which the Zhou were not even aware. According to Wang Chong, the prestige and influence demonstrated by obtaining such rare objects demonstrated the superiority of the Han to all earlier dynasties.[47]

The prestige of the exotic also figured in religion. Points of contact between men and spirits lay at the edges of the earth, either vertically on mountain peaks or horizontally on floating islands in the east or mountain ranges in the west. These realms of immortals and spirits contained the same extraordinary animals and plants that appeared in the human world as omens or tribute. Accounts of the immortal court of the Queen Mother of the West emphasize the trees of jade and other precious stones, as well as the unusual animals that filled her court. These nine-tailed foxes, rabbits grinding elixirs of immortality, dancing frogs, and bird messengers are also depicted in Han tomb art, both in wall carvings and in bronze "money trees."

From its origins in political and religious life, the cult of exotics spread to the Han elite and even to commoners. By the Eastern Han, foreign objects fascinated Chinese at every level of society. At the end of the first century A.D. the historian Ban Gu wrote to his kinsman Ban Chao, conqueror of Central Asia, describing the fabulous prices paid in the capital for Central Asian carpets and horses. In the middle of the second century A.D. Emperor Ling spent his leisure time in a nomad's tent that he had erected in his palace. He was also fond of barbarian clothing, food, music, and dances.[48] Private individuals copied this practice.

The white face powder (called "barbarian powder") that became a common form of makeup in Han China and later in Japan was adopted from non-Chinese peoples. Musical instruments, such as the *pipa*, came from Central Asia, and new varieties of fruits and dairy products were introduced into the Chinese diet from the west and the north. Finally, at the very end of the Han, the Buddhist religion moved into China both from Central Asia and overseas through the southeast. At first associated with the Queen Mother of the West as a saving divinity from the western edge of the world, the Buddha and his teaching became the most influential foreign exotic brought into China during the first centuries of our era.

7

KINSHIP

THE BREAKUP of extended families began with the destruction of the Zhou nobility by the Warring States, which tried to maximize the number of households providing taxes and adult male service. Qin in particular used tax policies to encourage the division of households and the establishment of the nuclear family as the basic social unit. The most common size for such households was five or six people. Early Han rulers continued this policy, and the small, nuclear family became the basic unit of residence and labor in Western Han society.

This policy was modified under the Eastern Han, when classicist theory and the cult of filial piety seriously influenced the court. The government acknowledged an ideal of multiple generations living together, though in practice this meant that families of brothers lived near one another (not in the same household) and perhaps were buried in a lineage graveyard. It produced a more integrated residential pattern without altering the nuclear family as the basic household unit. The great families stressed the importance of lineage in order to maintain alliances across numerous households, but the residential kin groups of the period consisted of husband and wife, children, and occasionally an elderly parent living in a household, with extended family living nearby in the case of great families.

Throughout early imperial China, kinship was marked by tension between the individual household and the patriline. This stemmed from a fundamental contradiction in the principles that defined these two domains. The lineage or patriline, as described in the ritual classics and laid out in ancestral temples, was defined by transmission from father to son to son across the generations. It was a world of men that women entered only as adjuncts to their husbands. The household, in contrast, was defined primarily by the relationship of husband to wife, and secondarily by that of parents to children. It was a realm in which women wielded great influence as wives and even greater power as mothers.

The lineage was the textually sanctioned unit advocated by literati who took an interest in kin structures, but the household was the unit in which people actually lived and established kin ties. The contradictions between these two models affected every aspect of the Chinese family, and extended outward into the spheres of economics, politics, and religion.

Gender in the Lineage and Household

From the perspective of the classical texts, a household represented just one bead in a long string of ancestors traced back from senior male to senior male until reaching an original male ancestor. This lineage was defined by the relations of father to son and brother to brother. Women were outsiders, necessary for reproduction but otherwise aliens within the husband's family. After marriage, a wife retained her natal surname and maintained links with her birth family, which were crucial for securing political alliances. But despite these natal ties, women were aliens in their birth homes as well. A daughter was not a permanent member of her father's household; she married out and lived with her husband's family. Even unmarried daughters who stayed at home generally did not inherit a share of the family land.[1]

This textual definition of a woman's place in the patriline did not guide everyday practice, however. Inside the household, women held considerable power, which flowed primarily from a mother's influence over her sons. In early imperial China the authority of age usually took precedence over the authority of gender, and filial obedience to both parents—his mother as well as his father—was a son's highest obligation. Although a woman, according to the celebrated "three forms of obedience," should always be subject to the men in her family, in actual Han households women commanded their sons, who were obliged to respect and obey them.[2]

A key demonstration of the authority of women can be found in the only surviving Han will, dating to 5 A.D. The will is written in the name of a widowed mother, who calls upon local officials as witnesses to validate it. She lists the members of the household and their relations, then dictates how the fields are to be distributed among her sons, and under what conditions the lands are to be held. The participation of officials as witnesses shows that the state regarded the widowed mother's authority over the disposition of the family's land as normal and proper. A similar case is recorded in a stone inscription erected in 178 A.D. that recounts how a widow surnamed Xu dictated the distribution of family land.[3] In both cases, the supposed obligations of widows to obey their sons, as defined by ritual, had little impact on actual practice.

The will also reveals some of the difficulties introduced when a widow remarried, for the treatment of each son depended on the relation of their respective fathers to the widow allocating the inheritance. In this case, the threat was mitigated by the fact that the woman remained in the household of her first husband. Her subsequent husbands lived with her family, rather than the other way around. Consequently, the well-being of the first husband's patriline—her highest concern according to the ritual texts—was not challenged. Just as the status of the sons depended on that of their father, so children of a second or third wife were always subordinate to those of the first.

Evidence of the mother's power also figures in Han poetry. "The Peacock Flies Southeast," written from the point of view of an oppressed daughter-in-law, narrates how her husband is controlled by his mother, who ultimately forces him to divorce his wife. Another poem concludes with a statement about an ideal woman: "When such a stalwart woman controls the house, she even surpasses a man." A further indication of the power of women over their husbands is indicated in the "Song of the Orphan," which describes a child forced to toil as a peddler after his uncle took over his upbringing upon the death of his parents. Brotherly devotion to the child's dead father should have led to the proper treatment of a nephew, but the sister-in-law used her influence to undermine it.[4]

A more serious problem than the sister-in-law was the stepmother, who came into the household when a man remarried after the death of his first wife. That a second or third wife would persecute the children of her husband's first marriage in order to advance her own biological children was so common that it was treated as a structural feature of the Chinese household. Anxiety over the problem of stepmothers and the care of children whose mother had died figured prominently in early Han stories and in Han art. Tales such as those of Min Sun and Jiang Zhangxun feature classic evil stepmothers. In the former, the stepmother persecutes the son of the first marriage until the father discovers her cruelty. In the latter, the mother attempts to kill the son after his father has died, until repeated failures convince her that Heaven is protecting the child.[5]

Given women's supposed tendency to favor their own children, the exemplary woman is one who protects the offspring of the first wife even at the expense of her own child. This not only preserves the lineage hierarchy, in which the first wife's offspring is senior, but more importantly signals a willingness to abandon her own interests, as embodied in her offspring. Thus when the two sons of the "righteous stepmother of Qi" were found next to a murdered corpse, each confessed to protect the other. Unable to judge, the officials asked the stepmother to select the guilty party: Weeping, she replied, "Kill the younger." An official asked, "The youngest son is the one people most love, yet now you desire to kill him. Why?" The mother replied:

> The younger one is my child; the elder is the son of the previous wife. When their father was ill and on the point of death he charged me, "Raise him [the elder] well and look after him." I said, "I will." Now having received a trust from him and agreed to it by saying, "I will," how could I forget that trust and be faithless to the promise? Moreover, to kill the elder and preserve the younger would be to abandon a public duty for the sake of a private love. To turn my back on my words and forget good faith would be to cheat the dead man. If I disregard my words, forget my pledge, and having already accepted [an obligation] then not keep faith, how can I live among men?[6]

The king pardoned both sons out of respect for the woman's devotion to duty, but this happy resolution does not soften the story's harsh lesson. Celebrating a woman for choosing to kill her own child in order to protect her husband's patriline, as indicated here in the appeal to the contradiction between "public duty" and "private love," offers a chilling demonstration of the moral convolutions entailed in defining kin ties exclusively through male transmission.

So great was the suspicion of women that certain anecdotes celebrated choosing a brother's lineage over a husband's, simply because this entailed the woman's rejection of her own affections and interests. Thus, when the virtuous aunt of Lu abandoned her own son to rescue her brother's, she once again justified the action in terms of rejecting "private love" in the name of "public duty." Similarly, a woman in Liang tried to rescue her elder brother's son from a burning house, but accidentally picked up her own son. By the time she had discovered her mistake, the flames were too advanced for her to return and rescue her nephew. When her companions tried to stop her from leaping back into the flames, she exclaimed: "Bearing the name of unrighteousness, what face can I have to meet my brothers and the men of the capital? I want to throw my son back into the fire, but this would disregard a mother's kindness. In this situation I can no longer live." She then dashed into the flames and perished.[7]

A correlate of the threat posed by the stepmother or sister-in-law was the danger that a widowed mother might herself remarry. This issue was already engraved by the First Emperor on a stone atop Mount Guiji: "A woman who has a child, if she remarries, betrays the dead and is unchaste."[8] The issue of remarriage was of great importance in the Han, for any patriline could face loss or extinction if a widow remarried and transferred her loyalties to the new family. Understandably, the natal families of widows often encouraged them to remarry, in order to establish new alliances, and women themselves doubtless chose in some cases to wed again. In such an event, she would be pushed by her new family to favor her new husband's sons over her sons from the previous marriage.

To avoid these difficulties, some texts argued that a woman should not remarry at all: "Good faith is the virtue of a wife. Once having been united with her husband she will not change for her entire life. Thus, if the husband dies she will not remarry."[9] The classic embodiment of this idea was the widow Gao Xing ("Lofty Conduct") of Liang. Celebrated for her beauty, she was widowed young and refused to remarry. The king of Liang sent a minister with betrothal gifts to take her as his wife. She replied:

"I have heard that the duty of a wife is that once she has gone out to marry she will not change. Thereby she keeps intact the moral integrity of chastity and good faith. To forget the dead and run after the living is unfaithful. Perceiving honor [the king] to forget the humble [her first husband] is unchaste. One who abandons duty and follows profit loses all means of being human." She took a mirror and knife and cut off her nose. She said, "I have become a mutilated person. I did not commit suicide because I could not bear for the children to be orphaned again. The king's seeking me was for my beauty, but now as this mutilated remnant I can probably escape."[10]

This gruesome story is not an invention—the histories record cases where widows cut off ears, fingers, or nose to avoid remarriage (Fig. 13). Some opted for suicide.

Kin structure, as depicted in these stories and in Han art, is the patriline formed by fathers and sons. The nuclear family—the dominant form of Han households—is fundamentally unsafe for the patriline because it incorporates women from outside. Relations with wives, in-laws, mothers, and stepmothers all threaten the sole reliable tie, that between father and son. Loyal to her natal family, to a future second husband, and to her biological children, a wife menaces both her spouse and his offspring. This is especially true of stepmothers, but all women are threats, even a mother, if she remarries after the death of her husband, or has too much influence over the behavior of her sons. The intensity of this suspicion of women is shown by the extraordinary acts of self-negation to which they are called in order to demonstrate their loyalty to a patriline. For male members of a patriline, physical mutilation and suicide were among the highest crimes, threats not only to the self but to the lineage. That women could have been celebrated for such actions shows their marginal position in classicist thinking.[11]

The wife in these stories stands in the same relation to the patriline as a household servant. An outsider tied to the kin group through the exchange of loyalty for employment or recognition, she is linked to the lineage in the same manner that assassins and ministers were tied to their lord in the Warring States period. It is no coincidence that the extreme acts by which the women in these stories prove themselves are the same self-negating acts by which exemplary assassins and loyal ministers of the Warring States proved their devotion to their lords.[12]

Fathers do not appear in these stories, and their responsibility to motherless orphans is never called a "public duty." Fathers needed no such parables on proper behavior because they were both the constituents of the patriline and its beneficiaries. The private love of men for their sons (and concern for their material self-interest) coincided with their public duty. For women, on the other hand, love and duty were sometimes antithetical, and the former might have to be sacrificed to the latter. To the extent that the Han kin system followed the teachings of the classics, it forced women into the position of outsider, condemned them as morally deficient for being in that position, and then offered them the possibility of redemption through renouncing their emotions, abandoning their in-

Fig. 13　The virtuous woman of Liang holding a mirror and knife to cut off her nose, as the ruler's messenger arrives.

terests, and if necessary committing self-mutilation, infanticide, or suicide.[13]

In practice, women successfully subverted these teachings at every turn. The most detailed evidence for the ability of women to pursue their own interests comes from accounts of the political power of imperial affines (relations by marriage). Just as mothers dominated private households, so dowager empresses wielded great authority during the Qin and Han empires. The First Emperor's mother was a powerful presence at court during his youth. The Han founder's widow also dominated the court and filled it with her kin. And Emperor Wu's mother controlled the early years of his reign. Starting with its fourth emperor, the Eastern Han was ruled by a succession of boys whose courts were guided by their mothers and her kin, or by the eunuchs who shared inner chambers with the imperial women. In many cases, imperial wives or concubines controlled their adult husbands as well. Particularly notable is the case of Emperor Cheng (r. 33–7 B.C.), whose reign was dominated by his inability to produce a male heir but who, according to the histories, killed two such heirs because they threatened the position of his favorite wife.[14]

Domination by dowager empresses or wives was made possible by the shift of authority from the official bureaucracy to the emperor's private chambers. With increasing concentration of power in the person of the emperor, the conduct of government business was moved from the outer offices and court assemblies into this "inner court." Policy decisions, with their decrees and proclamations, came to be handled by those gathered around the emperor. At first, these were the private secretaries who made up the secretariat. In time, even greater influence was wielded by eunuchs who looked after the emperor's bodily needs, or by the women of his harem and their kin. While none of these people had formal power, they controlled the conduct of business through immediate access to the person of the ruler.[15] This pattern was repeated in the centuries following the Han, in which the secretariat became the officially recognized center of power, only to be supplanted by newly emergent offices in even closer physical proximity to the emperor.

Gender and the Spatial Structuring of Power

From earliest times, Chinese political power was articulated in terms of the authority of the inner over the outer. Temples, palaces, and houses in early China and throughout its history were walled on the outside, and the first buildings encountered after entering the gate were the more public ones where men conducted their business. Here "insiders," that is, members of a family or the ruler and his household, would receive people from the outside. As a visitor moved toward the back, buildings became more "inner" and private, and access to them became more restricted. In a residential compound, these buildings would be the private chambers of the men and women of the house. In an imperial palace, these buildings would be the emperor's living quarters, which in the Han dynasty became the locus of the inner court.[16]

The earliest known expression of this pattern is the Western Zhou temple/palace compound at Fengchu in Shaanxi province.[17] The entry gate in the south-facing wall led into a front courtyard, along the north side of which was the front hall. Behind this hall were two smaller courtyards divided by a corridor that led to the back hall where the temple was located. Rows of side chambers lined the east and west walls. Thus, a single central axis through the gate, across the courtyard, up into the front hall, down through a corridor between the two rear courtyards, and finally to the back hall moved the ritual procession inward toward the temple at the rear of the complex.

The temple itself was arranged with the tablets of the most recent ancestors nearest the front, and with the shrine dedicated to the founding ancestor at the very back. Consequently this inward movement marked a movement backward in time as well, from the present day through the sequence of ancestors, to the origins of the ruling house. Since the authority of the Zhou kings was based on their access to the spirit power of potent ancestors, this movement inward toward the ancestors was also a movement to both the origin and center of the dynasty's power.[18]

The structural principles of this early Zhou temple complex provided the template for later Chinese palaces and dwellings, at least among the elite. Passages in the *Records of Ritual*, the *Transmissions of Master Zuo* (*Zuo zhuan*), and other Warring States texts describe dwelling compounds formed along a similar horizontal axis moving from an outer gate to private chambers, through alternating buildings and courtyards. While no examples of Han houses survive, models of individual buildings have been found in tombs, and images of walled compounds composed of alternating courtyards and buildings appear on several tomb walls.[19]

The significance of such a structure is suggested in a story in the *Analects* (*Lun yu*) telling of Confucius' encounter with his son in the family home:

Chen Kang asked Bo Yu [Confucius' eldest son], "Have you learned anything different [from what we have]?" Bo Yu replied, "Not yet. Once he [Confucius] was standing alone, and as I hastened respectfully past the courtyard he said, 'Have you studied the *Odes*?' I replied, 'Not yet.' He said, 'If you do not study the *Odes*, you will be unable to properly speak.' So I withdrew and studied the *Odes*. On another day when he was standing alone, I hastened respectfully past the courtyard and he said, 'Have you studied the *Rites*?' I replied, 'Not yet.' He said, 'If you do not study the *Rites*, you will be unable to properly stand.' So I withdrew and studied the *Rites*. I have learned these two things from him." Chen Kang withdrew and happily said, "Having asked one thing, I have learned three. I have learned about the *Odes* and the *Rites*, and I have also learned how the true gentleman keeps his son at a distance."[20]

Confucius as the ideal father stands in majesty overlooking the courtyard, like the ruler at a court assembly. His son respectfully scurries along the side corridors, speaking only when addressed. As Chen Kang notes, the lesson on the proper relations of father and son is clear, and it is mapped out in the placement and movement of people through the dwelling compound.

During the Warring States and early imperial periods, political power was walled off and rendered invisible, or visible only in the walls and towers that were its outer manifestation. This was true particularly of rulers, who for security and the cultivation of an aura of spiritual power were hidden from the outside world. In the case of the First Emperor, this tendency toward withdrawal and invisibility was treated as a sign of despotism and megalomania. But by the Western Han, the characterization of imperial power as hidden or "forbidden" to ordinary people was routine and built into the spatial organization of the empire. Power was hidden behind not one wall but a whole series: those of the city, the palace district, the palace itself, the court, and finally the inner chambers. Passage through each wall was controlled, and each movement closer to the center was reserved for a smaller number of people. Power and prestige were marked by the ability to move ever inward into the holy of holies that was the imperial presence.

At the same time, gender in China was becoming spatially structured according to a logic of outer and inner. However, it was the theoretically powerless women who occupied the inner spaces, while men were assigned to the outer public realm.[21] Thus, the Chinese world was marked by a contradictory set of equations in which power was located in the hidden depths of the interior, women were also located in the interior, but women were to be excluded from power. The institutional expression of this contradiction was that as power flowed inward toward the hidden emperor, it flowed away from male officials in the outer public realm and into the hands of women, their kin, and the eunuchs who shared their physical space. This reality, which represented a radical disjunction between the formal institutions of power and its actual locations, always came as a shock and a scandal, despite its regular recurrence.

This spatial ordering of political authority linked power with interiority, secrecy, and origins. Since women occupied the deepest interior and the place of greatest secrecy, and since they were the physical origins of male heirs, their place within the structure of the Chinese household represented both a restriction and a source of power. It was a hidden power, however, kept secret rather than acknowledged. Whenever knowledge of this hidden power seeped out into the public realm, it was greeted with outrage.

Children in Early Imperial Life

The Han dynasty was the first period in which childhood became a topic of conscious literary reflection.[22] Several Western Han authors—Jia Yi, Dong Zhongshu, and Liu Xiang—wrote about "fetal instruction" as a means of influencing the moral development of the child at the earliest possible opportunity. This idea, first articulated in the Warring States text *Words of the States (Guo yu)* and elaborated by Jia Yi as a means of assuring the development of the imperial heir, stipulated that the mother should be guided by proper ritual in what she saw, ate, heard, said, and did while pregnant. If she was "stimulated" by good things, then the child would be good; if by bad things, then bad. This emphasis on the decisive importance of origins probably grew out of the argument in the *Canon of Change (Yi jing)* and in military texts that a process could best be determined at the moment of its inception. Although it is unclear how widespread the practice of fetal education might have been, a manual on its techniques found in a Mawangdui tomb dated 168 B.C. indicates that at least the elite attempted to employ it.

During the Eastern Han, theories about child development and the ability of education to alter inborn endowments spread widely. At a time when a classicist education was the approved avenue to office and when powerful families dominated court appointments through control of recommendations, scholars debated the relative importance of heredity, early experience, and book learning in forming character. Biographies of leading officials and scholars routinely included long discussions of childhood actions or experiences that presaged or led to later eminence.[23]

Great emphasis was placed on literary prodigies who could recite and discourse on the classics in their early teens or even younger—Zhang Ba is described as understanding the principles of yielding and filial piety at the age of two, and Zhou Xie displayed such virtues at three months (Fig. 14). These examples led to debates about the significance of early achievements as signs of later intellectual and moral development. Critics of the cult of prodigies argued that "small vessels are quickly filled."[24]

The following account of childhood not only casts light on the ideal of education and scholarship in the Eastern Han but also the relations between adults and children in the period:

Fig. 14   Teacher on a dais instructing the sons of a household who are seated sequentially by age and size.

In the third year of *jianwu* [A.D. 27] Wang Chong was born. As a child when playing with his companions, he disliked all deception or bullying. His comrades loved to trap birds, catch cicadas, gamble for money, and play on stilts. He alone refused to do so, to the amazement of his father. At six, they began to teach him texts. He was respectful, honest, kind, and obedient, completely mastering ritual reverence. He was grave, earnest, and quiet, resolved on becoming an official. His father never beat him, his mother never criticized him, and fellow villagers never scolded him. When he was eight years old, he went to school, where there were over a hundred small boys. For offenses they had to bare the right shoulder, and were whipped for bad writing. Chong's writing progressed daily, and he never committed any offense. When he could write, his teacher gave him the *Analects* and the *Canon of Odes*. He daily read a thousand characters.[25]

Those under seven *sui* (six years old in Western terms) were exempted from the poll tax, and this seems to have been the standard division between infancy and childhood. Children were said to begin developing understanding at this age and could then enter school (although prodigies were an exception to this rule).[26] One did not become an adult until the age of twenty (for males), at which point a capping ceremony was held. Even here there were later demarcations, such as registration for military service that in some times and places was done at twenty-three or twenty-six.

Disaster relief edicts in the Eastern Han specified that aid would go only to those above the age of six, and the death of a child was not as significant as that of an adult. In the Qin code it was legal to kill a physically handicapped child. An Eastern Han stele to an adult named Zheng Gu refers to an older brother who died at the age of seven *sui* but is never mentioned by name and does not receive his own stone. He appears only as an incident in the funerary account of his younger brother. Children who died under the age of six were categorized as "early deaths for whom no mourning garments are worn." Deaths between the age of six and twenty, the age at which the attainment of full humanity is acknowledged with the capping ceremony, were divided into three categories of "early death."[27]

Children could not participate fully in the funerals of others because,

Fig. 15   Child seated on a dais, faced by infants playing with animals. The lower register depicts a musician, sleeve dancer, and juggler entertaining the household.

according to Zheng Xuan, a Han commentator, children "are not yet full people." While this statement represents how families formally viewed their children, in actual practice parents no doubt felt great affection for individual sons and even daughters and were not as callous as the ritual texts suggest. This idea is supported by Eastern Han stone inscriptions devoted to dead children which depict them playing with their toys and grievously mourn their deaths (Fig. 15).[28]

As for children's relations to their parents, the key term in Han sources is filial piety (*xiao*). This entailed honoring and obeying one's parents when they were alive, sacrificing to them after their death, and adhering to their guidance throughout one's life. Such conduct was held to be natural, as stated in the *Canon of Filial Piety* (*Xiao jing*): "Affection for parents grows up in early childhood, but in the act of nourishing parents daily become more severe. The sages proceeded from the severity to teach respect, and from the affection to teach love . . . This was the root. The Way of father and son is Heaven-conferred nature, and also the principle of duty between ruler and subject." Filial piety was thus the basis of being a proper subject. Not surprisingly, the *Canon of Filial Piety* was the first text studied in Han schools. In addition to inculcating the fundamental virtues of the son and the subject, it had the advantage of using only three hundred and eighty-eight different characters—all of them fairly common.[29]

The temple names of all Han emperors were preceded by the epithet *xiao*, indicating that they too were obedient sons. Given the Western Han's notion that the empire belonged to the Liu clan, and the Eastern Han's emphasis on filial piety as the foundation of all virtues, this routine application of the adjective "filially pious" to all emperors emphasized that they were members of a lineage and as such bound to revere and follow the precedents established by earlier rulers. The ultimate target of all imperial filial piety, and the supreme source of authoritative precedent, was the founder Gaozu. He alone did not receive the epithet *xiao*.

The emperor also had to be filial toward Heaven, whose "son" or "child" he was. Often during the Eastern Han, the emperor as "child of Heaven" was indeed a child himself, owing filial piety and obedience to a regent and a dowager empress. Some courtiers manipulated the imperial succession by enthroning an infant or young child who served as a puppet and figurehead for powers ruling from "behind the screen." These were generally the maternal relatives of the emperor, specifically his mother (or maternal grandmother) and her brothers. In this way, the "outer relatives," or relatives by marriage, dominated the imperial household and threatened the imperial patriline at its very core.

Adult Women and Men

As the position of women was discussed at length above, I shall here examine only the most prominent case of female authority, the history of the imperial house of Liu. With the death of Gaozu, his empress became regent in 188 B.C., and from the beginning she was depicted by Han loyalists as an unlawful usurper. She never declared herself ruler, but she issued edicts with unquestioned authority and elevated her own kin to the highest posts. When she died eight years later, her relations unsuccessfully attempted to eliminate the Liu house, thus causing her to become a watchword for treacherous outer relations.

Not every empress dowager took advantage of her station to this extent, but it became a fixed precedent that she approved the new heir in the absence of a clear claimant. The empress dowager also selected the regent of a child emperor, if she did not fill the role herself, and she usually chose a man from her own clan. This was how Wang Mang rose to power in the Western Han. In the Eastern Han, succession became a constant worry. After the first three rulers, virtually all the emperors acceded while still children. Since eight of the eleven empresses were childless, competition for power arose among offspring of concubines. No fewer than seven regents controlled the empire for a total of thirty-seven years.

Empresses thus came to be representatives of their natal clans and were chosen to link the Liu house to lineages that dominated different regions of the empire. Four different lineages supplied two empresses each, and through the empress's ability to secure court appointments for her relatives, these lineages obtained tremendous political influence and wealth during their periods of domination. However, rivalries with other families, the eunuchs, and the occasional emperor who reached adulthood shifted power among the lineages. Each fall of a lineage led to criminal proceedings, executions, and confiscations of wealth.

These "outer relatives" served as allies of the Liu house in their attempts to impose their will on the bureaucracy. Thus, Emperor Wu sought to increase his personal authority by transferring the conduct of business to the private chambers where his women dwelled, and he often employed relatives by marriage in important posts, particularly in the military. He established the precedent of making the highest military officer the chief of the inner court, and he filled this post with a relative by marriage. Guangwu similarly filled his inner court with "outer relatives" and used them as a private government staff at the beginning of the Eastern Han. Most of the political history of the Eastern Han consists of the struggle between eunuch factions and imperial affines for control of the inner court where actual authority resided.

One key female role in early imperial China was that of the concubine or secondary wife. Men could have only one legal wife, but those with money could keep other women in their households, who provided sexual services and cared for children. The role of concubine does not figure prominently in ritual texts, and it seems to have been largely a concession to conventional practice, although the emperor had a legal harem of hundreds or thousands of women. However, one Eastern Han stele from Sichuan is dedicated to a concubine who died at the age of fourteen. This provides our best account of the secondary wife.

> When she entered the household,
> She was diligent in care and earnest in attention.
> She nourished and ordered our familial Way,

Treating all our ancestors as lofty.
She sought good fortune without straying,
Her conduct omitting or adding nothing.
Keeping herself frugal, she spun thread,
And planted profitable crops in the orchards and gardens.
She respected the legal wife and instructed the children,
Rejecting arrogance, never boasting of her kindnesses.
The three boys and two girls
Kept quiet within the women's apartments.
She made the girls submissive to rituals,
While giving the boys power.
Her chastity exceeded that of ancient times,
And her guidance was not oppressive.
All our kin were harmonious and close,
Like leaves attached to the tree.[30]

Allowing for a level of hyperbole that was already criticized in Eastern Han times, we have here a useful sketch of what was hoped for in a secondary wife. It stresses spinning and the sale of garden crops. Even more important is the insistence on her adoption of the practices of her new clan (their "Way"), her reverence for the clan's ancestors, and her obedience to the legal wife. This lasted even into death. Another stele mourns the loss of a wife who, instead of being interred with the three sons who tragically preceded her in death, was buried instead with her mother-in-law to forever serve her in the afterlife.[31]

Early ritual handbooks depict a lineage in which women are subordinate and the eldest male member of the senior branch exerts considerable power. Likewise, the husband was to be master of his house. He was entitled to punish household members, but—theoretically at least—was not allowed to mutilate or kill them. Capital punishment, even for slaves, was reserved for the magistrate. The Qin code also privileged seniority within a family, effectively writing filial piety into law. An adult son's accusation of a parent could not be accepted as evidence, and the accuser himself could be punished. If a son beat his grandparents, he was tattooed and assigned to forced menial labor. The mere accusation of unfilial conduct might be punishable by death. A father was legally privileged in relation to his children: "A father stealing from his children is not a case of theft. Now a foster father steals from his foster children. How is he to be sentenced? It is warranted to be considered a case of theft." A father could also arrange to have the government banish, beat, or even execute his children.[32]

The power and position of a lineage chief derived from the accumulated force of his ancestors. The founder of an empire or a fief created a store of potency that passed to his successors but declined over time. One rich in potency enjoyed a long and brilliant posterity, while the posterity of one poor in potency soon faded. The clearest example of this was again the Liu house. The failure of the last three Western Han emperors to produce heirs proved to many that the potency of the line was exhausted, so it would soon be replaced. This argument was invoked to support Wang Mang's attempt to establish a new imperial lineage. Guangwu's restoration of the Han revived the dynasty in midcourse and gave it a new store of potency. At lower levels of society, potency, instead of dissipating, could accumulate over the generations, ultimately bearing fruit in successful offspring who lifted the whole line to empire-wide glory. The dynastic histories suggest that most men who attained prominence came from families that had been locally eminent for several generations.[33]

One expression of this belief that immediate ancestors assured success was the increasing emphasis in the Eastern Han on lavish burials for parents. A debate over elaborate versus moderate funerals had raged since at least the fourth century B.C., but in the Eastern Han the pendulum swung decisively in favor of great expenditure. Families sought to outdo one another in ostentatious spending on parents' funerals, along with protracted periods of mourning marked by severe austerities, and then used these displays to claim office on the basis of filial piety. Critics complained that many families spent little money on elderly parents when they were still alive, only to squander fortunes on their burials. Offspring erected stones and shrines inscribed with florid eulogies, absurdly exaggerating the greatness of the deceased father.[34] While these conspicuously wasteful funerals certainly were a contest for prestige, they may also have aimed to repay the ancestor for the material blessings gained through his potency, to secure the future support of ancestral spirits, and to assure the current generation of the excellence of the stock from which they sprang.

Not everyone agreed that a lineage could generate potency that resulted in virtuous and successful offspring. In debates on the value and purpose of education, some argued that learning and attainments depended on individual effort or endowment. Descended from a line of merchants and with a father and grandfather known for unruly behavior, the first-century Eastern Han scholar Wang Chong argued that brilliant men appeared individually and not as members of prominent families. Forty or fifty years later Wang Fu likewise denounced reliance on good connections and clan renown.[35] However, he and Wang Chong agreed that most people of their day attributed worth and attainments to clan background, and the biographies in the dynastic histories confirm that few men in the Eastern Han rose to high government office without an impressive pedigree.

Elders and Ancestors

To some extent in early imperial China, potency was measured by longevity. Confucius said that the benevolent lived long, and some Han thinkers held this to be literally true, while acknowledging inexplicable exceptions.[36] Thus, the endurance of both a lineage and an individual were traced back to a common source in the virtuous potency generated by correct and effective action. Veneration of the aged was a value in Chinese society that long antedated the Han.

The importance of caring for the elderly was suggested in the *Mencius*'s account of an ideal realm: "If mulberry is planted in every homestead of five *mu* of land, then those who are fifty can wear silk. If chickens, pigs, and dogs do not miss their breeding season, then those who are seventy can eat meat . . . Exercise care over education in the village schools, and discipline the people by teaching them the duties proper to sons and younger brothers, and those whose hair has turned grey will not carry loads on the roads."[37] While the last sentence suggests that respect for the aged might have been more common in ritual manuals than among the common people of the *Mencius*'s day, by the Han period reverence and care for elders were fundamental virtues.

Respect for elders took several forms. Regular awards of titles resulted in a rough association between rank and age, so that seating arrangements and distribution of food at state ceremonies tended to honor age. The laws also granted certain rights to the aged. In the Eastern Han a celebration was held each autumn at the Old Man Star Shrine south of the capital. During this feast those who had reached the age of seventy were given imperial staffs and fed by hand with rice gruel (on the assumption that they had lost their teeth). The staff had a model of a dove perched on its top, because the dove was said to never choke, a blessing to be imparted upon the staff's recipient. These staffs, as gifts from the emperor, granted the holder prestige and protection.

In one case found on a set of bamboo strips, an official struck an old man, thus causing him to drop his staff and break the dove. Since the object was the emperor's gift, the official was executed for breaking it. Han decrees asserted that villages gave precedence to elders, and they equated status based on age with status at court. The Eastern Han state-sponsored ritual compendia *Comprehensive Discourses of the White Tiger Hall* (*Bo hu tong*) also stated that the elderly were exempt from punishments, stressful mourning obligations, and compulsory labor service.[38]

The ideal life-span was seventy years. Confucius had reached seventy-two, Liu Xiang and Yang Xiong seventy-one. Stelae often recorded that those who died in their fifties had experienced an early death. But living out one's full span was a mixed blessing, for Han people were fully aware of the physical horrors of old age:

> The essential spirit dissipates,
> And the body's frame is ugly and vile.
> Irregular teeth rise and fall in cadence,
> While the bones are withered, the flesh grubby.
> Declining into old age, in desperate straits,
> No teeth to eat.
> Sick with piles, parched and tubercular,
> They go to dwell in darkness.
> The aged become hump-backed.
> The teeth have gaps and are loose.
> Nearing earth and far from Heaven,
> They descend to enter the Yellow Springs.[39]

The transience of youth and its pleasures was also a theme in the poetry of the period, especially the *Nineteen Old Poems*:

> Turning my carriage, I yoke the horses and go,
> On and on I travel down the long road.
> How desolate on every side,
> As an eastern wind rocks the grasses.
> Nothing I meet is familiar,
> How could this not hasten old age?

> Prosperity and decline each has its season,
> I grieve that I did not make a name for myself earlier.
> Human life lacks the permanence of metal and stone.
> How could we lengthen its years?
> We suddenly transform, in the way of all matter,
> But a glorious name is a lasting treasure.[40]

Another key element of early imperial kin structure was the memory of ancestors and their preservation in cult. The further back one could trace ancestry, the larger number of kin one could claim, and the more people one might appeal to in times of need. A family that could remember no further than one or two generations was linked to only a few households, but a lineage that traced its ancestry through multiple generations could bring together hundreds of households. Thus remembering and honoring ancestors was essential to structuring present-day society.

Because kin ties were defined by shared links to dead ancestors, ritual handbooks state that the shrine had two purposes: to remember one's ancestry and to determine how closely related each member of the lineage was. The system of ordering the lineage was known as the "Five Degrees of Mourning Attire." If a son mourned his father, he wore the most humble clothes (an unhemmed, coarse hemp garment) for the longest time (into the third year following death). If he mourned a paternal great grandfather's brother's wife, then he wore the least humble clothing (the finest hemp) for the shortest time (three months). The five degrees thus formed a system that was highly complex and totally inclusive. Someone who did not fit into any category was not a relative. The *Record of Ritual* states that if you are related to the deceased even by the fifth degree of mourning, then you must go vast distances to attend the funeral, but you should not attend the funeral of an unrelated person, even your nearby neighbor.[41] This is an extreme formulation, and we cannot know how closely such precepts were followed. The recent discovery at Mawangdui of a chart of kin ties inscribed with the mourning system suggests that lineage structure was taken seriously.

This ritual remembrance of the dead was reflected in Chinese depictions of human life span and survival across time. The Chinese term for longevity is *shou*, and its most common simile (as in the poem above) is "longevity like metal and stone." However, *shou* was not limited to physical life but also referred to descendants remembering an individual and preserving him in sacrificial cult. This is the longevity of a social identity made possible by the survival of a kin group, or in exceptional cases of literary works. Worshippers wished *shou* upon the spirit of Gaozu in services at his shrine, and the *Canon of Filial Piety* defines shrines as places where supreme reverence prevents forgetting ancestors. The *Canon of the Way and Its Power* (*Dao de jing*) likewise states, "Those who die but are remembered possess *shou*."[42] The poem cited above concludes that while the physical body will invariably "transform" and pass away, a glorious name is a treasure that may endure across the ages in cult or literature.

In Han ancestral cult, the soul of the deceased survived as long as the living cherished and cared for it. When the soul ceased to receive offerings, then it faded away. This fading was not left to chance. Ritual texts described a process of "structured amnesia" in which the oldest shrines were sequentially discarded. On the imperial level, the four most recent ancestors had shrines where they received offerings. When a new generation was added, the fourth shrine was discarded and the others were each moved back one place. As Kuang Heng, the chancellor under Emperor Yuan, said: "Setting up the four ancestral shrines marks your closeness to recent ancestors. As closeness fades, the shrines are eliminated in turn. The decline from near to far demonstrates that there is an ultimate end."[43]

The sole exception to the process of fading was the founder of the empire or fief, who could not be forgotten. So, ideally, there were five shrines to receive seasonal sacrifices. The Zhou dynasty is said to have had seven shrines—the four shrines of the immediate ancestors, one for the mythic creator of agriculture, Houji, who had founded the Zhou in receiving a fief, and one each for Kings Wen and Wu whose conquest of the Shang transformed the Zhou from a fief into a kingdom. Thus, the longevity of the spirit was directly tied to its contribution to the longevity of the line in having established a kingdom or other lasting form.

At the end of the Western Han, it was argued that the founder was not the only emperor who deserved perpetual remembrance. The first arguments were made in favor of Emperor Wu, who had attacked the Xiongnu, reformed the calendar, and established the sacrificial cults. Since his descendants still felt his influence generations after his death, it was proper that they should still worship at his altar.[44] The argument was accepted, and Emperor Wu was made a permanent ancestor, like Gaozu.

This move set a precedent. Western Han officials debated who should receive permanent remembrance in a cult, but in the Eastern Han they only debated who should *not* receive it. By the time of the penultimate ruler, Emperor Ling (r. 168–189), all seven previous adult emperors plus another emperor from the Western Han had been granted permanent cult status. None of them had founded an empire or gained land, and few had made any contribution at all, but it proved difficult to offer permanent worship to some and deny it to others.[45]

Below the imperial level, permanent remembrance of the dead was also fostered by the placement of inscribed stone stelae at the graveside. These were the public equivalent of the tablets kept in ancestral shrines. One inscription boasted: "By engraving the stone and erecting the stele, the inscription of merit is made vastly illustrious. It will be radiant for a hundred thousand years, never to be extinguished . . . Establishing one's words so that they do not decay is what our ancestors treasured. Recording one's name on metal and stone hands it down to infinity."[46]

Thus, in the course of the Han, ancestral remembrance that faded over time was replaced by a search for the permanence of metal and stone. Eternal ancestors secured permanent lineages and an undying state, but in the end everything perished nonetheless.

8

RELIGION

RELIGION in imperial China dealt with the realm of "spirits" (*shen*) and "shadow" (*yin*).[1] From earliest times, the Chinese offered sacrifices to a spirit world that paralleled the human. The two realms—the visible and invisible—were roughly parallel, and the dying moved from one to the other. Religious practice largely consisted of trying to control the flow of people and influences between these two realms: to secure the departure of the dead and prevent their return, and at the same time to guide the flow of energies, blessings, or information back to the human realm at licit points of contact between spirits and men.

These nodes of communication and exchange were sometimes personalized (as in divination, dreams, or trances), sometimes localized (as in sacred places or shrines), and sometimes generally visible as omens but subject to disputed interpretation (as in prodigies such as comets, eclipses, droughts, or the raining of blood).

Points of Contact

One point of contact between the visible and invisible realms was the sacrificial shrine or altar. Through ritual performances, the site of sacrifice was transformed into a sacred zone cut off from the mundane world. It was an arena of ritual time and space in which conventional physical processes and modes of perception ceased to operate. This ritual realm is invoked in a sacrificial hymn to the Han founder Gaozu written by one of his consorts:

Floating on high in every direction,
Music fills the hall and court.
The incense sticks are a forest of feathers,
The cloudy scene an obscure darkness.
Metal stalks with elegant blossoms,
A host of flags and kingfisher banners.
The "Seven Origins" and "Blossoming Origins" music
Are solemnly intoned as harmonious sounds.
So one can almost hear
The spirits coming to feast and frolic.
The spirits are seen off to the *zhu zhu* of the music,
Which refines and purifies human feelings.
Suddenly the spirits ride off on the darkness,
And the brilliant event concludes.
Purified thoughts grow hidden and still,
And the warp and weft of the world fall dark.[2]

The sacred space blurred ordinary sense perceptions with smoke, incense, music, and the forest of banners. The chief sacrificer prepared for his contact with the spirits by fasting and meditation. This extended deprivation not only cleansed the body but also induced a mental state more susceptible to perceiving uncanny phenomena. In the atmosphere of the ritual scene, the carefully prepared participants could hear the spirits come to feast with their living kin and then see them depart before the world settled into blackness. Such scenes are described in some of the songs of the Zhou *Canon of Odes* (*Shi jing*), where spirits grow drunk on sacrificial wine.[3]

A second point of contact between the visible and invisible was through spirit intermediaries who traveled through the *yin* realm and communicated with its inhabitants. A century or two before the Han, the "Nine Songs" now preserved in the *Songs of Chu* (*Chu ci*) evoked performances in which male and female shamans sang and danced for the gods in a form of divine courtship.[4]

During the Han, spirit intermediaries fell into trances or performed ecstatic dances to summon up the dead, cure diseases, and bring rain. Ritual specialists from the far southeastern region of Yue were especially favored at court for their extraordinary powers. The Western Han historian Sima Qian sneers at how religious figures duped Emperor Wu with

Fig. 16   The Queen Mother of the West seated on a mountain top.

Fig. 17   Two immortals playing the *liu bo* board game, seated on top of stylized mountains.

shadow plays and obscure words. One master of esoteric arts from the northeast named Luan Da gained the emperor's ear and was granted a seal of office and a marquisate of 2,000 households. Sima Qian observes: "Everyone on the seacoast of Yan and Qi [in the northeast] began waving his arms about, proclaiming that he possessed secret arts and could summon spirits and the immortals."[5]

The status of such figures declined over the course of the dynasty, and increasing restrictions were placed upon them. Men who married shamans were banned from holding office, although the ban was sometimes ignored. Spirit intermediaries were forbidden to ply their trade along the sides of roads, and in some cases were even banned from taking money.[6] Nevertheless, such people continued to perform religious services at all levels of Chinese society.

The visible and invisible also came together on the peaks of mountains, in high towers, or at the eastern or western ends of the earth. Both the First Emperor and Emperor Wu sought to encounter immortals by ascending mountains and building towers, and they sent expeditions across the Eastern Sea (the Pacific Ocean) in search of the floating islands of the immortals. The far west, in contrast, was the realm of the immortal Queen Mother of the West, who dwelt on the heights of Mount Kunlun, the axis mundi (Figs. 16 and 17). In a third-century B.C. text she was visited by King Mu of the Zhou, which provided a historical precedent for the aspirations of later emperors.

The belief that the realms of the living and of spirits were connected through vertical ascent also underlies the Han funerary practice of planting trees on the tops of tombs. Trees grew on mountains, and immortals dwelled in their branches. The bronze "money trees" of Sichuan depicted the Queen Mother of the West with her court in the branches of trees patterned on the "sun-trees" of the realms of the immortals. Fired clay trees featured winged immortals perched in the branches and human figures on the ground at their base.[7]

A fourth point of contact was divination—understanding and influencing future events. Cracking bones or plastrons (the flat lower plate of a turtle shell) to discern the will of the spirits began in Neolithic times and continued into the Han. In the *Canon of Change* (*Yi jing*), formulas were used to divine a course of action through the casting of yarrow stalks. Texts discovered in tombs reveal divinatory practices based on the day in which an activity was to be undertaken, in the manner of later Chinese almanacs. Related texts predicted the course of a disease on the basis of the day it had begun. A similar form of divination discovered at a Han tomb in Yinwan combined movement along a common cosmic chart with a calendar to divine what activities were suitable for a given day. All these modes of divination were based on the idea that time was not a continuous, homogeneous medium but a variable sequence in which each unit had a distinct nature and was thus suitable for different activities.[8]

Other forms of divination entailed reading elements of the natural environment, including wind or other meteorological phenomena (Fig. 18). A text discovered at Mawangdui presents pictures of comets, circles around the sun, and other visible patterns in the sky. To these images it appends texts stating what events they foretell. Stellar divination was widely practiced, particularly the form in which a diviner's board or cosmograph oriented the diviner within the universe to provide insight into the circumstances of the inquirer. Sima Qian's *Shi ji* contains a lengthy discussion of astrological divination based on the stars.[9]

Another category of divination was the reading of destiny in external forms. Physiognomy (physical appearance) could foretell the future of individuals, whether man or beast. A text discovered at Mawangdui describes the art of physiognomizing horses, and other texts mention its application to dogs. Military bamboo strips found at Juyan discuss the physiognomy of swords. Even the shapes of vessels and utensils could provide matter for divination, but the texts on this subject have been lost. Linked to physiognomy were early forms of geomancy—techniques for

Fig. 18   Thunder god on his cloud chariot, drawn by dragons, with the thunder drum mounted above.

reading the future from the shape of the earth, just as one read the shape of a face.[10]

Dreams were read as omens, and pre-Han texts refer to books on dream interpretation and specialists in their use. Spirits of the dead or gods appeared to the living in dreams and made demands of them, such as providing a proper burial or giving service in the realm of the dead. Sometimes they provided information, the accuracy of which validated the authority of the dream. Other dreams were coded symbols—for example, a dream of the sun presaged an audience with the ruler. Understanding such dreams required either the assistance of experts or recourse to a manual. In narratives the act of interpreting the dream guided the future, so that the ability to give a positive reading to a seemingly negative dream resulted in a happy outcome.[11] This is important, for Chinese divination was usually regarded more as a guide to action than as the report of a fixed fate. Divination provided not knowledge of a preordained future but understanding of trends so as to act upon events with the greatest efficacy.

Unusual events in nature (prodigies) were read as omens, most often as signals to the emperor. Some writers interpreted prodigies as warnings from a sentient and active Heaven, while others depicted them as mechanical products of hidden "resonances" among Heaven, Earth, and man. Any improper action, particularly the potent actions of the ruler, generated energies that upset the conventional processes or cycles of nature. Punishments that were too severe, women or ministers growing too powerful at court, or anything else disturbing the proper course of events generated forces that elicited corresponding disturbances in the natural world. This was likened to plucking a string on one musical instrument, and thereby causing strings of the same pitch on other instruments to vibrate.

Historical records assisted in interpreting prodigies, because past eclipses and similar phenomena could be matched with simultaneous faults in government. The *Spring and Autumn Annals,* interpreted as Confucius' prophecy of the rise of the Han, were a great resource for such information. It became the *urtext* (an original text from which all later versions derive) for manuals of omen interpretation, as the following statement from Dong Zhongshu (ca. 179–104 B.C.) explains: "The Way of the *Spring and Autumn Annals* is to cite the past in order to explain the future. For this reason, when a phenomenon occurs in the world, look to see what comparable events are recorded in the *Annals.* Find out the essential meanings of its subtleties and mysteries in order to see what causes are implied. Changes wrought in Heaven and on earth, and events that affect a dynasty will then all become clear."[12]

Dong Zhongshu and others sought to influence court policy by interpreting omens on the basis of their knowledge of history and the classical canon. However, because any sign had many possible meanings, major schools of interpretation grew up around such figures as Jing Fang and Liu Xiang. The Eastern Han historian and poet Ban Gu gathered these conflicting readings into an unsuccessful synthesis in his chapters on omens in the *Book of the Han.*[13] Given the diversity of readings, it is unlikely that attempts to use interpretations of omens as a means of guiding policy ever achieved the desired effect.

Prophecies based on omens and numerological calculations were central to the so-called apocryphal texts. These claimed to be esoteric transmissions of prophecies that Confucius or other sages had hidden in canonical texts. They first appeared in the second half of the first century B.C., flourished under Wang Mang, and enjoyed great influence in the Eastern Han. Many broached dangerous political issues, such as calculations of the number of years that the Han would last, prophecies of the rise of a new ruler (Wang Mang), or forecasts of his fall and the restoration of the Han. They also contained material on the mathematical structures of the world, the shape of history, and mythical acts and attributes of the ancient sages. Despite a series of bans, the apocrypha remained influential through the centuries of division after the fall of the Han, when they routinely provided divine sanctions for dynastic transitions.

One feature common to all these points of contact with the spirit world was the need for a religious specialist or the expertise transmitted in texts. Sacrifice had its ritual specialists; shamans and esoteric masters served as spirit intermediaries; and divination was best performed by an expert. While any literate person could consult the *Canon of Change,* he or she might well misunderstand its cryptic formulas, and so an expert was valuable here as well. The interpretation of omens required both a thorough knowledge of history and a familiarity with the traditions of omen lore. Most people living in the Han did not have the capability to bridge the gap between the two realms without assistance. However, such a capacity could be acquired through training or textual study, and it required no inherent magical powers.

State Cults

Ancestral worship, the primary state cult of the Shang and Zhou, was supplanted in the Warring States by cults to cosmic divinities or important natural sites, especially mountains and rivers. This reflected the need of rulers to marginalize the Zhou monarch, who remained the apical figure of ancestral worship and the cult of Heaven, and to assert their own sacral nature through worshipping powerful cosmic spirits or divinities linked to their states.[14] This shifted emphasis from the temple, where offerings were made to deceased human ancestors, to the outdoor altar, where sacrifices were presented to spirits of nature and the cosmos. The distinction between human cults performed under a roof and natural cults performed under the open sky remained essential in later Chinese religion.

During the Qin dynasty, the First Emperor granted priority to natural deities by continuing the established worship of the directional *di*—held on outdoor altars—and introducing the *feng* and *shan* sacrifices on the peaks of Mount Tai and a nearby hill. The idea of such sacrifices emerged in the late Warring States, when writers asserted that they had been performed by all rulers who had established "Great Peace" throughout the world. *Feng* meant "enfeoffment," and Han sources show that this sacrifice marked the claim of sovereignty over a given area. In the case of the *feng* sacrifice initiated by the First Emperor, it marked the claim to world sovereignty.

The sacrifice, the details of which were probably invented by the emperor and his counselors, entailed making offerings at the foot of the mountain and then burying a written message to a high god at the summit. Both before and after its performance, the First Emperor ascended other peaks in east China to place inscribed stelae proclaiming his achievements. The *feng* sacrifice was part of a series of mountain offerings asserting sovereignty over his new territories and proclaiming his triumphs to gods and men. Performing the sacrifice marked the establishment of world sovereignty, recognized in the realms of mortals and spirits.

Masters of esoteric arts from the state of Qi, where Mount Tai lay, gave another interpretation. According to them, the sacrifice served to attain immortality, like the Yellow Emperor. After making his sacrifices, ascending the peak, and burying his proclamation, the First Emperor (and the Han Emperor Wu, who repeated the sacrifice) should have encountered immortals with whom he could ascend into the sky to dwell for all eternity. In another explanation provided by Confucian classicists, the sacrifice was offered to the Zhou deity Heaven, thus conflating this ritual with the cult to Heaven.[15]

The *feng* and *shan* sacrifices were exceptional performances. The most important regular state cult in the Qin and Western Han was to the four (later five) *di*. These governed the directions, and each was named by the color linked to its direction: green for east, red for south, yellow for the center, white for west, and black for north. The first recorded worship of *di* as a directional god (the name had earlier been applied to the Shang high god) was in Qin in the seventh century B.C. Qin initiated a cult to the white *di*, probably because it was the westernmost state and hence under the patronage of that god. It later added cults for the yellow, green, and red *di*, perhaps as the ritual expressions of conquests in the central states, Chu, and the east. The cult to the black *di* was begun by the Han founder Gaozu in 205 B.C., and from that time forward the *di* were worshipped as a group representing all of space.

As in other domains, the early Han carried forward Qin religious practices, not only continuing the sacrifices but entrusting them to the same offices and using the same music. Even the title *huangdi*, coined by the First Emperor from Qin's high gods, was used by Han emperors. The

Han continued to link the cult of the *di* to authority over the land, as indicated in the Han ritual of enfeoffment. The Son of Heaven had an altar to the soil (*she*) composed of five colors of earth. In the enfeoffment ceremony, the new fiefholder took a lump of the colored earth appropriate to his region. If he were to receive territory in the east, he would take greenish earth; if in the south, it would be reddish. The recipient carried the earth to his new state and mixed it into his *she* altar. In this ritual, the central altar of the soil was a microcosm, and its distribution marked the radiation of authority from the court across the world.[16]

Emperor Wu introduced several new cults, most importantly those to the Grand Unity (Tai Yi) and the Empress Earth. The former was originally a deity from the state of Chu, where the Han house of Liu originated. This deity's role was primarily to ward off weapons and to assure victory in battle. Both the Warring States philosophy text *Master Zhuang* (*Zhuangzi*) and the early Han philosophical compendium *Master of Huainan,* two texts associated with Chu, describe Tai Yi as the embodiment of the state of non-differentiation that existed prior to the division of the world into Heaven and Earth, *yin* and *yang*. A picture buried at Mawangdui a quarter century prior to the reign of Emperor Wu shows Tai Yi supplanting the Yellow Emperor to rule over the five *di*.

The cult of Tai Yi, as established by Emperor Wu, seems to have been understood as a culmination in offerings to a single, high god of the sacrifices to the *di*. Emperor Wu's pairing of the cult to Tai Yi with a cult to Empress Earth suggests that Tai Yi was a sky god who stood in complementary opposition to the earth god. It is perhaps as a sky god, an embodiment of the primal unity described in the philosophical texts, that he could ritually encompass the five *di*. It is also quite likely that the *feng* sacrifice performed by Emperor Wu was addressed to Tai Yi.[17]

During the last forty years of the Western Han, and above all under Wang Mang, the cults of the *di,* Tai Yi, and Empress Earth were gradually supplanted by the cult of Heaven enacted in the annual *jiao* sacrifice. Heaven had been the high god of the Zhou, but details of the Zhou kings' rituals were lost in the centuries of royal eclipse. By collecting and reinterpreting scattered references to sacrifices in the canonical texts, Han theorists such as Dong Zhongshu invented a theory that the Zhou king had offered a sacrifice to Heaven on a circular altar in the suburbs south of the capital at the New Year or beginning of the agricultural season. This ritual, like that of the *feng* and *shan* sacrifices, had no textual foundation but was invented to ritually depict the nature of the empire. Its "origins" were then found in the historical record through the imaginative reading of sources. Dong Zhongshu advocated this sacrifice to the old Zhou high god to Emperor Wu, possibly as a Confucian alternative to the world-encompassing sacrifice that combined the Qin cult of the *di,* the Chu god Tai Yi, and sacrifices at the eastern peak sacred to Qi. The proposal was ignored at the time, but in the long run it was the *jiao* sacrifice to Heaven rather than the *feng* to Tai Yi that became the central state rite.

The cults of Tai Yi and of Heaven were each supported by a different segment of the literati. In 31 B.C. the classicist scholar-official Kuang Heng, a supporter of the cult of Heaven, suggested moving the then-ascendant cult of Tai Yi to the southern suburbs and the cult of Empress Earth to the northern ones. He argued that the cost and dangers of the emperor's traveling to distant shrines and the ancient precedent for royal sacrifices at the capital favored this move. In equating Tai Yi with the cult of Heaven and Empress Earth with the cult of Earth, he treated their cults as degenerated versions of the canonical cults (which were themselves commentarial inventions).

Although the text is not clear, it appears that the first *jiao* sacrifice in the southern suburbs was offered to Tai Yi. When the offerings failed to produce an heir, Kuang Heng fell into disgrace. After a storm damaged the old site of the Tai Yi cult, Emperor Cheng was tormented by bad dreams, so the cult was shifted back to its original site, where its recipient was Tai Yi. The cult of Heaven was not established as the primary state cult until the rule of Wang Mang. He justified his assumption of power as a dispensation from Heaven, and when the Eastern Han founder Guangwu later resumed the *feng* sacrifice, he explained it as a means of notifying Heaven of the restoration of order. Shortly afterward, Eastern Han scholars led by Ban Biao (3–54 A.D.) revived the Zhou doctrine of the "Mandate of Heaven."[18]

The establishment of the cult of Heaven was linked to a radical reduction in the scale of the imperial ancestral cult. Shrines to the Han founder Gaozu had been established in every commandery of the empire, along with numerous shrines to Emperor Wen. By 40 B.C. there were 167 imperial ancestral shrines in the provinces as well as 176 in the capital. According to Han records, these shrines were the scenes of 24,455 offerings per year and employed 67,276 people as guards, musicians, dancers, and so on. In 40 B.C., in response to a memorial from the same officials who advocated the establishment of the cult of Heaven, all the shrines in the provinces were eliminated, as were most of those in the capital.[19]

While this was rationalized as an economy measure, its timing suggests a new emphasis on the status of the emperor as Son of Heaven and a reduction in the importance of the imperial ancestors' potency, which had been proclaimed in the formula "All under Heaven belongs to the Liu clan." This move was also consistent with the classicists' insistence on sacrifice as a privilege of lineal descendants. In their view, forcing officials in the provinces to make sacrifices to the spirits of imperial ancestors, who were not their own kin, was a violation of filial piety.

The Cult of the Dead

The cult of the dead was much more widespread than the state cults, being practiced by emperor, nobility, powerful families, and perhaps even peasants. However, only the elite recorded their activities in writing and buried their dead in stone or brick tombs that survived the centuries. The tension in the kin system between the patriline and the household had its ritual correlate in the division of the cult of the dead between the ancestral temple, where the lineage was ritually constituted, and the tomb, where the joint burial of husband and wife along with replicas or images of their life together reconstituted the household in the world of the dead.

By the fourth century B.C. certain tombs had taken on physical aspects of the household or palace, and by the Eastern Han all tombs other than the very poorest were modeled on houses. In the late Warring States period the idea that the tomb was a replica of the house was not only visible in practice but had become articulated as a theoretical principle. Thus the chapter on ritual in the Confucian philosophical text *Master Xun* (*Xunzi*) says: "In the funeral rites one adorns the dead with the trappings of the living. On a grand scale one imitates what he had in life to send him off to the dead. As though dead, but as though still alive; as though gone, but as though still present, the end and the beginning are one. Thus the form of the grave and grave mound imitates the house. The form of the inner and outer coffins imitates the side, top, front, and back boards of a carriage. The cover over the coffin with its decorations imitates the screens, curtains, and hangings of a room. The wooden lining and frame of the tomb imitate the rafters and beams of a roof and a fence."[20]

The patterning of the tomb on the household grew ever more detailed and widespread. From the middle of the Western Han, tombs were dug into the walls of cliffs and divided into compartments corresponding to a reception hall, the private quarters where the corpse was placed, and side chambers for storage. In the front and side chambers were buildings of timber with tile roofs, and in the rear hall a building of stone with stone doors. Middling landowners were buried in hollow-brick tombs built in horizontal pit caves. These were often shaped like a house, with a gabled roof and a door-shaped front wall. The hollow bricks were often stamped with designs, and polychrome murals were painted in some tombs, including images on the ceiling of the sun, the moon, and stars, as well as the animals of the four directions, or stories from history and literature.

Shortly afterward, chamber tombs with arches built of small bricks gradually supplanted all other tomb types throughout the empire. Tombs of nobles and high officials were built on a large scale patterned on the elaborate dwellings in which they had lived. Murals and frescoes depicted scenes of the life of the tomb's denizens, or an idealized vision of the afterlife toward which they aspired.

Finally, a new type of tomb constructed from dressed stones with engraved designs appeared in the Eastern Han. Once again the layout of the burial chamber imitated the house of the tomb's inhabitant, and many of the stones depicted household scenes or incidents from the career of the tomb's occupant. By the late first century A.D. the notion that a tomb was to be a replica of a house had become so conventional that the Eastern Han scholar Wang Chong asked the rhetorical question, "What difference is there between a house and a tomb?"[21] This assumed that everyone knew that there was no difference whatsoever.

While women had only a marginal role in the patriline, the underworld household of the tomb was in many ways defined by the link of husband and wife, who were ultimately buried together. Husbands and wives not only resided in the tomb as a pair of corpses, but there were images of them sitting together, as well as scenes of intimacy and physical affection. Some scenes depict the female attendants of the wife. They are often shown spinning and weaving fabrics, as well as collecting mulberry leaves. Other women appear as entertainers—both dancers and musicians—and as workers in the kitchens where banquets are being prepared.[22] The tombs, like the households themselves, were filled with women playing key roles.

Deities depicted in order to transform the tomb into a cosmos were also often women. In several tombs, one stands at a half-open door welcoming the deceased to the world of the dead (Fig. 19). The most frequently depicted deities in Han tombs were the Queen Mother of the West and the pair Fu Xi and Nü Gua. Standing at the gateway between Heaven and Earth at the pinnacle of Mount Kunlun, the Queen Mother

Fig. 19 Woman at the doorway, greeting the deceased to the afterlife, with the Queen Mother of the West and a bird (messenger?) seated at the side.

of the West was the ruler of the immortal realm to which the tomb denizens aspired (Fig. 20). Fu Xi and Nü Gua were a spirit couple who joined together to structure the world, and thus provided the divine model for both the household and the joint burial.[23] The importance of these goddesses in the world of the tomb is noteworthy because in texts they are minor figures. This disjunction between text and tomb translates into the spirit world the social split between the state-sanctioned patriline and the household run by women, with their unsanctioned influence.

In elite tombs of the Western Zhou dynasty, bronze vessels were the same as those used in ancestral temples, though in lower ranking tombs they were often replaced by pottery substitutes. By the middle of the Eastern Zhou a millennium later, the substitution of cheap imitations, known as "spirit vessels," for costly originals was standard in all but the most elaborate aristocratic tombs.[24] This distinction between the ritual vessels of the living and those buried with the dead marks an early stage in a dramatic shift away from a world based on the shared existence of the living and the dead. While early Zhou ritual had demonstrated the links between living and dead kin, who in the odes feast together, by the late Warring States the *separation* of the living and the dead had become a major aim of funerary ritual.

Fig. 20   The Queen Mother of the West seated on her throne composed of the Tiger (west) and Dragon (east), surrounded by her animal court, including the nine-tailed fox, the toad of the moon, and her messenger bird. The deceased couple is in the lower corner.

In place of the Zhou assemblages of ritual vessels, the grave goods of the late Warring States and the Han were largely objects of daily use (clothing, lacquer bowls and plates, pottery, food) or models or images of such objects, and other items of worldly life (houses, granaries, animals, and tools). Among these replicas and images were those of human beings, both the people buried in the tomb and the servants, entertainers, cooks, agricultural laborers, and others essential to household life.[25] These figures provided the dead with a full and happy existence in the tomb, an existence based on miniature replicas or images of the world of the living. The *Master Xun* insisted on this "imitation" in the tomb—that objects buried with the dead, while patterned on those of the living, must be clearly distinct.

While these ritual texts do not usually discuss the reasons for separating the dead from the living, one passage in the *Records of Ritual* makes the motive explicit: "When a ruler attended the funeral of an official, he brought with him a shaman carrying a peach branch and reed broom [to expel evil spirits], as well as a soldier with a lance. This is because they dread the spirits. It is the reason why they distinguish them from the living." The dead as depicted in some Eastern Han tomb texts were frightening ghosts who inflicted disease or misfortune on the living unless they were securely imprisoned in a tomb.[26] A grave ordinance inscribed on a jar in the year 175 A.D. declares that "the family of Xu Wentai, including his sons, grandsons, and all later generations, no longer has any connection with the deceased." It then declaims in rhyming parallelism the necessary separation of the living and the dead:

High Heaven is blue [*cang cang*],
The underworld limitless [*mang mang*].
The dead return to the shadows [*yin*],
The living to the light [*yang*].
The living have their villages [*li*],
The dead their hamlets [*xiang*].
The living are subordinate to the western Chang'an [*an*],
The dead to the eastern Mount Tai [*shan*].
In joy they do not remember one another,
In bitterness they do not long for one another.

The text then states that if Xu is found guilty of any crimes in the underworld, a wax figure presumably buried with him should substitute for him in performing convict labor, so that Xu need never again impose on his living kin. It also states that earlier ancestors should not be allowed to compel the recently deceased to perform penal labor in their place. These passages provide our best evidence of an Eastern Han belief that the dead were subjected to judgment and penal servitude imposed by a bureaucratic government modeled on the Han.[27]

The "funeral narrative" found at Cangshan, which first asks the deceased to grant prosperity and longevity to his descendants and then describes the pleasures depicted in the tomb's images, ends with a chilling insistence on the need for absolute separation:

Having entered the dark world,
You are completely separated from the living,
After the tomb is sealed,
It will never be opened again.[28]

While the theme of the dead as a threat figures only in tombs from certain regions and social strata, it also figures in stories in the *Book of the Han* that describe how skeletons were pulverized and boiled in poisonous substances to prevent the deceased from menacing the living in their dreams. Burial was one method of removing the threat posed by the dead, but should this fail, the more drastic measures depicted in these stories could follow.[29]

It is uncertain why many Chinese came to perceive the dead as a threat. Both the political and ritual texts of the Warring States and early empires insisted on the need to maintain divisions in order to avoid collapse into chaos. Along with such divisions as those between Heaven and Earth or man and woman, the separation between the living and the dead was a fundamental boundary whose disappearance would lead to disorder. The reappearance of the dead in the human world signaled the collapse of this boundary, which could only result in catastrophe for the living.

Late Warring States and early imperial discussions of ghosts often focused on their role as avengers. In the fourth-century B.C. *Transmission of Master Zuo,* avenging ghosts such as Shen Sheng, Bo You, and other unhappy spirits came in dreams or visions to express their resentments, or even take life. The chapter of the Warring States philosophical text *Master Mo (Mozi)* seeking to prove the existence of ghosts frequently describes them as avenging spirits who returned to punish those who wronged them in life. Stories of avenging spirits also appear in the Western Han *Shi ji,* and they became a recurrent topic in Chinese history and fiction.

In addition, spirits appear to the living with demands for a proper burial, rescue from a coffin that has become flooded, or assistance on some other matter. Finally, ghosts appear to the mortally ill, in order to carry off the dying.[30] Spirits in Warring States and early imperial China appear in the human world when something has gone wrong, and they come to punish the living, to demand their aid, or to carry them off to the underworld. In a properly functioning world, the dead and the living are rigorously separated, so if the dead return, it is as harbingers of trouble.

When the dead are viewed as a threat to the living, constructing tombs on the model of houses can be understood as an effort to provide everything necessary for the deceased so they remain forever in their own world. But if they were trapped in a single household, the deceased would not be content. An entire world must be provided through images and replicas, so that the dead can enjoy all possible pleasures and remain happy in their tombs. The First Emperor's tomb, according to Sima Qian, contained a replica of the heavens on its ceiling and the entire earth on its floors. In describing the tombs of the rich and powerful, the Qin philosophical compendium, *Springs and Autumns of Master Lü,* says "They make their mounds like towns and cities."[31]

A clear example of the multiple roles of tombs—as household or world—is found at Mawangdui.[32] A banner draped over the inner coffin provides a model of the universe, with a watery underworld, a world of the living identified by a scene of offerings to the coffin found in the tomb, and a celestial plane marked by the sun and moon, along with associated beings. Inside this banner, the inner coffin became a complete universe where the soul could dwell. This banner-draped inner coffin is surrounded in turn by a second coffin whose decorations include images of horned spirits wielding weapons to kill harmful creatures, as well as auspicious hybrid animals and magical creatures. The third coffin contains an image of a jagged mountain peak flanked by dragons, divine animals, and immortals—possibly Kunlun, the magical mountain at the western edge of the world that was the realm of the Queen Mother of the West. These images suggest that the tomb or the coffin could also serve as a paradise of immortals. Given that immortals were aerial beings associated with the extreme west (Kunlun) or the extreme east (floating mountains on the Eastern Sea), these images once again suggest that this tomb magically included the entire world.

Finally, the coffins were surrounded by a wooden frame built into the tomb. This afterworld equivalent of the house was divided into four chambers with burial goods to provide a comfortable existence. The northern chamber copied the inner chamber of a house, with curtains, floor mats, eating and drinking vessels, bedroom furniture, a painted screen, and clothed figurines representing musicians and attendants. The other compartments contained stores of domestic utensils and food, along with numerous figurines representing servants. This pattern in which the outer layer provided the model of a house, while images within the house indicated that the grave was a complete universe, became a recurring pattern in Han funerary art.

Banners like those at Mawangdui, although simpler, have been found in several Han tombs. Labeled carvings on the coffin found at Guitoushan include the Gate of Heaven, Fu Xi and Nü Gua, the four directional animals, the sun and the moon, numerous immortals, and replicas of buildings such as a Grand Granary. The recurring figures on coffin lids of Fu Xi and Nü Gua holding aloft the sun and the moon also figure as a reduced version of the Mawangdui image of the universe, with the three realms of Heaven, man, and Earth linked together in the sweeping lines of the deities (Fig. 21). The celestial realm is indicated by the sun and moon, the human world by the human upper halves of the deities, and the earth by their lower bodies formed from snakes. Images on tomb ceilings and walls include the sun and moon, constellations, the animals of the four quarters, spirits of the wind and the rain, the Queen Mother of the West, and immortals. Images of the Queen Mother of the West and her immortal court also appear on many objects buried in tombs, such as bronze "money trees." These images may indicate that the household alone could not provide a complete existence for the deceased, who would be satisfied only in the plenitude of an entire world. They may also have served as charts for cosmic journeys.[33]

The underworld had its own bureaucracy. Carved on lead tablets, deeds of grave ownership identify dimensions, purchase date, purchase price, and witnesses for underworld bureaucrats. These officials include the Emperor of Heaven, Director of Life Spans, Duke of the Hills, Commune Chief of the Tomb Gate, Underworld 2,000-Picul-Wage Officers, and most commonly the Earl of the Tomb. The texts stipulate that any objects buried in the plot became the property in the underworld of the tomb's occupant, and any other corpses buried there became his slaves. Other tomb-protecting texts called upon the Yellow Emperor or his Emissary to command spirit armies to repulse demonic incursions. Still others beg underworld officials to make sure that the life span computations were correct and that the deceased was not taken prematurely, or in the place of another of the same name. One story of such a bureaucratic mix-up and the eventual resurrection of the error's victim has been found in a Qin tomb, and similar tales became a virtual literary subgenre in the centuries after the Han.[34]

While the tomb became a major cultic site in the Han, temple sacrifices to ancestors were performed by powerful lineages up to the end of the dynasty. Han documents and Sima Biao's third-century A.D. monograph on ritual describe the two ancestral temples in Luoyang and the offerings there. Emperors were presented at these temples at the time of their accession, debates were held on the ordering of the tablets, and records describe the music and dances performed. Prayers offered there when the

Fig. 21 Fu Xi and Nü Gua embracing, intertwining their snake bodies below
while holding aloft the sun and the moon.

capital was forcibly returned to Chang'an in 190 A.D. are preserved in the
collected writings of Cai Yong (133–192 A.D.).[35]

The surviving fragments of Cui Shi's *Monthly Ordinances of the Four
Categories of People (Si min yue ling)*, a handbook on running an estate
and a large household, indicates that great families continued to make offerings at ancestral temples as well as graves in the second century: "On
the day of the [New Year] offering, they present wine to cause the spirits
to all descend. Then all members of the household, both noble and base,
without exception for young or old, are arrayed in front of the ancestors
in order of age." This array of the extended household in front of all the

ancestors could take place only in an ancestral temple, where the tablets were present and in order. Like the imperial temple sacrifices, these were conducted at intervals throughout the year. At several points the text stipulates that offerings at the graves should take place the day *after* offerings in the temple, suggesting the ritual priority of the latter. Unlike the temple offerings, these grave rituals also included offerings to non-kin.[36]

The linkage of temple sacrifices to grave sacrifices, with ritual priority for the former, is also shown in Sima Biao's account of imperial sacrifices in the late Eastern Han. This third-century text notes that the second emperor of the Eastern Han established the precedent that the emperor should not erect a mausoleum at the site of his tomb but simply place a tablet in the temple of the Eastern Han's founder. Grave sacrifices were thus offered only to selected women and to emperors who died before reaching adulthood and thus could not be placed in the ancestral temple. Cai Yong's *Solitary Judgments* (*Du duan*) stipulates: "Underage emperors who died without reaching adulthood were excluded from the temple." Sima Biao adds that this exclusion was due to the fact that these emperors had not truly reigned, since their mothers had ruled as regents.[37]

The temple remained the most important site for ancestral worship because it was the key ritual site for the patriline, while the grave was reserved for individuals and the household. Imperial graveside offerings were reserved for women and children, who were not full members of the lineage, while temple offerings indicated both membership in the lineage and political authority. Temple offerings were the occasion for gathering the true family, meaning male members of the patriline, while graveside offerings could involve more distant forms of sociability including political superiors, teachers, friends, village elders, or remote kin. This secondary status of the grave is suggested in the organization of the clan cemeteries that began to appear in the Eastern Han, for these were only loose assemblages of graves without any overarching structure expressing the organization of the lineage.[38]

Because the temple was described in canonical ritual texts, while records of graveside ritual did not antedate the Qin, Eastern Han intellectuals celebrated the former as characteristic of high antiquity and denigrated the latter as a development of the late Warring States, or even an innovation of the First Emperor of Qin. Thus Cai Yong wrote: "In ancient times they did not sacrifice at graves. When it came to the time of the First Emperor of Qin, he removed the mausoleum from the capital and erected it at the side of his grave. The Han followed Qin without change." This follows the model of much Eastern Han writing, which lumps the Western Han together with Qin as a period of error, while celebrating their own age for its restoration of ritual correctness. In this schema, graveside offerings are a deviant Qin innovation perpetuated by the Western Han, while temple rites derive from the classics.[39]

Modern scholars have generally analyzed Han grave rites in terms of a supposed belief in two souls: the *hun,* a refined "cloud" soul associated with *yang,* and the *po,* a turbid "new moon" soul associated with *yin.* The *hun* was supposed to ascend to Heaven, while the *po* stayed underground. But the opposition of *hun* and *po* appears only in a couple of scholastic texts, the *Records of Ritual* and the *Master of Huainan,* following the tendency of Han intellectuals to link all phenomena to *yin/ yang* or the five phases.[40] The latter text, in particular, presents an extract of Daoist cosmology with no relation to rituals of the tomb or grave. In the written materials most closely related to burial—the stone inscriptions of the Eastern Han—the terms *hun* and *po* are used interchangeably or combined in a compound.

For Warring States and Han writers, the key issue was not the nature of the soul but the appropriate forms of ritual, in particular whether burials should be elaborate and expensive or plain and frugal. Early Confucians, influenced by Zhou society in which the ancestral cult was the key religious activity and the definition of nobility, emphasized elaborate funerals. Mohist writers, by contrast, denounced lavish burials as a waste of resources. Since the elite poured vast sums into their burials, the competition for prestige meant that "when commoners or people of low status die, the entire fortune of their family was exhausted on the funeral."[41]

The Warring States philosophical text *Master Xun* retorted that multiple coffins, lavish grave goods, elaborate decorations, and funerary garments defended social order by maintaining hierarchy in death ritual. The *Springs and Autumns of Master Lü* riposted that lavish burials were self-defeating, because they invited grave robbers: "If someone erected a stele on top of the grave mound stating, 'There are many precious jewels and goods here. One should certainly open it. When you open it, you will become rich. All your descendants will ride chariots and eat meat,' then people would laugh at it and consider it deluded. And yet the excessive burials in our day are just like this."[42] Many Han sources repeat this argument, which indicates that it was not heeded.

Writers in the tradition of the Warring States philosophical text *Master Zhuang (Zhuangzi)* argued that fancy coffins and expensive stone or brick walls prevented the body from reuniting with the earth. However, decay was what most people wanted to prevent. The corpse of Lady Dai at Mawangdui was preserved with skin and hair intact by careful encasement in multiple layers of charcoal and other materials that kept out moisture. Elsewhere, jade plugs were used to block up the orifices and thereby prevent vital energies from seeping away. Those with greater wealth pursued this procedure to its logical conclusion in jade suits that covered the entire body. Numerous examples have been found, most notably one from Mancheng composed of more than 2,500 plaques sewn together with gold thread. The Red Eyebrow peasant rebels who began the uprising against Wang Mang opened up the imperial tombs in pursuit of treasure: "In the tombs that the bandits had opened, all the corpses dressed in jade casings looked as if they were still alive." In an irony anticipated by the *Springs and Autumns of Master Lü,* the precious objects intended to grant the deceased eternal life in the tomb led to their bodies being abandoned to the elements.[43]

Great families of the Eastern Han extended the cult of the dead to funerary shrines. Services at these structures were attended not only by family members but also by clients, associates, or friends. They gave a religious aspect to the networks formed through education and government service that increasingly linked many powerful families against the eunuch-dominated court. Long after the tomb was sealed up, images in the shrines could be viewed by both descendants and associates. These images proclaimed the moral or political program that the deceased had espoused and inculcated in his posterity. Those in the best preserved of these shrines, belonging to the Wu family in Shandong, offer a microcosm of a complete, ideal world. The gables depict the realms of the immortals at the edges of the world, and the walls portray the world of men. The latter are in turn divided into images of sage rulers and moral exemplars from history and scenes from the life of the deceased, including official processions, combats with bandits, and a scene of homage.[44]

Regional Cults

Regional cults existed in both official and popular versions. Official cults included sacrifices by agents of the state to the major mountains and rivers, as well as to the constellations that were the celestial counterparts of earthly regions. However, most regional cults lacked state sanction, and as a result they do not figure in official records. Such cults were often tied to local immortals, landmarks, or seasonal feasts, and were organized by associations of shamans, sometimes hereditary, or of merchants who financed the rites.

In stories in the *Comprehensive Meaning of Customs* (*Feng su tong yi*), local organizations of religious practitioners, generally called "shamans" as a term of opprobrium, collect money from local populations to support a cult to a deity not sanctioned by the state. This is invariably described as a form of swindling the people. One cult provides a mountain god with human "brides" who are then banned from "remarrying" mortal men. A newly arrived official in the area demonstrates the impotence of the supposed divinity, bans the cult, and executes its organizers. In one case the cult is sponsored not by shamans but by local businessmen, and the recipient of the sacrifices is a historic figure who helped to thwart the Lü clan's attempt to replace the Liu lineage.[45]

Stelae texts depict cults to mountain spirits such as the Lord Spirit of White Rock, recipient of seasonal sacrifices on White Rock Mountain in Hebei. These sacrifices included incense, jade, and silk. Participants sought official recognition, but the sacrifices continued whether or not this was obtained. Stelae also tell of cults to immortals, such as the Eastern Han inscription from Shaanxi that records the story of Tang Gongfang's encounter with a "perfected man" who taught him how to understand animals and to travel great distances in the blink of an eye. When Tang Gongfang incurred the wrath of a local official, he beseeched the perfected man for help: "The [perfected man] accompanied him home and gave Gongfang, his wife, and children an elixir to drink, saying 'Now you can leave.' But his wife loved her home and could not bear to depart. The master said to her, 'Are you not saying that you would like to take your entire household with you?' The woman answered, 'That would be my greatest desire.' They started to anoint the pillars of the house with the elixir and gave it to the domestic animals. A moment later a great wind arose and a black cloud came to meet Gongfang, his wife, children, home, and animals, and in a great whirlwind it took them all up together." As the stele records, Tang Gongfang then became a focus of prayer in the region, where his cult continued into the twentieth century.[46]

A couple of other inscriptions commemorating local cults to immortals have been discovered. The *Arrayed Biographies of Immortals* (*Lie xian zhuan*) speaks of many such cults. In southern Sichuan dozens of shrines were erected to Ge You, who had supposedly obtained immortality there.

The immortal Kou Xian was worshipped in every house in his home county. The biographies record that these cults had tens of thousands of followers and lasted for many generations.[47]

Some modern scholars believe that the dead were guided to the lands of the immortals by magic charts placed on the lids of coffins or the ceilings of tombs, or by illustrations of "psychopomps" (guides for the souls of the dead). However, in Han accounts as in later religious Daoism, immortals were beings who *avoided* death. The standard formula in later times was to "become an immortal in one's fleshly body." Often winged or having undergone some physical transformation, they lived a very long time (but not forever) at the edges of the earth, in the mountains, or in other regions that lay beyond. But having escaped death, immortals also rejected the status of ancestor that created and defined kin groups. The tension between immortals and families is suggested in the story of Tang Gongfang by the wife's unwillingness to depart without taking the entire household and farm.

This opposition between kinship—based on the cult of the dead—and immortality is clearer in a remark of Emperor Wu upon hearing how the Yellow Emperor had become an immortal. "Ah! If I could only become like the Yellow Emperor, I would think no more of my wife and children than of a cast-off slipper."[48] Thus, the role of immortals in tombs was possibly not to serve as guides to their paradises but as markers of the extreme limits of the earth, who transformed the grave into an entire world.

Organized Religious Movements

Religious practices of the common people enter historical records only where they threaten the state. Many of the beliefs and practices described above—shamanic spirit intermediaries, sacrifice to ancestors, local cults—figured in the lives of ordinary people. Texts discovered in tombs show that ordinary people also lived surrounded by potentially dangerous spirits whom it was necessary to identify and to guard against using assorted magical procedures. Such demons figured in accounts of the origin of diseases and in the lore of strange and dangerous creatures that haunted uninhabited regions such as mountains and bodies of water.[49]

There were also cults related to the economic activities of commoners. The agrarian altars of the grain and soil were the primary religious site for towns and even cities. Crafts whose technical difficulty made them seem most susceptible to divine intervention—metallurgy, ceramics, and lacquerwork—had their own mythology and patron deities. Some religious or magical practices, such as the carving of the animals of the four directions onto molds for coins, have left material traces. The second century B.C. *Fifty-two Recipes to Cure Disease* (*Wushier bing fang*) discovered at Mawangdui details an exorcism to ward off diseases caused by a rebel god, the Lacquer King. He had been charged to assist workers but instead created a skin disease, the dermatitis that is actually induced by lacquer, which is derived from a plant related to poison oak. The fourth-century A.D. *Record of the Lands South of Mount Hua* (*Huayang guo zhi*) mentions a mountain-top temple dedicated to the divine Iron Ancestor in a region with many iron works.[50]

However, the truly distinctive commoner religions that appeared from the late Western Han were large-scale movements which, from the perspective of the state, led to public disturbances and rebellions. One of the earliest worshipped was the Queen Mother of the West. During a drought in the northeast in 3 B.C., crowds began to run from town to town carrying emblems woven of straw or hemp. Often disheveled or barefoot, they broke down doors or gates and at night staged torch-lit processions across the roofs of towns. Spreading across twenty-six commanderies and kingdoms up to Chang'an, they held services to the Queen Mother and passed around a written message that said: "The Mother tells the people that those who wear this talisman will not die. Let those who do not believe her words look below the hinges of their gates, and there will be white hairs there to show that this is true."[51] When the drought broke, the movement subsided and the cult vanished from the historical record.

The most important religious movements were the Yellow Turbans, the Five Pecks of Grain, and Buddhism. The first two were organized into military units, reflecting the late Han decline in social order, against which local communities organized for self-defense. The Yellow Turbans led by Zhang Jue taught that disease resulted from sin and could be healed by confession. They believed that the Han lineage was exhausted and aimed to establish a new dynasty under the rising "Yellow Heaven." The movement was widespread through the northeast and even penetrated the imperial guard. Their rebellion in 184 set off the civil war that ended the Han.

The Five Pecks of Grain movement was led by Zhang Lu in what is now Sichuan. Like Zhang Jue (probably unrelated), he preached that disease could be cured through repentance. Records indicate many outbreaks of epidemics in this period, in part explaining the rise of major movements that claimed healing powers. The movement was named "Five Pecks" because each member had to give five pecks of grain to the community, which would be used to provision charity houses for adepts and travelers. This cult also proclaimed an imminent age of Great Peace, but unlike the Yellow Turbans, it originally espoused the reform of the Han house rather than its replacement. The cult's followers also worshipped the divinized Laozi, who was periodically incarnated to rescue the world and who had received sacrifice from the imperial house since 166 A.D. Zhang Lu took control of Sichuan but was defeated by Cao Cao in 215. Cao Cao enfeoffed his sons, and in the fourth century A.D. later followers of the Zhangs established a Daoist state in this area.[52]

Buddhism entered China during the Eastern Han, following both the overland trade routes through Central Asia and the sea lanes from Southeast Asia. The first reference to it dates from 65 A.D., where it is mentioned along with Daoism and alchemy. At the end of the Han a monastery patronized by an imperial prince was established in Luoyang. Depictions of the Buddha have been found in Han tombs, usually occupying a location that in other tombs was filled by the Queen Mother of the West. This suggests that the Buddha was conceived as a divinity from the West in the image of the Queen Mother, who answered prayers and rescued believers from suffering. However, there is little evidence of any awareness of Buddhist doctrine in the Han.[53]

In conclusion, one should note what has *not* been discussed in this chapter. It has said nothing of a systematic mythology with elaborate tales of the origins of the universe or the deeds of the gods. While such tales figure in the written literature, they are not abundant and deal largely with human culture heroes who created the technologies and practices needed for a civilized existence. It has also said nothing of a creator divinity or a pure, transcendent realm. Neither existed in Han China. The spirits of whom we have records were fed by sacrifices from humans, usually their descendants or natives of their home regions, which resulted in a relation of mutual dependence between the visible and shadow worlds.

The vast majority of spirits in the Han empire, as in later China, were either people who had died or escaped death as immortals. The worlds of the living and the dead, of men and spirits, were separate but parallel. People passed from one to the other, and sometimes might pass back again. For those who believed in an afterlife, it was much like the world of the living. And for many people, as in all times and places, death was the inevitable absolute terminus. Thus, another of the *Nineteen Old Poems* concludes:

> Through the ages mourners in their turn are mourned,
> Neither sage nor worthy can escape.
> Seeking by diet to obtain immortality,
> Many have been the dupes of drugs.
> Better far to drink good wine,
> And clothe our bodies in silk and satin.[54]

9

LITERATURE

THE CREATION of a unified empire transformed Chinese intellectual life. In the Qin dynasty and the early Western Han, works in history, philosophy, and poetry were produced that attempted to comprehensively depict the new unified world. These texts were the intellectual equivalents of empire. Then, by the late Western Han, the Confucian canon—the Zhou textual heritage defined by the "six classics" (*Odes*, *Documents*, *Ritual*, *Music*, *Spring and Autumn Annals*, and *Changes*)—emerged as the all-encompassing textual embodiment of Han imperial ideals. Like many other aspects of Qin and Han history, Chinese intellectual life was divided into two epochs by this establishment of the Zhou classics as foundational texts of the realm.

The application of the term "Confucian" in the Han is problematic, however, as several modern scholars have shown. The term *ru*, which has been translated as "Confucian," had a broader sense than simply the followers of Confucius. And even the self-proclaimed followers of Confucius rejected major parts of what had previously defined "the Way of Confucius." Moreover, these acolytes did not share a philosophical orthodoxy among themselves, as would later "Confucians" in the Song and Yuan dynasties.[1] Although these criticisms all have some degree of truth, I shall—for the four reasons given below—continue to use the term "Confucian" to describe those people who were devoted to the Zhou textual heritage.

First, even those who question the translation of *ru* as "Confucian" agree that one major sense of the term referred to specialists in the classical Zhou heritage, both its rituals and its texts. Second, when *ru* appeared as a category in comprehensive philosophical and bibliographic systems in the Han, users of the term identified the *ru* as those who "take the six classics as their model" and devote themselves to their commentaries.[2] Third, while it is true that Han *ru* changed major elements of the "Way of Confucius," this kind of reworking and reevaluation was already happening among Warring States followers of the sage and would continue throughout Chinese history. The tradition that evolved under the rubric of Confucianism was a protean one, but to rename it with every change of emphasis or interpretation would obscure more than it would reveal. Finally, the diverse intellectual, literary, and bibliographic changes sketched in this chapter, the establishment of memorizing the classics as the basis of education, and the triumph of the cult of Heaven in religious rites, taken together, fixed the six classics as the center of the Chinese intellectual universe.

Rival Traditions of "the Way"

Philosophical texts produced in the Warring States period asserted their authority by claiming to possess a comprehensive wisdom, generally called the Way. During this time of political turmoil, the variant interpretations of the Way hardened into polemical traditions, each claiming that its own wisdom was all-encompassing and drawn from ancient sages, while dismissing rival doctrines as partial truths of limited applicability. The competing texts produced by the various traditions were to be read as a literary expression of the Zhou realm's political fragmentation into warring regions. The Confucian version of this ideal is exemplified by a passage from the *Master Xun* (*Xunzi*), a third-century B.C. compilation of the teachings of Xun Kuang of Qi, a major Warring State:

> Now the feudal lords have different governments and the hundred schools different theories, so inevitably some are right and others wrong, some well-governed and some in chaos . . . Master Mo was blocked by the idea of utility and thus insensible to refined culture. Master Song [Xing] was blocked by the idea of [limiting] desires, and thus insensible to fulfillment. Master Shen [Dao] was blocked by the idea of law and thus insensible to the value of worthy men. Master Shen [Buhai] was blocked by the idea of the force of position and thus insensible to wisdom. Master Hui was blocked by the idea of fine words and thus insensible to realities. Master Zhuang was

blocked by the idea of Heaven and thus insensible to the human . . . Each of these is one corner of the Way. The Way embodies the constant and exhausts all changes. A single corner cannot give an idea of it . . . Confucius was benevolent, wise, and not blocked. Therefore, though studying confused methods, he was still sufficient to have been one of the ancient kings. His school alone obtained the Way of Zhou [*zhou dao*, also "the complete Way"].[3]

This philosophical disunity led Li Si (d. 208 B.C.), a scholar who had studied under Xun Kuang and later became the chief minister of Qin, to propose to the First Emperor that he should suppress private ownership and transmission of nontechnical writings—including the philosophers, the *Odes*, and the *Documents*—and make the state the sole source of education and truth. Like the philosophical texts he criticized, Li Si privileged the comprehensive over the partial, but he identified all-encompassing truth with Qin-imposed unity. The rival traditions, he claimed, were self-seeking factions that threatened public order through the pursuit of private glory. Qin's task was to provide a unitary tradition by linguistic and philosophical standards. Philosophy—like laws, measures, and script—should be dictated from the center and enforced by the emperor's servants.[4]

The notion that rival philosophical traditions were fragments of a whole continued into the early Han, in the work of Sima Tan (d. 110 B.C.). As grand historian to Emperor Wu, he initiated the comprehensive Han history *Shi ji*, a project taken over and completed by his son, Sima Qian, who inherited his father's position at court. Sima Tan was the first person to divide the intellectual field into a limited number of doctrinally defined schools, which included "the traditions of Yin/yang, Classicists [Confucians], Mohists, Names, Law, and the Way and Its Power." Sima Tan credits all of these schools, except the last one, with knowing one part of the Way, and he sees this partiality as causing errors.

In his view, the tradition that avoids the trap of incompleteness by incorporating the best features of all the other traditions and embracing constant change and adaptation is "the Way and Its Power," or Daoism. Sima Tan traced the Daoist tradition back to the legendary Zhou official Laozi, supposedly an older contemporary of Confucius. The myth of Laozi's career had developed in the late Warring States period to account for the existence of a text known as the *Canon of the Way and Its Power* (*Dao de jing*), and some modern scholars doubt that he ever existed.

However, the *Canon of the Way and Its Power*, along with the *Master Zhuang*, provided the foundation texts for the Daoist tradition.

In Sima Tan's words, "The Daoists cause people's refined spirit energies to be undivided, their actions to accord with the formless, and to nourish all things. Their technique follows the general order of yin/yang, selects the good points of the classicists and Mohists, and extracts the essential points of the School of Names and Legalists. Moving with the seasons, changing in response to things, it establishes customs and bestows tasks, and there is nothing that is not appropriate."[5] In this program of the perfection of the body/self, the basing of actions on the formless origin of things, and the following of natural patterns, Daoism would eventually become one of the so-called pillars of Chinese thought, along with Confucianism and Buddhism.

Canon and Commentary

A major development in late Warring States intellectual life was the establishment of a privileged category of texts, called *jing*, through the addition of commentaries, called *zhuan*. Each philosophical tradition from this period condemned intellectual disputation as a form of social breakdown, while claiming that its own doctrines for creating social order represented the original principles employed by the ancient sages. The textual categories *jing* and *zhuan* came to identify these principles and the modes of explaining them.

The character *jing* had originally indicated something running throughout an area and serving to regulate it, with the associated meaning of "strong" and "unbending." A derived sense of *jing* included the idea of "boundary" or "demarcation," as in the creation of the grid that defined the city and the marketplace. When the character was paired with *wei*, meaning "weft," it referred to the warp of a fabric. Eventually, these two characters *jing* and *wei* would be used to translate the terms "longitude" and "latitude." In other passages, the character *jing* functioned simply as a verb meaning "to put in order" or "to rule." When used as a noun, it meant "guiding principle" or "constant norm."[6]

In the late Warring States period, *jing* began to appear in titles of texts and chapters and to be applied to a certain body of works. This use of *jing* indicated that the texts were constant or universal and that they provided order or structure to the world. For example, the final chapter of the *Master Zhuang* states that the Mohists "all recite the Mohist canon

[Mo jing]." The first nine chapters of the collection of essays on government, the Master Guan (Guanzi), are entitled "Discussion of Constant
Principles" (Jing yan) and deal with methods for obtaining and using
power. The character jing is frequently preceded by a numeral that enu-
merates principles of statecraft. In the Master Han Fei, to take one example, a chapter entitled the "Eight Constant Principles" (Ba jing) gives
maxims on government. The term was also applied to texts that presented the fundamental principles of any practice.[7]

The character jing appeared in the title of classic Daoist texts associated with Laozi and the Yellow Emperor (supposedly the first ruler of the
Han people) that were recovered from Han tombs at Mawangdui in the
late twentieth century. In addition to the Canon of the Way (Dao jing),
these include the Canon of Virtuous Power (De jing), the Constant Model
(Jing fa), and the Sixteen Canons (Shi liu jing). These texts present principles of social order, which they derive from the cosmic Way. When the
catalogue of the imperial library was compiled in the late Western Han,
several geographic works, such as the Canon of the Mountains and Seas
(Shan hai jing), and major medical texts were also identified as jing, and
the latter were linked to the Yellow Emperor.

Texts or chapters entitled jing were often accompanied by zhuan (meaning "transmission, tradition") or shuo (meaning "explanation"). Six chapters of the Master Han Fei entitled Collected Explanations (Chu shuo)
begin with brief principles of government, followed by references to anecdotes that demonstrate the principles. The principles are called jing
and the anecdotes shuo. The major term for commentaries, however,
was zhuan. The Eastern Han dictionary Explanations of Simple and
Compound Graphs (Shuo wen jie zi) glosses this character as a carriage
used in relays to deliver messages, while the Eastern Han dictionary Explaining Names (Shi ming) defines it as the stations at which such carriages changed horses. This dictionary also states that as a literary term
zhuan means "to hand down and show to later men."[8]

These definitions suggest that zhuan derived from a figurative sense in
which the message of the canon, obscure because of its subtlety and archaic language, was delivered or conveyed to the world at large. The term
also marks a hierarchical relationship between the canonical text and its
commentary. According to early texts, officers who delivered messages
through the relay system were of low status; and in another context, the
term zhuan is prescribed as a humble self-referent for the lowest rank of
nobility when addressing the Son of Heaven. Thus, by analogy, while the
canons were the textual legacy of the sages, the commentaries were de-

rived from the lower-status worthies who devoted themselves to transmitting the ideas and intentions of the sages. Neither form of text could be understood without the other, but a clear hierarchy was implied.

The *jing* texts of the late Warring States were all recent compositions, many written with their own appended explanations. But the central texts of the *ru* tradition, known as the Five Canons—the *Odes*, *Documents*, *Rites*, *Spring and Autumn Annals*, and *Changes*—which originated centuries earlier, were also transformed into canons through the addition of commentary. Indeed, virtually any text could, in theory, become a *jing* if a *zhuan* was appended. When the Eastern Han scholar Wang Chong argued that *jing* need *zhuan*, he meant that only with a commentary could a classic text be understood. But in practice, adding a commentary certified a text as canonical by showing its hidden depths or flexible application to many situations.[9]

Thus, the Zhou *Odes* were interpreted by the *Master Xun* as the wisdom of ancient sages that revealed truths about institutions and practices of its own day. Commentaries on the *Spring and Autumn Annals* explained this chronicle from the court of Lu as a philosophy of government expressed through a coded set of quasi-legal judgments. This ideal government was considered a prophecy of, and a model for, Han institutions. Similarly, commentators on the *Documents* reread political speeches dealing with particular issues as depictions of a model kingship.

Encyclopedias

In contrast with canons that offered universal principles in gnomic language requiring explication, or commentaries that read evolving, hidden meanings into archaic texts, several works from the Qin-Han empires claimed to be encyclopedias of all significant knowledge. The two major examples are the *Springs and Autumns of Master Lü* (*Lü shi chun qiu*), composed under the auspices of Qin's chief minister in the middle of the third century B.C., and the *Master of Huainan* (*Huainanzi*), sponsored by the king of Huainan at the beginning of the reign of Emperor Wu of the Western Han.

These two texts share many features. They are collective works by numerous scholars gathered around a political patron, after whom the text is named. The works assemble maxims and principles from all the philosophic traditions and attempt to synthesize them into a coherent whole. They adapt natural models for this synthesis, both texts involving the dimension of time, so that the text serves as a microcosm of the world. Finally, both texts emphasize the ideal of political and doctrinal unity.

Eminent men of the Warring States had competed for prestige by surrounding themselves with individuals with useful or amusing talents. Patronage of scholars by political figures grew out of this practice, and the great sponsored compendia of the Qin and early Han were a further step in the process. The Han biographies of Lü Buwei and Liu An claim that they assembled thousands of scholars. Gao You's late Eastern Han preface to his commentary on the *Master of Huainan* also insists on the large number of scholars gathered at Liu An's court and lists eight men who shared in organizing the project. This emphasis on vast participation in the writing of the encyclopedia is part of their program of comprehensiveness.[10]

Naming the books for a political patron rather than a teacher also indicates their public nature. In the myths of the ancient sages, Warring States philosophers had linked the notion of comprehensive wisdom with the ideal of political and intellectual unification, and in so doing they had identified intellectual dispute as a sign of decay. Legalist thinkers in the same period had also called for the abolition of scholastic disputation in the name of the state's intellectual hegemony. The pattern of the *Springs and Autumns of Master Lü* and the *Master of Huainan*, in which a chief minister or king assembled scholars from the competing traditions to synthesize their positions into a harmonious whole, responded to these ideas: intellectual unification paralleling the empire's geographical unification was a major goal in these early imperial compendia.

Although originating as collections of essays by multiple authors, the texts were reworked into more elaborate structures to suggest both comprehensiveness and natural foundations. The *Springs and Autumns of Master Lü* was modeled on the annual cycle, as indicated by its title and the organization of its first section. The *Master of Huainan* took its form from models of the heavens sketched in such Warring States works as the *Canon of the Way and Its Power*, the *Master Zhuang*, and manuscripts found at the Mawangdui tombs. In both encyclopedias, the organization breaks down in later sections, which fill in omissions, elaborate points already made, or pursue numerological significance in the arrangement of chapters. Nevertheless, it is clear that the authors tried to find natural models and thereby to establish their universal authority.

The *Springs and Autumns of Master Lü* is composed of three sections—twelve registers (*ji*), eight overviews (*lan*), and six assessments (*lun*). Only the *ji*, which form the core of the book and correspond to the months of the year, are strictly calendrical, and they were probably written first as an independent work. This is indicated by the presence after the last *ji* of a postface discussing the nature of the work—a common practice from the late Warring States through the Han. The postface refers to the work as the "Twelve Registers" and argues that it encompasses the triad of Heaven, Earth, and man.[11]

The registers are named for the months of the year, and each begins with the relevant section from the calendar of royal activities commonly known as the "Monthly Ordinances." These opening sections are followed by essays that extend the strictures of the royal calendar into a theory of kingship. The sections on Spring are followed by essays on the supreme significance of life, the importance of the ruler's valuing his own health, and the ruler's duty to impartially further the lives of other beings. The essays appended to Summer deal primarily with the need to further life through respect for teachers, the cultivation of ritual, and the practice of music. The essays of Autumn deal largely with military affairs. Those of Winter begin with discussions of funerals and then switch to advocacy of personal austerity, the checking of accounts, the selection and rewarding of personnel, and the making of long-range plans.

The ruler's adaptation to the shifting of the seasons provides a framework in which the theories advocated by the philosophical traditions all find their place. While themes from the different traditions are scattered throughout the text, the Spring section is dominated by ideas from the Yangist and syncretist chapters of the *Master Zhuang*, the Summer section by the educational program of the Confucians, the Autumn section by the military treatises and chapters on warfare from the philosophical schools, and the Winter section by Mohist strictures on funerals and economy, and by legalist teachings on the assessment and employment of talent. The ideal of a comprehensive doctrine in which the limited teachings of each school find their place is achieved by subsuming them under the calendar of royal activities. The king, who embodies and enacts the cycle fixed by Heaven, becomes the point in which the schools converge.

The *Master of Huainan* adopts its pattern not from the seasons but from Daoist explanations of the origin and nature of the universe. The first chapter deals with the universal Way, which is both the origin of all things and the model for comprehensiveness. The second chapter develops the principles of division and transformation by which the universe and all things within it were formed. The third chapter deals with

Heaven, the fourth with Earth, and the fifth traces the annual cycle in a version of the "Monthly Ordinances." The sixth chapter then presents the principle of "resonance" that links Heaven, Earth, and all natural phenomena. The seventh deals with the origin and nature of the human body, the eighth with the sage, and the ninth with the ruler.

Having ascended from the primal unity, through first divisions into Heaven and Earth, the structure of space and time, and the origins of man, to the highest forms of man in the sage and ruler, this encyclopedia, like the *Springs and Autumns of Master Lü*, loses a clear sense of structure. Nevertheless, the passage in the early chapters, from original unity to the sage, provides a universal model for the incorporation of all philosophical and technical traditions.

The *Springs and Autumns of Master Lü* was composed just two decades before Qin's final campaigns of conquest, and its link to the ambition of political unification is clear. The text insists repeatedly on the importance of rulers and the value of unification, arguing that in antiquity before the appearance of rulers, or in distant lands that have no monarchs, people lived like animals. Kin ties, hierarchical relations, ritual conduct, implements and tools, and all other features of civilization depend upon rulers for their introduction and maintenance. But the functions of the ruler could be carried out only if one man rules over all. The absence of a universal ruler, with his comprehensive laws, measures, standards of judgment, and ideals, would lead to chaos and war.[12]

Histories

Composed in the decades following the presentation at the Western Han court of the *Master of Huainan*, the historical opus *Shi ji* also aimed to give textual expression to the project of empire. The *Shi ji*'s primary author was Sima Qian (c. 145– c. 86 B.C.), son of Sima Tan, who was grand historian to Emperor Wu. When Sima Qian offended the emperor by trying to intercede for a general who had lost in battle, the emperor sentenced him to castration—a sentence that usually led to an honorable suicide rather than the alternative of disgrace.

In a letter to his friend Ren An, Sima Qian justified his decision not to commit suicide by describing the goals of the vast history he hoped to finish before his death: "I have gathered old traditions abandoned by the world, examined people's conduct, investigated the principles of success and failure or rise and decline . . . I desire thereby to exhaust [*jiu*] the interchanges between Heaven and man, completely trace [*tong*] the changes from ancient times to the present, and thus complete [*cheng*] the words of a single school/family."[13]

The aspiration to cover all human history and society, from the Yellow Emperor down to Sima Qian's own day, defines the *Shi ji*. He takes as his historical model the *Spring and Autumn Annals*, but he includes periods both before and after those covered in that ancient work. Sima Qian suggests a motive for this historical range by including his father's essay on the "Six Schools" in the postface that tells how he came to write the *Shi ji*. This essay celebrated the Daoists for "evolving with the times," "changing in response to things," and thus "being suitable to all affairs." Thus among the six schools, the Daoists embodied the ideal of comprehensive wisdom to which Sima Qian aspired for his own work.

The theme of comprehensiveness also figures in Sima Qian's decision to structure the work around the principle that the world had been ruled by a chain of universal monarchs since the creation of the state by the Yellow Emperor. Each of his first twelve chapters (the "Fundamental Chronicles") is devoted to a world-ruling monarch or dynasty. Reading the unified Han empire back into the beginning of history, Sima Qian assumes that an undivided sovereignty passed from king to king without interruption from the Yellow Emperor to his own ruler, Emperor Wu. The idea of the single ruler, advocated in late Warring States polemics as the foundation of intellectual unity, here reappears as the unifying principle of history.[14]

In addition to the "Fundamental Chronicles," with its thread of sovereignty running throughout, other categories of chapters include the "Tables," which are charts linking the history and noble lineages of each principality to the sequence of kings; the "Monographs," which trace the evolution of the rituals, music, pitch pipes, calendars, and sacrifices that gave visible and audible form to the idea of empire; the "Hereditary Households," which deal with fiefs and, along with the "Tables," incorporate an earlier multistate reality into an imperial ideal; and the "Traditions," which, in describing officials, diplomats, generals, merchants, manufacturers, philosophical masters, scholars, poets, diviners, assassins, and gangsters—all commoners—provide a portrait of the wider society in the Warring States, Qin, and early Han.

Though not itself a canon, the *Shi ji* adopts the structure of canon and commentary. Sima Qian's opening twelve chapters form a chronicle of events in imitation of the *Spring and Autumn Annals*. The term *ji* (**kieg*) that he applied to these chapters was nearly homophonous with *jing* (**kieng*) and shared a common range of meanings: "guiding thread," "norm," "rule," or "regulation." Most of the remaining chapters bear the character *zhuan*, meaning commentaries. While the narratives and anecdotes in Sima Qian's *zhuan* have little in common with the explication of graphs in the *Gongyang* commentary to the *Annals*, they resemble the material of the *Transmissions of Master Zuo* (*Zuo zhuan*), which Sima Qian describes as the most accurate record of Confucius' explanation of the *Annals*. The biographies of commoners in the *Shi ji* thus play the role of commentary to canon, adding substance, detail, and drama to the briefer, drier chronicles.[15]

Sima Qian's work also aimed to be comprehensive as an anthology of earlier texts. The account of Confucius includes many passages of the *Analects* (*Lun yu*), historically situated to provide a context. Other biographies—such as those of Qu Yuan, Jia Yi, and Sima Xiangru—consist largely of works composed by these figures. Sima Qian also borrowed much material from the *Transmissions of Master Zuo*, although he rewrote its archaic language, and his history of the Warring States is made up of extensive quotations from the kinds of texts later edited to form the *Stratagems of the Warring States* (*Zhanguo ce*). Philosophical works such as the *Mencius* are also quoted or adapted to provide material. In short, although the *Shi ji* was composed by Sima Qian and his father, its frequent use of quotation and the incorporation of other works turn the history into a multi-voiced encyclopedia of the literature known in the early Han.

The multi-voiced nature of the work also serves to offer historical lessons, through an ironic interplay between quoted assertions and factual narrative. Examples of this are the contrast between the inflated claims of the First Emperor's stone inscriptions and Sima Qian's narration of the events of his reign, or the discrepancy between promises of the Masters of Esoteric Arts to Emperor Wu and the results obtained. Similarly, by describing historical figures primarily through the voices of their contemporaries and by dividing narratives into multiple chapters written from the perspective of different participants, the *Shi ji* demonstrates objectivity and a universal perspective that the use of Sima Qian's own voice alone would have lacked.[16]

Sima Qian cast himself in the role of a new Confucius by writing judgments into the fabric of history. But with the triumph of the Confucian canon as state orthodoxy, the *Shi ji,* with its supposed Daoist slant, became the target of criticism. Ban Biao and his son Ban Gu, who carried on the task of writing Han history in the first century A.D., adopted Sima Qian's work as a structural model, but they rejected his vision of universality and criticized his failure to adhere to the virtues of Confucianism.[17]

Although Sima Qian had claimed that he intended to write his history to praise the Han, his actual treatment of Han rulers—notably the founder Gaozu and the contemporary Emperor Wu—was highly critical. In contrast, Ban Gu in his poetry treated the first three Eastern Han emperors as brilliant rulers, if not sages, who had moved toward the creation of a Confucian state. Because this celebration of the Eastern Han entailed a critique of the Western Han rulers, whom Sima Qian also disparaged, Ban Gu was able to use much of Sima Qian's text even while casting aspersions on his hostility to the ruling house.

Ban Gu also criticized Sima Qian because "his moral judgments had hugely deviated from those of Confucius." Although Sima Qian adopted Confucius and the *Annals* as his model, he also patterned himself on less canonical authors, such as the Warring States poet Qu Yuan. More importantly, the inclusion of his father's essay, which proclaimed the superiority of Daoism, led to the charge that Sima Qian himself was in reality a devotee of Daoist philosophy. Finally, Sima Qian's categorization of several chapters—treating the Han founder's rival Xiang Yu as a ruler, and the leader of the anti-Qin rebellion Chen She as a "hereditary household"—and his inclusion of sometimes laudatory biographies of assassins, gangsters, and merchants were regarded as clear evidence of moral deviance.

The composition of Ban Gu's *Book of the Han* (*Han shu*) marked an institutional shift in the nature of historiography. The *Shi ji* had been a familial endeavor of Sima Tan and Sima Qian, and Ban Biao had also written his history as a private, literary work. Although Ban Gu, like his father, had at first worked alone and was even arrested for "privately rewriting the state's history," he was subsequently commissioned by Emperor Ming to write a history of the Han.[18] This marked the origin of the official historiography that became a standard feature of imperial Chinese dynasties.

Historians were appointed by the state to compile annals of rulers and biographical memoirs of individuals, works that would ultimately form chapters in "dynastic histories." The Eastern Han History Bureau was located in the Eastern Lodge in Luoyang, and a fragment of the collection of biographies composed under the auspices of the bureau has survived under the title *Han Records from the Eastern Lodge* (*Dong guan Han ji*). This bureaucratization of the writing of official histories, which reached its full extent under the Tang, represented a serious decline in the quality of dynastic histories.

Poetry

In addition to Sima Qian, the other great writer of the age of Emperor Wu was Sima Xiangru (ca. 180–117 B.C.), who developed a poetic language to express the ideal of all-inclusiveness. His "rhapsodies" incorporated elements from the *Songs of Chu* (*Chu ci*)—most prominently, flights in the company of gods and immortals and romantic encounters with goddesses. The use of unusual graphs to evoke exotic creatures, minerals, and plants linked his poetry to the theme of tribute—the presentation of rare objects to the ruler as a testament to his power. Sima Xiangru's poems and essays emphasize the power of words to cast a spell on the reader or even to call objects into existence, a power linked to the religious uses of language from which the rhetoric of the rhapsody derived.[19]

For most of the Western Han period, when poetry was above all a product of the court, Sima Xiangru was recognized as the greatest writer—the very model of a poet. However, with the rise of the Confucian canon, many aspects of his art were rejected, a trend epitomized in the career of Yang Xiong (53 B.C.–18 A.D.). During his youth, Yang Xiong wrote rhapsodies that adopted both the style and subjects of Sima Xiangru. However, later in life he rejected this form of poetry because it lacked moral seriousness and because its fantastic images and romanticized language did not adhere to the Confucian ideal of writing, in which words must be a direct expression of experience and character.[20]

In his *Canon of Supreme Mystery* (*Tai xuan jing*) Yang Xiong argues that poetry should be a moral instrument of persuasion. He embraces as his model the Zhou writers whose verses are preserved in the *Canon of Odes* (*Shi jing*). Confucian works since the Warring States period—such as the *Mencius*, the *Master Xun*, and the "Mao Preface"—had elaborated the theory that these odes were the direct and sincere expression of the moral purpose of their authors, the sage kings of the early Zhou, or of historians writing under their influence.[21] Because verse was meant to be morally direct and persuasive, the language should be clear and intelligible, avoiding elaborate phrases and ornaments that obscured its purpose. Excessive ornament and artificial language were the great fault of "writers of ornate language" (ci ren) like Sima Xiangru and his followers. While their effusive verbiage could cast a spell on the audience, it could not lead individuals to appropriate conduct. Thus, Yang Xiong concluded that such works were "beautiful writing, but of little use." Ban Gu adopted the same principles in his poetry, when he criticized Sima Xiangru and the Western Han capital that admired his work.

Although odes emerged as the exemplary model for verse at the end of the Western Han, men of literary ambition did not compose odes (or at least few have been preserved). Named authors of Han songs, as preserved in the histories, are largley rulers, concubines, and generals. These are personal testaments in which the author sings of his or her emotional response to a situation, usually tragic in nature. Most of the songs precede a suicide or a final parting. Many simply describe the situation and declare the sentiments of the speaker without metaphor or ornament. An example is the song sung by the Han founder Gaozu's great rival, Xiang Yu, to his concubine Yu, prior to his last battle and ultimate suicide:

> My strength uprooted hills,
> My energy dominated the age.
> But the times were unpropitious,
> And Dapple [his horse] runs no more.
> When Dapple runs no more,
> What then can I do?
> Ah Yu, my Yu,
> How can I save you?[22]

Most Han songs are not attributed to known authors but are known as either "music bureau" songs or the Nineteen Old Poems. Music bureau songs received their name from the government department founded or revived by Emperor Wu to compose songs to accompany state sacrifices, banquets, court receptions, and army parades. These songs were written by professional musicians of low status. Apart from the temple hymns, they reflect the kind of oral, folk traditions found throughout the world, and they may have been related to early Chinese popular compositions. Among their features are impersonality and detachment in presentation, stereotyped situations or plots, lack of introspection, ahistoricity, abrupt transitions, use of commonplace phrases, recurring refrains, and colloquialism. But it would be incorrect to speak of these compositions as folk songs. They were written for performance at court, and they exhibit a mix of classical and vernacular languages. Because they had to be performed and understood without recourse to a written text, however, the language was simplified and repetitious. Moreover, they were often adapted from more popular compositions that were popular with the ruler or court. This accounts for the overlap of their features with true folk compositions.[23]

The simplest of the court compositions resemble work chanties, such as the song "South of the River."

> South of the river we can pick lotus,
> The lotus leaves, how they fill the pond.
> Fish play among lotus leaves.
> Fish play east of lotus leaves.
> Fish play west of lotus leaves.
> Fish play south of lotus leaves.
> Fish play north of lotus leaves.[24]

This piece seems to be patterned on songs that provided a vocal replication of the rhythm of physical work, maintaining the pace of repetitive tasks and relieving boredom. Other music bureau songs are more elaborate and even dramatic, but they still copy popular songs in their abrupt transitions in point of view and content, the absence of a clear temporal sequence when telling a story, composite structures that suggest alternation between soloists and a chorus, and the frequent use of repeated lines or phrases.[25]

Still other music bureau songs show evidence of being aimed at a highly literate segment of the court audience. References to historical or literary figures imply textual study on the part of the author and his intended audience. Others tell of spirit flights and meetings with immortals, a distinctly elite concern. In addition to their differences in subject matter, such poems replace the composite structure and shifting point of view of the folklike songs with a more sequential narrative told from a single, or sometimes a double, point of view. A classic example is the following poem:

Green, green the grass by river,
Endlessly my longing follows the distant road.
The distant road, beyond imagining,
And yet last night I saw him in a dream.
In a dream I saw him by my side,
Suddenly I woke, and he was in another land.
Another land, each of us in different realms,
Tossing and turning I could see him no more.
Withered mulberry feels Heaven's wind,
The ocean's water feels Heaven's cold.
Entering the house, each is naturally loved,
But who deigns to speak to me?
A traveler comes from far away,
He brings me a double carp [letter box].
I shout at the servant, "Cook the carp."
Inside there is a white silk letter.
I kneel down and read the letter.
What, after all, is within?
First it says, "Try and eat more."
Last it says, "I will always remember you."[26]

Here, the singer is a woman whose husband is serving in the army at the frontier (as indicated in the title of the poem). The entire poem narrates the woman's thoughts and experiences, with a second voice entering at the end in the words of her husband's letter. The passionate sorrow of the first voice, poetically expressed by beginning some lines with the last words of the preceding ones, provides a striking contrast with the prosaic but ultimately heart-breaking contents of the letter.

This more explicitly lyric verse in which the author meditated on his own experience or imaginatively projected himself into "the voice of another" developed further in the so-called ancient poems of the Eastern Han.[27] These poems feature two conventional speakers: neglected women and young men who aspired to an official career. Frustrated in their hopes, these figures mourn time's passing and dwell on aging and death. The tone of the poems consequently varies between melancholic brooding, outright lamentation, and injunctions to "seize the day" through the pleasures of wine and music. Devoted to the poet's inner experience and meditations on human mortality, they reduce narrative elements to a minimum. Instead, the poet describes the situation, such as a scene that has been witnessed, and then elaborates the emotions aroused. The poems are marked as *texts* to be read, with visual links provided by grammatical or semantic parallels between lines and couplets replacing the repetition often used in music bureau songs.

The music bureau was sometimes condemned by Confucian scholars for employing the sort of popular music that had developed in the late Warring States—the "music of Zheng and Wei" which Confucius had denounced as licentious. The bureau was abolished at the end of the Western Han, as part of the ritual reforms and money-saving policies associated with the rising influence of classicist thought. However, since Confucian poetic theorists had also asserted that Zhou kings had collected folk songs to learn the state of public morality, the music bureau song remained a legitimate form of verse and became a standard subgenre of lyric (*shi*) poetry. While the obsession of the "ancient poems" with mortality and physical pleasure did not follow the Confucian moral program, their simplicity of language and direct expression of the poet's feelings and aspirations were in line with the proclaimed ideals of Eastern Han verse. At the end of the Han, the Cao clan and some of their followers adapted the techniques and themes of the "ancient poems" and music bureau songs to create the first lyrics composed by named literati.

The Confucian Library

Perhaps the clearest evidence of the impact of Confucian classicism on Han literature was the catalogue of the imperial library. It was composed by Liu Xiang and his son Liu Xin, working under Wang Mang at the end of the Western Han. Ban Gu included it, in modified form, in the *Book of the Han* as the "Monograph on the Arts and Letters." Libraries and their systems of categorization offer a window onto the structure of an intellectual universe, because they reveal a society's organization of the branches of knowledge. The Lius structured their catalogue on the assumption that the texts of the Confucian canon were both the models of proper writing and the origin of all other categories of text. They identified this canon with the sage kings, and they traced each category of text back to a department or office in the Zhou kingdom.

Because the catalogue presumes the unity of knowledge as an ideal, it treats any multiplicity of versions or overlap of texts as a problem to be corrected. The Lius explain the existence of corrupt texts in the rhetoric of inter-school polemics:

Long ago Confucius died and the subtle words were cut off. His seventy disciples perished, and the great truth was perverted. Therefore the *Annals* split into five versions, the *Odes* into four, and the *Changes* was transmitted in variant traditions. In the Warring States period diplomats and persuaders argued over what was true and false, and the words of the masters became a jumbled chaos. This disturbed Qin state, so it burned writings in order to make idiots of the common people. The Han arose and repaired the damage wrought by Qin. On a large scale they assembled texts and strips, and they broadly opened the path for the offering up of documents.[28]

The Lius credit a series of Han emperors for taking the lead in gathering the texts together, and they list the scholars who worked in the compilation of the final catalogue. Their account of the creation of the imperial library catalogue thus parallels the *Springs and Autumns of Master Lü* and the *Master of Huainan*, in which the completeness of the work was achieved by rulers who gathered scholars in order to put together a comprehensive work and restore lost unity.[29]

The centrality accorded to the canonical texts as the basis of all writing is shown in the catalogue's title, which divides texts into canonical arts (*yi*) and all other "letters" (*wen*). The canons come directly from sage rulers, whereas other categories are attributed to offices in an imagined early state. Just as officers derived their authority from the monarch, so the lesser forms of writing traced their limited share of the truth back to the texts of the sages. All non-canonical categories were justified by a quotation from a classic or from the writings of Confucius, making it clear that the philosophy and verse which emerged in the Warring States were derivatives of the Confucian canon. "The different philosophical traditions all cling to their own strengths . . . but if you join their essential conclusions they are all branches or channels of the Six Canons."[30]

Although the Warring State philosophers were the literary expression of the fragmentation of power, they nevertheless preserved elements of the canon's truth, according to the Lius. When a true king returns to the world, under the Han, he will draw the classics back into the original unity from which they have split off. The same model applies to poetry:

In ancient times when the feudal lords and hereditary officials had exchanges with neighboring states they used subtle words to move one another. When saluting with bows they invariably cited an *Ode*

to make known their aspirations, and they thereby separated the
worthy from the unworthy and observed flourishing or decline. After the Spring-and-Autumn period, the Way of Zhou was gradually
ruined, and the *Odes* for paying respects and making inquiries were
no longer practiced among the states. Men of honor who studied the
Odes were lost among the commoners, so the rhapsodies of worthy
men disappointed in their aspirations arose.[31]

The "Monograph" then quotes Yang Xiong's praise for the "rhapsodies
of the men of *Odes*" over the "rhapsodies of the men of ornate language"
and calls for the restoration of the canonical ideal of morally serious
verse under the Han emperors.

The parallel between texts and government is explicit in these passages. The canons are equated with the early sage kings, and the emergence of the philosophical masters and new forms of verse are explained
as expressions of political turmoil. The Han's political rise led to an improvement of literature through the revival of earlier principles, if not
necessarily earlier literary forms. The Lius developed this idea of the parallel between government and texts by tracing textual categories back to
political offices in the Zhou state. Thus, Confucian philosophical texts
derive from the minister of the masses and of education; Daoist texts
from the historian-astrologer; yin/yang from the calendrical office of Xi
and He; legalist philosophies from judicial officials; those of the school of
names from ritual officials; Mohist texts from officials in charge of the
ancestral temple; those of the school of alliances from the office of emissary; and so on.[32]

Mapping texts onto political offices reflects not only the equation of intellectual authority with political authority but also the ideal of restoring
unity to a fragmented world. The catalogue emphasizes that it was written by a group of officials, each of whom possessed a form of limited,
specialized expertise. Only when these were combined under the sponsorship of the ruler could they produce a complete, annotated account of
the textual realm. Thus the ultimate unity of the textual realm in the catalogue parallels the unity of the imperial state under the ruler.

However, despite this ideal of unity, the catalogue does not gloss over
the inadequacy of existing texts. This is true primarily of canonical texts,
which survived in multiple forms. The *Canon of Change* was the best
preserved because Qin did not suppress it, but even it existed in a half
dozen versions by the Han dynasty. Every other canon was divided into

competing traditions of commentary, often appended to varying canonical texts. The master philosophers were fragmentary and partial. Verse had lost its links to government and had become a genre in which commoners employed elaborate language and flights of fantasy to express individual despair. Military texts had become devoted to the general's arts of maneuver and deception. Divination had passed into the hands of technical specialists unable to master the subtlety of astronomy and calendars. The arts of health and longevity had been corrupted by specialists who employed them as technical tricks for the prolongation of life.[33]

This attack on specialization indicates a final theme of the catalogue, the superiority of encompassing skills to limited, technical ones. This idea, developed in the self-justifications of the philosophical traditions, figures in the composition of the catalogue. The work was divided into seven categories. The first four—the collective, the canons, the masters, and verse—were compiled by Liu Xiang and Liu Xin. The remaining three—military, numbers and divination, and formulas and techniques of longevity—were each compiled by a specialist in the field: a military officer, the grand astrologer, and the emperor's attending physician. Thus, literary and generalist skills, including the all-encompassing canons, were handled by the literary officials in charge of the project, while technical disciplines were entrusted to specialists. The categories are listed hierarchically, with the generalist headings preceding the technical ones. Moreover, philosophical writings and verse are treated as generic outgrowths of the canon, while the technical works are not traced back to canonic models.

The technical categories are also marked by a distinctive form of corruption. While the masters degraded canonical texts through partiality, and the poets through lack of political purpose and an obsession with ornament, both remained elements of the canonical heritage and were redeemable when a sage government returned. The technical arts, by contrast, corrupted canonical principles by their very existence, and the monograph suggests no program for their redemption.

The depiction of textual specialization and the hierarchy of genres in the bibliographic catalogue differs from that articulated in the Warring States. In this earlier period, the philosophers had distinguished themselves from the mantic traditions by claiming to possess a generalizing intellect that encompassed and guided the technical arts. They thereby equated their status to that of administrators or kings. However, in the shift toward writing comprehensive texts and rereading existing texts as universal, the philosophical masters were themselves demoted to the status of parts of the encompassing whole which the canon embodied.

In this new intellectual order, fashioned to express the unitary empire, the canon was identified with the monarch and a unified wisdom, of which all other texts were fragments. The older, Warring States hierarchy articulated by the philosophers survived in the ranking of the "literary" arts above the technical disciplines, but philosophers were now placed in a subordinate position within a larger order defined by the canon and its commentaries. Similarly, poetry and history, and indeed all forms of writing, were read within an intellectual universe established by the state canon that was understood as the textual form of the Han empire.

IO

LAW

LAW IS A protean term connected to many aspects of life in ancient China. It was a set of authoritative propositions closely linked to religious beliefs and practices, a system of rules and punishments by which the state sought to impose its standards, an extension of the kin structure that underwrote the authority of the aged, a form of language, a type of career, a means of expelling undesirable elements of the population to the frontier, and a way to recruit labor for state service.

Written codes first emerged in the Warring States period, when tax and service obligations were extended to lower levels of urban society and to peasants in the hinterland. Local officials responsible for enforcing these obligations required written laws and regulations stipulating procedures for keeping accounts, the penalties for crimes, and other aspects of administration. But far from being merely the tools of rational administration or of brutal *realpolitik,* these codes were embedded within the religious and ritual practices of the societies from which they emerged.

Law and Religion

Stories in the *Transmissions of Master Zuo (Zuo zhuan),* set in the seventh through fifth centuries B.C., depict Zhou aristocrats ritually invoking powerful spirits with blood sacrifices and calling upon these spirits to enforce the terms of their oaths. Such covenants, sanctified through smearing the lips of participants with the blood of sacrificial animals and burial of the covenants in the ground to transmit them to the spirit world, were used to form alliances between states or lineages. They also dictated the agreed-upon rules to be observed by all who joined these leagues. The recent discovery of some of these buried covenant (*meng*) texts from Houma, Wenxian, and Qinyang, along with the rereading of received texts in light of these discoveries, shows how such texts provided a religious foundation for a new political authority based on writing.[1]

In addition to covenants, a second form of writing that sacralized the earliest legal codes was inscription on bronze vessels of the type used in the religious cults of the Shang and Zhou. These inscriptions had served, among other purposes, to communicate with ancestors and to render permanent any gifts of regalia or grants of political authority made by the ruler. In the late Western Zhou and Spring and Autumn periods, several inscriptions record decisions in legal cases, most commonly disputes over land. A vessel discovered in the cache at Dongjia village records the punishment of a cowherd, who was sentenced to whipping and tattooing. By the sixth century B.C., according to the *Transmissions of Master Zuo*, the states of Zheng and Jin used bronze vessels to consecrate their new legal codes. Thus, inscriptions on sacred vessels that had fixed power and privilege under the Zhou were adapted to codify the powers of the emerging territorial states.[2]

The sacralization of law in covenants and bronzes did not end with the development of more elaborate codes written on bamboo or wooden strips. Han texts narrate several occasions in the Qin-Han interregnum and the early Han when ceremonies accompanied by blood sacrifice were used to consecrate new laws. But by this time the emphasis had shifted to the *text* of the oath as the binding force—a recognition of the power of sanctified writing.[3]

The religious links of early legal codes are also indicated by the recent discovery of substantial samples of late Warring States law in tombs of officials at Yunmeng (Qin state) and Baoshan (Chu state). This shows that legal texts figured in funerary ritual. It is unclear whether the documents were buried because they were powerful, sacred texts that would protect the deceased in the afterlife or whether they were an element in the program of equipping the tomb with all the materials needed to continue the deceased's mode of living in the world beyond. In either case, in the still overlapping realms of funerary cult and political authority, these legal texts played a role reminiscent of the Zhou bronzes. The deceased held them through the gift of the ruler, and they were signs and tools of the holder's power over his subordinates. Both binding and empowering, the texts were carried into the afterlife to preserve the status of the deceased.

The legal texts at Yunmeng and Baoshan were successors not just of the Zhou bronzes but also of the covenants. Like these ritual oaths, the legal texts were buried in the earth for transfer to the spirit realm. But more important, the texts played a pivotal role in the creation of the state by transmitting the policies of the ruler directly to leading political actors, who in turn transmitted them to their own subordinates and kin. The names on the buried covenant texts were heads of locally powerful families who had come into the presence of the ruler of the emerging state and sworn loyalty to his person and lineage. These oaths bound not only the family heads but the lesser members of their lineages. Similarly, the laws of the Warring States were inscribed on ritual texts bestowed upon political actors, who were bound to the ruler through the receipt of these sacred objects and who in turn imposed the rules on their subjects. The physical bestowal of the written statutes and associated documents at or in the wake of the ceremony of appointment was central to the law's function, and this ritualization of the code was carried forward in funerary rites.

This focus of laws on the ruler's control of officials is clear in the legal texts from Yunmeng, where the common people appear only in a secondary role. In these documents, the first and longest section in the groupings used by modern editors ("Eighteen Statutes") deals almost entirely with rules for official conduct, guidelines for keeping accounts, and procedures for the inspection of officials. The second section ("Rules for Checking") dictates the maintenance of official stores and the records thereof. The contents of the third section ("Miscellaneous Statutes") closely resembles those of the first two. The fourth section ("Answers to Questions Concerning Qin Statutes") defines terms and stipulates procedures so that officials could interpret and execute items of the code in the manner intended by the court. The fifth section ("Models for Sealing and Investigating") instructs officials in the proper conduct of investigations and interrogations so as to secure accurate results and transmit them to the court.[4]

The emphasis on the control of local officials reappears in the text "On the Way of Being an Official" found in the same tomb. The official is charged to obey his superiors, limit his own wants, and build roads so that directives from the center can arrive rapidly and without modification. It praises loyalty, absence of bias, deference, and openness to the actual facts of cases as the highest of virtues. It attacks personal desires, acting on one's own initiative, resisting superiors, and concentrating on private business as the worst of faults. In short, it proclaims the new ideal of the official as a conduit who transmits the facts of his locality to the court and the decisions of the court to the countryside without interposing his own will or ideas.[5] This is the sort of official that was to be created through the dictates of the legal documents in the same tomb.

Principles underlying the early legal codes are also linked to the ritual practices of the period. Two of particular significance are the idea of punishment as *do ut des* (the exchange of one thing for another) and the importance attributed to titles and names.[6]

Divination materials found with the legal texts in the fourth-century B.C. Baoshan tomb reveal a system of curing/exorcism through sacrifice that follows the Shang pattern. The physician/diviner ascertains the identity of the spirit causing the disease, its relation to the patient, and the type and number of sacrifices necessary to assuage it. The ritual is a mechanical form of exchange with no moral dimension. A similar process of identification of the spirit culprit and mechanical ritual expulsion or appeasement informs the "Demonography" found in the Yunmeng tomb. This text's title *jie* is a technical term in legal documents meaning "interrogation" but also refers to the commanding of spirits through the use of written spells; in Zhou documents this term meant "to obligate oneself to the spirits by means of a written document." Here a term used for written communications with the spirits was applied to the legal practice of making written records of testimony by witnesses. This close connection between religious and legal language figures throughout the texts from Yunmeng.[7]

Texts on demon control share with legal documents not only a common vocabulary but also a common mode of practice. In both spheres—religious and legal—order and control are maintained through the process of identifying malefactors and applying graded responses sufficient to counteract the threat or compensate for damage. Legal punishments incorporated the minute, mathematical gradations that had characterized sacrificial responses to threatening spirits since the Shang. This parallel between exorcism and punishment was noted in a passage from the text of political philosophy *Master Han Fei* (*Han Feizi*), written under the Qin or early Han: "Ghosts' curses causing people to fall ill means that ghosts harm people. People's exorcising the ghosts means that people harm ghosts. People's breaking the law means that people harm their superiors. Superiors' punishing the people means that the superiors harm the people."[8]

The Yunmeng documents include a "Book of Days" (*ri shu*)—a text for determining which days were favorable or unfavorable for certain activities—which contains a guide to thief catching (a legal concern) through divination. The guide describes how the physical appearance of the thief can be determined based on the day when the crime occurred. Other strips deal with appropriate days to take up a post and indicate the consequences of holding audiences at various times of the day. Since these mantic texts were buried together with the legal materials, it is likely that the deceased official or his subordinates employed them in their everyday administrative activities, further blurring the line between legal and religious practice.[9]

The link between law and religion in early imperial China also entailed bringing the actions of government into conformity with Heaven and nature. For example, executions could legally take place only in autumn and winter, the seasons of decay and death. If a man condemned to death survived the winter, due to a procedural delay or dilatory action, then he was no longer liable to execution. One story tells of Wang Wenshu, a harsh official in the time of Emperor Wu who had just executed several thousand households of locally powerful families. "When the beginning of spring came, Wang Wenshu stamped his foot, sighing, 'If only I could make the winter last one more month it would suffice to finish my work!'"[10]

A related practice was the regular granting of general amnesties for all but the most serious criminal offenses. Such amnesties were bestowed on happy occasions pertaining to the imperial household, such as the birth of a son or establishment of an heir. They were also granted in response to natural calamities thought to derive from excessive severity. In his role as a giver of life, the emperor patterned his amnesties on the life-giving potency of Heaven, his spiritual father and divine equivalent.[11]

The idea that human misconduct disturbed the natural order led to certain legal precepts pertaining to punishment. Punishments were imposed to *bao* (requite or pay back) the deed, implying a restoration of the natural balance disturbed by the crime. To be efficacious, a punishment should not be either too severe or too lenient; if the punishment was not in balance with the crime, the natural order would not be restored. On the basis of this theory, scholars would in some cases argue that particular natural disasters or unusual phenomena resulted from inappropriate punishments, or failure to punish at all.[12]

Law and Administration

While law in the Warring States and early empires remained embedded in the religious practices and ideas of the period, it was above all a tool of administration used to preserve social order. In this role, law went beyond simply enjoining certain actions, prohibiting others, and enforcing both with penal sanctions. An entire model of the social structure was built into the patterns of rewards and punishments stipulated in legal codes. The judicial practices of the period trace the lineaments of a properly functioning society as understood by the ruler and his agents.

One of the clearest examples of this is the differentiation of rewards and punishments based on the status of those involved. The semi-divine status of the emperor found legal expression in the designation of offenses against his person or property as the most heinous of crimes. Inflicting damage on an imperial dwelling or tomb, for example, was punishable by death. If an artisan's error caused a wheel or axle on the imperial chariot to break, the artisan was executed. Even accidentally breaking an imperially bestowed gift, such as a dove staff, could lead to capital punishment for an official.

This ranking of misdeeds and punishments also applied to ordinary households. Crimes committed by kin were more serious than those committed by a stranger, and crimes of juniors against seniors were more serious than the reverse. Because the Qin code gave legal sanction to the authority of parents, a son's denunciation of his father could not be accepted as evidence, and the denouncer could be punished for making the accusation. A father could steal from his children with impunity, but if a grandchild beat his grandparents, he was tattooed and assigned to forced menial labor. The father could use the legal system to mete out punishments to his own family, even banishing or executing them. Routine, low-level violence of fathers against children in the name of discipline appears to have been the norm. Wang Chong's first-century A.D. biography notes how remarkable it was that his father never flogged him. Later writings show that such beatings were a regular aspect of education in China for over two millennia.

One of the most striking features of Qin law to survive into the Han was "mutual implication" (*lian zuo*). Punishment for certain major crimes did not end with the individual but was extended to family, neighbors, and, in the case of an official, to superiors, subordinates, or the man who had recommended him for office. But the most important links were those among kin, and the range of collective punishments offers important evidence of the limits of kinship that were regarded as socially or legally significant by the state.

Collective punishment of kin was known by the technical term "destruction of the lineage" (*mie zu*). In the Spring and Autumn period "destruction of the lineage" had referred to a political event in which one noble clan eliminated another through killing or enslaving thousands of people. The phrase began to change meaning in the Warring States as indicated in the buried covenant texts, where it referred to the destruction of individual families who violated the terms of the oath. Shortly thereafter it came to include the punishing of family members for failures of their kin in military service. Thus, by the Qin and Han dynasties, "destruction of the lineage" had become a legal tool in the government's effort to delimit, register, and control the individual households that were the foundation of the state's power.[13]

This extended familial liability for crimes paralleled in significant ways a moral obligation to avenge kin, as prescribed in the classicist texts. First, the practice of vengeance entailed collective responsibility. A memorial written in the early Eastern Han described how reciprocal vengeance among the people led to the destruction of entire families. In some cases an avenger did not kill the actual offender but rather his wife and children or one of his other relatives. Sometimes a relative of the offender would voluntarily present himself to the avengers in the hope of rescuing his kinsman. Since the obligation to avenge was based on ties of kinship, the roles of avenger and victim were played by the collective kin unit rather than isolated individuals.

The state's use of collective punishment mirrored or inspired this social practice, and the groups delineated by punishments in law were those who acted for revenge in local feuds.[14] Thus collective legal liability was to some degree the state's mode of participation in a vengeful society constituted through reciprocal blood debts. In a world where people's kin were obliged to avenge them, anyone who killed a person had best destroy the family too, and the state could not exempt itself from this kill-or-be-killed rule. In many cases the targets of revenge were officials who had performed legal executions.

Collective responsibility was not just a means for the state to terrify people through the enormity of the punishment but also a method to secure their participation in mutual surveillance. If kin or neighbors reported the crimes of those to whom they were linked, they not only escaped punishment but could receive rewards. The early imperial state sought to control a large population with a small number of officials; so, as noted by the reforming Qin chief minister Shang Yang, governing the state depended on the participation of the entire population, as in the passage quoted on page 48.[15]

Through collective responsibility and mutual surveillance the state sought to fashion a people who would actively enforce the legal dictates of their masters. In such a system the people would judge their fellows; or, more precisely, they would judge those to whom they were bound in kinship or membership in local units of collective responsibility. In the state advocated by Shang Yang, a man would stand in judgment of those whom, in the world of the classicists, he would be obliged to avenge.

The punishments in the legal texts also suggest a social hierarchy constituted through reciprocal obligations of gift and debt. Rather than stipulating fixed punishments, the law indicated that each crime produced an obligation to be redeemed through the performance of certain acts or certain payments. People of different status had different means for paying off the obligation created through violation of the legal codes. The status of the individual determined the appropriate punishment as much as did the nature of the crime. In the Qin code and in the Baoshan materials, the underlying principle was that the relation of the culprit to the ruler determined the form of punishment. This relationship was marked by the receipt of gifts from the ruler that entered into reciprocal exchanges built into the penal codes.[16]

The clearest example is the granting of titles of rank. These ranks were received from the ruler in exchange for service, at first for military service and then for the payment of sums to the state. Titles were the chief reward that common people could receive, and holders of titles could surrender them for a reduction of punishment.[17] This meant that any crime committed by a title-holder would be punished less severely—or more precisely, that the title could be returned to the ruler in exchange for a reduction of the normal penalty. This exchange of status for a lesser punishment was worked out in a highly elaborated form in the Qin legal order.

Under the Qin code, violations by officials were usually punished with fines, measured as a certain number of suits of armor. These individuals, already protected by their titles, thus enjoyed the added privilege of redeeming any misconduct with forced contributions to the army. Most scholars assume that this was a financial penalty, since money had to be relinquished in order to purchase the suits of armor. So not only could those who received titles from the ruler use them to redeem their crimes, but those who received cash in the form of a salary from the ruler could return it to him in order to escape servitude. This principle is not absolute, however, for individuals without office accused of cash-related crimes or failures in military duties also paid fines in the form of armor. People with neither rank nor office could redeem crimes only through labor service for a fixed term or through state slavery. Once again, the punishment reflected the ties of the individual to the ruler, for labor service was the primary obligation of a peasant.[18]

Mutilating punishments, which dated back at least to the Shang and Zhou, fell outside the scheme of status-based reciprocity because they could not be avoided through payments. But even for these archaic punishments, graded degrees of mutilation were adapted to the position and privileges of the criminal. Mutilations, ranging from shaving beards and hair (a temporary stripping away of manhood) through tattooing and cutting off the nose or foot to castration or death, were used to make minute distinctions in the scale of punishments and balance them against past rewards.

In addition to receiving titles as a mark of their incorporation into the state, common people also received the gift of a family name. In the Zhou state a family name had been an aristocratic privilege, but in the Warring States this was extended to commoners. Consequently, the term "Hundred Surnames" (*bai xing*) that had previously indicated "the aristocracy" came to mean "commoners." Membership in society, as defined by law, entailed being registered within a lineage and household. The "Models for Sealing and Investigations" from the Yunmeng legal documents states that any testimony must begin with the name, status (rank), and legal residence of the witness. Even the earlier cases from Baoshan provide many examples of this practice.[19]

Once the common people were granted ranks and family names like those that had previously defined the nobility, the meaning of these attributes changed. Just as the process of universalizing military service had transformed a mark of nobility into a token of servitude, so the universalizing of naming, titling, and registration stripped these attributes of their authority. When the Zhou nobility received titles and surnames from the king, they inscribed these in reports to their ancestors, who granted them power and status not wholly dependent on the king. By contrast, the names and titles of the Warring State peasant, although showing status as a legally free member of the political order, were inscribed on registers whose ultimate recipient was the ruler of the state. To have one's name and title inscribed meant being a subject under the law.

Population registers, and the maps associated with them, came to represent authority in a way that transcended their power as legal documents. They magically embodied the people and territory they represented. For example, when Jing Ke attempted to assassinate the First Emperor, his pretext for appearing at court was to surrender territory to Qin through the formal presentation of the relevant population registers and maps. The force in law of such documents has been demonstrated by a tomb text entitled "Statute for forming arable plots" dated to 309 B.C. [20]

By the late Warring States period, population registration had also become an element of religious practice. The clearest evidence is a story found in a third-century B.C. Qin tomb at Fangmatan, which tells of a man who committed suicide to avoid the disgrace of an unjust execution. Legal petitions addressed to the "Master of Life Spans" led to his body's being exhumed at the command of a scribe of the god and gradually restored to life.[21] This story depicts an underworld bureaucracy which keeps registers and communicates with mortals in texts based on terrestrial legal documents. It is also significant that the underworld administration was invoked to correct a death resulting from failings of earthly legal procedure.

"Spirit registrars" controlling the human life span also figure in the Warring States texts *Master Mo* and *Words of the State,* and the early Han philosophical compendium the *Master of Huainanzi.* The fourth-century B.C. Chu silk manuscript likewise contains evidence of a bureaucratic pantheon.[22] An even more elaborate underworld bureaucracy operating through codes and laws appears in Han tomb texts for the control of the spirit world.

Qin texts also discuss the handling of documents, the administration of granaries and storehouses, and the loaning of grain or oxen to peasants. Han wooden strips from the northwestern sites of Dunhuang and

Juyan provide details of administrative concerns and procedures, including rules for keeping records and making reports, maintaining equipment, annually testing soldiers in archery (with rewards for good performance), obtaining a certificate for travel, granting leave so that a soldier could return home to bury a parent, paying taxes, and issuing circulars describing wanted criminals.[23] All these documents show the pervasive role of law in early imperial administration.

Law and Language

As James Boyd White has elaborated, law is not only a system of rules and sanctions but also a specialized form of language and rhetoric. Legal systems generate their own technical vocabulary and usages, the mastery of which is essential for participation in the legal process.[24] Because local Qin and Han officials were also the chief judges in their districts, they were required to learn the distinct linguistic usages of the legal code. Similarly in the central court, those in charge of drafting legal regulations had to become specialists in legal language. However, the links between law and language in early imperial China were not simply a matter of mastering technical language but of controlling society through the regulation of language.

The most elaborate accounts of the relations among law, administration, and language were those under the rubric of "forms and names" (*xing ming*), as discussed in the Qin text *Master Han Fei*.[25] The ruler is advised to hold himself quiet and allow the ministers to describe the administrative tasks they will accomplish (that is, to "name" themselves). These declarations should be written down to provide a "tally" or "contract" against which performance will be measured. Later, if the claim and performance match, then the official will be rewarded; if not, he will be punished.[26] This prescription for the use of contracts and annual verifications in the *Master Han Fei* corresponds to descriptions of actual administrative practice.

In both theory and practice, the use of rules and punishments is based on the matching of language to reality. Successful law and administration stemmed from the correction of words so that they matched actions. A related idea had appeared earlier in the theory attributed to Confucius of rule through the "rectification of names." In reply to a question of what policy he would advocate for the state of Wei, Confucius stated that he would begin by rectifying names. If names were not correct, then words would not correspond to the world, affairs would not be regulated, rites and music would not flourish, punishments would be incorrect, and the people would not know how to behave. As this list is clearly sequential, the correct use of names is the foundation of the system of rites that in turn makes possible the adequacy of legal punishments and social order.[27]

This idea developed in several ways, but the one most relevant to a theory of law and language was elaborated in the *Gongyang Commentary* to the *Spring and Autumn Annals*. It read the *Annals* as a coded text in which the choice of title or the mention of a person's name indicated judgments equivalent to a ruler's rewards and punishments. In this interpretation, the text was the blueprint for an imaginary kingdom of Lu, which Confucius ruled as the "uncrowned king" through a legal system consisting entirely of the correct application of names.[28] This mode of reading the text explicitly identified the power of rectified language with that of legal judgments. Law, in this tradition of commentary, was the quintessential expression of the social powers of language.

By the first century of Han rule, most scholars at the imperial court had accepted this idea of the *Annals* as the textual expression of law as perfected language. When asked why Confucius wrote the *Spring and Autumn Annals,* the historian Sima Qian quotes the classicist scholar of the *Annals* Dong Zhongshu (ca. 179–104 B.C.): "When the Way of Zhou declined and was abandoned, Confucius was chief magistrate in Lu . . . Confucius knew that his words would not be employed and his way not put into practice. He judged the rights and wrongs of 242 years [the span covered in the *Annals*] to create a standard for the world. He criticized the Son of Heaven, demoted the feudal lords, and punished the high officials, all in order to carry out the tasks of the king." By the Eastern Han, a text attributed to the same Dong Zhongshu taught how to use the coded judgments of the *Annals* to make actual legal decisions. To the extent that this and similar texts were used, the identification of the *Annals* as the textual form of the purified language of law had become a political reality.[29]

Linking the *Annals* to Confucius' supposed role as a judge is significant. Law, along with religion and government, is one of the spheres in which language most frequently plays a performative role. The declarations of the judge, like those of the official or the priest, *produce* social realities. His pronouncement of guilt creates the fact of guilt in a way that the words of ordinary people cannot. When the *Annals* assigns guilt or innocence, or grants or withholds a certain status, it acts as judge. Parables in the fourth-century B.C. *Transmissions of Master Zuo* also treated historians as judges. This notion that historians pass judgment on the past is commonplace in the West, but the *Gongyang Commentary* and its Han followers treat the figure of speech as a literal reality. Confucius' supposed role as a judge and his imposition of punishments was central to the myth that had developed around him by the early Han.[30]

Law as purified language figured not only in philosophy, commentary, and history but also in the legal texts. The clearest examples of this appear in the Qin legal documents from Yunmeng. Many passages on these strips consist of definitions for technical legal terms. In discussions of the family as a legal entity they gloss terms dealing with the household: "'Household' [*hu*] means 'those who dwell together' [*tong ju*]. They implicate dependents [*li*, servants and slaves], but dependents do not implicate the household. What is meant by 'people of the house' [*shi ren*]? What is meant by 'dwelling together' [*tong ju*]? 'Dwelling together' means only those on the household register. 'People of the house' means the entire household, all those who would be mutually implicated with a criminal."[31]

From other Han sources we know that these terms were also part of conventional language. A decree of Emperor Hui (r. 195–188 B.C.) uses *tong ju* in semantic parallel with the graph *jia* "family." This shows that the terms were synonyms, both meaning "family" in a loose sense.[32] Similarly, *hu* in Han texts has the sense of "household" or "family." What the legal documents do is impose a technical definition on words and phrases that possessed a range of meanings in conventional speech. In the example above, shared residence rather than blood ties defined the legal "family" for the Qin government, whatever might have been the conventional usages of the period. Similar passages from the strips give technical meanings to other graphs, or stipulate whether a given person or case fits into a particular legal category. These are practical manifestations of the philosophical vision of law as a form of rectified language that imposes social order.

Sima Qian's chapter on legal specialists at the imperial court points out the drawbacks of this vision. Speaking of "cruel officials" who use law to impose state authority on powerful families, he quotes philosophical passages on the limits of law and the counterproductive nature of relying on it. He invokes the by-then standard argument against the Qin empire that the severity of its laws and the ruthlessness with which they were imposed led to Qin's collapse.[33] (His animus against rigorous use of the law was not unrelated to his being castrated for arguing that the letter of the law should not be imposed on a general who had been forced to surrender to the Xiongnu.)

Sima Qian then paints a largely negative portrait of officials who employed the full severity of the law. One of the recurring formulas by which he describes them is that they "applied the letter of the law and made no exceptions even for the emperor's in-laws." Others are "too severe in applying the letter of the law" or "manipulate the letter of the law to devise ways to convict people."[34] In short, one of the bases of his critique was that law was a rigorous language which gave power to those who mastered its subtleties and permutations but did not always achieve justice as he or others perceived it. Like the texts cited above, Sima Qian's negative view nevertheless defines law as a distinct form of technically regulated and hence powerful language.

The central figure in Sima Qian's chapter is Zhang Tang. This man, who for a period dominated the court of Emperor Wu, was a specialist in the drafting of legal documents. Like others in the chapter, he is accused of excessive severity in imposing the letter of the law and of manipulating the technical language of legal documents to secure the results he desired. However, his biography also contains distinctive features. First, it includes a childhood narrative that identifies him as a prodigy in the use of legal language and procedure.

> Once his father went out and left Tang, who was still a child, to mind the house. When he returned he found that a rat had stolen a piece of meat. He was enraged and beat Tang for his negligence. Tang dug up the rat's hole, caught the rat, and recovered the remains of the meat. He proceeded to indict the rat, beat it until it confessed, write out a record of its testimony, compare these with the evidence, and draw up a proposal for punishment. After this he took the rat and the meat out into the courtyard. There he held a trial, presented the charges, and executed the rat. When his father saw what he was doing and examined the documents, he found to his astonishment that the boy had carried out the entire procedure like a veteran prison official.[35]

Such accounts of childhood deeds that reveal character and future career featured in many early Chinese biographies, notably that of Confucius, who as a child played at laying out ritual vessels. The story of the boy Zhang Tang reads almost as a parody of such accounts, but it also treats law as a distinctive, life-defining activity marked by the preparation of documents and the formal correctness of language. Moreover, it presents the standard forms of investigation and interrogation as described in the Qin legal documents (and deals with the thieving of rats, which similarly figures in Qin laws).

The second notable feature of Zhang Tang's biography is that once he recognized the emperor's fondness for classical studies and literature, he began to support his decisions with quotations from the classics. He even recruited scholars who were thoroughly versed in the *Canon of Documents* and the *Spring and Autumn Annals* to act as his secretaries so that he could cite these works to greatest effect. Sima Qian notes that many of these students of the classics became his fiercest "claws and teeth" in the rigorous imposition of penalties.[36] Here the theory of Confucius' writing as a mode of legal judgment and the theory of law as a technical language of government converge. The same pattern also figures in other biographies, such as that of the leading classicist scholar of Emperor Wu's court, Gongsun Hong. This demonstrates the close ties between the technical languages of law and of commentary on the classics that developed under the Han.

Another passage that illuminates, from a negative angle, the importance of legal language is the Eastern Han historian and poet Ban Gu's (32–92 A.D.) complaint about the length and complexity of the Han code as it evolved across the centuries. Having supposedly been introduced as a radically simplified version of the Qin code in 200 B.C., by the late first century A.D. it had grown into tens of thousands of articles totaling more than seven million characters. Ban Gu asserted: "[Legal] documents filled tables and cupboards, so even knowledgeable officials could not examine them all. Therefore local officials disagreed, and sometimes the same crime elicited completely different judgments."[37] As in many cultures where elaborate legal systems have evolved, Ban Gu insisted that the search for a rigorous language to cover all cases inevitably broke down due to the multiplication of possibilities.

Law and Punishments

Early imperial law, in the narrowest sense, was a set of rules for behavior and of punishments imposed for their violation. Both Chinese and Western scholars have long noted that early Chinese writers regarded punishment as the defining aspect of law. The monograph on law in Ban Gu's *Book of the Han* is entitled "The Monograph on Punishments" and devotes its first half to the history of the military as the highest form of punishment.

Early Chinese law was largely a system of criminal law, but legal disputes over property and inheritance can be found in this period. The Han will discovered in a tomb in modern Jiangsu shows official participation in the inheritance of property, a fact already suggested by "grave purchase agreements" buried in tombs. Although these were religious documents intended to secure the position of the deceased in the afterlife, we can now confirm that they were patterned on actual practice. The legal texts also deal with such issues as the disposal of the dowry of a married woman convicted of a crime, the rights of slaves to marry, and the relations of parents and children. Nevertheless, the transmitted discussions of law and the bulk of our evidence deal with criminal law and its punishments.[38]

The early imperial state used three primary types of punishments: the death penalty, physical mutilation, and hard labor. Imprisonment was not a punishment in itself but rather a means of detaining suspects and witnesses during the legal process. However, imprisonment could last for a long period if the legal process dragged on, and at least one of the legal specialists described by Sima Qian contrived to hold suspects indefinitely in prison if he thought that the emperor did not desire their execution. Ban Gu also notes that if officials found a case doubtful and could not come to a decision, they would hold people in prison indefinitely.[39] Without possessing any legal grounding, protracted imprisonment was a fact of life.

The highest sanction was capital punishment, of which the most common form was beheading. This was often followed by exposing the head, the corpse, or both in the market. Much rarer was the practice of cutting the condemned in half at the waist by using a large blade hinged on a block. For particularly heinous crimes, which included the execution of three or nine (magical numbers indicating totality) sets of relatives, the primary culprit was subject to all punishments: first he was tattooed, then his nose cut off, then both feet, and finally he was beaten to death, after which his head was hung in the market and the corpse chopped to pieces in the same place. The number of crimes punishable by execution in the Han was very high, though amnesties or commutation into military service at the frontier were also frequent outcomes of capital crimes.[40]

The second category of punishments, mutilation, was much debated and modified over the centuries of Han rule. Originally these punishments had consisted of tattooing the criminal's face, cutting off his nose, amputating one or both feet, and castrating him. In 167 B.C. all of these except castration were formally abolished and replaced by punishments that would not leave the convicted party marked and maimed for life. Tattooing was replaced by shaving the head, wearing an iron collar, and doing labor service. Cutting off the nose or the feet was replaced by a specified number of strokes on the back or buttocks with the bastinado (cane). However, the weight of the bastinado and number of blows usually led to death through abundant bleeding, so what had been proclaimed as an act of mercy in fact represented a significant increase in severity.

The number of strokes and weight of the bastinado were consequently reduced in 156 B.C. and again in 151. But as these punishments grew bearable, officials complained that they could not deter violations. In response, the number of crimes punished by death was increased, so that there were more than a thousand capital crimes in the later Han. Castration may have been abolished as an independent punishment either before or shortly after the abolition of the other mutilating punishments, but it continued to be used sporadically as an exceptional form of death-sentence commutation (which was normally military service at the frontier). It was again abolished in the second decade of the second century A.D. and does not appear to have been used after that date.[41]

The most common punishment in early imperial China was hard labor ranging from one to five years. Each duration was identified by a particular task, such as "wall building and keeping guard," "gathering firewood for sacrifice," or (for women) "pounding grain." These archaic categories did not describe the actual work performed, however, which included constructing roads and bridges, serving in government workshops, diking rivers, transporting grain, and producing iron. All periods of service were preceded by beating with the bastinado, and the more serious ones involved temporary mutilation. A man sentenced to a five-year term had his head shaved and wore an iron collar, while those sentenced to four years had only the beard and mustache shaved.[42]

Another type of punishment commonly used in the Qin was banishment. This punishment may have been frequently invoked because Qin had underpopulated and newly conquered regions that benefited from sending people to live there. A striking case appears in the "Models for Sealing [Houses] and Investigating": "A, a commoner of X village, said in his denunciation, 'I request to have the feet of my own son C, a commoner of the same village, fettered and to have him banished to a border prefecture in Shu [Sichuan], with the injunction that he must not be allowed to leave the place of banishment.'" The official approved the request and provided detailed instructions on how the son was to be escorted. Banishment became less common in the Han, except for those reprieved from death sentences and sent to the frontiers.[43]

In addition to amnesties, many punishments in Qin and Han China were eligible for redemption, a practice to which the Chinese applied the same term as a slave buying his or her freedom. The Qin legal documents frequently refer to the possibility of redemption from banishment, hard labor, mutilation, castration, and even the death penalty.[44] In most cases redemption took the form of a surrender of titles or the payment of a fine. If the fine could not be paid, redemption might be imposed in the form of a period of labor service. Fines in the strict sense were levied primarily on officials for failures in the performance of their duties, with the fine being measured in terms of the purchase of suits of armor, as we have seen. In the Han, payments were conventionally made in gold.

It is difficult to generalize about punishments during this period. On the one hand, executions, mutilations, and even the treatment of hair and clothing that substituted for mutilations entailed a strong element of public display of the state's power over the bodies of its people, as well as the separation from the human community of those who committed major crimes. On the other hand, many punishments took the form of an exchange of services, money, or ranks that was carefully articulated in terms of differential relations. Using labor service as a form of punishment, as well as banishing convicts to frontiers or newly conquered regions, shows that punishments also provided human resources to the state. This is not unlike the use of galley slaves and chain gangs in early modern Europe or the United States. Although Han writers insisted on the disastrous consequences of Qin's excessively detailed regulations and cruel punishments, the records from their own period do not suggest that the Han made any significant improvement in these areas.

Law and Investigations

The essential elements of judicial procedure in early imperial China are fairly well documented. There was no sharp distinction between administrative and legal authority, and in general the chief administrator of a region was also the chief judge: the district magistrate was judge of his district, and the commander of his commandery. A general had the power to punish his troops, even to execute them. Stone inscriptions and textual references tell of specialist legal counselors assisting officials at the local level, but they provide no details.

At the central court, several officials handled legal cases. The superintendent of ceremonies, as chief administrator of the towns associated with the imperial tombs, was high judge for the area around the capital. The primary legal official, however, was the commandant of justice. He acted as judge in all cases pertaining to the imperial house, feudal kings or marquises, and high officials. He also resolved doubtful cases sent up by local officials. Finally, the emperor himself was highest judge, ultimate arbiter, and the source of all laws. While most emperors were happy to delegate to legal officials the actual work of rendering judgments, they could personally intervene or empower specific officials (such as the "cruel clerks" cited above) to act on their behalf.[45]

The central court also supervised the judicial activities of local officials. One method was granting convicted parties or their families the right to appeal judgments, although we have no records of the procedure. The court also established traveling regional inspectors in 106 B.C. Among the matters that these men examined was the fairness and impartiality of the judgments in each administration. They were particularly charged to search for collusion between local officials and the great families of their districts or commanderies. Most of the legal specialists were ordered to attack these families and curb their influence. The court's worry about such collaboration of its own agents with regional powers was not unfounded. In the cities, the equivalent cases of corruption and collusion usually involved gangsters. Han histories tell of protracted collaboration between local officials and gangsters and of the destruction of these illicit leagues by agents from the court.[46]

From scattered references, of which the most detailed example is Zhang Tang's prosecution of the rat, scholars have reconstructed a rough picture of the conduct of legal investigations and trials. More detailed information has been obtained from Qin legal documents, particularly the "Models on Sealing and Investigation." These consist of boilerplate forms showing local officials how to write up reports of investigations and trials, which were sent to the central government. While these models may be based on actual cases, they were used as a procedural guide for local officials.

Many of the models insist on a forensic examination of the scene of the crime and the victims, specifying the details to be studied. A model case on a death by hanging gives a detailed description of the house, the location of the body, the type and size of the rope, the disposition and state of the different body parts, the clothes worn by the victim, the size of the beam from which he was hanged, and even the condition of the soil that prevented footprints. This is followed by a general injunction on methods of investigation:

> When investigating, it is essential carefully to examine and consider the physical traces. One should go alone to the place where the corpse is and consider the knot of the rope. If at the place of the knot there are traces of a noose, then observe whether the victim's tongue protrudes or not, how far the head and feet are distant from the place of the knot and the ground, and whether he had discharged feces and urine or not. Then untie the rope and observe whether mouth and nose emit a sigh or not. Then observe the condition of the blood congealing along the trace of the rope. Try to free the head from the knot in the rope. If you can free it then [text missing] his clothes and completely observe his body, from underneath the hair on his head down to the perineum. If the tongue does not protrude, if mouth and nose do not emit a sigh, if there is no congealed blood along the trace of the rope, if the knot in the rope is so tight that it cannot be slipped off [text missing] Since he has been dead for a long time, the mouth and nose may not produce a sigh. People who kill themselves must first have had reasons. Question the members of his household so that they will reply as to the reasons.[47]

Other accounts include the examination of a tunnel used to break into a house, the study of a fetus and the body of the mother when a fight has induced a miscarriage, and the consultation of a medical specialist to determine which diseases could produce a given physical state.

In addition to investigations of the material and bodily traces of a crime, many cases involved accusations by neighbors or family members. Suspects were arrested by the posthouse chief or constabulary, often retired military men who served the local government. The local administrator then interrogated witnesses and accused:

> In all cases of interrogating one should first listen fully to their words and note these down, letting each of them set out his or her statement. Although the investigator knows that one is lying, there is no need to question pressingly at each point. When a statement has been completely taken down and does not cohere, then question pressingly on the required points. Having questioned pressingly, one listens to everything, notes down the explanatory statements, and then looks further at other unexplained points and questions pressingly on these. When one has questioned pressingly to the ultimate limits of the case, but the suspect has repeatedly lied, changed testimony, and not confessed, then bastinado those whom the statutes allow to be bastinadoed. When you bastinado, be sure to note down: "Report—Because X repeatedly changed testimony and provided no explanatory statement, X has been interrogated with the bastinado."[48]

Physical evidence and testimony converged in a grand confrontation of all concerned parties and the investigating official. Each party gave an account, and the investigating official combined these with the physical evidence to provide a coherent and satisfactory version of events. At points where accounts or physical traces conflicted, further questioning was applied. Changes in testimony or internal contradictions provided the leads for further interrogation. Ultimately, the confession of the accused was necessary, and obdurate refusal to confess in the face of the evidence would lead to beatings and perhaps other forms of torture. However, beating was only a last resort, and its use had to be noted in the report.

In this procedure the official remained silent but kept an exact account of the witnesses' words and then matched the accounts for internal consistency and their relation to material evidence. This corresponded to the ruler's use of "forms and names" to control his ministers. Here, the local official stood in the position of the ruler, and the witness in the position of the minister. The witness named himself and gave an account of his actions, which were transformed into writing, just as the aspirant officer did in the presence of the ruler. Meanwhile, the local official sat silently and measured everything against his knowledge of the facts. This model of administration through a hierarchical series of staged personal encounters moving from the local level to the central court was fundamental to early imperial government.

These texts also show the idea in Chinese legal theory and practice that the judge should be a detective. Through his ability to read the hidden meanings of physical traces and human speech, the ideal judge penetrated the veil of confusion and deceit to arrive at a truthful account of events and a just disposition of the concerned parties. This vision of the judge as a sagely reader of signs also figures in a case found in a Han tomb at Zhangjiashan, wherein an official assigned to discover who had contaminated a meal deduced the failings of an entire household.[49] The judge as a detective figured prominently in later Chinese theater and fiction, where Judge Di (Dee) or Judge Bao became stock embodiments of the aspiration for truth and justice. As the new Qin and Han materials have revealed, this model of justice as the result of sagely ability to read the meaning of signs had already emerged at the beginning of the imperial period.

Law and Labor

Under the Qin, several categories of lawbreakers, along with other social delinquents such as merchants, were forcibly dispatched to the frontiers. Under the Han, as frontier garrisons were increasingly filled with reprieved convicts, physical transfer to the frontier for military service became conflated with the banishment of criminals. Military action at the frontiers thus became a means of exporting internal violence and pacifying the interior. The army served not only to suppress external enemies of the imperial order but also to expel disruptive members of society to regions that in the Han imagination lay beyond the reach of civilization.[50]

The evidence for this comes from many sources. In 109 B.C. Emperor Wu recruited men condemned to death for use in an expeditionary army, and further uses of convicts in expeditions are recorded in 105, 104, 100, and 97 B.C., as well as under later emperors. Emperor Wu's decree of 100 B.C. stated that convicts were to establish a base at Wuyuan. Han wooden strips also show that, from the time of Emperor Wu, convicts were stationed in frontier garrisons, and they increased as a percentage of the total forces throughout the Western Han.[51]

Following the abolition of universal military service by the Eastern Han, the use of convicts dramatically increased. This was not simply an increase in quantity but also a qualitative shift in terms of organization. In 32 A.D., the year after the abolition, the Eastern Han founder Guangwu established the office of the left inspecting commandant of the black turban. Several biographies show that this officer's staff administered punishments. The title also indicates a military role, and in 91 A.D. its holder was indeed sent out on an expedition. A petition referred to a man placed under the commandant as a "reprieved convict," the formula applied to convicts sent to the frontier for military service. Similarly, a memorial requesting the pardon of several former officials called them "reprieved convicts of the left [inspecting] commandant." These show that those placed under this office were convicts who had their death sentences commuted and were sent to the frontier as garrison troops. Thus in addition to those reprieved in the decrees, convicts were routinely sent to the frontiers through this office.[52]

In addition to this evidence of an office devoted to sending convicts to the frontier, documents indicate that garrisons were manned largely by convicts. In 45 A.D. Guangwu established three camps with associated fields at the frontier and ordered that these be filled with reprieved convicts. When Ban Chao returned to court in 102 A.D. after thirty-one years campaigning in Central Asia, a friend apologized that the veteran commander had not received a higher office. In reply, Ban Chao observed that he was not fit for an office at court: "The officers and soldiers beyond the frontiers are not filial sons and obedient grandsons. They have all been transported to fill the frontier camps because of their crimes."[53]

A memorial by Yang Zhong in 76 A.D. indicates the scale of this practice. He wrote that, since the beginning of the reign of Emperor Ming in 58 A.D., officials had repeatedly scoured the prisons and condemned innocent men in order to obtain recruits for the frontier; those sent out numbered in the tens of thousands. The "Fundamental Chronicles" and biographies indicate an average of one decree every five years up to 154 A.D. sending pardoned convicts to the frontier. Although no decrees are listed after 154, biographies cite individuals sent as convicts to the frontier after that date.[54]

We cannot calculate the exact number of men transported, but one can get an idea of the order of magnitude from figures in the "Monograph on Punishments" in the Book of the Han: "Now in the commanderies and princely states, those executed annually are numbered in the tens of thousands. In the empire there are more than two thousand prisons, and the bodies of the unjustly slain pile one on the other."[55] The phrase "numbered in the tens of thousands" is a literary trope, although it echoes the statement of Yang Zhong. However, the figure of two thousand prisons looks more like a genuine number. If it is correct, and given the high number of crimes punishable by death under Han law, officials could easily have provided tens of thousands of convicts for frontier service. In 87 A.D. an official named Guo Geng sent up a memorial asking that those who committed a capital crime before an amnesty but not captured until afterward ought also to be sent to the frontier. Such men, he argued, numbered in the tens of thousands. He also gave the clearest explanation of the rationale of the system, arguing that it both "preserved life [through pardons] and benefited the frontiers."[56] Ban Chao's remark that all the soldiers at the frontier were transported convicts might well have been no exaggeration.

Forced labor was the foundation of the Qin and Han states. Monumental public works such as palaces, temples, and imperial tombs—as well as more overtly utilitarian projects such as canals and roads—required all sorts of skills. Unskilled manual toil figured prominently in leveling ground, moving mountains, piling up earth, and so on. Some tasks were extremely dangerous and resulted in numerous fatalities, particularly in the iron casting foundries that were run by the state monopoly in certain periods. For such types of work, convict labor was essential to the state.[57]

The early empires employed four types of manual labor: peasant corvée, hired, convict, and slave. Each of these had different legal and social characteristics and was consequently suitable for different types of work. Adult males in free households owed one month's labor per year. Such work was devoted to diverse tasks, and the legal texts mention repairing walls of government buildings, mending roads and bridges, excavating ponds, and digging or dredging canals. Corvée labor was most frequently employed in local projects such as flood control, irrigation, or roads, but it was also used to build imperial tomb mounds, construct walls around the capital, and repair breaks in the dikes of the Yellow River. However, such work crews changed each month, and peasants were unavailable during times of crucial agricultural work. If peasants were forced to work away from their native area, the state provided food and tools. Consequently, the use of corvée labor could lead to costly delays in major projects.

Given these limitations, convict labor became crucial to the state. These men and women could work throughout the year until a project was finished. They could be transported across great distances to projects that might take weeks to reach, because once there, they could remain indefinitely. Most important, they could perform the most arduous and dangerous of jobs which might entail the deaths of thousands of laborers. With so many types of crime, and the entire empire to draw upon, the convict population provided a bottomless supply of expendable labor. Several Han tombs contain wall tiles depicting convicts in neck collars, wooden fetters, and iron manacles. One scene even depicts a group of convicts having their heads shaved.

The labor of convicts was as diverse as that of corvée workers, and in some cases the two groups worked together, although the convicts were distinguished by their shaved heads, red caps, and physical restraints. Many convicts were employed in building the tombs of emperors, which often required years of labor by tens of thousands of men. Inscriptions also show that the Qin employed convicts, some of them skilled artisans who had fallen afoul of the law, in factories that produced weapons. Under the Han, skilled labor was done mostly by wage-labor artisans, while convict labor was largely devoted to state iron and copper mines and metal casting facilities. Estimates based on scattered textual references and archaeological remains indicate that somewhere between ten thousand and fifty thousand convicts were employed in the iron processing facilities of the state monopoly. Such work included the mining and the smelting of iron into ingots at the site to facilitate its being shipped across the empire. These activities were extremely dangerous, and deaths were frequent.

The lives of convicts were hard. They received an adequate diet of about 3400 calories per day for hard physical labor, but it consisted almost entirely of grain. They were beaten for the smallest infraction, although officials faced a stiff fine if convicts died within twenty days of a beating. Any further criminal violation by a convict warranted the death penalty. The physical condition of these men and women can be reconstructed in part from skeletons found in three large convict cemeteries dating from the Qin, the reign of the Han emperor Jing (r. 156–141 B.C.), and the late Eastern Han (ca. 86–170 A.D.). All three cemeteries seem to have been used for decades, largely for the remains of those who died while building imperial palaces and tombs. In all three cases more than 90 percent were young men. Seven percent had died from the trauma of sudden blows, almost always to the skull. The jawbones and teeth from the Eastern Han cemetery show a high frequency of advanced gum disease and dental abscesses, probably due to malnutrition. Many of the skeletons still wore their iron collars and leg fetters. The Western Han collars weighed from two and a half to three and a half pounds and had a long spike that would have made it impossible for the convict to bend over very far without impaling himself. Presumably this was removed for certain tasks.

Most of the skeletons were accompanied by notations on brick or some other material with their name and sometimes fuller information on their place of origin, crime, rank, and day of death. These show that convicts were transported from all over the empire to work on these imperial projects. At one major imperial construction site, from one to six people died per day. This seems to have been considered an acceptable rate of mortality, because only once is there a record of an emperor complaining that too many men were dying to build his tomb.[58]

In addition to corvée workers and convicts, the state also drew on a pool of slave labor created through the enslavement of family members of convicted criminals. Archaeologically recovered Qin documents indicate that the state enslaved the women and children of anyone sentenced to three years of hard labor or worse, as well as those castrated for rape. The children of government slaves were slaves from birth. Finally, thousands of prisoners of war were enslaved to the state. However, slaves in this period were largely employed in domestic duties such as cleaning, cooking, mending, running errands, and caring for animals. References to slaves in agriculture or industry are quite rare.[59]

While there is no evidence that slaves worked state-owned land, a Han tomb at Fenghuangshan indicates that about a dozen slaves, mostly female, had been used in private agriculture by the tomb's occupant, and a few texts mention the use of private slaves in large-scale craft production. But not a single surviving imperially produced Qin or Han object mentions a slave as its manufacturer; and other than the First Emperor, there is no indication that any emperor employed slaves in building his tomb. This suggests that for wealthy private individuals, who did not have access to convict labor, employing slaves in certain kinds of work could be more efficient than hiring laborers. For the state, however, convicts provided a steady supply of expendable, cheap labor, whereas slaves were permanent property not to be lightly discarded.

This preference for the use of convicts in the greatest imperial construction projects and in the crucial state monopolies shows that while slaves were legally the lowest form of humanity, it was upon convicts' expendable backs that the material foundations of the early imperial state were built.

CONCLUSION

WHEN AN official named Song Yi submitted the following memorial in 88 A.D., the Han state was at the height of its power: "Since the rise of the Han there have been repeated offensive expeditions, but their gains never matched their losses. [The Eastern Han founder] Guangwu, having experienced the trials of warfare, understood the order of Heaven and Earth. So following [the nomads] coming to surrender, he nourished them under a loose rein. The people at the frontier were able to live and their service was halted; up to today it has been more than forty years. Now the Xianbei are obedient and capture heads of Xiongnu numbered in the tens of thousands. China enjoys this great achievement, and the common people know nothing of its toil. In this the Han has reached its apogee. And the reason it is so is because the barbarians attack one another, with no loss to the Han armies."[1]

This passage celebrates the success of the Eastern Han's military reforms at the end of the first century A.D. The key policy was to pit nomads against one another and use them as cavalry. In the next decade this practice would defeat the Northern Xiongnu and end forever the Han's greatest external threat. Song Yi does not mention the widespread use of convicts and volunteers, but this also kept the peasantry undisturbed. At this time, Ban Gu was writing his rhapsodies celebrating the establishment of a ritually proper regime in a canonical capital, and Wang Chong was praising the Han as the greatest of dynasties because its influence spread far beyond that of the ancient Zhou.

But over the next century the entire system disintegrated, and the policies initiated by the Eastern Han founder Guangwu played a key role in the dynasty's collapse. The chief problem with relying on alien troops was loyalty. Nomads joined the Han army, but because their tribal ties were not dissolved, they were never fully incorporated into the military hierarchy. Instead, the Han government relied on the standing frontier commands to keep them under control. As more and more tribes moved inside the frontiers, this burden proved too great for the relatively small armies in the frontier camps. Loyalty was also weak among the convicts and professionals who spent their lives at the frontier and were linked to the Han state only through the person of their commander.

Another reason for the failure of the Eastern Han army in the second century was its success in the first. Just as the armies of the Warring States and early Western Han had been designed to fight Sinitic rivals, so those of the Eastern Han had been aimed at the northern Xiongnu. With their defeat, many of the "inner barbarians" who had helped the Han in the first century turned against it. The Southern Xiongnu, Wuhuan, and Xianbei lost their chief motive for submission to the Han, as well as their chief source of bonuses for military service. So the Wuhuan and Southern Xiongnu turned increasingly to internal pillage for income, while the Xianbei replaced the Xiongnu as the chief external threat. To the west, the problem was even more severe, for this area suffered through the disastrous Qiang wars.[2]

Every army is intended to fight a certain type of war or counter a particular kind of threat. The entire Eastern Han defense faced north, providing a screen against small-scale raids and a warning in case of invasions. Its large cavalry forces were assembled for offensive expeditions against a united foe with substantial armies. Such dispositions were of little use against the Qiang, located to the west beyond the Han's border defenses. These nomads lacked any overarching political order and did not form large confederacies. The consequences of any defeat were thus limited, and victories, however small, soon led to major rebellions as scattered groups assembled under a successful leader. For the same reasons, peace agreements with the Qiang could not last for long. Moreover, scattered groups of Qiang lived throughout the western and northwestern territories, as well as beyond the frontier. There was no clear geographic boundary between the Qiang and the Han, and under the Eastern Han the Qiang were resettled in the old capital region. The only defense against such an adversary was to move Han farmers and soldiers into the provinces, so that no settlements were left exposed to low-level attacks and the Qiang could be absorbed into the Han economy and polity.

But whenever the Han attempted such a policy, it ended in failure. In 61 B.C. Zhao Chongguo proposed founding military colonies in the west-

ern regions. However, as soon as the colonists had pacified the area, they
were allowed to return to their former homes. A few years later there
was another attempt to settle a permanent agricultural population in the
region, and others between 101 and 104 A.D.[3] But when the Qiang wars
exploded on a large scale in 110 A.D., the government pulled its troops
back to Chang'an. Local officials sent out from the interior, lacking all
knowledge of the region, ordered the abandonment of three commanderies, the confiscation of crops, and the leveling of homes so that no one
would return. By 111 the population of the entire former capital region
in Guanzhong was in flight. An attempt was made between 129 and 132
to restore the abandoned commanderies and establish military colonies,
but when Qiang uprisings resumed in 137, no significant repopulation
had taken place.[4]

Throughout the Eastern Han, particularly in the second century A.D.,
the population of Guanzhong and the old capital region drastically declined under the continuous pressure of Qiang onslaughts (Maps 15 and
16). Even in the early decades of the first century, the northwest frontier

**Population
Distribution
of China
in 2 A.D.**
(One dot represents
25000 persons)

MAP 15

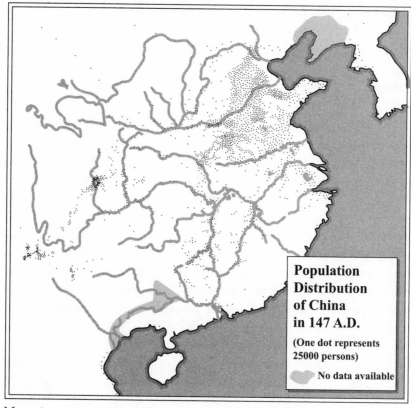

**Population
Distribution
of China
in 147 A.D.**

(One dot represents
25000 persons)

No data available

MAP 16

regions had been seriously depopulated.[5] The policies of resettling barbarians inside China and sending convicts to the frontier may have been
in part an attempt to repopulate these regions. However, these measures
did little to check the demographic decline of the frontier. Census evidence shows that, with one exception, all commanderies in the west and
northwest suffered significant losses, many of them more than 80 or 90
percent. While the figures are unreliable, a change of this magnitude, especially when contrasted with the relative stability and even some in-
creases in inner provinces, probably indicates an actual decline in the
Han population in the border regions.[6]

Contemporary observations support these statistics. Wang Fu (ca. 90–
165 A.D.) noted: "Now in the border commanderies for every thousand *li*
there are two districts, and these have only a few hundred households.
The Grand Administrator travels about for ten thousand *li*, and it is
empty. Fine soil is abandoned and not cultivated. In the central provinces
and inner commanderies cultivated land fills the borders to bursting and

one cannot be alone. The population is in the millions and the land is completely used. People are numerous and land scarce, and there is not even room to set down one's foot." Writing several decades later, Cui Shi described a situation that was virtually identical.[7]

The Eastern Han government made futile attempts to prevent people from leaving the frontier regions and to encourage those who had left to return. The *Book of the Later Han* (*Hou Han shu*) states, "Under the old system [under the Han] frontier people were not allowed to move inward." In 62 A.D. Emperor Ming offered a payment of twenty thousand cash to any refugee from the frontier who returned to his old home. As clear evidence for this ban on inward movement, Zhang Huan, who came from Dunhuang in the far northwest, was allowed to move to an inner commandery in 167 A.D. only as a special reward for meritorious service.[8]

But these attempts to stabilize the frontier population failed. Between 92 and 94 A.D., Emperor He proclaimed geographic quotas to correlate the number of people recommended as "filially pious and incorrupt" (the primary route to office) with the population of a region. For every twenty thousand registered people, a commandery would be allowed to recommend one man per year. For a population between ten thousand and twenty thousand, a commandery was granted one recommendation every three years. But in 101 A.D. frontier commanderies with a population of between ten thousand and twenty thousand were allowed to recommend one man every year. Those with a population of between five thousand and ten thousand could recommend one every other year. And those with fewer than five thousand were granted one every three years. This change shows that the populations of frontier districts were low and declining. Even the reduced limits were too high for many commanderies. Wang Fu observed that because of low population, the commanderies in his region had been unable to recommend even a single man for more than a decade. An examination of the geographic origins of the "filially pious and incorrupt" recorded in the *Book of the Later Han* and on stone inscriptions bears out his complaint.[9]

The conduct of the Eastern Han government in the Qiang wars demonstrates a fundamental weakness of the regime: its single-minded focus on the Guandong region. The scale of the Qiang disasters and the collapse of Han civilization in the west and northwest were direct consequences of the eastern government's ultimate decision to leave the frontier commanderies defenseless and to remove population from the region. This lack of interest in the security of the west and northwest, which can be observed throughout the Eastern Han, stems from the shift of power to the new capital in the east.

When the Western Han capital was based in Guanzhong, the government pursued a policy of forcibly resettling population into new towns for the maintenance of imperial tombs. Through resettlement, powerful provincial families lost their local basis of influence and fell under the sway of the imperial court. Grain and other foodstuffs were eventually imported from the more productive Guandong region to maintain the demographic and economic well-being of Guanzhong.

The Western court regarded the area "east of the passes" with a mixture of suspicion and contempt. Jia Yi (201–169 B.C.) observed to the emperor: "The reason for which you have established the Wu, Hangu, and Jin passes is largely to guard against the enfeoffed nobles east of the mountains."[10] In the *Discourses on Salt and Iron* (*Yan tie lun*) Sang Hongyang (executed 80 B.C.) remarked: "People have a saying, 'A provincial pedant is not as good as a capital official.' These literati all come from east of the mountains and seldom participate in the great discussions of state affairs."[11] Although men from Guandong played a larger role in Western Han government after Emperor Wu's death, only when the capital moved to Luoyang did the situation truly change.

The Eastern Han founder Guangwu and most of his followers came from just south of Luoyang, and the rest of his closest adherents came from the great families of Guandong. Moving the capital from Guanzhong to Guandong transferred political power to their region. This break with the past was made self-consciously and deliberately, without regard to strategic considerations, particularly the fact that the newly reunited Xiongnu were drawing near Luoyang.

Throughout the Eastern Han the court entertained many proposals to abandon territory in the north or west, leaving the old capital region vulnerable. In 35 A.D. officials urged that everything to the west of the Gansu corridor be abandoned, but this was blocked by Ma Yuan, a man from the northwest.[12] In 110 A.D., in the wake of the Qiang uprisings, a proposal called for the abandonment of all of Liang province (from the western end of the Gansu corridor at Dunhuang east to the borders of the capital region around Chang'an) and even some of the old imperial tombs. Opponents of this idea argued that the warrior traditions of the western people were essential to the security of the empire, and that moving them toward the interior would incite rebellion.

A better plan, they suggested, was for court officials to select men from among the sons and younger brothers of the important families of provinces outside Guandong and give them appointments as supernumerary officials. This would "on the outside encourage their endeavors and on the inside restrain them, to guard against any evil schemes."[13] In short, appointees from the north or west would be held as hostages to their elders' faithfulness. Several other proposals to abandon the west were submitted, and on two occasions the government forced the closing of frontier commanderies. With the easterners' dominance of the court came a decline in the status of military expertise, which was associated with the west, so that the court lost its links with military commanders on the frontier.[14]

Wang Fu described at length the easterners' indifference toward the west in his account of the Qiang wars. His *Discourses of a Hidden Man* (*Qian fu lun*) includes diatribes against the negligence and cowardice of eastern officials serving in western commanderies. In addition to attacking their proposals to abandon the frontier, he excoriated their disinclination to resist the Qiang. According to Wang Fu, these officials from inner provinces were ignorant of war and thought only of fleeing to safety. Being from the court, they focused solely on the expense of fielding an army while ignoring the losses sustained by the people, whom they plundered. They purportedly caused more losses than the Qiang.

Against proposals to abandon commanderies he argued: "If you lose Liang province, then the Three Adjuncts will be the border. If the people of the Three Adjuncts move inward, then Hongnong will be the border. If the people of Hongnong move inward, then Luoyang will be the border. If you carry on like this you will reach the edge of the Eastern Sea, and that too will be your border."[15] This prophecy was fulfilled at the end of the Han empire.

The collapse of the Eastern Han in the interior was less dramatic than the fall of the frontier, but no less devastating. The Eastern Han regime had attempted to achieve internal security through demilitarization by eliminating universal military service. Three developments eventually filled this vacuum: the remilitarization of provincial governors, the evolution of long-standing commands into semiprivate armies based on personal ties between troops and commanders, and the appearance of private armies under the control of great families. The long-term consequence of these developments was rule by warlords.

By the end of the Western Han the office of provincial governor had grown from a mere inspector into the chief local administrator. As the

Fig. 22 Han forces fighting and capturing bandit/barbarian enemies.

governors' power increased under the Eastern Han, they were able to appoint and dismiss officials within their provinces without the approval of the court. Holders of the office thus became autonomous regional lords who, though subject to dismissal, held sway within their own jurisdiction. Their powers included military duties, and in the second century A.D., when barbarian incursions and banditry led to constant combat, the governor replaced the grand administrator as the person in command of the state's emergency levies (Fig. 22). As civil order decayed and provincial forces spent more time in the field, they took on the characteristics of semiprivate standing armies.

This development was a major change in Han local administration and an important step in the fall of the Eastern Han. The Han dynasty had based its administration on the commandery and the district—a two-tier structure that fragmented local power into small units to avoid threats to the central government. The provincial governor, however, became a third tier, with command of large populations, great wealth, and significant armed forces—resources that could challenge the authority of the imperial government. In the second half of the second century A.D., governors became semi-independent warlords. When Liu Yan took office as governor of Yi province, he massacred important local families, gave his own sons major positions, recruited personal followers from among refugees, and defied imperial commands. In similar fashion, Liu Yu established his own little kingdom as governor of You province. He pacified local barbarians, sheltered refugees, encouraged crafts, and gathered armies. Liu Biao pursued an identical course of action in Jing province.[16]

By the late Eastern Han, governors had obtained the power to recruit troops on their own initiative. This in effect recognized their right to command private armies. In 178 A.D. when the provinces of Jiaozhi and Nanhai (in southern Guangdong and Vietnam) rebelled, Zhu Jun was sent out as governor and empowered to recruit "household troops" (one of the earliest uses of the term) to form an army. The commentary identifies these troops as his servants and slaves. In 189 A.D. He Jin sent Bao Xin to his home near Mount Tai to recruit troops for the purge of the eunuchs. By the time Bao Xin returned, He Jin had been slain. Bao Xin went back to Mount Tai, recruited twenty thousand men, and joined forces with Cao Cao, the warlord who ultimately conquered the Yellow River Valley and whose son formally brought the Han dynasty to an end.[17] The delegation to individuals of the power to recruit private armies in their home regions shows that the central government had lost its ability to rule the population. Only through the personal networks of eminent families in their home regions could the state mobilize a military force.

Recruits in the provinces developed strong ties to those who recruited them. In 88 A.D. a certain Deng Xun had recruited Xiongnu soldiers to act as guards against the Qiang. Contrary to normal practice, he allowed these tribesmen and their families to live in his fortress, and he even let them into his own garden. They swore personal loyalty to Deng Xun and allowed him to raise several hundred of their children as his personal followers.[18] This was an exceptional case at the time, but by the end of the dynasty such ties between recruits and their commanders were common.

In 189 A.D., when Dong Zhuo declined to leave his army at the northwestern frontier and take up an appointment at court, he wrote: "The righteous followers from Huangzhong and the Han and barbarian troops under my command all came to me and said, 'Our rations and wages have not yet been completely paid, and now our provisions will be cut off, and our wives and children will die of hunger and cold.' Pulling back my carriage, they would not let me go." When the court attempted to have him yield his command to Huangfu Song, he replied: "Though I have no skill in planning and no great strength, I have without cause received your divine favor and for ten years have commanded the army. My soldiers both great and small have grown familiar with me over a long time, and cherishing my sustaining bounty they will lay down their lives for me. I ask to lead them to Beizhou, that I may render service at the frontier."[19]

This second passage points out another feature of the Eastern Han's collapse: the proliferation of long-term commands in the field. In the Western Han, generals had been appointed to command an expedition, after which the army was disbanded and the general returned to his regular post. The "Monograph on Officials" of the *Book of the Later Han* states, "Generals are not permanently established."[20] However, the Eastern Han created permanent armies stationed at fixed camps. Although in the first century A.D. the size of armies was kept small and commanders were regularly rotated, prolonged crises on the frontier required generals to remain with their armies in the field for years. These armies—which now were composed of barbarians, convicts, and long-term recruits–became the loyal creatures of their commanders.

Such men had no place in Han society and no home or family to which they could return. Instead, they formed families at the frontier, and their lives centered on the person who was, as Dong Zhuo observed, the source of their livelihood. The Han court never acknowledged this shift. In Dong Zhuo's biography his title changed frequently in the ten years prior to 189 A.D., but his own testimony shows that he and his army stayed together for the entire period.

We also have the following account from an official named Gong Ye: "All the commanderies of Guanxi [Guanzhong] are practiced in war and in recent years have often fought with the Qiang. So even women bear halberds and wield spears, clasp bows in their arms and carry arrows on their backs. How much more the stalwart and brave soldiers! . . . These strongest and bravest of the empire are dreaded by the common people. To possess the people of Bing and Liang provinces [the northwest], the volunteers from the Xiongnu and the Tuge, and the people of Huangzhong, with a brilliant commander leading them and using them as his claws and teeth, is like setting tigers and rhinoceroses upon dogs and sheep."[21] Not only were frontier armies loyal to their commanders, with no ties to the court, but they had even become detached from the values of the sedentary Chinese civilization.

Another path leading to private armies was the development of a dependent tenantry. The absorption of the old category of "clients" into this new servile group meant that labor and military service were largely transferred from the state to great families.[22] In the early Eastern Han, Ma Yuan commanded the services of several hundred families attached to him as clients.[23] Military service was probably included in these obligations. Drawing from these service-providing dependents, the great families were able to assemble armies of hundreds or thousands of men.

Such armies of tenants had overthrown Wang Mang at the end of the Western Han, and the military capacity of dependent populations existed, as a latent possibility, right up to the Eastern Han dynasty's collapse. Like the government's commandery troops, they could be raised in times of emergency. With the decay of internal order and the outbreak of civil war, these dependents began to form full-time private armies recruited from what was becoming a hereditary soldiery. At the same time the dwellings of the great families became fortified compounds with walls and watchtowers (Fig. 23).

The Eastern Han government gave up all attempts to restrict the rise of a dependent tenantry, and in so doing abandoned direct administration of the countryside. Furthermore, as power shifted to the inner court of affines and eunuchs, the imperial house became separated from the great

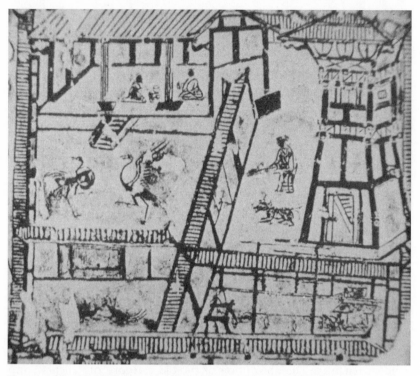

Fig. 23   The fortified compound of an Eastern Han great family, with walls and a watchtower. Auspicious birds dance on the wall, while a dog stands in the courtyard. Tools of domestic labor can be seen in the lower right.

families who controlled the outer court. This steady implosion of imperial power ruptured the ties that bound the court to the countryside. As social order steadily deteriorated in the second century A.D., the court discovered that it had lost the ability to mobilize armies and enforce its own rule.

To counter the threat of rebellious "inner barbarians" and ultimately the millenarian rebel movements, the imperial government required military resources that only those who had developed personal ties to the soldiery could muster: provincial governors, generals on the frontier, resettled tribal chieftains, great landlords, and, in a few cases, leaders of religious rebels. While each type of commander had secured support in a different way, all of them had one thing in common: in an age of general social breakdown, they could call upon their own armed followers for security. These various warlords were key political actors in the long centuries of disunion that would follow the demise of the Han.

DATES AND USAGE

ACKNOWLEDGMENTS

NOTES

BIBLIOGRAPHY

INDEX

DATES AND USAGE

In this book, the history of the Qin state is divided into "pre-imperial Qin," which refers to the period prior to the completion of its conquest of China in 221 B.C., and "imperial Qin," which refers to the period from 221 until its fall. "Warring States Qin" is sometimes used to refer to the specific period from 418 to 221 B.C. The name "Han" refers to the empire that existed from 206 B.C. to 221 A.D., with an interregnum under the Xin dynasty of Wang Mang from 9 to 25 A.D. The Han is divided into the "Western Han" (also known as "Former Han"), which reigned from 202 B.C. to 9 A.D., and the "Eastern Han" (also known as the "Later Han"), which reigned from 25 to 220 A.D. The terms "Western" and "Eastern" refer to the relative locations of their capitals in Chang'an and Luoyang, respectively.

B.C.

897 Qin state established

770 Zhou capital moved east to Luoyang

672 Pre-imperial Qin's first incursions into the central regions of the Zhou realm

481 Beginning of Warring States period

359 Beginning of the reforms of Shang Yang, including building of Xianyang

350 Legal recognition of private ownership of land in Qin

338 Shang Yang executed

316 Qin completes conquest of Shu and Ba (in modern Sichuan)

312 Qin defeats Chu at Danyang to turn its southern conquests into a single block

310 Qin begins construction of Chengdu in Sichuan

168 Loss of the Ordos region in the bend of the Yellow River
169 Beginning of the "Great Proscription" against the anti-eunuch group
184 Beginning of the Yellow Turban rebellion
189 Dong Zhuo seizes Luoyang
197 Yuan Shu declares himself emperor
215 Cao Cao defeats the Five-Pecks-of-Rice movement in Sichuan
216 Cao Cao declared King of Wei
220 Formal abdication of the last Han ruler and foundation of the Wei

ACKNOWLEDGMENTS

I WOULD like to acknowledge my great debt to all the scholars whose research has been incorporated into this history. Their names are listed in the notes and bibliography. I also wish to express my appreciation to Timothy Brook, an anonymous reviewer for Harvard University Press, and Susan Wallace Boehmer for their numerous suggestions on how to improve this book. Finally, I would like to thank my wife, Kristin Ingrid Fryklund, for all her work in the preparation of the manuscript. Any remaining errors and, unless otherwise noted, all translations are my own.

NOTES

Introduction

1. On the Chinese script and the language(s) it has been used to record, see Qiu, *Chinese Writing*; De Francis, *The Chinese Language: Fact and Fantasy*; Norman, *Chinese*; Ramsey, *The Languages of China*.

1. The Geography of Empire

1. "The real history of China is not so much the history of the rise and fall of great dynasties as the history of the gradual occupation of the Chinese earth by untold generations of farming folk." Buchanan, *Transformation of the Chinese Earth*, pp. 5–6. Worster, *Rivers of Empire*, ch. 2, "The Flow of Power in History."

2. Skinner, "Marketing and Social Structures in Rural China"; "Regional Urbanization in Nineteenth-Century China"; "Cities and the Hierarchy of Local Systems." For a discussion of regions in the early imperial period, see Lewis, *Construction of Space*, ch. 4.

3. Lewis, "Warring States Political History," pp. 593–597.

4. The full details of this are elaborated in Barbieri-Low, *Artisans in Early Imperial China*, ch. 6.

5. *Shang shu zheng yi*, ch. 6, "Yu gong."

6. *Wuzi zhi jie*, ch. 2 "Liao di," pp. 17a–20a.

7. *Xunzi ji jie*, ch. 10, "Yi bing," p. 181.

8. Wang, *Lun heng ji jie*, ch. 23, p. 457; *Shi ji* 106, p. 2823; Hulsewé, *Remnants of Ch'in Law*, p. 206.

9. *Xunzi ji jie*, ch. 5, "Wang zhi," pp. 102–103; ch. 15, "Jie bi," p. 260; ch. 12, "Zheng lun," pp. 219–220.

10. *Shi ji* 129, pp. 3261–3270, esp. pp. 3264, 3266. See a related passage in *Han shu* 28b, pp. 1640–1671.

11. *Shi ji* 6, p. 281; 129, p. 3267; *Han shu* 64b, p. 2818. See also *Han shu* 28b, p. 1663; *Hou Han shu* 4, p. 167. *Hou Han shu* 3, p. 155.

12. *Xunzi ji jie,* ch. 4, "Ru xiao," pp. 91–92.

13. Lewis, *Construction of Space,* pp. 192–199. The quotation from the *Springs and Autumns of Master Lü* is on p. 199. On the references to the inspection and cleansing of customs in the first emperor's stone inscriptions, see Kern, *The Stele Inscriptions of Ch'in Shih-huang,* pp. 44, 48.

14. For a detailed account of Qin-Han history, see Loewe, ed., *The Cambridge History of China,* Vol. 1: *The Ch'in and Han Empires,* chs. 1–5.

15. *Shi ji* 7, p. 315. Lawson, *New Perspectives on Chu Culture;* Cook and Major, *Defining Chu;* Knechtges, "The Emperor and Literature."

16. *Shi ji* 6, p. 277.

17. Cottrell, *The First Emperor of China,* chs. 3–4.

18. Sage, *Ancient Sichuan and the Unification of China. Shi ji* 29, p. 1408.

19. Hsu, "The Changing Relationship between Local Society and Central Political Power."

20. *Han shu* 24a, p. 1137.

21. *Han shu* 30, p. 3024.

22. *Quan Hou Han wen* (Complete Writings of the Later Han) 46, p. 12a.

23. *Xian Qin Han Wei Jin Nanbeichao shi,* p. 347.

2. A State Organized for War

1. *Shi ji* 68, pp. 2230, 2232. For other references in surviving texts see *Xunzi ji jie,* ch. 10, p. 181; *Han Feizi ji shi,* ch. 17, p. 907; *Han shu* 23, p. 1096; 24, p. 1126; 28b, p. 1641.

2. Lewis, *Sanctioned Violence,* pp. 54–61.

3. Ibid., pp. 62–64.

4. Lewis, "Warring States Political History," pp. 634–635.

5. Ibid., pp. 607–608.

6. Ibid., p. 621.

7. Ibid., pp. 639–641.

8. The following derives much from Pines, "The Question of Interpretation: Qin History in the Light of New Epigraphic Sources."

9. Lewis, "Custom and Human Nature in Early China." See, for example, von Falkenhausen, "Mortuary Behavior in Pre-Imperial China." Qiu, *Chinese Writing,* pp. 78–89; von Falkenhausen, *Suspended Music,* pp. 189–190.

10. [*Chun qiu*] *Gongyang zhuan zhu shu,* ch. 22, Zhao year 5, p. 11a, ch. 14, Wen year 12, p. 3b; ch. 22, Zhao year 1, p. 3b.

11. *Zhanguo ce,* ch. 24, p. 869. A closely related passage appears in the materials cognate to the *Stratagems* discovered at Mawangdui. *Zhanguo zongheng jia shu,* in *Mawangdui Han mu boshu,* vol. 3, p. 52. The Han critique of Qin in

terms of custom is discussed in Lewis, *Construction of Space,* pp. 201–210. On Qin as characterized by the absence of humanity, ritual, and duty, see also *Xunzi ji jie,* ch. 10, p. 186; ch. 17, p. 295; *Zhanguo ce,* ch. 20, p. 696; ch. 14, p. 503. For other remarks that describe Qin as animals or barbarians see ch. 2, p. 50; ch. 20, p. 696. The idea of Qin as the enemy of All under Heaven with no apparent critical intent also figures in *Han Feizi ji shi,* ch. 1, pp. 1–3. On this idea, see Pines, "Changing View of Tianxia in Pre-Imperial Discourse."

12. *Huainanzi,* ch. 21, p. 376.

13. *Shi ji* 15, p. 685. On the same page Sima Qian noted, "At first Qin was a small state in a remote region. The Chinese treated it as an outsider, on the same level as the Rong and Di." He also notes the security of Qin's terrain. See also *Shi ji* 122, p. 3149.

14. *Shi ji* 68, p. 2234. On the Jique Palace and Shang Yang's role in establishing Qin's new capital at Xianyang, see Wu, *Monumentality in Early Chinese Art and Architecture,* pp. 105–108.

15. *Shi ji* 6, pp. 277–278.

16. *Jiazi xin shu jiao shi,* pp. 303, 315, 317. For another version of this essay, with the order rearranged, see *Han shu* 48, p. 2244.

17. Other Han writers adopted this critique of Qin custom and law as a means of criticizing Han legal practice, or other aspects of Han administration such as a perceived failure to listen to remonstrance. See *Han shu* 48, p. 2251; 51, pp. 2351, 2362, 2369–2370.

18. [*Chun qiu*] *Guliang zhuan zhu shu,* ch. 9, Xi year 33, pp. 16b–17a.

19. *Han Feizi ji shi,* ch. 1, pp. 1–4.

20. *Shi ji* 87, pp. 2543–2544. *Han Feizi ji shi,* ch. 3, p. 187. This story depicts Qin possessing "the music of the central states" in the seventh century B.C., and using it to trap a barbarian king whose people had no such music. *Shi ji* 81, p. 2442 treats a reference to striking pots and pans as definitive of Qin music as an insult.

21. *Shuihudi Qin mu zhu jian,* p. 15.

22. *Han shu* 64b, p. 2821.

23. *Yunmeng Shuihudi Qin mu,* pp. 25–26. The letters are translated in Shaughnessy, "Military Histories of Early China," p. 181. *Shi ji* 7, p. 300. On popular resistance to Qin occupation, in this case in the state of Hann, see also *Zhanguo ce,* ch. 5, pp. 204–205.

24. *Shuihudi Qin mu zhu jian,* p. 135. See the discussion in Pines, "The Question of Interpretation." On these alliances and the fundamental inequality of the "horizontal" ones, see Lewis, "Warring States Political History," pp. 632–634.

25. This is the central theme of Hsu, *Ancient China in Transition.* Wu, ed., *Qin jian Ri shu ji shi,* pp. 291–311.

26. Lewis, "Warring States Political History," pp. 629–630. *Shuihudi Qin mu zhu jian,* p. 203.

27. *Shang Jun shu zhu yi*, ch. 15, p. 323. *Shi ji* 87, p. 2541. Li Si's rebuttal is on pp. 2541–2545. *Shi ji* 63, p. 2155.

28. Pines, "Friends or Foes."

29. Lewis, "Warring States Political History," p. 630.

30. The most interesting reflection on the *Shang Jun shu*, although one that is replete with theoretical excesses and historical errors, is the first part of Dean and Massumi, *First and Last Emperors.*

31. *Shang Jun shu zhu yi*, ch. 3, p. 56. For various forms in which the fact of a universally mobilized peasantry was reflected in thought, see Lewis, *Sanctioned Violence*, pp. 64–67.

32. *Shang Jun shu zhu yi*, ch.13, pp. 285–286; ch. 20, pp. 443; ch. 5, p. 135. On warfare as that which the people hate, see ch. 18, p. 378.

33. *Shang Jun shu zhu yi*, ch. 3, p. 61; ch. 18, p. 378.

34. *Shang Jun shu zhu yi*, ch. 4, p. 93; ch. 13, pp. 276, 281; ch. 20, p. 445.

35. *Shang Jun shu zhu yi*, ch. 2, pp. 20, 21–22, 23, 25, 27. *Shang Jun shu zhu yi*, ch. 24, pp. 497–498. See also ch. 25, p. 509.

36. *Shang Jun shu zhu yi*, ch. 5, pp. 140–141; ch. 24, p. 498. See also Lewis, *Sanctioned Violence*, pp. 92–94.

37. *Shang Jun shu zhu yi*, ch. 1, p. 10. On the idea that the ruler was defined through his mastery of change, particularly the changing of laws, see Lewis, *Writing and Authority*, pp. 39–40.

38. *Shang Jun shu zhu yi*, ch. 26, pp. 527–528, 533, 536–537. Hulsewé, *Remnants of Ch'in Law*, pp. 120–182.

39. *Shang Jun shu zhu yi*, ch. 4, p. 93. *Shang Jun shu zhu yi*, ch. 8, p. 210; ch. 13, p. 276; ch. 20, pp. 434, 436.

40. Dean and Massumi, *First and Last Emperors*, pp. 19, 42.

3. The Paradoxes of Empire

1. These reforms are discussed in Bodde, *China's First Unifier*; Bodde, "The State and Empire of Ch'in," pp. 52–72; Cottrell, *The First Emperor of China*, chs. 6–7.

2. Kern, *The Stele Inscriptions of Ch'in Shih-huang. Shi ji* 6, pp. 261–262.

3. Hulsewé, *Remnants of Ch'in Law*, pp. 19, 42–43, 57–58, 88–89, 93–94, 161.

4. *Han shu* 24b, p. 1152.

5. *Shi ji* 110, p. 2886; 6, p. 241.

6. Hulsewé, *Remnants of Ch'in Law*, pp. 44–45, 54–55, 83–86, 178. Loewe, *Records of Han Administration*, pp. 110–114; *Han shu* 4, p. 123; 5, p. 143; 8, p. 245; *Shi ji* 49, p. 1973; 106, p. 2833; 107, p. 2850; 122, p. 3135.

7. *Shi ji* 88, pp. 2565–2566; 6, p. 280.

8. *Shi ji* 8, pp. 379, 380–381.

9. *Shi ji* 8, pp. 341–348, 391.

10. Ch'ü, *Han Social Structure,* pp. 66–75; Wang, "An Outline of the Central Government of the Former Han Dynasty," pp. 137–143.

11. Nishijima, "The Economic and Social History of Former Han," pp. 598–601.

12. Lewis, "The Han Abolition of Universal Military Service."

13. Lewis, *Writing and Authority,* ch. 8.

14. *Shi ji* 6, p. 283.

15. *Shi ji* 6, pp. 280–281; *Jiazi xin shu jiao shi,* pp. 15–19.

16. *Shi ji* 6, pp. 242, 248, 256, 263.

17. *Shi ji* 6, pp. 245, 250, 252.

18. *Wu lu,* in *Tai ping yu lan,* ch. 156, p. 3a; *San guo zhi* 53, p. 1246 n. 2; *Jin shu* 6, p. 157; 53, p. 1457. *Liang Jiang Wentong wenji,* ch. 1, p. 5; *Li Bo ji jiaozhu,* vol. 1, p. 97.

19. *Shi ji* 117, pp. 3056–3060; 29, p. 1413.

4. Imperial Cities

1. Steinhardt, *Chinese Imperial City Planning,* pp. 46–53; Wu Hung, "The Art and Architecture of the Warring States Period," pp. 653–665. For a more detailed discussion of the cities of early imperial China, with fuller documentation, see Lewis, *Construction of Space,* ch. 3.

2. *Shi ji* 30, pp. 1418, 1430.

3. Lewis, *Writing and Authority,* pp. 79–83, 287–336, 358, 495 n. 60–62.

4. Wu, *Monumentality in Early Chinese Art,* pp. 102–110. The material presented from here through note 12 is discussed in Lewis, *Construction of Space,* pp. 153–159. Wang Chong, *Lun heng ji jie,* ch. 13, p. 273.

5. See the citations in Lewis, *Construction of Space,* ch. 3, n. 69.

6. See the citations in Lewis, *Construction of Space,* ch. 3, n. 73. *Li ji zhu shu,* ch. 10, p. 25b; Finsterbusch, *Verzeichnis und Motivindex der Han-Darstellungen,* plates #34, 103, 124, 128, 141, 151, 155, 164, 179, 198, 223, 240, 459, 625, 639, 652, 1016, 1017, 1018.

7. Wu, *Monumentality,* p. 106.

8. See the citations in Lewis, *Construction of Space,* ch. 3, n. 80.

9. *Shi ji* 6, pp. 239, 241 (the commentary states that walled roads let the emperor travel invisibly), 251, 256, 257, 264.

10. *Wen xuan* 1 "Xi du fu," pp. 10, 11; 2, "Xi jing fu," p. 30. The term "forbidden" was already an epithet for imperial parks and forests in the Han. See *Wen xuan* 1 "Xi du fu," pp. 6, 12; 2 "Xi jing fu," p. 35; 6 "Wei du fu," pp. 121, 123.

11. Lewis, *Construction of Space,* pp. 159–160.

12. Barbieri-Low, *Artisans in Early Imperial China,* ch. 3.

13. Bielenstein, "Lo-yang in Later Han times," pp. 58–59; *Wen xuan* 2 "Xi jing fu," p. 34; Lim, *Stories from China's Past,* p. 101.

14. Barbieri-Low, *Artisans in Early Imperial China,* ch. 3.

15. Lewis, *Construction of Space,* pp. 160–161.

16. *Shi ji* 85, p. 2510; 68, p. 2231.

17. Lewis, *Construction of Space,* pp. 161–162.

18. Ibid., pp. 162–163.

19. *Shi ji* 124 and *Han shu* 92; Lewis, *Sanctioned Violence,* pp. 80, 88–91, p. 281 n. 137; James J. Y. Liu, *The Chinese Knight Errant;* Ch'ü, *Han Social Structure,* pp. 161, 188–198, 232, 245–247; *Wen xuan* 1 "Xi du fu," p. 5; 2 "Xi jing fu," pp. 34–35; *Shi ji* 86, pp. 2522, 2523, 2525, 2528; 95, pp. 2651, 2673; 124, p. 3181, 3183–3184; 129, p. 3271; *Han shu* 94, pp. 3698, 3699; *Han Feizi ji shi,* ch. 19, pp. 1057, 1058, 1091, 1095 (2); *Hou Han shu* 28a, p. 958; 67, p. 2184. The term *you xia* later was applied to swashbuckling martial artists who figure prominently in Chinese literature, in which context the term is sometimes translated "knight errant," as in the title of the book by Liu cited in this note. To apply the term to these figures in the Han is anachronistic. It is also important to note that in our own popular culture the term "gangster" also has romantic overtones and can imply a degree of approbation for violent "Robin Hood" figures like those described by Sima Qian.

20. Lewis, *Sanctioned Violence,* pp. 147, 154, 155, 224, 321 n. 49; Lewis, *Construction of Space,* pp. 164–165; Hayashi, *Chugoku kodai no seikatsu shi,* pp. 110–111.

21. Harper, "Warring States Natural Philosophy," pp. 874–875; Harper, *Early Chinese Medical Literature,* pp. 43–44, 152–153, 155–159, 166, 168, 174–175, 177; Lewis, *Construction of Space,* pp. 165–169; *Yan tie lun,* p. 68; *Qian fu lun jian,* ch. 3, "Fu chi," p. 125. On the Discourses of a Hidden Man see Kinney, *The Art of the Han Essay: Wang Fu's Ch'ien-fu Lun.*

22. *Shi ji* 6, p. 241; 27, pp. 1289–1290.

23. *Shi ji* 6, p. 256; *Sanfu huang tu,* pp. 4–7.

24. *Shi ji* 6, p. 239; *Wen xuan* 2 "Xi jing fu," pp. 27, 28, 29 (2), 31.

25. *Shi ji* 6, pp. 239, 244, 256.

26. *Shi ji* 6, p. 239; 28, pp. 1396, 1397, 1399, 1403; *Sanfu huang tu,* p. 5.

27. *Lü shi chun qiu jiaoshi,* ch. 10, pp. 535–536; Wu, "Art and Architecture," pp. 709–717; *Shi ji* 6, p. 265.

28. *Shi ji* 28, pp. 1358–1360, 1364, 1375–1377.

29. *Shi ji* 28, pp. 1367–1368, 1371–1374, 1377. *Wen xuan* 1 "Dong du fu," p. 22.

30. In English see Steinhardt, *Chinese Imperial City Planning,* ch. 3; Wu, *Monumentality,* ch. 3; Wang Zhongshu, *Han Civilization,* chs. 1–2; Xiong, *Sui-Tang Chang'an,* ch. 1; Hughes, *Two Chinese Poets;* Bielenstein, "Lo-yang in Later Han

Time"; Hotaling, "The City Walls of Han Ch'ang-an." *Shi ji* 99, p. 2723; *Han shu* 43, pp. 2126–2128.

31. Knechtges, "The Emperor and Literature"; Sukhu, "Monkeys, Shamans, Emperors, and Poets."

32. *Shi ji* 7, pp. 311, 322, 327–328; 8, pp. 341, 342, 347, 350, 358, 371, 372, 381, 382, 386–387; 50, p. 1987. On the divine paternity of sages in Warring States and Han myth, see Lewis, *Writing and Authority,* pp. 219, 447 n. 117.

33. *Shi ji* 7, p. 315. Sima Qian lists Xiang Yu' "turning his back on the passes and longing for Chu" as the first reason for his defeat. See *Shi ji* 7, p. 359.

34. *Shi ji* 8, pp. 385–386. *Shi ming shu zheng bu,* ch. 2, p. 10b; *Zuo zhuan zhu,* Zhuang year 28, p. 242.

35. *Zhou li zhushu,* ch. 41, pp. 24b–25a; Steinhardt, *Chinese Imperial City Planning,* pp. 33–36; Xu, *The Chinese City in Space and Time,* pp. 31–39; Wheatley, *The Pivot of the Four Quarters,* pp. 411–419.

36. Wu, *Monumentality,* pp. 157–162.

37. *Shi ji* 28, pp. 1378–1380.

38. *Shi ji* 28, pp. 1382, 1384, 1386, 1387, 1388, 1389, 1393–1395, 1397–1398, 1402–1404.

39. Powers, *Art and Political Expression in Early China,* pp. 160–161, 171–180.

40. *Wen xuan* 1 "Xi du fu," p. 16; 2, "Xi jing fu," p. 28.

41. *Wen xuan* 3 "Dong jing fu," p. 67; *Han shu* 99b, p. 4193.

42. *Xian Qin Han Wei Jin Nanbeichao shi,* vol. 1, p. 454. On the absence of physical traces of the Han capital in later times, see Yang, *A Record of Buddhist Monasteries in Lo-yang,* p. 133. On meditations on vanished capitals as a literary topos see Owen, *Remembrances,* pp. 58–65.

5. Rural Society

1. *Huainanzi,* ch. 11, p. 185. On the philosophical tradition of Shen Nong, see Graham, *Disputers of the Tao,* pp. 64–74; Graham, "The Nung-chia School of the Tillers and the Origins of Peasant Utopianism in China."

2. Bodde, *Festivals in Classical China,* pp. 223–241, 263–272.

3. *Lü shi chun qiu jiao shi,* ch. 26, pp. 1731–1732, 1756; Cho-yun Hsu, *Han Agriculture,* pp. 7–9. Hsu, *Han Agriculture,* pp. 109–128, 298–299, 300, 307.

4. Hsu, *Han Agriculture,* pp. 297–298, 300.

5. Lewis, *Construction of Space,* pp. 101–104.

6. A good survey of Qin and Han labor service based on the most recent finds is Barbieri-Low, *Artisans in Early Imiperial China,* ch. 5, sec. 1 "The Conscripted Artisan."

7. Lewis, "The Han Abolition of Universal Military Service," pp. 34–39.

8. On the duties of the magistrate and his staff, see Bielenstein, *The Bureaucracy of Han Times*, pp. 99–104.

9. Gao, *Han bei ji shi*, p. 489.

10. Hulsewé, *Remnants of Ch'in Law*, pp. 26–27.

11. Ibid., pp. 162–163.

12. Nishijima, "The Economic and Social History of Former Han," pp. 552–553; Loewe, "The Structure and Practice of Government," pp. 484–486; Loewe, "The Order of Aristocratic Ranks in Han China."

13. *Han shu* 24a, p. 1132; Hsu, *Han Agriculture*, pp. 160–163.

14. *Hou Han shu* 49, p. 1644; Hsu, *Han Agriculture*, p. 214.

15. Hulsewé, *Remnants of Ch'in Law*, pp. 52–53. *Shi ji* 30, p. 1441.

16. *Mao shi zheng yi*, ch. 1.2, #2, "Ge tan," p. 2b; ch. 2.1, #27, "Lu yi," p. 4b; ch. 4.2, #75, "Zi yi," p. 4b; ch. 5.3, #107, "Ge lü," p. 2b; ch. 8.1, #154, "Qi yue," pp. 11b–14a; ch. 8.2, #156, "Dong shan," p. 7a; ch. 15.2, #226, "Cai lu," pp. 6a–6b. Lewis, *Construction of Space*, pp. 104–105. For depictions in Han tomb art of women gathering mulberry leaves and producing cloth, see Lim, *Stories from China's Past*, pp. 95–98, 152, 155; Finsterbusch, *Verzeichnis und Motivindex*, vol. 2, figs. 33, 594, nachtrag 5; Hayashi, *Chūgoku kodai no seikatsu shi*, pp. 75–78; Wu, *Monumentality in Early Chinese Art*, p. 233. While the role of women in cloth production became a cliché, they also toiled in agriculture and in many types of artisanal workshops. See Barbieri-Loew, *Artisans in Early Imperial China*, ch. 2, sec. 8, "Female Artisans."

17. *Xunzi ji shi*, ch. 18, pp. 316–317.

18. *Lun heng ji jie*, ch. 27, p. 543. For a more detailed discussion of the great families of Han China, with fuller documentation, see Lewis, *Construction of Space*, ch. 4, sec. 3, "Regions and the Great Families."

19. *Yan tie lun*, p. 118.

20. Lewis, *Construction of Space*, pp. 215–216.

21. *Hou Han shu* 43, pp. 1467–1468, n. 1. See also *Lun heng ji jie*, ch. 27, p. 537. *Hou Han shu* 43, pp. 1474–1475, n. 2.

22. Lewis, *Construction of Space*, pp. 217–218.

23. Wakefield, *Fenjia*; Yan, *The Flow of Gifts*, pp. 39–42, 109, 115–119, 178–209, esp. p. 196; Kipnis, *Producing Guanxi*, pp. 87–90, 99, 138; Ma, *Mawangdui gu yi shu kaoshi*, p. 1008; Harper, *Early Chinese Medical Literature*, p. 423. Quarrels between mothers-in-law and daughters-in-law were also cited in the passage on Qin from Jia Yi quoted above. Ebrey, "Early Stages," pp. 18–29; Holzman, "The Cold Food Festival in Early Medieval China," pp. 51–79; Wu, *The Wu Liang Shrine*, pp. 30–37.

24. *Hou Han shu* 32, pp. 1119–1120.

25. Lewis, *Sanctioned Violence*, ch. 2.

26. *Hou Han shu* 8, p. 330; 48, pp. 1598–1599; 67, p. 2189; *zhi* 10, p. 3221; *Han shu* 60, p. 2660.

27. Lewis, *Construction of Space*, pp. 219–220.

28. *Han shu* 90, p. 3647; 92, p. 3700; *Shi ji* 122, p. 3133.

29. *Hou Han shu* 31, p. 1114; 33, p. 1155, n. 2 quotes Xie Cheng's history; 70, p. 2281; *San guo zhi* 11, p. 343; 36, p. 947.

30. Lewis, *Construction of Space*, pp. 221–222. Ebrey, "The Economic and Social History of the Later Han," pp. 637–640; Ebrey, "Later Han Stone Inscriptions," pp. 325–353.

31. Lewis, *Construction of Space*, pp. 220–221.

32. Ibid., pp. 222–223.

33. On Qin *fu lao*, see *Shuihudi Qin mu zhu jian*, pp. 143, 193, 230. On Han, see *Shi ji* 8, p. 362; *Han shu* 24a, p. 1139; 71, p. 3046; 89, p. 3629. On terms for women, see *Han shu* 45, p. 2166; *Hou Han shu* 43, p. 1457.

34. *Lun heng ji jie*, ch. 7, p. 164.

35. *Han shu* 71, p. 3040. See also *Dong guan Han ji jiao zhu*, ch. 15, pp. 598–599; *Hou Han shu* 82a, pp. 2720–2721. For lists joining villagers and patriline as a group, and sometimes including retainers or dependents, see *Han shu* 21, p. 792; *Hou Han shu* 41, p. 1395; 81, pp. 2690, 2696; *San guo zhi* 11, p. 341.

36. *Shi ji* 129, pp. 3271–3272; Scott, *The Moral Economy of the Peasant*, ch. 6.

37. Lewis, *Construction of Space*, pp. 225–226; Lim, *Stories from China's Past*, pp. 110–111, plate 25. The "Fundamental Chronicles" of the Han dynastic histories are filled with references to the emperor's gifts to his officials and to the poor.

38. Lewis, *Construction of Space*, pp. 226–227.

39. *Li shi*, ch. 7, pp. 5b–7b; 11, pp. 4a–6a; *Li xu*, ch. 12, pp. 5b–18b.

40. Lewis, *Construction of Space*, p. 228.

41. *Li ji zhu shu*, ch. 12, pp. 16a–16b. For an application of this passage to local cults at the end of the Han, see Ying, *Feng su tong yi*, p. 325.

6. The Outer World

1. Barfield, *The Perilous Frontier*, ch. 1; Lattimore, *Inner Asian Frontiers of China*, chs. 15–16; Wiens, *China's March to the Tropics*.

2. Di Cosmo, "The Northern Frontier in Pre-Imperial China"; Di Cosmo, *Ancient China and Its Enemies*, ch. 1.

3. Di Cosmo, *Ancient China and Its Enemies*, ch. 2.

4. Ibid., pp. 131–138.

5. Lewis, "Warring States Political History," pp. 629–630. Di Cosmo, *Ancient China and Its Enemies*, pp. 138–158; Waldron, *The Great Wall of China*, ch. 2.

6. The most persuasive version of this model is Barfield, *The Perilous Frontier*.

7. This case is argued in Di Cosmo, *Ancient China and Its Enemies*, esp. pp. 167–174.

8. *Shi ji* 6, p. 252; 88, pp. 2565–2566; 110, pp. 2886, 2888.

9. *Shi ji* 110, pp. 2890–2891.

10. On the populations of the Tarim basin and their relation to the surrounding lands, see Mallory and Mair, *The Tarim Mummies*, chs. 1–2, 8–9; Barber, *The Mummies of Ürümchi*, chs. 6–10.

11. On the *he qin* policy, see Di Cosmo, *Ancient China and Its Enemies*, pp. 190–227; Barfield, *The Perilous Frontier*, pp. 45–67; Yü, *Trade and Expansion in Han China*, pp. 10–12, 36–43; Yü, "Han Foreign Relations," pp. 386–389, 394–398. *Han shu* 48, p. 2265, n. 3; *Jiazi xin shu jiao shi*, ch. 4, pp. 433–478.

12. *Han shu* 94a, pp. 3762–3763.

13. *Shi ji* 110, pp. 2896, 2902; *Han shu* 94a, pp. 3756–3757; 3762–3763.

14. *Han shu* 49, pp. 2281–2293; Lewis, "The Han Abolition of Universal Military Service," pp. 45–48.

15. *Shi ji* 110, pp. 2879, 2892; 112, p. 2954; Di Cosmo, *Ancient China and Its Enemies*, pp. 267–281. For pre-Qin accounts of lack of honor among the northern peoples, see *Zuo zhuan zhu*, Xi year 8, p. 322.

16. *Shi ji* 110, p. 2879; Di Cosmo, *Ancient China and Its Enemies*, pp. 274–276.

17. Di Cosmo, *Ancient China and Its Enemies*, pp. 304–311. *Han shu* 49, p. 2284.

18. *Shi ji* 27, pp. 1305–1306, 1326, 1328

19. Di Cosmo, *Ancient China and Its Enemies*, pp. 216–227.

20. Barfield, *The Perilous Frontier*, pp. 56–60.

21. *Hou Han shu* 89, p. 2952.

22. For details on what follows, see Lewis, "The Han Abolition of Universal Military Service."

23. *Shi ji* 123, p. 3157; *Han shu* 61, p. 2687.

24. *Han shu* 61, p. 2692.

25. Rashke, "New Studies in Roman Commerce with the East."

26. *Shi ji* 123, p. 3172.

27. *Han shu* 22, pp. 1060–1061.

28. Yü, "Han Foreign Relations," pp. 381–383, 394–398.

29. *Hou Han shu* 88, p. 2931.

30. *Han shu* 96a, pp. 3886, 3893.

31. See, for example, *Han shu* 96b, p. 3928. Yü, "Han Foreign Relations," pp. 417–418. *Han shu* 96b, pp. 3908–3909; *Hou Han shu* 88, p. 2931; *Jin shu* 122, p. 3055.

32. *Han shu* 69, pp. 2979, 2986; 87, p. 2883.

33. *Hou Han shu* 87, p. 2869; *Han Shu* 69, p. 2972.

34. *Hou Han shu* 87, pp. 2876; 2878–2879; *Jin shu* 56, p. 1533.

35. *Han shu* 94b, p. 3804; *Hou Han shu* 87, p. 3878.

36. Yü, "Han Foreign Relations," pp. 427–428; Lewis, "The Han Abolition of Universal Military Service," pp. 59, 63–64; *Hou Han shu* 87, pp. 2876–2878; *Han shu* 69, p. 2985.

37. Lewis, "The Han Abolition of Universal Military Service," pp. 57–61.

38. Yü, "Han Foreign Relations," pp. 428–430; *Hou Han shu* 4, p. 185; 87, pp. 2880, 2898.

39. *Hou Han shu* 65, p. 2138.

40. *Hou Han shu* 87, pp. 2898–2899; 4, p. 170; 5, pp. 206, 211, 237; *zhi* 23, pp. 3514, 3515, 3521.

41. *Hou Han shu* 90, pp. 2981–2982.

42. Yü, "Han Foreign Relations," pp. 439–440.

43. *Hou Han shu* 7, pp. 310, 315; 38, p. 1286; 73, p. 2353.

44. *Hou Han shu* 8, pp. 354, 356; 73; pp. 2353–2354; 90, p. 2984.

45. Yü, "Han Foreign Relations," pp. 446–460.

46. *Shi ji* 117, p. 3025. Translation from Watson, *Chinese Rhyme-Prose,* p. 41.

47. Wang Chong, *Lun heng ji jie,* ch.19, pp. 387–398.

48. *Quan Hou Han wen,* ch. 25, p. 4a; *Hou Han shu zhi* 13, p. 3272.

7. Kinship

1. *Li ji zhu shu,* ch. 37, "Yue ji," pp. 11b–12a; *Shi ji* 24, p. 1187. See also *Li ji zhu shu,* ch. 37, pp. 14a, 19a. For a more detailed discussion of the kin system of early imperial China, with fuller documentation, see Lewis, *Construction of Space,* ch. 2 and pp. 105–106.

2. *Lie nü zhuan,* ch. 1, p. 10a–p. 11b. On the three obediences, see *Li ji zhu shu,* ch. 26, p. 19b; *Da Dai li ji jie gu,* ch. 13, p. 254.

3. Bret Hinsch, "Women, Kinship, and Property as Seen in a Han Dynasty Will," pp. 1–21; *Li shi,* ch. 15, pp. 10b–11b. Certain details of the account of the will in Hinsch's article are based on readings which have since been corrected.

4. *Xian Qin Han Wei Jin Nanbeichao shi,* pp. 256, 283–286, 270–271.

5. *Yan shi jia xun hui zhu,* pp. 8b–10a. Wu Hung, "Private Love and Public Duty: Images of Children in Early Chinese Art," pp. 79–110; Wu, *The Wu Liang Shrine,* pp. 256–258, 264–266, 278–280, 291–292.

6. *Lie nü zhuan,* ch. 5, pp. 6a–6b.

7. *Lie nü zhuan,* ch. 5, pp. 5a, 9a–9b.

8. *Shi ji* 6, p. 262.

9. *Li ji zhu shu,* ch. 26, pp. 18b–19a.

10. *Lie nü zhuan,* ch. 4, p. 9a.

11. *Yan shi jia xun hui zhu,* ch. 4, pp. 9a–9b. *Li ji zhu shu,* ch. 63, p. 12b; *Da Dai li ji jie gu,* ch. 13, p. 253. *Lie nü zhuan,* ch. 5, p. 5a.

12. Wu, "Private Love and Public Duty," pp. 86, 90–91, 94. Lewis, *Sanctioned Violence,* pp. 70–78.

13. *Han shu* 40, p. 2038; *Hou Han shu* 81, p. 2684, 2685–2686. *Yan shi jia xun hui zhu,* ch. 3, pp. 6b–7b; ch. 3, pp. 6b–7b.

14. Ch'ü, *Han Social Structure,* pp. 57–62, 77–83, 168–174, 210–229, 237–240.

15. Wang, "An Outline of the Central Government of the Former Han Dynasty," pp. 166–173; Ch'ü, *Han Social Structure,* pp. 179–171, 216–217, 234–235.

16. Boyd, *Chinese Architecture and Town Planning,* p. 48; Bray, *Technology and Gender,* pp. 52–53.

17. Thorp, "Origins of Chinese Architectural Style," pp. 26–31; Hsu and Linduff, *Western Zhou Civilization,* pp. 289–296; Chang, *The Archaeology of Ancient China,* pp. 353–357; Rawson, "Western Zhou Archaeology," pp. 390–393; Knapp, *China's Old Dwellings,* pp. 30–32.

18. Wu, *Monumentality,* pp. 84–88; von Falkenhausen, "Issues in Western Zhou Studies," pp. 148–150, 157–158, 162, 166, 170–171.

19. Finsterbusch, *Verzeichnis und Motivindex der Han-Darstellungen,* vol. 2, figs. 34, 311, 508s-t, 593, 594; Lim, *Stories from China's Past,* pp. 104–105. Lewis, *Construction of Space,* pp. 116–117. *Li ji zhu shu,* ch. 24, pp. 12a, 17b; ch. 26, p. 22a; *Lun yu zheng yi,* ch. 22, p. 409. Harper, "Warring States Natural Philosophy and Occult Thought," pp. 841, 847–852; Kalinowski, "The Xingde Text from Mawangdui," pp. 125–202; Yates, "The Yin-Yang Texts from Yinqueshan, pp. 82–84, 88–90, 93; Major, "The Meaning of Hsing-te [Xingde]," pp. 281–291; Major, *Heaven and Earth in Early Han Thought,* pp. 86–88. *Huainanzi,* ch. 3, p. 40.

20. *Lun yu zheng yi,* ch. 20, pp. 363–364.

21. Lewis, *Construction of Space,* pp. 114–115.

22. Kinney, *Representations of Childhood and Youth in Early China,* ch. 1; Kinney, "Dyed Silk," pp. 17–44.

23. DeWoskin, "Famous Chinese Childhoods," pp. 57–76.

24. Kinney, *Representations of Childhood and Youth,* ch. 2.

25. *Lun heng ji jie,* ch. 30, pp. 579–580; Kinney, "Dyed Silk," pp. 37–38.

26. *Han shu* 24a, p. 1122; *Bo hu tong,* ch. 4, p. 16b.

27. Hulsewé, *Remnants of Ch'in Law,* p. 139. *Hou Han shu* 7, pp. 301, 319. Gao, *Han bei ji shi,* p. 227; Hertz, *Death and the Right Hand,* p. 84.

28. *Yi li zhu shu,* ch. 31, pp. 14a–14b; *Li ji zhu shu,* ch. 19, pp. 14b–20b; ch. 32, p. 9b; ch. 43, p. 2b. Wu, "Private Love and Public Duty," p. 80.

29. *Xiao jing zhu shu,* ch. 5, pp. 4b–6a. Kinney, *Representations of Childhood*

and Youth, p. 15, 25; *Han shu* 7, p. 223; 12, p. 299; 71, p. 3039; *Hou Han shu* 32, pp. 11225–11226.

30. *Li shi,* ch. 12, p. 16a.

31. Cai, *Cai Zhonglang wen ji,* ch. 4, p. 11b.

32. Hulsewé, *Remnants of Ch'in Law,* pp. 125, 141, 147, 148–149, 195–197.

33. *Guliang zhuan zhu shu,* ch. 8, Xi year 15, p. 12b; *Han shu* 22, p. 1050. Ebrey, "The Economic and Social History of Later Han," pp. 633–635.

34. Wang, *Qian fu lun jian,* ch. 12, pp. 120, 130, 133–134; *Han shu* 67, p. 2908; *Hou Han shu* 39, p. 1314; *Guanzi jiao zheng,* ch. 17, p. 290; Poo, "Ideas Concerning Death and Burial in Pre-Han China," pp. 25–62; Nylan, "Confucian Piety and Individualism in Han China," pp. 1–27; Powers, *Art and Political Expression,* pp. 136–141; Loewe, "The Conduct of Government and the Issues at Stake," pp. 300–301; Ch'en, "Confucian, Legalist, and Taoist Thought in Later Han," pp. 802–804. On the actual techniques and costs of producing funerary monuments, and the distances from which workers and materials might be brought, see Barbieri-Low, *Artisans in Early Imperial China,* ch. 2, sec. 5, "Stone Funerary Workshops"; and ch. 3, sec. 2, "Marketing Territory."

35. Ebrey, "The Economic and Social History of Later Han," pp. 633–635.

36. *Lun yu zheng yi,* ch. 6, p. 127.

37. *Mengzi zheng yi* IA, ch. 1, pp. 33–35.

38. Bodde, *Festivals in Classical China,* pp. 361–380; Loewe, "The Wooden and Bamboo Strips Found at Mo-chü-tzu (Kansu)," pp. 13–26. *Han shu* 6, p. 156; *Bo hu tong shu zheng,* pp. 208, 314, 520; Hulsewé, *Remnants of Han Law,* pp. 298–302.

39. Jiao, *Jiao shi yi lin,* ch. 1, p. 38. On the physical decay of old age, see also Wang, *Lun heng ji jie,* ch. 2, p. 32.

40. *Xian Qin Han Wei Jin Nanbeichao shi,* pp. 331–332.

41. *Li ji zhu shu,* ch. 8, pp. 21a–21b.

42. *Han shu* 22, p. 1043; *Laozi dao de jing,* ch. 1, #33, p. 19; *Xiao jing zhu shu,* ch. 8, p. 2a; Yü, "Life and Immortality in the Mind of Han China," pp. 83, 87, 111, 121–122; Brashier, "Longevity like Metal and Stone," pp. 214–217.

43. *Han shu* 73, p. 3118; Keightley, "The Quest for Eternity in China," pp. 18–21.

44. *Han shu* 73, p. 3126. For an opposing position, see *Han shu* 75, pp. 3156–3157.

45. *Hou Han shu, zhi* 9, p. 3197; Cai, *Cai Zhonglang wen ji,* ch. 8, pp. 5a–5b.

46. *Li shi,* ch. 7, p. 16b.

8. Religion

1. Teiser, "Introduction," *Religions of China in Practice,* pp. 21–36, esp. 32–36.

2. *Han shu* 22, p. 1046; *Xian Qin Han Wei Jin Nanbeichao shi*, p. 145.

3. *Mao shi zheng yi*, ch. 16.3, pp. 6a–10b; 17.2, pp. 1a–8a; 15a–20b.

4. Waley, *The Nine Songs*, "Introduction"; Hawkes, *The Songs of the South*, pp. 38, 42–51, 95–101; Lewis, *Writing and Authority*, pp. 184–185.

5. *Shi ji* 28, pp. 1384–1391, 1399–1400.

6. Loewe, *Chinese Ideas of Life and Death*, ch. 10; Ch'ü, *Han Social Structure*, pp. 55, 375; Poo, *In Search of Personal Welfare*, pp. 185–200; *Han shu* 6, p. 2003; *Hou Han shu* 11, pp. 479, 480; 41, pp. 1397, 1413; 47, p. 1573; 57, p. 1841; *Dong guan Han ji jiao zhu*, ch. 21, p. 863; Ying, *Feng su tong yi*, pp. 338–339; *Li ji zhu shu*, ch. 9, p. 18b.

7. Erickson, "Money Trees of the Eastern Han Dynasty," pp. 1–116; Lewis, *Construction of Space*, pp. 157–158; Major, *Heaven and Earth in Early Han Thought*, pp. 102, 158, 196, 204. For images see Elisseeff, *New Discoveries in China*, p. 91; Rawson, *Mysteries*, pp. 177–178, 190, 192; Wu, "Mapping Early Taoist Art," pp. 84–88; Bagley, *Ancient Sichuan*, pp. 272–277.

8. Loewe, *Divination, Mythology and Monarchy in Han China*, ch. 8, 10; Harper, "Warring States Natural Philosophy and Occult Thought," pp. 843–866; Poo, *In Search of Personal Welfare*, pp. 44–52, 69–101; Loewe, *Chinese Ideas of Life and Death*, ch. 9; Lewis, "Dicing and Divination in Early China."

9. Harper, "Warring States Natural Philosophy and Occult Thought," pp. 839–843; Loewe, *Divination, Mythology and Monarchy*, ch. 3, 9; *Shi ji* 27.

10. Csikszentmihalyi, *Material Virtue: Ethics and the Body in Early China*, pp. 130–141; Lewis, *Construction of Space*, pp. 63–65; Knoblock, *Xunzi*, vol. 1, pp. 196–200; Sterckx, *The Animal and the Daemon in Early China*, p. 155.

11. For English discussions of dreams and their interpretation in early China see Ong, *The Interpretation of Dreams in Ancient China*; Brown, ed., *Psycho-Sinology: The Universe of Dreams in Chinese Culture*, esp. Ong, "Image and Meaning: The Hermeneutics of Traditional Dream Interpretation"; Strickmann, "Dreamwork of Psycho-Sinologists: Doctors, Taoists, Monks." Moffett, "Prediction in the *Zuo-zhuan*," contains translations of many dream accounts in the *Zuo zhuan*, the richest source of such stories in early China. Diény, "Le saint ne rêve pas," pp. 127–128, n. 2, lists major works on the subject in Chinese and German.

12. *Han shu* 27a, p. 1331–1332.

13. *Han shu* 27a-e; Queen, *From Chronicle to Canon*, chs. 5, 9.

14. Bilsky, *The State Religion of Ancient China*, pp. 14–16, 58–60, 66, 126–127, 162–169, 183–190, 135–146, 274–276, 296–308, 318–324.

15. Lewis, "The Feng and Shan Sacrifices of Emperor Wu of the Han."

16. *Shi ji* 28, pp. 1358, 1360, 1364, 1365, 1378; *Han shu* 25a, pp. 1196, 1199. Lewis, "Feng and Shan Sacrifices," p. 55.

17. Li, "Formulaic Structure in Chu Divinatory Bamboo Slips," p. 84; Li, "An Archaeological Study of Taiyi (Grand One) Worship," pp. 1–39; *Huainanzi*, ch. 3, p. 39; ch. 7, p. 111; ch. 8, p. 119; ch. 9, p. 127; ch. 14, p. 235 (2); ch. 21, p. 369; *Zhuangzi ji shi*, ch. 32, p. 453; ch. 33, p. 473; *Xunzi ji jie*, ch. 13, p. 236.

18. *Han shu* 25b, pp. 1254–1259; Lewis, "The Feng and Shan Sacrifices," p. 67; Loewe, "The Concept of Sovereignty," pp. 735–737.

19. Loewe, *Chinese Ideas of Life and Death*, pp. 140–141.

20. Poo, *In Search of Personal Welfare*, pp. 165–167; Wang, *Han Civilization*, chs. 8–9; Wu, "Art and Architecture of the Warring States Period," pp. 707–744; Wu, *Monumentality*, pp. 110–121; von Falkenhausen, "Sources of Taoism, pp. 1–12. For a more detailed discussion, see Lewis, *The Construction of Space*, ch. 4, sec. 5, "Household and Tombs." *Xunzi ji shi*, ch. 13, pp. 243–246.

21. Wang, *Lun heng ji jie*, ch. 23, p. 467.

22. Lim, *Stories from China's Past*, pp. 109 (fig. 3), 126–131, 138, 139 (photo at bottom center), 141, 143, 144, 189, 190; Powers, *Art and Political Expression*, pp. 51, 288, 291, 293, 306; James, *Guide*, pp. 163, 202, 226–230; Finsterbusch, *Verzeichnis und Motivindex*, vol. 2, #191, 192, 212, 261, 268, 277, 310, 338, 363, 508a, 508q, 508s, 508t, 538, 552, 594, 641, 786, 793.

23. Wu, "Beyond the Great Boundary," pp. 90, 101; Wu, *The Wu Liang Shrine*, pp. 246–247; Lewis, *Writing and Authority*, pp. 197–209; von Glahn, *The Sinister Way*, pp. 58–59. This last discusses the demonic character of the Queen Mother in certain traditions.

24. Von Falkenhausen, "Sources of Taoism," pp. 3–5; Rawson, "Western Zhou Archaeology," pp. 364–375, 433–440.

25. Wang, *Han Civilization*, pp. 206–210.

26. *Li ji zhu shu*, ch. 9, p. 18b; Seidel, "Post-mortem Immortality—or the Taoist Resurrection of the Body," pp. 223–237; Seidel, "Traces of Han Religion in Funeral Texts Found in Tombs," pp. 21–57.

27. Ikeda, "Chūgoku rekidai boken ryakko," p. 273, no. 7. For discussions of this and related texts, and what they reveal about Han ideas regarding the afterlife, see von Glahn, *The Sinister Way*, pp. 49–57. "Jiangsu Gaoyou Shaojiagou Han dai yizhi de qingli," pp. 20–21. *Li shi*, ch. 12, pp. 16b–17a.

28. Wu, "Beyond the 'Great Boundary,'" pp. 93–98.

29. *Han shu* 53, pp. 2428–2430. See also *Jing fa*, p. 61; Wang, *Lun heng ji jie*, ch. 4, pp. 83–84; ch. 10, p. 214; ch. 21, p. 434.

30. *Mozi jian gu*, ch. 8, pp. 139–141, 142–143, 143–144; Wang, *Lun heng ji jie*, ch. 22, pp. 449–450; ch. 23, p. 461 (3), 464 (4); ch. 25, p. 505; Cohen, "Avenging Ghosts and Moral Judgment in the Ancient Chinese Historiography: Three Examples from *Shi-chi*," pp. 97–108.

31. *Lü shi chun qiu jiaoshi*, ch. 10, pp. 535–536.

32. Wu, "Art in Ritual Context: Rethinking Mawangdui," pp. 111–144.

33. James, *Guide*, pp. 4–13, 23–27, passim. Finsterbusch, *Verzeichnis und motivindex*, figures 32a, 45, 101–102, 106, 127, 137, 150, 158, 161, 167, 172, Hebei appendix 3–4; Wu, "Beyond the 'Great Boundary,'" pp. 88–90. Lim, *Stories from China's Past*, pp. 20–21, 34–35, 155–156, 158–181; Loewe, *Ways to Paradise*, chs. 2, 4, and 5; Wu, *The Wu Liang Shrine*, chs. 3–4. On cosmic journeys from the tomb, see Cook, *Death in Ancient China*.

34. Poo, *In Search of Personal Welfare,* pp. 167–170; Seidel, "Traces of Han Religion," pp. 28–30; Harper, "Resurrection in Warring States Popular Religion," pp. 13–28.

35. Brashier, "Han Thanatology and the Division of 'Souls,'" pp. 152–153, n. 100; *Hou Han shu* 4, p. 167; 5, p. 205; 6, p. 250; 7, p. 288; 61, pp. 2029–2030; *zhi* 9, p. 3197; Cai, *Du duan,* ch. 2, pp. 5a–7b; *Dong Guan Han ji jiao zhu,* pp. 165–166; Cai, *Cai Zhonglang wen ji,* ch. 8, pp. 4a–5a.

36. Cui, *Si min yue ling ji shi,* pp. 1, 3, 25, 53, 68 (2), 84, 98, 104, 109.

37. *Hou Han shu, zhi* 9, p. 3197. See also *Du duan,* ch. 2, p. 7a.

38. Wu, *The Wu Liang Shrine,* pp. 30–37.

39. Cai, *Du duan,* ch. 2, pp. 5a–b; Wang, *Lun heng ji jie,* ch. 23, p. 467.

40. *Huainanzi,* ch. 9, p. 127.

41. *Mozi jian gu,* ch. 6, p. 106.

42. *Xunzi ji jie,* ch. 19, pp. 231, 233–234, 237–238, 239–241, 246, 247–248; *Lü shi chun qiu jiao shi,* ch. 10, p. 536.

43. Wang, *Han Civilization,* pp. 181–182; Loewe, *Ways to Paradise,* pp. 13–14; *Hou Han shu* 11, pp. 483–484. See also *Han shu* 99c, p. 4194.

44. Wu, *The Wu Liang Shrine;* Liu, Nylen, and Barbieri-Low, *Recarving China's Past.*

45. Ying, *Feng su tong yi jiao shi,* pp. 333–334, 339, 350.

46. Brashier, "The Spirit Lord of Baishi Mountain," pp. 159–231; *Li shi,* ch. 3, pp. 9b–11a.

47. Little and Eichman, *Taoism and the Arts of China,* pp. 150–151; *Lie xian zhuan,* ch. 1, pp. 6, 8, 10, 11, 13, 14, 14–15, 17, 18; ch. 2, pp. 4, 5, 6–7, 8, 10, 12, 13, 15. Similar cults in Sichuan are described in Chang, *Huayang guo zhi jiao zhu.* See, for example, pp. 64, 77, 96–97, 124, 145, 181, 182, 200, 201, 242, 244, 279, etc.

48. *Shi ji* 28, p. 1394.

49. Harper, "A Chinese Demonography of the Third Century B.C.," pp. 459–498; von Glahn, *The Sinister Way,* chs. 2–4.

50. Barbieri-Low, *Artisans in Early Imperial China,* ch. 2, sec. 6, "Workshop Labor Environment"; sec. 7, "Religious Beliefs of Artisans."

51. *Han shu* 11, p. 342; 26, pp. 1311–1312; 27, pp. 1476–1477; 84, p. 3432; Loewe, *Ways to Paradise,* ch. 4.

52. Kleeman, *Great Perfection,* ch. 2; Goodman, *Ts'ao P'i Transcendent,* pp. 74–86.

53. Demiéville, "Philosophy and Religion from Han to Sui," pp. 820–826.

54. *Xian Qin Han Wei Jin Nanbeichao shi,* p. 332.

9. Literature

1. On the meaning(s) of the term *ru,* see Zufferey, *To the Origins of Confucianism;* Cheng, "What Did It Mean to Be a *Ru* in Han Times?" Eno, *The Confu-*

cian *Creation of Heaven;* Nylan, "A Problematic Model: The Han 'Orthodox Synthesis' Then and Now," pp. 18–19. On the divergences between Han "Confucianism" and its earlier versions, see Nylan and Sivin, "The First Neo-Confucianism," Sivin, *Medicine, Philosophy and Religion in Ancient China,* p. 6; Wallacker, "Han Confucianism and Confucius in Han." On the absence of a philosophical orthodoxy, in addition to the works already cited, see Kern, *The Stele Inscriptions of Ch'in Shih-huang,* p. 9; Nylan, "Han Classicists Writing in Dialogue about Their Own Tradition"; Nylan, "The Chin-wen/Ku-wen Controversy in Han Times."

2. *Shi ji* 130, p. 3290; *Han shu* 30, pp. 1701, 1716–1717, 1728.

3. *Xunzi ji jie,* ch. 15, pp. 258, 261–263. See also *Han Feizi ji shi,* ch. 19, p. 1067.

4. *Shi ji* 87, pp. 2546–2547.

5. *Shi ji* 130, pp. 3288–3293.

6. Lewis, *Writing and Authority,* pp. 297–299.

7. *Zhuangzi ji shi,* ch. 33, p. 467; *Guanzi jiao zheng,* pp. 1–47 (see also Rickett, tr., *Guanzi,* vol. 1, p. 4); *Han Feizi ji shi,* ch. 18, pp. 996–1039; Graham, *Later Mohist Logic, Ethics and Science,* pp. 22–24, 243–244.

8. *Han Feizi ji shi,* chs. 9–14. For the principles as *jing,* see pp. 526, 576, 621, 676, 715, 761. *Shuo wen jie zi zhu,* ch. 8a, p. 25a; *Shi min shu zheng,* ch. 5, p. 13b; ch. 6, pp. 7b, 13a.

9. Nylan, *The Five "Confucian" Classics.*

10. Lewis, *Writing and Authority,* pp. 77–79; *Shi ji* 85, p. 2510; *Han shu* 44, p. 2145; *Huainanzi,* p. 1.

11. *Lü shi chun qiu jiao shi,* p. 648.

12. *Lü shi chun qiu jiao shi,* ch. 17, pp. 1123–1124, 1132.

13. *Han shu* 62, p. 2735. On aspects of this passage, see Durrant, *The Cloudy Mirror,* pp. 124–129; *Shi ji* 130, p. 3285; *Guo yu,* ch. 18, pp. 559–564. On the *Shi ji* as a comprehensive world model, see also Hardy, *Worlds of Bronze and Bamboo;* Lewis, *Writing and Authority,* pp. 308–317.

14. *Shi ji* 130, p. 3319.

15. Nylan, *The Five "Confucian" Classics,* ch. 6; *Shi ji* 14, pp. 509–510.

16. Durrant, "Ssu-ma Chi'en's Portrayal of the First Ch'in Emperor," pp. 35–46.

17. *Han shu* 62, pp. 2737–2738; *Hou Han shu* 40a, pp. 1325–1327.

18. *Hou Han shu* 40a, pp. 1333–1334.

19. Lewis, *Writing and Authority,* pp. 317–325; Knechtges, *The Han Rhapsody,* ch. 2; Rouzer, *Articulated Ladies,* pp. 45–52, 121–122; Knechtges, "Ssu-ma Hsiang-ju's 'Tall Gate Palace Rhapsody,'" pp. 47–64; Harper, "Wang Yen-shou's Nightmare Poem," pp. 239–283.

20. Yang, *Yangzi fa yan,* ch.2, pp. 4–5. On these passages and their context, see Knechtges, *The Han Rhapsody,* ch. 5.

21. Van Zoeren, *Poetry and Personality,* chs. 1–4; Lewis, *Writing and Author-ity,* pp. 155–176.

22. *Shi ji* 7, p. 333. For at least one example of "ode" written by a literary man, see Han shu 73, pp. 3110–3114.

23. Cai, *The Matrix of Lyric Transformation,* ch. 2; Birrell, *Popular Songs and Ballads of Han China,* intro.; Frankel, "The Development of Han and Wei Yüeh-fu as High Literary Genre"; "Yüeh-fu Poetry." For the most thorough critique of the idea that these were folk songs, see Egan, "Were Yüeh-fu Ever Folk Songs?" and "Reconsidering the Role of Folk Songs in Pre-T'ang Yüeh-fu Development." My discussion of the stylistic features of the songs derives largely from Cai's book cited at the beginning of this note. On the manner in which these putative Han songs were defined as genres and fitted into a "history" of Chinese literature by later poets and anthologists, see Owen, *The Making of Early Chinese Classical Poetry.*

24. *Xian Qin Han Wei Jin Nanbeichao shi,* p. 256.

25. Ibid., pp. 257–258.

26. Ibid., p. 192. On the dispute over the attribution of this poem, see Birrell, *Popular Songs and Ballads,* p. 125.

27. On using "the voice of others" as an attribute of Music Bureau poetry, see Allen, *In the Voice of Others.* On how the "ancient songs" established as a set and were dated to the Han, see Owen, *The Making of Early Chinese Classical Po-etry,* pp. 33–41.

28. *Han shu* 30, p. 1701.

29. Lewis, *Writing and Authority,* pp. 325–332.

30. *Han shu* 30, pp. 1728, 1732, 1737, 1738, 1740, 1743, 1745, 1746, 1755–1756, 1762, 1765, 1769, 1771, 1773, 1775, 1780.

31. *Han shu* 30, p. 1756.

32. *Han shu* 30, pp. 1728, 1732, 1734, 1736, 1737, 1738, 1740, 1742, 1743, 1745, 1755, 1762, 1775, 1780.

33. *Han shu* 30, pp. 1704, 1706, 1708, 1710, 1715, 1717, 1719, 1728, 1732, 1734–1735, 1736, 1737, 1738, 1740, 1742, 1743, 1745, 1756, 1762–1763, 1765, 1767, 1769, 1771, 1773, 1776, 1778, 1779, 1780.

10. Law

1. Lewis, *Sanctioned Violence,* pp. 43–50; Liu, *Origins of Chinese Law,* ch. 5.

2. Lewis, *Writing and Authority,* p. 20.

3. Lewis, *Sanctioned Violence,* pp. 67–80.

4. See the translation of the legal documents in Hulsewé, *Remnants of Ch'in Law.*

5. *Shuihudi Qin mu zhu jian,* pp. 281–293.

6. Ibid., pp. 26–27, 181, 182, 183, 261–262, 263.

7. Harper, "Warring States Natural Philosophy and Occult Thought," pp. 854–856; Harper, "A Chinese Demonography," pp. 470–498; Katrina McLeod and Robin Yates, "Forms of Ch'in Law," n. 57; *Zuo zhuan zhu*, Cheng year 5, pp. 822–823; *Guo yu*, pp. 405–406.

8. *Han Feizi ji shi*, ch. 6, p. 357.

9. *Yunmeng Shuihudi Qin mu*, strips 827 verso–814 verso, 886–895; Hulsewé, "The Wide Scope of Tao 'Theft' in Ch'in-Han Law," pp. 182–183; Yates, "Some Notes on Ch'in Law," p. 245.

10. *Shi ji* 122, p. 3148.

11. Mcknight, *The Quality of Mercy*, ch. 2.

12. *Han shu* 56, pp. 2500–2502; Hulsewé, "Ch'in and Han Law," pp. 522–523.

13. Hulsewé, *Remnants of Han Law*, pp. 271–272. Lewis, *Sanctioned Violence*, pp. 80–94.

14. Lewis, *Sanctioned Violence*, pp. 49–50, 91–94.

15. *Shang Jun shu zhu yi*, ch. 5, pp. 140–141.

16. For what follows see Lewis, *Writing and Authority*, pp. 23–26.

17. *Shuihudi Qin mu zhu jian*, pp. 92, 93–94, 101–102, 102–103, 103, 136–147; Lewis, *Sanctioned Violence*, pp. 61–64.

18. *Shuihudi Qin mu zhu jian*, pp. 97, 113–148; Hulsewé, *Remnants of Ch'in Law*, pp. 14–18.

19. *Shuihudi Qin mu zhu jian*, pp. 247–249; *Baoshan Chu jian*, pp. 17–39.

20. Hulsewé, *Remnants of Ch'in Law*, pp. 211–215; Sage, *Ancient Sichuan and the Unification of China*, pp. 131–133.

21. Harper, "Resurrection in Warring States Popular Religion," pp. 13–28.

22. Riegel, "Kou-mang and Ju-shou," pp. 57–66; Barnard, *The Ch'u Silk Manuscript*, pp. 207–210; *Huainanzi*, ch. 8.

23. Loewe, *Records of Han Administration*.

24. White, *Heracles' Bow, The Legal Imagination, Justice as Translation*.

25. Yates, "New Light on Ancient Chinese Military Texts," pp. 220–222; Wang and Chang, *The Philosophical Foundation of Han Fei's Political Theory*, pp. 59–60; Makeham, *Name and Actuality*, pp. 69–75.

26. Lewis, *Writing and Authority*, p. 33.

27. *Lun yu zheng yi*, ch. 7, p. 129; ch. 15, p. 271; ch. 16, pp. 280–293; ch. 20, p. 364; Makeham, *Name and Actuality*, chs. 2–4.

28. Lewis, *Writing and Authority*, pp. 139–144.

29. *Shi ji* 130, p. 3297; *Han shu* 30, p. 1714; *Shi ji* 122, p. 3139; Queen, *From Chronicle to Canon*, chs. 6–7.

30. *Zuo zhuan zhu*, Xuan year 2, pp. 662–63; Xiang year 25, p. 1099; Lewis, *Writing and Authority*, pp. 130–131, 222–224.

31. *Shuihudi Qin mu zhu jian*, pp. 160, 238.

32. *Han shu* 2, p. 85; 50, p. 1307; *Hou Han shu* 25, p. 886; 52, p. 1722; 60b, p. 1980.

33. *Shi ji* 122, p. 3131.

34. *Shi ji* 122, pp. 3133, 3135, 3136, 3139, 3140, 3141, 3145, 3150, 3151, 3152.

35. *Shi ji* 122, p. 3137.

36. *Shi ji* 122, pp. 3139, 3143.

37. *Han shu* 24, p. 1101.

38. Kleeman, "Land Contracts and Related Documents," pp. 1–34; *Shuihudi Qin mu zhu jian*, p. 224; Wilbur, *Slavery in China during the Former Han Dynasty*, pp. 158–164.

39. *Shi ji* 122, pp. 3150, 3153; *Han shu* 23, p. 1106.

40. Hulsewé, "Ch'in and Han Law," pp. 532–533.

41. *Han shu* 4, p. 125; 23, pp. 1097, 1099–1101.

42. Hulsewé, *Remnants of Ch'in Law*, pp. 14–18; Hulsewé, "Ch'in and Han Law," p. 533.

43. *Shuihudi Qin mu zhu jian*, pp. 91, 92, 13, 143, 150, 177, 178, 204, 261, 276. Hulsewé, *Remnants of Ch'in Law*, p. 195.

44. *Shuihudi Qin mu zhu jian*, pp. 84–85, 91, 143, 152, 164, 178, 179, 200, 231. For the Han, see Hulsewé, *Remnants of Han Law*, pp. 205–214.

45. Hulsewé, "Ch'in and Han Law," pp. 528–530.

46. *Han shu* 90, pp. 3673–3674; 92, pp. 3705–3706, 3706–3707; *Qian fu lun jian*, ch. 5, pp. 173–197; Lewis, *Sanctioned Violence*, pp. 90–91.

47. Hulsewé, *Remnants of Ch'in Law*, pp. 200–201.

48. *Shuihudi Qin mu zhu jian*, pp. 246–247.

49. *Zhangjiashan Han mu zhu jian*, pp. 225–226. The historicity of this case is called into question by its resemblance to a case described in *Han Feizi ji shi*, ch. 10, pp. 595–596.

50. *Shi ji* 6, p. 253; *Han shu* 6, p. 205; Chü, *Han Social Structure*, pp. 328–329, n. 21; Bodde, "The State and Empire of Ch'in," pp. 29, 38, 59, 65–66, 88.

51. *Han shu* 6, pp. 193, 198, 200, 203, 205; 70, pp. 3010, 3017; 76, 3208, 3214; Lewis, "The Han Abolition of Universal Military Service," p. 54.

52. *Hou Han shu* 4, p. 171; 43, pp. 1470–1471; 58, p. 1871; 65, p. 2147; 67, p. 2192.

53. *Hou Han shu* 23, p. 3533; 47, p. 1586.

54. *Hou Han shu* 48, pp. 1597–1598. *Hou Han shu* 2, p. 111; 18, p. 681; 20, p. 737; 47, p. 1576.

55. *Han shu* 23, p. 1109.

56. *Hou Han shu* 46, pp. 1544–1545.

57. Barbieri-Low, in the final chapter of his *Artisans in Early Imperial China*.

58. Ibid.

59. Wilbur, *Slavery in China during the Former Han Dynasty*, pp. 121–126.

Conclusion

1. *Hou Han shu* 41, pp. 1415–1416.

2. De Crespigny, *Northern Frontier*, chs. 2–4, 7.

3. *Han shu* 69, pp. 2985–2992; *Hou Han shu* 97, pp. 2877, 2885.

4. *Hou Han shu* 87, pp. 2887–2888, 2894; Wang, *Qian fu lun jian*, ch. 24.

5. *Han shu* 94b, p. 3826; *Hou Han shu* 1b, p. 64; 76, pp. 2460–2461; monograph 10, p. 3221.

6. Lewis, "The Han Abolition of Universal Military Service," pp. 64–65.

7. Wang, *Qian fu lun jian*, p. 285.

8. *Hou Han shu* 2, p. 109; 65, p. 2140.

9. *Hou Han shu* 4, p. 189; 37, p. 1268; Wang, *Qian fu lun jian*, p. 288.

10. *Jiazi xin shu jiao shi*, ch. 3, p. 357.

11. *Yan tie lun*, p. 63.

12. *Hou Han shu* 14, p. 835.

13. *Hou Han shu* 58, p. 1866.

14. De Crespigny, *Northern Frontier*, pp. 324–326, 425–426.

15. Wang, *Qian fu lun jian*, pp. 257, 258.

16. *Hou Han shu* 73, pp. 2354–2356; 74b, pp. 2419–2421; 75, pp. 2432–2433.

17. *Hou Han shu* 71, p. 2308; *San guo zhi* 12, p. 384.

18. *Hou Han shu* 16, pp. 609–610.

19. *Hou Han shu* 72, p. 2322.

20. *Hou Han shu* 24, p. 3563.

21. *Hou Han shu* 70, p. 2258.

22. Ch'ü, *Han Social Structure*, pp. 133–134.

23. *Hou Han shu* 24, p. 828.

BIBLIOGRAPHY

Allen, Joseph R. *In the Voice of Others: Chinese Music Bureau Poetry*. Ann Arbor: University of Michigan Press, 1992.

Bagley, Robert, ed. *Ancient Sichuan: Treasures from a Lost Civilization*. Seattle: Seattle Art Museum, 2001.

Baopuzi nei pian jiao shi (Annotated Elucidations of the "Inner Chapters of the Master Who Embraces Simplicity"). Annotated by Wang Ming. Beijing: Zhonghua, 1980.

Baoshan Chu jian (The Chu State Strips from Baoshan). Beijing: Wenwu, 1991.

Barber, Elizabeth Wayland. *The Mummies of Ürümchi*. New York: W. W. Norton, 1999.

Barbieri-Low, Anthony. *Artisans in Early Imperial China*. Seattle: University of Washington, 2007.

Barfield, Thomas J. *The Perilous Frontier: Nomadic Empires and China*. Cambridge: Basil Blackwell, 1989.

Barnard, Noel. *The Ch'u Silk Manuscript*. Canberra: Australian National University Press, 1973.

Bielenstein, Hans. *The Bureaucracy of Han Times*. Cambridge: Cambridge University Press, 1980.

——— "Lo-yang in Later Han times." *Bulletin of the Museum of Far Eastern Antiquities* 48 (1976): 1–142.

Bilsky, Lester. *The State Religion of Ancient China*. Taipei: The Chinese Association for Folklore, 1975.

Birrell, Anne. *Popular Songs and Ballads of Han China*. London: Unwin Hyman, 1988.

Bo hu tong shu zheng (Correct Subcommentaries on the "Comprehensive Discourses of the White Tiger Hall"). Annotated by Wu Zeyu. Beijing: Zhonghua, 1994.

Bodde, Derk. *China's First Unifier: A Study of the Ch'in Dynasty as Seen in the Life of Li Ssu (280?–208 B.C.)*. Leiden: E. J. Brill, 1938.

—— *Festivals in Classical China: New Year and Other Annual Observances During the Han Dynasty*. Princeton: Princeton University Press, 1975.

—— "The State and Empire of Ch'in." In *The Cambridge History of China, Vol. 1: The Ch'in and Han Empires, 221 B.C.–A.D. 220*. Ed. Michael Loewe. Cambridge: Cambridge University Press, 1986.

Boyd, Andrew. *Chinese Architecture and Town Planning: 1500 B.C.–A.D. 1911*. Chicago: University of Chicago Press, 1962.

Brashier, K. E. "Han Thanatology and the Division of 'Souls.'" *Early China* 21 (1996): 125–158.

—— "Longevity like Metal and Stone: The Role of the Mirror in Han Burials." *T'oung Pao* 81.4–5 (1995): 201–229.

—— "The Spirit Lord of Baishi Mountain: Feeding the Deities or Heeding the Yinyang." *Early China* 26–27 (2001–2002): 159–231.

Bray, Francesca. *Technology and Gender: Fabrics of Power in Late Imperial China*. Berkeley: University of California Press, 1997.

Brown, Carolyn T., ed. *Psycho-Sinology: The Universe of Dreams in Chinese Culture*. Lanham, MD: University Press of America, 1988.

Buchanan, Keith. *The Transformation of the Chinese Earth: Perspectives on Modern China*. London: G. Bell & Sons, 1970.

Cai, Yong. *Cai Zhonglang wen ji* (Collected Literary Works of Cai Yong). Si bu cong kan ed.

—— *Du duan* (Solitary Judgments). In *Han Wei cong shu*, Vol. 1. Taipei: Xin Xing, 1977.

Cai, Zongqi. *The Matrix of Lyric Transformation: Poetic Modes and Self-Presentation in Early Chinese Pentasyllabic Poetry*. Ann Arbor: University of Michigan Press, 1996.

Chang, Kwang-chih. *The Archaeology of Ancient China*. 4th ed., revised and enlarged. New Haven: Yale University, 1986.

Chang, Qu. *Huayang guo zhi jiao zhu* (Annotated Commentary to the "Record of the States South of Mt. Hua"). Chengdu: Ba Shu Shu She, 1984.

Ch'en, Ch'i-yun. "Confucian, Legalist, and Taoist Thought in Later Han." In *The Cambridge History of China, Vol. 1: The Ch'in and Han Empires*.

Cheng, Anne. "What Did It Mean to Be a *Ru* in Han Times?" *Asia Major,* Third Series 14:2 (2001): 101–118.

Ch'ü, T'ung-tsu. *Han Social Structure*. Seattle: University of Washington Press, 1972.

Chun qiu fan lu yi zheng (Proving the Meaning of the "Abundant Dew on the Spring and Autumn Annals"). Annotated by Su Yu. Beijing: Zhonghua, 1992.

Cohen, Alvin. "Avenging Ghosts and Moral Judgment in the Ancient Chinese

Historiography: Three Examples from *Shi-chi*." In *Legend, Lore, and Religions in China: Essays in Honor of Wolfram Eberhard on His Seventieth Birthday*. Ed. Sarah Allan and Alvin P. Cohen. San Francisco: Chinese Materials Center, 1979.

Cook, Constance A. *Death in Ancient China: The Tale of One Man's Journey*. Leiden: E. J. Brill, 2006.

Cook, Constance A., and John S. Major, eds. *Defining Chu: Image and Reality in Ancient China*. Honolulu: University of Hawaii Press, 1999.

Cottrell, Arthur. *The First Emperor of China*. New York: Holt, Rinehart, and Winston, 1981.

Csikszentmihalyi, Mark. *Material Virtue: Ethics and the Body in Early China*. Leiden: E. J. Brill, 2004.

Cui, Shi. *Si min yue ling ji shi* (Collected Elucidations of the "Monthly Ordinances of the Four Categories of People"). Annotated by Miao Qiyu and Wan Guoding. Beijing: Nongye, 1981.

Da Dai li ji jie gu (Analytic Exegesis of the "Elder Dai's Record of Ritual"). Beijing: Zhonghua, 1983.

de Crespigny, Rafe. *Northern Frontier: The Policies and Strategy of the Later Han Empire*. Canberra: Australian National University Press, 1984.

De Francis, John. *The Chinese Language: Fact and Fantasy*. Rep. ed. Honolulu: University of Hawaii Press, 1986.

Dean, Kenneth, and Brian Massumi. *First and Last Emperors: The Absolute State and the Body of the Despot*. Brooklyn: Autonomedia, 1992.

Demiéville, Paul. "Philosophy and Religion from Han to Sui." In *The Cambridge History of China, Vol. 1: The Ch'in and Han Empires, 221 B.C.–A.D. 220*. Cambridge: Cambridge University Press, 1986.

DeWoskin, Kenneth J. "Famous Chinese Childhoods." In *Chinese Views of Childhood*. Ed. Anne Behnke Kinney. Honolulu: University of Hawaii Press, 1995.

Di Cosmo, Nicola. *Ancient China and Its Enemies: The Rise of Nomadic Power in East Asian History*. Cambridge: Cambridge University Press, 2002.

——— "The Northern Frontier in Pre-Imperial China." In *The Cambridge History of Ancient China: From the Origins of Civilization to 221 B.C.* Ed. Michael Loewe and Edward Shaughnessy. Cambridge: Cambridge University Press, 1999.

Diény, Jean-Pierre. "Le saint ne rêve pas: De Zhuangzi à Michel Jouvet." *Études Chinoises* 20:1–2 (Printemps-Automne 2001): 127–200.

Dong guan Han ji jiao zhu (Annotated Commentary on the "Han Records from the Eastern Tower"). Annotated by Wu Shuping. Zhongzhou: Guji, 1987.

Durrant, Stephen W. *The Cloudy Mirror: Tension and Conflict in the Writings of Sima Qian*. Albany: State University of New York Press, 1995.

——— "Ssu'ma Ch'ien's Portrayal of the First Ch'in Emperor." In *Imperial Rul-*

ership and Cultural Change in Traditional China. Ed. Frederick P. Brandauer and Chun-chieh Huang. Seattle: University of Washington Press, 1994.

Ebrey, Patricia. "The Early Stages in the Development of Descent Group Organization." In *Kinship Organization in Late Imperial China: 1000–1940.* Ed. Patricia Ebrey and James L. Watson. Berkeley: University of California Press, 1986.

———— "The Economic and Social History of Later Han." In *The Cambridge History of China, Vol. 1: The Ch'in and Han Empires, 221 B.C.–A.D. 220.* Cambridge: Cambridge University Press, 1986.

———— "Later Han Stone Inscriptions." *Harvard Journal of Asiatic Studies* 40:2 (1980): 325–353.

Egan, Charles H. "Reconsidering the Role of Folk Songs in pre-T'ang *Yüeh-fu* Development." *T'oung Pao* 86 (2000): 47–99.

———— "Were *Yüeh-fu* Ever Folk Songs? Reconsidering the Relevance of Oral Theory and Balladry Analogies." *CLEAR* 22 (Dec. 2000): 31–66.

Elisseeff, Danielle. *New Discoveries in China: Encountering History through Archaeology.* Secaucus, NJ: Chartwell Books, 1983.

Eno, Robert. *The Confucian Creation of Heaven: Philosophy and the Defense of Ritual Mastery.* Albany: State University of New York Press, 1990.

Erickson, Susan N. "Money Trees of the Eastern Han Dynasty." *Bulletin of the Museum of Far Eastern Antiquities* 11 (1994): 1–116.

Finsterbusch, Käte. *Verzeichnis und Motivindex der Han-Darstellungen.* 2 vols. Wiesbaden: Otto Harrasowitz, 1971.

Frankel, Hans. "The Development of Han and Wei *Yüeh-fu* as a High Literary Genre." In *The Vitality of the Lyric Voice: Shih Poetry from the Late Han to the T'ang.* Ed. Stephen Owen and Shuen-fu Lin. Princeton: Princeton University Press, 1986.

———— "*Yüeh-fu* Poetry." In *Studies in Chinese Literary Genres.* Ed. Cyril Birch. Berkeley: University of California Press, 1977.

Gao, Wen. *Han bei ji shi* (Collected Explanations of Han Inscriptions). Kaifeng: Henan University Press, 1985.

[*Chun qiu*] *Gongyang zhuan zhu shu* (Commentaries and Subcommentaries to the "Gongyang Commentary to the *Spring-and-Autumn Annals*"). In *Shisan jing zhu shu* (The Thirteen Classics with Commentaries and Subcommentaries), Vol. 7. Taipei: Yiwen, 1976.

Goodman, Howard L. *Ts'ao P'i Transcendent: The Political Culture of Dynasty-Founding in China at the End of the Han.* Seattle: Scripta Serica, 1998.

Graham, A. C. *Disputers of the Tao: Philosophical Argument in Ancient China.* La Salle, IL: Open Court, 1989.

———— *Later Mohist Logic, Ethics and Science.* Hong Kong: Chinese University of Hong Kong, 1978.

—— "The *Nung-chia* School of the Tillers and the Origins of Peasant Utopianism in China." *Bulletin of the School of Oriental and African Studies* 42 (1971): 66–100.

Guanzhong cong shu (Collecteana of Guanzhong). Compiled by Song Liankui. Reprint of 1934 edition. Taipei: Yiwen, 1970.

Guanzi jiao zheng (Annotated and Corrected "Master Guan"). In *Xin bian zhu zi ji cheng* (New Compilation of the Comprehensive Collection of the Various Masters), Vol. 5. Taipei: Shijie, 1974.

[*Chun qiu*] *Guliang zhuan zhu shu* (Commentaries and Subcommentaries to the "Guliang Commentary to the *Spring and Autumn Annals*"). In *Shisan jing zhu shu* (The Thirteen Classics with Commentaries and Subcommentaries), Vol. 7. Taipei: Yiwen, 1976.

Guo yu (Words of the States). Shanghai: Guji, 1978.

Han Feizi ji shi (Collected Elucidations of the "Master Han Fei"). Annotated by Chen Qiyou. Shanghai: Renmin, 1974.

Han shi wai zhuan ji shi (Exoteric Transmission of "Han Ying's Commentary on the *Odes*"). Annotated by Xu Weiyu. Beijing: Zhonghua, 1980.

Han shu (The Book of the Han). Beijing: Zhonghua, 1962.

Hardy, Grant. *Worlds of Bronze and Bamboo: Sima Qian's Conquest of History.* New York: Columbia University Press, 1999.

Harper, Donald. "A Chinese Demonography of the Third Century B.C." *Harvard Journal of Asiatic Studies* 45:2 (1985): 459–498.

—— *Early Chinese Medical Literature: The Mawangdui Medical Manuscripts.* London: Kegan Paul, 1998.

—— "Resurrection in Warring States Popular Religion." *Taoist Resources* 5:2 (December 1994): 13–28.

—— "Wang Yen-shou's Nightmare Poem." *Harvard Journal of Asiatic Studies* 47:1 (1987): 239–283.

—— "Warring States Natural Philosophy and Occult Thought." In *The Cambridge History of Ancient China*. Ed. Michael Loewe and Edward L. Shaughnessy. Cambridge: Cambridge University Press, 1999.

Hawkes, David. *The Songs of the South: An Anthology of Ancient Chinese Poems by Qu Yuan and Other Poets.* New York: Penguin Books, 1985.

Hayashi, Minao. *Chūgoku kodai no seikatsu shi* (History of Daily Life in Ancient China). Tokyo: Yoshikawa Bunkan, 1992.

Heng, Chye Kiang. *Cities of Aristocrats and Bureaucrats: The Development of Medieval Chinese Cityscapes.* Honolulu: University of Hawaii Press, 1999.

Hertz, Robert. *Death and the Right Hand.* Tr. Rodney Needham and Claudia Needham. Aberdeen: Cohen & West, 1960.

Holzman, Donald. "The Cold Food Festival in Early Medieval China." *Harvard Journal of Asiatic Studies* 46:1 (1986): 51–79.

Hotaling, Stephen. "The City Walls of Han Ch'ang-an." *T'oung Pao* 64 (1978): 1–36.

Hou Han shu (Book of the Later Han). Beijing: Zhonghua, 1965.

Hsu, Cho-yun. *Ancient China in Transition: An Analysis of Social Mobility, 722–222 B.C.* Stanford: Stanford University Press, 1965.

——— "The Changing Relationship between Local Society and Central Political Power in Former Han: 206 B.C.–8 A.D." *Comparative Studies in Society and History* 7 (July 1965): 345–370.

——— *Han Agriculture: The Formation of Early Chinese Agrarian Economy.* Seattle: University of Washington Press, 1980.

Hsu, Cho-yun, and Katheryn M. Linduff. *Western Zhou Civilization.* New Haven: Yale University, 1988.

Huainanzi (The Master of Huainan). In *Xin bian zhu zi ji cheng* (New Compilation of the Comprehensive Collection of the Various Masters), Vol. 7. Taipei: Shijie, 1974.

Huang Di nei jing ling shu jiao zhu yu yi (Annotation, Commentary, and Translation of the "Numinous Pivot of the Internal Classic of the Yellow Emperor"). Annotated by Guo Aichun. Tianjin: Tianjin Kexue Jishu, 1989.

Hughes, E. R. *Two Chinese Poets: Vignettes of Han Life and Thought.* Princeton: Princeton University Press, 1960.

Hulsewé, A. F. P. "Ch'in and Han Law." In *The Cambridge History of China, Vol. 1: The Ch'in and Han Empires, 221 B.C.–A.D. 220.* Cambridge: Cambridge University Press, 1986.

——— *Remnants of Ch'in Law: An Annotated Translation of the Ch'in Legal and Administrative Rules of the 3rd Century B.C.* Leiden: E. J. Brill, 1985.

——— *Remnants of Han Law,* Vol. 1. Leiden: E. J. Brill, 1955.

——— "The Wide Scope of *Tao* 'Theft' in Ch'in-Han Law." *Early China* 13 (1988): 166–200.

Ikeda, On. "Chūgoku rekidai boken ryakkō." (A Brief Examination of Chinese Grave Contracts Through Successive Dynasties). *Tōyō bunka kenkyûsho kiyō* 86:6 (1981): 193–278.

James, Jean. *A Guide to the Tomb and Shrine Art of the Han Dynasty.* Lewiston, NY: Edwin Mellen, 1996.

"Jiangsu Gaoyou Shaojiagou Han dai yizhi de qingli" (The Han Site at Shaojiagou in Gaoyou in Jiangsu Province). *Kaogu* 10 (1960): 18–23.

Jiao, Yanshou. *Jiao shi yi lin* (Master Jiao's Forest of the Changes). Cong shu ji cheng ed. Changsha: Shangwu, 1937.

Jiazi xin shu jiao shi (Annotated Elucidations of "Master Jia's New Writings"). Annotated by Qi Yuzhang. Taipei: Qi Yuzhang, 1974.

Jin shu (Book of the Jin). Beijing: Zhonghua, 1974.

Jing fa (Canonical Model). Beijing: Wenwu, 1976.

Juyan xin jian (New Wooden Strips from Juyan). Beijing: Zhonghua, 1994.

Kalinowski, Marc. "The *Xingde* Text from Mawangdui." *Early China* 23–24 (1998–1999): 125–202.

Keightley, David N. "The Quest for Eternity in Ancient China: The Dead, Their

Gifts, Their Names." *Ancient Mortuary Traditions of China*. Ed. George Kuwayama. Los Angeles: Far Eastern Art Council—Los Angeles County Museum of Art, 1991, pp. 12–24.

Kern, Martin. *The Stele Inscriptions of Ch'in Shih-huang: Text and Ritual in Early Chinese Imperial Representation*. New Haven, CT: American Oriental Society, 2000.

Kinney, Anne Behnke. *The Art of the Han Essay: Wang Fu's Ch'ien-fu Lun*. Tempe: Center for Asian Studies, Arizona State University, 1990.

——— "Dyed Silk: Han Notions of the Moral Development of Children." In *Chinese Views of Childhood*. Ed. Anne Behnke Kinney. Honolulu: University of Hawaii Press, 1995.

——— *Representations of Childhood and Youth in Early China*. Stanford: Stanford University Press, 2004.

Kipnis, Andrew B. *Producing Guanxi: Sentiment, Self, and Subculture in a North China Village*. Durham: Duke University Press, 1997.

Kleeman, Terry. *Great Perfection: Religion and Ethnicity in a Chinese Millennial Kingdom*. Honolulu: University of Hawaii Press, 1998.

——— "Land Contracts and Related Documents." In *Chûgoku no Shûkyô Shisô to Kagaku*. Tokyo: Kokusho Kankôkai, 1984.

Knapp, Ronald G. *China's Old Dwellings*. Honolulu: University of Hawaii Press, 2001.

Knechtges, David. "The Emperor and Literature: Emperor Wu of the Han." In *Imperial Rulership and Cultural Change*. Ed. Frederick P. Brandauer and Chun-chieh Huang. Seattle: University of Washington Press, 1994.

——— *The Han Rhapsody: A Study of the Fu of Yang Hsiung*. Cambridge: Cambridge University Press. 1976.

——— "Ssu-ma Hsiang-ju's 'Tall Gate Palace Rhapsody'." *Harvard Journal of Asiatic Studies* 41:1 (1991): 47–64.

Knoblock John, tr. *Xunzi: A Translation and Study of the Complete Works*, Vol. 1. Stanford: Stanford University Press, 1988.

Ko, Dorothy. "Pursuing Talent and Virtue: Education and Women's Culture in Seventeenth- and Eighteenth-Century China." *Late Imperial China* 13:1 (June 1992): 9–39.

Laozi dao de jing zhu (Commentary on Laozi's "Canon of the Way and its Power"). Annotated by Wang Bi. In *Xin bian zhu zi ji cheng* (New Compilation of the Comprehensive Collection of the Various Masters), Vol. 3. Taipei: Shijie, 1974.

Lattimore, Owen. *Inner Asian Frontiers of China*. New York: American Geographical Society, 1940.

Lawton, Thomas, ed. *New Perspectives on Chu Culture During the Eastern Zhou Period*. Washington, DC: Smithsonian Institution, 1991.

Lewis, Mark Edward. *The Construction of Space in Early China*. Albany: State University of New York Press, 2006.

———— "Custom and Human Nature in Early China." *Philosophy East and West* 53:3 (July 2003): 308–322.

———— "Dicing and Divination in Early China." *Sino-Platonic Papers* 121 (July 2002).

———— "The *Feng* and *Shan* Sacrifices of Emperor Wu of the Han." In *State and Court Ritual in China*. Ed. Joseph McDermott. Cambridge: Cambridge University Press, 1999.

———— "The Han Abolition of Universal Military Service." In *Warfare in Chinese History*. Ed. Hans van de Ven. Leiden: E. J. Brill, 2000.

———— *Sanctioned Violence in Early China*. Albany: State University of New York Press, 1990.

———— "Warring States Political History." In *The Cambridge History of Ancient China: From the Origins of Civilization to 221 B.C.* Ed. Michael Loewe and Edward Shaughnessy. Cambridge: Cambridge University Press, 1999.

———— *Writing and Authority in Early China*. Albany: State University of New York Press, 1999.

Li, Daoyuan. *Shui jing zhu* (Commentary to the "Water Classic"). Taipei: Shijie, 1974.

Li, Ling. "An Archaeological Study of Taiyi (Grand One) Worship." *Early Medieval China* 2 (1995–1996): 1–39.

———— "Formulaic Structure in Chu Divinatory Bamboo Slips." Tr. William Boltz. *Early China* 15 (1990): 71–86.

Li, Xueqin. *Eastern Zhou and Qin Civilizations*. Tr. K. C. Chang. New Haven: Yale University Press, 1985.

Li Bo ji jiaozhu (Annotated Commentary to the "Collected Poems of Li Bo"). Shanghai: Guji, 1980.

Li He shi ji (Collected Poems of Li He). Beijing: Renmin Wenxue, 1984.

Li ji zhu shu (Commentaries and Subcommentaries to the "Records of Ritual"). In *Shisan jing zhu shu* (The Thirteen Classics with Commentaries and Subcommentaries), Vol. 5. Taipei: Yiwen, 1976.

Li shi (Elucidation of Clerical Graph Inscriptions). Compiled by Hong Gua. In *Shike shiliao congshu* (Collecteana of Historical Resources Carved on Stone). Vols. 1–3. Taipei: Yiwen, 1966.

Li xu (Sequel to the Elucidation of Clerical Graph Inscriptions). In *Shike shiliao congshu*. Vol. 3. Taipei: Yiwen, 1966.

Liang Han jin shi ji (Records on Metal and Stone from the Two Han Dynasties). In *Shike shiliao congshu*. Vols. 4–5. Taipei: Yiwen, 1966.

Liang Jiang Wentong wenji (Collected Writings of the Two Jiangs). Si bu cong kan ed.

Lie nü zhuan jiao zhu (Annotated Commentary to the "Arrayed Biographies of Women"). Si bu bei yao ed.

Lie xian zhuan (Arrayed Biographies of Immortals). In *Zheng tong Dao zang*

(Daoist Canon from the Zhengtong Reign Period). Shanghai: Shangwu, 1923–1926.

Lim, Lucy, ed. *Stories from China's Past: Han Dynasty Pictorial Reliefs and Archaeological Objects from Sichuan Province, People's Republic of China.* San Francisco: Chinese Culture Foundation, 1987.

Little, Stephen and Shawn, Eichman. *Taoism and the Arts of China.* Chicago: Art Institute of Chicago, 2000.

Liu, Cary, Michael Nylan and Anthony Barbieri-Low. *Recarving China's Past: Art, Archaeology, and Architecture of the "Wu Family Shrines."* New Haven: Yale University Press, 2005.

Liu, James J. Y. *The Chinese Knight Errant.* London: Routledge & Kegan Paul, 1967.

Loewe, Michael. *Chinese Ideas of Life and Death: Faith, Myth and Reason in the Han Period.* London: George Allen & Unwin, 1982.

—— "The Concept of Sovereignty." In *The Cambridge History of China, Vol. 1: The Ch'in and Han Empires, 221 B.C.–A.D. 220.* Cambridge: Cambridge University Press, 1986.

—— "The Conduct of Government and the Issues at Stake, A.D. 57–167." In *The Cambridge History of China, Vol. 1: The Ch'in and Han Empires, 221 B.C.–A.D. 220.* Cambridge: Cambridge University Press, 1986.

—— *Divination, Mythology and Monarchy in Han China.* Cambridge: Cambridge University Press, 1994.

—— "The Orders of Aristocratic Ranks of Han China." *T'oung Pao* 48:1–3 (1960): 97–174.

—— *Records of Han Administration.* 2 vols. Cambridge: Cambridge University Press, 1967.

—— "The Structure and Practice of Government." In *The Cambridge History of China, Vol. 1: The Ch'in and Han Empires, 221 B.C.–A.D. 220.* Cambridge: Cambridge University Press, 1986.

—— *Ways to Paradise: The Chinese Quest for Immortality.* London: George Allen & Unwin, 1979.

Loewe, Michael, ed. *The Cambridge History of China, Vol. 1: The Ch'in and Han Empires, 221 B.C.–A.D. 220.* Cambridge: Cambridge University Press, 1986.

Lu, Jia. *Xin yu jiaozhu* (Annotated Commentary to the "New Words"). Annotated by Wang Liqi. Beijing: Zhonghua, 1986.

Lü shi chun qiu jiao shi (Annotated Elucidation of the "Springs and Autumns of Master Lü"). Annotated by Chen Qiyou. Shanghai: Xuelin, 1984.

Lun yu zheng yi (True Meaning of the "Analects"). In *Xin bian zhu zi ji cheng* (New Compilation of the Comprehensive Collection of the Various Masters), Vol. 1. Taipei: Shijie, 1974.

Ma, Jixing. *Mawangdui gu yi shu kaoshi* (Critical Elucidation of the Ancient Medical Texts from Mawangdui). Changsha: Hunan Kexue Jishu, 1992.

Major, John. *Heaven and Earth in Early Han Thought: Chapters Three, Four, and Five of the Huainanzi*. Albany: State University of New York Press, 1993.

——— "The Meaning of *Hsing-te* [*Xingde*]." In *Chinese Ideas about Nature and Society*. Ed. Charles Le Blanc and Susan Blader. Hong Kong: Hong Kong University, 1987.

Makeham, John. *Name and Actuality in Early Chinese Thought*. Albany: State University of New York Press, 1994.

Mallory, J. P., and Victor Mair. *The Tarim Mummies: Ancient China and the Mystery of the Earliest People from the West*. London: Thames and Hudson: 2000.

Mao shi zheng yi (The Correct Meaning of the "Mao Commentary to the Odes"). In *Shisan jing zhu shu* (The Thirteen Classics with Commentaries and Subcommentaries), Vol. 2. Taipei: Yiwen, 1976.

McKnight, Brian. *The Quality of Mercy: Amnesties and Traditional Chinese Justice*. Honolulu: University of Hawaii Press, 1981.

McLeod, Katrina, and Robin Yates. "Forms of Ch'in Law." *Harvard Journal of Asiatic Studies* 41:1 (1981): 111–163.

Mengzi zheng yi (True Meaning of the "Mencius"). In *Xin bian zhu zi ji cheng* (New Compilation of the Comprehensive Collection of the Various Masters), Vol. 1. Taipei: Shijie, 1974.

Moffett, J. C. P. "Prediction in the *Zuo-zhuan*." Ph.D. diss. Edinburgh University, 1991.

Mozi jian gu (Itemized Exegesis on the "Master Mo"). Annotated by Sun Yirang. In *Xin bian zhu zi ji cheng* (New Compilation of the Comprehensive Collection of the Various Masters), Vol. 6. Taipei: Shijie, 1974.

Nishijima, Sadao. "The Economic and Social History of Former Han." In *The Cambridge History of China, Vol. 1: The Ch'in and Han Empires, 221 B.C.– A.D. 220*. Cambridge: Cambridge University Press, 1986.

Norman, Jerry. *Chinese*. Cambridge: Cambridge University Press, 1988.

Nylan, Michael. "The *Chin-wen/Ku-wen* Controversy in Han Times." *T'oung Pao* 80 (1994): 82–144.

——— "Confucian Piety and Individualism in Han China." *Journal of the American Oriental Society* 116:1 (1996): 1–27.

——— *The Five "Confucian" Classics*. New Haven: Yale University Press, 2001.

——— "Han Classicists Writing in Dialogue about their Own Tradition." *Philosophy East and West* 47:2 (April 1997): 133–188.

——— "A Problematic Model: The Han 'Orthodox Synthesis' Then and Now." In *Imagining Boundaries: Changing Confucian Doctrines, Texts, and Hermeneutics*. Ed. Chow Kai-wing, Ng On-cho, and John B. Henderson. Albany: State University of New York Press, 1999.

Nylan, Michael, and Nathan Sivin. "The First Neo-Confucianism: An Introduction to Yang Hsiung's 'Canon of Supreme Mystery' (*T'ai hsüan ching*, 4

B.C.).” In *Chinese Ideas about Nature and Society: Studies in Honour of Derk Bodde*. Hong Kong: Hong Kong University Press, 1987.

Ong, Roberto K. “Image and Meaning: The Hermeneutics of Traditional Dream Interpretation.” In *Psycho-Sinology: The Universe of Dreams in Chinese Culture*. Ed. Carolyn T. Brown. Lanham, MD: University Press of America, 1988.

——— *The Interpretation of Dreams in Ancient China*. Bochum: Studienverlag Brochmeyer, 1985.

Owen, Stephen. *The Making of Early Chinese Classical Poetry*. Cambridge: Harvard University Press, 2006.

——— *Remembrances: The Experience of the Past in Classical Literature*. Cambridge: Harvard University Press, 1986.

Pines, Yuri. “Changing Views of *Tianxia* in Pre-Imperial Discourse.” *Oriens Extremus* 43:1–2 (2002): 101–116.

——— “Friends or Foes: Changing Concepts of Ruler-Minister Relations and the Notion of Loyalty in Pre-Imperial China.” *Monumenta Serica* 50 (2002): 35–74.

——— “The Question of Interpretation: Qin History in the Light of New Epigraphic Sources.” *Early China* (forthcoming).

Poo, Mu-Chou. “Ideas Concerning Death and Burial in Pre-Han China.” *Asia Major*, 3rd ser., 3:2 (1990): 25–62.

——— *In Search of Personal Welfare: A View of Ancient Chinese Religion*. Albany: State University of New York Press, 1998.

Powers, Martin J. *Art and Political Expression in Early China*. New Haven: Yale University Press, 1991.

Qiu, Xigui. *Chinese Writing*. Tr. Gilbert Mattos and Jerry Norman. Berkeley: The Society for the Study of Early China, 2000.

Quan Hou Han wen (Complete Writings of the Later Han). In *Quan shanggu Sandai Qin Han Sanguo Liuchao Wen* (Complete Writings of High Antiquity, the Three Dynasties, Qin, Han, Three Kingdoms, and the Six Dynasties). Compiled by Yan Kejun (1762–1843 A.D.). Beijing: Zhonghua, 1958.

Queen, Sarah. *From Chronicle to Canon: The Hermeneutics of the Spring and Autumn According to Tung Chung-shu*. Cambridge: Cambridge University Press, 1996.

Qun shu zhi yao (Ordered Essentials of the Collected Texts). Si bu cong kan ed.

Ramsey, S. Robert. *The Languages of China*. Rep. ed. Princeton: Princeton University Press, 1989.

Rashke, Manfred B. “New Studies in Roman Commerce with the East.” In *Aufstieg und Niedergang der Römischen Welt, Geshichte und Kultur Roms im Spiegel der Neuren Forschung* II, 9. Ed. Hildegard Temporini and Wolfgang Haase. Berlin: Walter de Gruyter, 1978.

Rawson, Jessica. "Western Zhou Archaeology." In *The Cambridge History of Ancient China: From the Origins of Civilization to 221 B.C.* Ed. Michael Loewe and Edward Shaughnessy. Cambridge: Cambridge University Press, 1999.

Rawson, Jessica, ed. *Mysteries of Ancient China: New Discoveries from the Early Dynasties.* London: British Museum Press, 1996.

Riegel, Jeffrey K. "Kou-mang and Ju-shou." *Cahiers d'Extrême-Asie: Special Issue, Taoist Studies II* 5 (1989–1990): 55–83.

Rouzer, Paul. *Articulated Ladies: Gender and the Male Community in Early Chinese Texts.* Cambridge: Harvard University Press, 2001.

Sage, Steven F. *Ancient Sichuan and the Unification of China.* Albany: State University of New York Press, 1992.

[Jiao zheng] Sanfu huang tu ([Annotated and Corrected] Yellow Map of the Capital Region). Taipei: Shijie, 1974.

San Guo zhi (Record of the Three Kingdoms). Beijing: Zhonghua, 1959.

Schelach, Gideon, and Yuri Pines. "Power, Identity and Ideology: Reflections on the Formation of the State of Qin." In *Asian Archaeology.* Ed. Miriam Stark. London: Blackwell, 2005.

Scott, James. *The Moral Economy of the Peasant.* New Haven: Yale University Press, 1976.

Seidel, Anna. "Post-mortem Immortality—or the Taoist Resurrection of the Body." In *Gilgul: Essays on Transformation, Revolution and Permanence in the History of Religions.* Leiden: E. J. Brill, 1987.

————— "Traces of Han Religion in Funeral Texts Found in Tombs." in *Dōkyō to shûkyō bunka.* Ed. Akizuki Kan'ei. Tokyo: Hirakawa, 1987.

Shang Jun shu zhu yi (Commentary and Vernacular Translation of the "Book of Lord Shang"). Annotated by Gao Heng. Beijing: Zhonghua, 1974.

Shang shu zheng yi (The Correct Meaning of the "Canon of Documents"). In *Shisan jing zhu shu* (The Thirteen Classics with Commentaries and Subcommentaries), Vol. 1. Taipei: Yiwen, 1976.

Shaughnessy, Edward L. "Military Histories of Early China: A Review Article." *Early China* 21 (1996): 159–182.

Shi ji (Records of the Grand Historian/Astrologer). Beijing: Zhonghua, 1959.

Shi ming shu zheng bu (Corrected and Supplemented Subcommentary to "Explaining Names"). Annotated by Wang Xianqian. Shanghai: Guji, 1984.

Shui yuan (Garden of Persuasions). In *Han Wei cong shu* (Collecteana of the Han and Wei Dynasties), Vol. 1. Taipei: Xin Xing, 1977.

Shuihudi Qin mu zhu jian (Bamboo Strips from the Qin Tomb at Shuihudi). Beijing: Wenwu, 1978.

Shuo wen jie zi zhu (Commentary on "Explanations of Simple and Compound Graphs"). Compiled by Xu Shen. Annotated by Duan Yucai. Taipei: Yiwen, 1974.

Sima fa zhi jie (Direct Explanations of the "Methods of the Commander"). Annotated by Liu Yin. In *Ming ben wu jing qi shu zhi jie* (Ming Edition of the Direct Explanations of the Seven Military Classics), Vol. 1. Taipei: Shi Di Jiaoyu, 1972.

Sivin, Nathan. *Medicine, Philosophy and Religion in Ancient China: Researches and Reflections.* Aldershot, Ashgate: Variorum Series, 1995.

Skinner, G. William. "Cities and the Hierarchy of Local Systems." In *The City in Late Imperial China.* Ed. G. William Skinner. Stanford: Stanford University, 1977, pp. 275–351.

———— "Marketing and Social Structures in Rural China," 3 parts. *Journal of Asian Studies* 24.1 (1964): 3–44; 24.2 (1964): 195–228; 24.3 (1965): 363–399.

———— "Regional Urbanization in Nineteenth-Century China." In *The City in Late Imperial China.* Ed. G. William Skinner. Stanford: Stanford University Press, 1977, pp. 211–252.

Sou shen ji (Record of Collected Spirits). Beijing: Zhonghua, 1979.

Steinhardt, Nancy S. *Chinese Imperial City Planning.* Honolulu: University of Hawaii Press, 1990.

Strickmann, Michel. "Dreamwork of Psycho-Sinologists: Doctors, Taoists, Monks." In *Psycho-Sinology: The Universe of Dreams in Chinese Culture.* Ed. Carolyn T. Brown. Washington, D.C., Woodrow Wilson International Center for Scholars, 1988.

Sukhu, Gopal. "Monkeys, Shamans, Emperors, and Poets: The *Chuci* and Images of Chu during the Han Dynasty." In Constance Cook and John Major, eds., *Defining Chu.* Honolulu: University of Hawaii Press, 1999.

[*Shi yi jia zhu*] *Sunzi* ([Ten Schools of Commentary on] Master Sun). Shanghai: Guji, 1978.

Taiping huan yu ji (Record of the World from the Taiping Reign Period). Hongxing Shan Fang, 1803.

Taiping yu lan ([Florilegium for] Imperial Inspection in the Taiping Reign Period). Taipei: Shangwu, 1935.

Teiser, Stephen. "Introduction: The Spirits of Chinese Religion." In *Religions of China in Practice.* Ed. Donald S. Lopez, Jr. Princeton: Princeton University Press, 1996.

Thorp, Robert L. "Origins of Chinese Architectural Style: The Earliest Plans and Building Types." *Archives of Asian Art* 36 (1983): 22–39.

Twitchett, Denis. "The T'ang Market System." *Asia Major* 12:2 (1966): 202–248.

Van Zoeren, Steven. *Poetry and Personality: Reading, Exegesis, and Hermeneutics in Traditional China.* Stanford: Stanford University Press, 1991.

von Falkenhausen, Lothar. "Issues in Western Zhou Studies: A Review Article." *Early China* 18 (1993): 145–171.

——— "Mortuary Behavior in Pre-Imperial China: A Religious Interpretation." In *Religion in Ancient and Medieval China*. Ed. John Lagerwey. Hong Kong: Chinese University of Hong Kong Press, 2004.

——— "Sources of Taoism: Reflections on Archaeological Indicators of Religious Change in Eastern Zhou China." *Taoist Resources* 5:2 (1994): 1–12.

——— *Suspended Music: Chime-Bells in the Culture of Bronze Age China*. Berkeley: University of California Press, 1993.

von Glahn, Richard. *The Sinister Way: The Divine and the Demonic in Chinese Religious Culture*. Berkeley: University of California Press, 2004.

Wakefield, David. *Fenjia: Household Division and Inheritance in Qing and Republican China*. Honolulu: University of Hawaii Press, 1998.

Waldron, Arthur. *The Great Wall of China: From History to Myth*. Cambridge: Cambridge University Press, 1990.

Waley, Arthur, tr. *The Nine Songs: A Study of Shamanism in Ancient China*. London: George Allen & Unwin, 1955.

Wallacker, Benjamin E. "Han Confucianism and Confucius in Han." In *Ancient China: Studies in Early Civilization*. Ed. David T. Roy and Tsien Tsuen-hsuin. Hong Kong: The Chinese University Press, 1978.

Wang, Chong. *Lun heng ji jie* (Collected Explanations of the Balanced Discourses). Annotated by Liu Pansui. Beijing: Guji, 1957.

Wang, Fu. *Qian fu lun jian* (Interpretation of the Discourses of the Hidden Man). Annotated by Wang Jipei. Beijing: Zhonghua, 1979.

Wang, Yü-ch'üan. "An Outline of the Central Government of the Former Han Dynasty." *Harvard Journal of Asiatic Studies* 12 (1949): 134–187.

Wang, Zhongshu. *Han Civilization*. New Haven: Yale University, 1982.

Watson, Burton, tr. *Chinese Rhyme-Prose: Poems in the Fu Form from the Han and Six Dynasties Periods*. New York: Columbia University Press, 1971.

Wen xuan (Selections of Refined Literature). Hong Kong: Shangwu, 1978.

Wheatley, Paul. *The Pivot of the Four Quarters*. Edinburgh: Aldine, 1971.

White, James Boyd. *Heracles' Bow: Essays on the Rhetoric and Poetics of Law*. Madison: University of Wisconsin Press, 1985.

——— *Justice as Translation: An Essay in Cultural and Legal Criticism*. Chicago: University of Chicago Press, 1990.

——— *The Legal Imagination* (abridged ed.). Chicago: University of Chicago Press, 1973.

Wiens, Herold. *China's March to the Tropics*. Washington, D.C.: Office of Naval Research, U.S. Navy, 1952.

Wilbur, C. Martin. *Slavery in China during the Former Han Dynasty, 206 B.C.– A.D. 25*. New York: Russell and Russell, 1943.

Worster, Donald. *Rivers of Empire: Water, Aridity, and the Growth of the American West*. New York: Oxford University Press, 1985.

Wright, Arthur F. "The Cosmology of the Chinese City." In *The City in Late Im-*

perial China. Ed. G. William Skinner. Stanford: Stanford University Press, 1977, pp. 33–74.

Wu, Hung. "The Art and Architecture of the Warring States Period." In *The Cambridge History of Ancient China.* Ed. M. Loewe and E. L. Shaughnessy. Cambridge: Cambridge University Press, 1999.

———. "Art in Ritual Context: Rethinking Mawangdui." *Early China* 17 (1992): 111–144.

———. "Beyond the 'Great Boundary': Funerary Narrative in the Cangshan Tomb." In *Boundaries in China.* Ed. John Hay. London: Reaktion Books, 1994.

———. "Mapping Early Taoist Art: The Visual Culture of Wudoumi Dao." In *Taoism and the Arts of China.* Ed. Stephen Little. Chicago: The Art Institute of Chicago, 2000.

———. *Monumentality in Early Chinese Art and Architecture.* Stanford: Stanford University Press, 1995.

———. "Private Love and Public Duty: Images of Children in Early Chinese Art." In *Chinese Views of Childhood.* Ed. Anne Behnke Kinney. Honolulu: University of Hawaii Press, 1995.

———. *The Wu Liang Shrine: The Ideology of Early Chinese Pictorial Art.* Stanford: Stanford University Press, 1989.

Wu, Xiaoqing, ed. *Qin jian Ri shu ji shi* (Collected Elucidations of "Almanacs" from Qin Strips). Changsha: Yuelu, 2000.

Wu yue chun qiu (Spring and Autumn Annals of Wu and Yue). Si bu bei yao ed.

Wuzi zhi jie (Direct Explanations of the "Master Wu"). Annotated by Liu Yin. In *Ming ben wu jing qi shu zhi jie* (Ming Edition of the Direct Explanations of the Seven Military Classics), Vol. 1. Taipei: Shi Di Jiaoyu, 1972.

Xian Qin Han Wei Jin Nanbeichao shi (Poems of the Pre-Qin, Han, Wei, Jin, and Northern and Southern Dynasties). Annotated by Lu Qianli. Taipei: Xuehai, 1993.

Xiao jing zhu shu (Commentaries and Subcommentaries on the "Canon of Filial Piety"). In *Shi san jing zhu shu* (The Thirteen Classics with Commentaries and Subcommentaries), Vol. 8. Taipei: Yiwen, 1976.

Xiong, Victor Cunrui. *Sui-Tang Chang'an: A Study in the Urban History of Medieval China.* Ann Arbor: Center for Chinese Studies, University of Michigan, 2000.

Xu, Yinong. *The Chinese City in Space and Time: The Development of Urban Form in Suzhou.* Honolulu: University of Hawaii Press, 2000.

Xunzi ji jie (Collected Explanations of the "Master Xun"). In *Xin bian zhu zi ji cheng* (New Compilation of the Comprehensive Collection of the Various Masters), Vol. 2. Taipei: Shijie, 1974.

Yan, Yunxiang. *The Flow of Gifts: Reciprocity and Social Networks in a Chinese Village.* Stanford: Stanford University Press, 1996.

Yan, Zhitui. *Yan shi jia xun hui zhu* (Collected Commentaries on the "Family Instruction of the Yan Clan"). Annotated by Zhou Fagao. Taipei: Zhongyang Yanjiuyuan Lishi Yuyan Yanjiusuo, 1960.

Yan tie lun (Discourse on Salt and Iron). Shanghai: Renmin, 1974.

Yang, Hsüan-chih. *A Record of the Buddhist Monasteries in Lo-yang.* Tr. Yi-t'ung Wang. Princeton: Princeton University Press, 1984.

Yang, Xiong. *Yangzi fa yan* (The Model Words of Master Yang). In *Xin bian zhu zi ji cheng* (New Compilation of the Comprehensive Collection of the Various Masters), Vol. 2. Taipei: Shijie, 1974.

Yanzi chun qiu ji shi (Collected Explanations of the "Springs and Autumns of Master Yan"). Annotated by Wu Zeyu. Beijing: Zhonghua, 1962.

Yates, Robin. "New Light on Ancient Chinese Military Texts: Notes on Their Nature and Evolution, and the Development of Military Specialization in Warring States China." *T'oung Pao* 74 (1988): 212–248.

——— "Some Notes on Ch'in Law." *Early China* 11–12 (1985–87): 243–275.

——— "The Yin-Yang Texts from Yinqueshan: An Introduction and Partial Reconstruction with Notes on their Significance in Relation to Huang-Lao Taoism." *Early China* 19 (1994): 75–144.

Yi li zhu shu (Commentaries and Subcommentaries on the "Ceremonies and Rituals"). In *Shi san jing zhu shu* (The Thirteen Classics with Commentaries and Subcommentaries), Vol. 3. Taipei: Yiwen, 1976.

Ying, Shao. *Feng su tong yi jiaoshi* (Annotated Explanations of the "Comprehensive Meaning of Customs"). Annotated by Wu Shuping. Tianjin: Tianjin Renmin, 1980.

Yü, Ying-shih. "Han Foreign Relations." In *The Cambridge History of China, Vol. 1: The Ch'in and Han Empires, 221 B.C.–A.D. 220.* Cambridge: Cambridge University Press, 1986.

——— "Life and Immortality in the Mind of Han China." *Harvard Journal of Asiatic Studies* 25 (1964–65): 80–122.

——— *Trade and Expansion in Han China: A Study in the Structure of Sino-Barbarian Economic Relations.* Berkeley: University of California Press, 1967.

Yue jue shu (Book on the Destruction of Yue). Shanghai: Shangwu, 1956.

Yunmeng Shuihudi Qin mu (The Qin Tomb from Shuihudi at Yunmeng). Beijing: Wenwu, 1981.

Zhangjiashan Han mu zhu jian (The Bamboo Strips from the Han Tomb at Zhangjiashan). Beijing: Wenwu, 2001.

Zhanguo ce (Stratagems of the Warring States). Shanghai: Guji, 1985.

Zhanguo zong heng jia shu (Book of the Warring States Vertical and Horizontal Alliances). In *Mawangdui Han mu boshu* (Silk Texts from a Han Tomb at Mawangdui), Vol. 3. Beijing: Wenwu, 1983.

Zhou li zhu shu (Commentaries and Subcommentaries on the "Rituals of

Zhou"). In *Shisan jing zhu shu* (The Thirteen Classics with Commentaries and Subcommentaries), Vol. 3. Taipei: Yiwen, 1976.

Zhuangzi ji shi (Collected Explanations of the "Master Zhuang"). In *Xin bian zhu zi ji cheng* (New Compilation of the Comprehensive Collection of the Various Masters), Vol. 3. Taipei: Shijie, 1974.

[*Chun qiu*] *Zuo zhuan zhu* (Commentary on the "Transmissions of Master Zuo on the *Spring and Autumn Annals*"). Annotated by Yang Bojun. Beijing: Zhonghua, 1981.

Zufferey, Nicolas. *To the Origins of Confucianism: The Ru in Pre-Qin Times and during the Early Han Dynasty*. Bern: Peter Lang, 2003.

INDEX